THE NEW
PALGRAVE

GENERAL
EQUILIBRIUM

THE NEW PALGRAVE

GENERAL EQUILIBRIUM

EDITED BY

JOHN EATWELL · MURRAY MILGATE · PETER NEWMAN

W·W·NORTON

NEW YORK · LONDON

Published simultaneously in Canada by
Penguin Books Canada Ltd.
2801 John Street
Markham, Ontario L3R 1B4

ISBN   0-393-02728-7

ISBN   0-393-95853-1   PBK.

W. W. Norton & Company, Inc.
500 Fifth Avenue
New York, NY 10110

W. W. Norton & Company, Ltd.
37 Great Russell Street
London WC1B 3NU

Printed in Great Britain

1   2   3   4   5   6   7   8   9   0

Contents

Contents

Acknowledgements

The following contributors (articles shown in parentheses) acknowledge support from public bodies or permission to reprint copyright material:

Gerard Debreu (Existence of General Equilibrium), support from the National Science Foundation.
Roy Radner (Uncertainty and General Equilibrium) for material previously published in the *American Economic Review*, vol. LX, May 1970, in the *Journal of Economic Theory*, vol. 26, 1982, and in *Handbook of Mathematical Economics*, ed. K.J. Arrow and M. Intriligator, vol. II, 1982, Amsterdam: North-Holland Publishing Company.
John Roberts (Large Economies), support from the National Science Foundation through grant SES83-08723.

General Preface

The books in this series are the offspring of *The New Palgrave: A Dictionary of Economics*. Published in late 1987, the *Dictionary* has rapidly become a standard reference work in economics. However, its four heavy tomes containing over four million words on the whole range of economic thought is not a form convenient to every potential user. For many students and teachers it is simply too bulky, too comprehensive and too expensive for everyday use.

By developing the present series of compact volumes of reprints from the original work, we hope that some of the intellectual wealth of *The New Palgrave* will become accessible to much wider groups of readers. Each of the volumes is devoted to a particular branch of economics, such as econometrics or general equilibrium or money, with a scope corresponding roughly to a university course on that subject. Apart from correction of misprints, etc. the content of each of its reprinted articles is exactly the same as that of the original. In addition, a few brand new entries have been commissioned especially for the series, either to fill an apparent gap or more commonly to include topics that have risen to prominence since the dictionary was originally commissioned.

As *The New Palgrave* is the sole parent of the present series, it may be helpful to explain that it is the modern successor to the excellent *Dictionary of Political Economy* edited by R.H. Inglis Palgrave and published in three volumes in 1894, 1896 and 1899. A second and slightly modified version, edited by Henry Higgs, appeared during the mid-1920s. These two editions each contained almost 4,000 entries, but many of those were simply brief definitions and many of the others were devoted to peripheral topics such as foreign coinage, maritime commerce, and Scottish law. To make room for the spectacular growth in economics over the last 60 years while keeping still to a manageable length, *The New Palgrave* concentrated instead on economic theory, its originators, and its closely cognate disciplines. Its nearly 2,000 entries (commissioned from over 900 scholars) are all self-contained essays, sometimes brief but never mere definitions.

Apart from its biographical entries, *The New Palgrave* is concerned chiefly with theory rather than fact, doctrine rather than data; and it is not at all clear how theory and doctrine, as distinct from facts and figures, *should* be treated in an encyclopaedia. One way is to treat everything from a particular point of view. Broadly speaking, that was the way of Diderot's classic *Encyclopédie raisonée* (1751–1772), as it was also of Léon Say's *Nouveau dictionnaire d'économie politique* (1891–2). Sometimes, as in articles by Quesnay and Turgot in the *Encyclopédie*, this approach has yielded entries of surpassing brilliance. Too often, however, both the range of subjects covered and the quality of the coverage itself are seriously reduced by such a self-limiting perspective. Thus the entry called '*Méthode*' in the first edition of Say's *Dictionnaire* asserted that the use of mathematics in economics 'will only ever be in the hands of a few', and the dictionary backed up that claim by choosing not to have any entry on Cournot.

Another approach is to have each entry take care to reflect within itself varying points of view. This may help the student temporarily, as when preparing for an examination. But in a subject like economics, the Olympian detachment which this approach requires often places a heavy burden on the author, asking for a scrupulous account of doctrines he or she believes to be at best wrong-headed. Even when an especially able author does produce a judicious survey article, it is surely too much to ask that it also convey just as much enthusiasm for those theories thought misguided as for those found congenial. Lacking an enthusiastic exposition, however, the disfavoured theories may then be studied less closely than they deserve.

The New Palgrave did not ask its authors to treat economic theory from any particular point of view, except in one respect to be discussed below. Nor did it call for surveys. Instead, each author was asked to make clear his or her own views of the subject under discussion, and for the rest to be as fair and accurate as possible, without striving to be 'judicious'. A balanced perspective on each topic was always the aim, the ideal. But it was to be sought not *internally*, within each article, but *externally*, between articles, with the reader rather than the writer handed the task of achieving a personal balance between differing views.

For a controversial topic, a set of several more or less synonymous headwords, matched by a broad diversity of contributors, was designed to produce enough variety of opinion to help form the reader's own synthesis; indeed, such diversity will be found in most of the individual volumes in this series.

This approach was not without its problems. Thus, the prevalence of uncertainty in the process of commissioning entries sometimes produced a less diverse outcome than we had planned. 'I can call spirits from the vasty deep,' said Owen Glendower. 'Why, so can I,' replied Hotspur, 'or so can any man;/ But will they come when you do call for them?' In our experience, not quite as often as we would have liked.

The one point of view we did urge upon every one of *Palgrave*'s authors was to write from an historical perspective. For each subject its contributor was asked to discuss not only present problems but also past growth and future prospects. This request was made in the belief that knowledge of the historical development of any theory enriches our present understanding of it, and so helps to construct better theories for the future. The authors' response to the request was generally so positive that, as the reader of any of these volumes will discover, the resulting contributions amply justified that belief.

Peter Newman
Murray Milgate
John Eatwell

Preface

The essays in this volume deal with a central theme of modern economic theory – the economy considered as a system of many interrelated markets. Fifty years ago matters were quite different; the economic theory actually used then was predominantly partial equilibrium in nature, taking one market at a time.

Looking back, the situation seems to have been ripe for change, although it did not appear so then. In the mid-1930s Abraham Wald had published a series of papers which gave the first proofs that (under rather severe conditions) a model as complex as Cassel's version of Walrasian general equilibrium *could* have economically sensible solutions, i.e. that it was a logically consistent model. Soon afterwards John von Neumann proved existence of balanced growth paths in his own model, which is the profound source of many important strands in modern general equilibrium theory.

In their review articles of *The General Theory of Employment, Interest and Money* (1936), John Hicks and Oscar Lange showed that the Keynesian system could itself be formalized as a working model of general aggregative equilibrium. But since it was not based on formal optimization by its individual economic agents, it was not Walrasian in character. Hence, no one except Hicks made any connection from Keynes to Walras. His epochal *Value and Capital* of 1939 did many remarkable things, of which two are especially relevant here. First, he generalized the methods of comparative static analysis from single to multiple markets, and thus freed Walrasian theory from the charge of sterility. Secondly, he took a major step towards dynamizing formal general equilibrium theory by regarding commodities available at different times as different commodities, thus making their choice part of the agent's optimizing problem. This required that all agents form expectations of the prices of such future commodities, and so led to the first formal (but primitive) treatment of expectations in a general equilibrium setting.

The disturbances of the Second World War delayed the advent of general equilibrium theory by perhaps a decade, but once started its victory was rapid and complete. Building on innovations in game theory and convexity theory, in the early 1950s Arrow, Debreu and McKenzie each began to attempt proofs of Walrasian equilibrium more satisfactory than those of Wald. This *could* have been a mere matter of mathematical aesthetics, but in the process something rather remarkable happened.

For in setting out their models of general equilibrium with enough clarity to permit exact proofs of consistency, these pioneering theorists were forced to say *exactly* what they meant. So it came to pass that one of the virtues of the prevalence of general equilibrium theory is that to know what one is talking about is today rather less uncommon than it used to be.

The Editors

General Equilibrium

LIONEL W. McKENZIE

General equilibrium theory is in contrast with partial equilibrium theory where some specified part of an economy is analysed while the influences impinging on this sector from the rest of the economy are held constant. In general equilibrium the influences which are treated as constant are those which are considered to be noneconomic and thus beyond the range of economic analysis. Of course, this does not guarantee that these influences will in fact remain constant when the economic factors change, and the usefulness of economic analysis for predictive purposes may depend on to what degree influences treated as noneconomic are really independent of the economic variables.

The institution whose phenomena are the primary subject matter of economic analysis is the market, made up of a group of economic agents who buy and sell goods and services to one another. In partial equilibrium theory the group of agents may be confined to those who are involved in one industry, either buying or selling its product or buying or selling the materials and productive services used in making its product. However, in general equilibrium theory all the agents involved in exchanges with each other should ideally be included and all their sales and purchases should be allowed for. However, it may happen that the activities of many agents are only treated in the aggregate and the list of goods and services may be reduced by aggregation. The aggregation of agents and commodities into a few categories is especially important when general equilibrium theory is applied to special areas of public policy such as the government budget, money and banking, or foreign trade. Much of the theory developed for these subjects is general equilibrium theory in aggregated form.

The general equilibrium implies that all subsets of agents are in equilibrium and in particular that all individual agents are in equilibrium. The conscious development of a formal general equilibrium theory stated in mathematical terms seems to have been inspired by a formal theory of the equilibrium of the individual consumer faced with a given set of trading opportunities or prices. This theory was developed by the marginal utility, or neo-classical, school of economists in

1

the third quarter of the 19th century, independently, by Gossen (1854), Jevons (1871), and Walras (1874–7), who used mathematical notations, and by Menger (1871) who did not. The step was taken in the most effective way by Walras.

THE EQUILIBRIUM OF AN EXCHANGE ECONOMY. Walras assumed that the utility derived from the consumption of a good was given as a function of the amount of that good alone that was consumed and independent of the amounts consumed of other goods. He also assumed that the first derivative of the utility function was positive and decreasing up to a point of satiation when one exists. He then gave a rigorous derivation of the demand for a good by a consumer from the maximization of utility subject to a budget constraint. The demand functions give the equilibrium quantities traded by the consumer as a function of market prices. As Walras saw, this is a crucial step in the development of a general equilibrium theory for an economy. It has remained in a generalized form the cornerstone of general equilibrium theory since Walras.

The simplest problem of general equilibrium arises in the theory of the exchange economy without production. In this economy the budget constraint of the trader is established by his initial stocks and the list of prices. Then the individual demand function represents the equilibrium of the single trader in face of a given price system. The market demand function is the sum of the individual demand functions, and the equilibrium of the market occurs at a price for which the sum of demands, including offers as negative demands, is equal to 0 for each good, or, if free disposal is allowed, is not positive for any good. This idea was expressed in classical economic theory by the equality of supply and demand in each market, but its expression in a set of equations to be satisfied by the list of equilibrium prices was due to Walras, although Cournot (1838) had foreshadowed the Walrasian analysis in his discussion of the international flow of money and Mill (1848) in his discussion of foreign trade.

Suppose there are n goods to be traded and there are m traders. Let w_i^h be the quantity of the ith good held initially by the hth trader. Let $u^h(x)$ where $x = (x_1, \ldots, x_n)$ be the utility to the hth trader of possessing the quantities $x_1, \ldots, x_n$ of the n goods traded. Then the hth trader is in equilibrium at the prices $p = (p_1, \ldots, p_n)$ and the quantities x^h if $u^h(x)$ is a maximum at x^h over all values of x which satisfy $\Sigma_1^n p_i x_i \leqslant \Sigma_1^n p_i w_i^h$. If smoothness and concavity conditions are met by the utility function, and the goods are divisible, the maximizing x will be unique and will define a function $f^h(p)$ over an appropriate price domain. Since the set of commodity bundles x at which the utility functions is maximised does not change when the prices p are multiplied by a positive scalar, this function will satisfy $f^h(p) = f^h(\alpha p)$ for $\alpha > 0$.

The market demand function is $f(p) = \Sigma_1^m f^h(p)$. Then the market equilibrium for a trading economy is given by a price vector p and an allocation of goods $(x^1, \ldots, x^m)$ such that $x^h = f^h(p)$ and $\Sigma_1^m x^h = \Sigma_1^m w^h$, or, assuming free disposal, $\Sigma_1^m x^h \leqslant \Sigma_1^m w^h$. The first condition expresses the equilibrium of the individual trader and the second condition is the equality of supply and demand. Thus there are n scalar equations $\Sigma_{h=1}^m f_i^h(p) = \Sigma_{h=1}^m w_i^h$ to determine the n equilibrium prices p_i. The given data are the consumer tastes, expressed in the utility functions u^h, and the initial stocks of goods w^h.

It is clear that the market demand function satisfies the homogeneity condition $f(\alpha p) = f(p)$ for $\alpha \geqslant 0$. Thus equilibrium prices are only determined up to multiplication by a positive number. This reflects the fact that the equilibrium of the consumer is not affected if prices are multiplied by α and market equilibrium is the simultaneous equilibrium of all consumers at the same prices. It is often convenient to adopt some normalization of prices. Walras chooses a good whose price is known to be positive in equilibrium and gives this good, which he calls the numeraire, the price 1. Another convention which is useful when free disposal is assumed, so that prices are necessarily non-negative, is to choose p such that $\Sigma_1^n p_i = 1$. Then the domain of definition for the demand functions may be taken to be all p such that $p_i \geqslant 0$ and $\Sigma_1^n p_i = 1$.

There is an analogy between the equilibrium of the trading economy and the equilibrium of mechanical forces. Indeed, one of the inspirations for the theory of Walras appear to have been a treatise on statics by Poinsot (1803, 1842). According to the principle of virtual work an infinitesimal displacement of a mechanical system, which is at equilibrium under the stress of forces and subject to constraints, does no work. In the economy at equilibrium an infinitesimal displacement of the allocation of goods $(x^1, \ldots, x^m)$ cannot increase the utility of one trader unless it reduces the utility of another. This is an easy implication of the fact that utility is maximised over the budget constraint, provided no one is saturated. This means that a new allocation to a trader cannot preserve his utility level if its value at the equilibrium prices falls. On the other hand, the utility level of a trader cannot increase unless his allocation becomes more valuable at the equilibrium prices. But then the new allocations $x^{h'}$ would satisfy

$$\sum_{h'=1}^{m} \sum_{i=1}^{n} p_i x_i^{h'} > \sum_{h=1}^{m} \sum_{i=1}^{n} p_i w_i^h$$

which is impossible since the total allocation cannot exceed the total supply of goods. Indeed, if each trader holds all goods in his equilibrium allocation and the utility functions are differentiable, which implies that goods are divisible, an infinitesimal reallocation would have no effect on utility levels if it has no effect on the levels of individual budgets. This property of market equilibrium was first recognized by Pareto (1909), and an allocation of goods with the property that no displacement of it can benefit one consumer unless it harms another is said to be Pareto optimal. The implication from competitive equilibrium to Pareto optimality requires that no consumer be locally satiated. It is also true that a Pareto optimal allocation may be realized as a competitive equilibrium given an appropriate distribution of initial stocks, but the conditions are more severe. The first general theorems were proved by Arrow (1951).

EQUILIBRIUM WITH PRODUCTION. The next step in developing the general equilibrium of an economy is to introduce production under the condition that the output matures without a lapse of time. This step was taken by Walras who introduced linear activities which list the quantities of productive services required to produce one unit of a good. There may be many alternative activities for the production of any given good and a choice is made among them in order to minimize the cost of production at given market prices. Let $z = (z_1, \ldots, z_r)$ be a list of quantities of productive services and let $g^i(z)$, $i = 1, \ldots, n$, be production functions for the n goods. Since linear activities are assumed, the production functions will satisfy $\alpha g^i(z) = g^i(\alpha z)$. In particular, we may consider the unit isoquant or the set A_i such that $g^i(z) = 1$ for z in A_i. Then the activities which minimize cost at given prices q are represented by production coefficients $a^i(q)$, contained in A_i, where $q'a^i(q) \leqslant q'z$ for z in A_i. Equilibrium in the production sector is given by price vectors p and q and activity vectors $a^i(q)$ where $p_i \leqslant \Sigma_{j=1}^r q_j a_j^i(q)$ for all i and equality holds if the ith good is produced.

In an equilibrium of the production sector any quantities y of outputs may be produced provided quantities z of productive services are available where $z_j = \Sigma_{i=1}^n y_i a_j^i(q)$. In order to include the productive sector in a market equilibrium the utility functions of consumers must be extended to include productive services among their arguments. They may be written $u^h(x, z)$. If we reinterpret x_i as the quantity of a good traded rather than the quantity consumed, the initial stocks may be suppressed. This is convenient since it is not clear how initial stocks labour services can be specified. Then the individual consumer is in equilibrium given prices p and q for goods and productive services when the quantities traded (x^h, z^h) maximize $u^h(x, z)$ over all (x, z) such that $\Sigma_1^n p_i x_i - \Sigma_1^r q_i z_i \leqslant 0$. The maximizing quantities need not be unique in general, so it is necessary to represent demand by a correspondence that takes a set of trades as its value and write $(x^h, z^h) \in f^h(p, q)$ when (x^h, z^h) is a maximizer given prices p and q.

As before market equilibrium is achieved when all economic agents are in equilibrium at the same prices and supply is equal to demand. Since risk is not present in this economy, the productive services involved in organizing production need not be given a distinguished role. Activities may be treated as conducted by the whole set of owners of the productive services involved in them. Then if it should happen that $p_i > \Sigma_{j=1}^r q_j a_j^i(q)$ for the ith good, there will be an opportunity for some owners of productive services to earn larger returns producing the ith good than those prevailing generally as given by q. Thus productive services will leave other activites and flow to this activity, so equilibrium does not obtain for owners of productive services. This equilibrium now requires, on the one hand, equilibrium of each economic agent as consumer of goods and provider of productive services, that is, $(x^h, z^h) \in f^h(p, q)$, and, on the other hand, equilibrium of each economic agent as a participant in production, that is, $p_i \leqslant \Sigma_{j=1}^r q_j a_j^i(q)$, with equality if the ith good is produced. However, market equilibrium also requires that $\Sigma_{h=1}^m z_j^h = \Sigma_{h=1}^m \Sigma_{i=1}^r x^h a_j^i(q)$, that is, the supply of productive services must equal the quantities needed to produce the quantities of goods demanded. As before, if surplus productive services may be freely disposed of, the equality in the last equation may be replaced by an inequality.

The demand functions $f_i^n(p, q)$ and the supply functions $f_{n+j}^h(p, q)$ express the equilibrium of the household sector. Therefore, the relation $\Sigma_{i=1}^{n} p_i f_i^h(p,q) = \Sigma_{j=1}^{r} q_j f_{n+j}^h(p,q)$ holds for all values of p and q in the price domain. Let x_i be the amount of the ith good produced and let z_j be the amount of the jth factor used in production. Then equilibrium in the production sector implies that

$$\sum_{i=1}^{n} p_i x_i = \sum_{j=1}^{r} \sum_{i=1}^{n} q_j x_i a_j^i = \sum_{j=1}^{r} q_j z_j.$$

Let $f(p,q) = \Sigma_{h=1}^{m} f^h(p,q)$. Then household equilibrium implies $\Sigma_{i=1}^{n} p_i f_i(p,q) = \Sigma_{j=1}^{r} q_j f_{n+j}(p,q)$. Let excess demand for a good be $e_i(p,q) = f_i(p,q) - x_i$, and excess demand for a productive service be $e_{n+j}(p,q) = z_j - f_{n+j}(p,q)$. Then equilibrium in the production and household sectors together implies that $\Sigma_{i=1}^{n} p_i e_i(p,q) + \Sigma_{j=1}^{n} q_j e_{n+j}(p,q) = 0$, or the value of excess demand is zero whatever price system is set. This relation is referred to as Walras's Law.

If there is free disposal, prices must be non-negative. Otherwise, disposal would be profitable. Also with free disposal the condition for equilibrium of the market is $e(p,q) \leqslant 0$. Then Walras's Law immediately implies $p_i e_i(p,q) = q_j e_{n+j}(p,q) = 0$, and if any good or productive service is in excess supply in equilibrium, its equilibrium price must be 0. This might be termed Wald's Law, since he made a crucial use of it in the first rigorous proof that equilibrium exists in a competitive economy (Wald, 1935, 1936a).

A production sector composed of activities with single outputs is the model used by Walras who was responsible for the first fully developed general equilibrium theory. The natural generalization of this model is to introduce more than one output. Then the kth activity is represented by an output vector $b^k = (b_1^k, \ldots, b_n^k)$ and an input vector for productive services $a^k = (a_1^k, \ldots, a_r^k)$. Assume that activities may be replicated and are independent of each other. Then if (a^k, b^k) is a possible intput–output combination for the kth activity, so is $(\alpha a^k, \alpha b^k)$ where α is any non-negative integer. Indeed if all inputs and outputs are divisible it is possible for α to take as its value any real number.

This model of the production sector which embraces the transformation of productive services into goods and services is due to Walras in the context of a theory of general equilibrium. It is convenient to think of the market as held periodically to arrange for the delivery of goods and services over a certain basic period of time. This view of the market, which is also a device of Walras, leads to a theory of temporary equilibrium. The theory was further elaborated by Hicks (1939) and in recent years by other authors. In order to explain the demand and supply of products and productive services in the periodic market it is necessary to introduce some assumptions on the formation of expectations for the prices which will prevail in future markets. The simplest assumption is that the prices arrived at in one market are expected to prevail in future markets. This type of expectation formation is sometimes referred to as static expectations. Walras usually appears to assume static expectations. Hicks introduced a notion of elasticity of expectations to allow expectations of future prices to depend on the change of prices from one temporary equilibrium to another. In recent work analysis has proceeded upon more general assumptions, using various formal properties of dependencies between past prices and expected prices. A quite different approach to expectations which enjoys much current popularity is to assume that expectations are correct, at least in a stochastic sense. The rationale of this approach is that any persistent bias in forecasts of future prices implies that there are unexploited opportunities for profit from further trading which eventually should be recognized.

The model of the production sector as a set of potential linear activities was subsequently used by Cassel (1918) in a simplified Walrasian model which preserved the demand functions and the production coefficients but which did not deduce the demand functions from utility functions or preferences. The model was generalized to allow joint production in a special context by von Neumann (1937). It was given a thorough elaboration and analysis in a model where intermediate products are introduced explicitly by Koopmans (1951). In the Walrasian picture intermediate products were eliminated through the combination of activities so that activities were described as transforming productive services directly into final products whether consumer goods and services or capital goods. However, such a description of the economy depends for its relevance on prices which do not change from one temporary equilibrium to another, so that the choice of activities is not changing.

In the general linear model of production it is no longer adequate to treat the choice of activities as a process of cost minimization given the price vectors p and q. Cost minimization must be replaced by the condition that no activity may offer a profit and no activity which is used in competitive equilibrium may suffer a loss. This is exactly the condition '*ni benefice ni perte*' which Walras used to define equilibrium in production, initially in a model with fixed coefficients of production. However, this condition was first used in a general production model by von Neumann, so it might be termed von Neumann's Law for an activities model of production. Koopmans explored the relation between efficient production and von Neumann's Law. He established an equivalence between the proposition that an output is efficient and the proposition that prices exist such that von Neumann's Law is satisfied when the activities used are those needed to produce this output. Moreover, if each good or service is either desired in unlimited quantities or freely disposable the prices must be non-negative. Thus under these demand and supply conditions any competitive equilibrium must include an efficient output from the production sector. The activities approach to the production sector of a competitive economy was used by Wald and then by McKenzie (1954) in proofs of existence for competitive equilibrium. It was also used by Scarf (1973) in an algorithm for finding a competitive equilibrium given the technology, the resources, and the demand functions.

An alternative model of the production sector emphasizes the productive organization or firm rather than the activities or technology. A set of actual or potential firms is given and each firm is endowed with its own set of possible input–output combinations. The set of possible input–output combinations achievable by the economy, independently of resource availabilities, is the sum of the sets of input–output combinations achievable by the firms. The condition for equilibrium in the production sector is that each firm maximizes its profits, that is, the value of the input–output combination over its production possibility set, given the prices of inputs and outputs. This view of production was explicit in a partial equilibrium context in Cournot. It was at least implicit in the work of Marshall (1980) and Pareto, and became quite explicit in a general equilibrium context in the work of Hicks (1939) and Arrow and Debreu (1954).

In the Hicksian model a firm is associated with each economic agent who is a consumer and who may be a worker and owner of resources, but who also may be an entrepreneur. As an entrepreneur he owns a possible production set based on his personal characteristics and perhaps some other non-marketed resources. Of course, most of these individual enterprises will be inactive. A difficulty with this model is that it seems unrealistic to treat the entrepreneur as a profit maximiser unless all the resources which he himself supplies have market prices so that they could equally well be bought by him from the market or sold by him to the market. But if that is the case we are back to the concept of the entrepreneur used by Walras and it seems more realistic to refer to activities, which are impersonal, rather than to individual enterprises.

In the model of Arrow and Debreu, which is the first complete general equilibrium model in which the existence of equilibrium was rigorously proved, the production sector is made up of firms which are described as joint stock companies. Each firm has a production possibility set based on resources which it owns and the ownership of the firm is spread in a prescribed way over a set of consumers. The production sector is in equilibrium when each firm has chosen an input–output combination from its production possibility set which maximizes profit at the market prices. Since the outputs of one firm may be inputs of another and the resort to integrated activities which convert productive services directly into products is not available in a model based on firms, it is convenient to distinguish inputs from outputs by signs rather than be lists. Let Y_j denote the production possibility set of the jth firm, and let $y = (y_1, \ldots, y_n)$ denote an element of this set. There are n goods and services in the economy, and $y_i < 0$ denotes an input, while $y_i > 0$ denotes an output. Let y^j be the input–output vector of the jth firm. Then equilibrium in the production sector requires that the condition $p \cdot y^j \geqslant p \cdot y$ for all $y \in Y_j$ hold for all j, where j indexes the set of firms, and p is the market price vector.

The Arrow–Debreu approach to the production sector involves a major difficulty. It is not well adapted to handle the formation of new firms and the dissolution of old ones. If firms are based on the assembly of a set of resources jointly owned by the shareholders, it becomes critical to give the principle which underlies such an assembly. If the firm's resources are priced and traded, so the firm's production may be treated like an activity, there is no difficulty since von Neumann's Law may be applied. Otherwise, the rules governing the entry and exit of firms are unclear. The problem is similar to the general problem of coalition formation in the theory of cooperative games.

A FORMAL MODEL. A formal model of the competitive economy, presented in the form of a series of axioms, was developed in the 1950s. It was intended that the axioms should be interpretable to apply to real economic systems, albeit in some approximate sense. However, as a formal mathematical model the implications of the axioms could be developed independently of the applications. The selection of axioms was influenced by the possibility of making useful interpretations, but also by the facility with which results can be derived.

Two closely related sets of assumptions were developed. One, developed primarily by McKenzie (1959), is a formalization of the Walrasian theory and uses a linear model of production. The other, developed primarily by Arrow and Debreu, is a formalization of the Hicksian theory where the production sector is described as an assembly of firms. On the side of consumers and the market there are no significant differences at a fundamental level, although there are sometimes differences of approach. A history of the problem of existence of equilibrium for the formal models may be found in Weintraub (1983).

In the fully developed McKenzie model (see McKenzie, 1981) two assumptions are made for the consumption sector, two for the production sector, and two assumptions relate the consumption and production sectors. On the consumption side there is a finite number m of consumers indexed by h, and each consumer has a set X_h of trades which are feasible for him. There are n goods and the sets X_h are contained in R^n, the n dimensional Euclidean space. The convention is used that quantities supplied by consumers are negative and quantities received by consumers are positive. The consumer has preferences defined on X_h by a correspondence P_h. The preference correspondence P_h takes as its value at $x \in X_h$ the subset of X_h each of whose members is preferred to x. This subset may be empty. The assumptions on the consumers which hold for all h, are

(1) X_h is convex, closed and bounded below.
(2) P_h is open valued relative to X_h and lower semicontinuous. Also x is not in convex hull $P_h(x)$.

Convexity of X_h implies that a good is divisible if someone can consume it in more than one quantity. X_h bounded below means that the consumer is not able to supply an indefinite quantity of any good. Closedness and boundedness are needed to provide compact feasible sets.

On the production side there is an activities model with no limitation on the number of activities. The activities are linear and give rise to a possible production set Y contained in R^n. If $y \in Y$, the negative components of y denote quantities of inputs and the positive components denote quantities of outputs. The assumptions on Y are

(3) Y is a closed convex cone.
(4) $Y \cap R^n_+ = \{0\}$. R^n_+ is the set of non-negative vectors in R^n.

That Y is a convex cone is equivalent to the production set being generated by linear activities. It means that if y and y' are producible, that is, elements of Y, then $\alpha y + \beta y'$ is also producible, that is, an element of Y, for any non-negative numbers α and β. Thus producible goods are divisible. Closedness is needed for the compactness of the feasible set. Assumption (4) is not restrictive. It is a recognition that goods which are never scarce are irrelevant to problems of economizing.

Finally two assumptions relate the consumption sector and the production sector. Let X be the total possible consumption set, that is, $X = \Sigma_{h=1}^{m} X_h$. The first relation is

(5) relative interior $X \cap$ relative interior $Y \neq \phi$.

Here the relative interior of a set is relative to the smallest linear subspace that contains it. This assumption insures that someone has income at any price vector which is consistent with equilibrium in the production sector, that is, satisfies von Neumann's Law. The second relation is an assumption that the economy is irreducible. Let I_1 and I_2 refer to nonempty subsets of consumers such that $I_i \cup I_2$ includes all consumers and $I_1 \cap I_2 = \phi$. Let $X^1 = \Sigma X_h$ for $h \in I_1$, and similarly for I_2. Let $\bar{X}_h$ be the convex hull of X_h and the origin of R^n. The irreducibility assumption is

(6) However I_1 and I_2 may be selected, if $x^1 = y - x^2$ with $x^1 \in X^1$, $y \in Y$, and $x^2 \in \bar{X}^2$, then there is also $\tilde{y} \in Y$ and $w \in \bar{X}^2$, such that $\tilde{x}^1 = \tilde{y} - x^2 - w$ and $\tilde{x} \in P(x^h)$ for all $h \in I_1$.

Assumption (6) guarantees that everyone has income if anyone has income. The meaning of having income is that the consumer is able to reduce his spending at the market price vector below the cost of his allocation and remain within his possible consumption set X_h.

Competitive equilibrium is defined by a price vector p, an output vector y, and vectors $x^1, \ldots, x^m$ of consumer trades. There is equilibrium in the production sector if von Neumann's Law holds, that is,

(I) $y \in Y$ and $p \cdot y = 0$, and for any $y' \in Y$, $p \cdot y' \leqslant 0$.

When y satisfies (I) it is not possible for the owners of inputs to withdraw them from activities where they are being used and employ them in other activities, whether in use or not, so that the receipts from the resulting outputs allow some inputs to earn larger returns while none of them earns less. This is the same condition for equilibrium in production that was given by Walras, or, for that matter, by Adam Smith (1776).

There is equilibrium in the consumer sector if the x^h satisfy

(II) $x^h \in X_h$ and $p \cdot x^h \leqslant 0$, and $p \cdot z > 0$ for any $z \in P_h(x^h)$, $h = 1, \ldots, m$.

When x^h satisfies condition (II), there is no preferred bundle of goods, including goods or services that are supplied by the consumer, which is available to him under his budget constraint. This is essentially the same condition used by Walras, except that he assumed that preferences could be represented by a strictly concave utility function. Thus he is able to refer to maximization of the utility function over the budget set uniquely at x^h.

Finally, there is market equilibrium when

(III) $\Sigma_{h=1}^{m} x^h = y$.

This is the condition that markets clear which was used by Walras.

If there is free disposal, Wald's Law may be derived directly from equilibrium in the production sector. The possibility of free disposal is recognized by the inclusion of disposal activities in the production cone, that is, an activity y^i for $i = 1, \ldots, n$ which has $y^i_i = -1$ and $y^i_j = 0$ for $j \neq i$. The condition $p \cdot y^i \leqslant 0$ implies that $p_i \geqslant 0$ must hold. Then if disposal occurs the condition $p \cdot y^i = 0$ implies that $p_i = 0$.

On the basis of Assumptions 1 through 6 it is possible to prove that a competitive equilibrium exists. This was first achieved in a model with assumptions for the demand sector put directly on preferences, in the manner of Walras, by Arrow and Debreu. At the same time McKenzie proved existence for a model with assumptions put on the demand functions rather than directly on preferences. Also McKenzie assumed a linear technology rather than a set of firms. This was a generalization of a model of Wald in which joint production was absent and very special assumption was made that the market demand functions satisfied the weak axiom of revealed preference. The weak axiom says if x is demanded at p and x' and p', then $p \cdot x' \leqslant p \cdot x$ implies that $p' \cdot x' < p' \cdot x$. This is a consistency requirement on choice under budget constraints. Wald's assumption was a deep insight. He anticipated the statement of this principle by Samuelson (e.g. 1947) who applied it to the demand of the individual consumer to derive most of the propositions of demand theory. Wald showed that the weak axiom assumed for the market leads to uniqueness of equilibrium. Subsequently it was shown by Arrow and Hurwicz (1958) that the weak axiom is implied by the assumption that all goods are gross substitutes. They also proved that the weak axiom confined to a comparison of choices between the equilibrium prices and other prices implies the global stability of a process of price adjustment in which the prices of goods are increased if excess demand exists and lowered if excess supply exists. Wald (1936b) wrote another paper on equilibrium in an exchange market which used assumptions closer to those of Arrow and Debreu, but this paper unfortunately was lost.

The only important distinction between the approach of Arrow and Debreu (see Debreu, 1962) and the approach expressed in Assumptions 1 through 6 is the use of a set of firms rather than a set of activities to generate the production set. Mathematically, through the introduction of entrepreneurial factors the approaches can be reconciled. However, the intentions of the two approaches are quite different. The linear model is intended to represent free entry into any line of production by cooperating factors, however organized in a legal sense, where economies of scale are sufficiently small to allow approximate linearity to be achieved by the multiplication of producing units. The lumpiness which is present is compared to that resulting from goods which are in fact indivisible, although they are treated as divisible. This leads to a reasonable approximation to real markets only if units are small compared with the levels of trade. This view of the competitive economy is consistent with the analysis of Marshall as well as Walras. Of course, it has to be recognized that in real economies some sectors cannot be approximated in this way. However, when linearity becomes a bad approximation to the production sector, convexity has in all likelihood become an equally bad approximation to the production sets of firms.

Recently an explicit modelling of the approach of the firms economy to the activities economy has been given by Novshek and Sonnenschein (1980). They use the model of quantity adjusting firms developed in a partial equilibrium context by Cournot to find an equilibrium for the firms economy. Then they let the firm size shrink and show that the Walrasian equilibrium of an activities economy is approached in the limit.

TWO INTERPRETATIONS OF THE FORMAL MODEL. Two basic interpretations of the general equilibrium model were described by Hicks and referred to as the spot economy and the futures economy. The spot economy is a market held on 'Monday' at which all transactions are arranged that involve delivery during the 'week'. This is the economy described by Walras. The equilibrium of the spot economy is called temporary equilibrium in the modern literature. Some effort has been devoted to an analysis of the path followed by such an economy through a succession of temporary equilibria. The role of expectations in the spot economy is critical, as Hicks recognized.

The futures economy on the other hand has a single market in which all future transactions are negotiated at once. Hicks does not treat this economy in detail, but turns to a sequence of spot markets with trading that is guided by expectations. In the futures economy goods available in different periods would be treated as different goods, so that the number of goods would be finite only if the economic horizon is finite. If there is perfect foresight the futures economy is a reasonable alternative and there is no reason why markets should reopen. However, when the future is uncertain and the available futures contracts are for sure delivery, or at least do not exist in sufficient variety to take account of all contingencies, there is no assurance that the contracts entered into will remain desirable or indeed can be executed. For this reason Hicks chose to do a dynamic analysis of a sequence of temporary equilibria in the main body of his work.

In order to avoid the problem of the feasibility of plans and the need to reopen markets, Debreu (1959) following a lead of Arrow (1953) introduced a specification of goods by the event in which they are made available. The set of events would have to discriminate all the circumstances that might make delivery impossible or undesirable, so there would be no motive for traders to reopen markets. Despite this complexity, it is a consistent model which may have relevance to the real world. In order to keep the set of goods finite they assume a finite horizon and a finite set of events, in addition to assuming a finite list of goods in terms of location and physical characteristics.

With this interpretation of the formal model there is no room for borrowing and lending since payments are cleared only once, at the beginning of time. Uncertainty is present since there is no assumption that the event realized at any future time is known. Rather it will be revealed when the time arrives. There is no reason for spot markets to arise since the transactions which have been made for the future event that is revealed are the ones each trader desired at the prices paid in those circumstances. Thus if a spot market were opened no transactions would take place.

Of course it is idealization to suppose that all relevant events could be described in advance, or, if they could, that it would be feasible to establish markets discriminating between them. An alternative is to use a succession of markets in which temporary equilibria are established while some trading in futures contracts takes place. However, the limiting cases of the pure spot economy or the pure futures economy have an analytical tractability that the mixed cases lack and for this reason they remain of great importance.

TEMPORARY EQUILIBRIUM. Once a sequence of markets is contemplated, rather than a single comprehensive market, plans for future trades become relevant and, therefore, expectations of the prices at which they can be made. Also money stocks and loans become useful in making financial preparations for the trading that is planned. Also, if there may be forward trading as well as spot trading, arbitrage is possible, and speculative trading arises which expresses disagreement among consumers about probable price levels on future spot and forward markets.

These complications were handled by Walras without an explicit analysis of demand by consumers for goods in the future using utility functions in which these goods appear. Rather he reduces the demand for future goods to a demand for assets in general which would provide the means for future purchases. On the other hand, he carefully distinguished between stocks of goods and their services, and the investments of the consumer are treated as if they were made directly in the stocks of goods whose services are sold to the entrepreneurs, or directly to consumers in the case of services of consumer goods.

The spirit of this analysis is to choose a period short enough that it is not too great a distortion of reality to suppose that all trades for this period can be concluded in advance as in the Arrow–Debreu model for the entire horizon, but the forms of industrial organization are abstracted from, so that attention may be concentrated on the productive activities and the ultimate beneficial owners of the resources whose services are used in them. Also to give the future some role in the decisions of the consumers but not a role requiring detailed analysis, Walras assumed that present market prices are expected to persist. In contrast, Hicks and Arrow–Debreu deal explicitly with intertemporal planning by firms and consumers. In a succession of markets this allows Hicks to analyse the effects of changes in expectations on the present market prices and the plans of agents.

The theory of Walras provides the most complete and detailed model of temporary general equilibrium that has ever been given, an impressive performance since it was also the first formal model of general equilibrium. He was able to deal with money, production, lending, and capital accumulation, and in his model an interest rate, price levels, and prices of capital goods and their services are all determined. He showed that the system was not overdetermined, and probably not underdetermined either, in that the number of independent functional relationships and the number of economic quantities to be determined are equal. He was not able to give a proof that an equilibrium in non-negative real variables exists for his model. However, proofs have since been given for simplified versions of it.

A fundamental difference between temporary equilibrium and equilibrium over a horizon is that part of the consumers' demand for goods in the temporary equilibrium is intended for investment rather than for consumption within the period while in the economy of the classical existence theorem consumers' demand is entirely aimed at consumption within the horizon. This raises two problems. One is to distinguish between resources devoted to this period's consumption and resources reserved for the support of consumption in future periods. The other is to explain how the decision to reserve a certain quantity of resources for future use is made. Walras went further to make the distinction between current and future use than any of his successors. They, on the other hand, have done much more analysis of the relation between investment and expectations. The Walrasian assumption on expectations was usually to project the prices arrived at in the current market into the future. This assumption is only appropriate for a stationary, or a steadily progressive, state of the economy. Of course, it has often been remarked that it is only in these conditions that expectations are likely to be correct.

Walras distinguished between consumption goods and services which are consumed in one use and consumption goods which are in effect capital goods providing consumer services, that is, having more than one use. Among the consumption goods which serve as capital goods he included consumption goods which are held in stocks to provide, as Walras put it, services of availability. Thus part of a person's income for a period may be invested in new stocks of consumer goods as well as in capital goods which are intended for use in productive activities. By the same token some of the productive activities which occur may occur in the household rather than in the factory, and these should satisfy the same profit conditions as the productive activities that occur in the firms.

The Walrasian approach to temporary equilibrium is entirely appropriate only to steady states where underlying circumstances, technology, tastes, and resources are constant, perhaps with capital stocks and population expanding at uniform rates. Then the comparative statics that can be done is a comparison of different steady states. On the other hand, in the Hicksian model where expectations of price changes are allowed, it is possible to consider the effect on the temporary equilibrium of changes in price expectations which need not duplicate changes in current prices. However, the approach of Walras allows him to ignore the consumer's portfolio problem and treat the consumer as only making a saving decision, since all assets of equal value are treated as indifferent with equal rates of return after allowing for depreciation and insurance costs. When there is uncertainty, the treatment of all assets as indifferent in this fashion is not justified even by the mean-variance theory of portfolio selection. The variances and covariances of asset returns must be taken into account. Thus Walras's theory of investment requires that expectations be held with certainty, although he only explicitly assumes certainty within the horizon of a single period, after allowing for fully insurable risks.

There are two features of the Walrasian theory of investment which are quite effective, even by modern standards. One is the analysis of the demand for money. Money is needed during the period to make payments which are planned in advance and the cost of this money service is simply the interest on a loan of that amount for the period. This is very close to the treatment of the demand for money for transactions purposes in modern theory. The demand for money as an asset is merged with the general demand for assets, since any net money balance at the end of the period will be expected to be lent at the current interest rate for the next period, either to others or implicitly to oneself. This represents a cash balance approach to monetary theory where cash balances are only wanted for transactions purposes. It leads to a strict quantity theory of the price of money in terms of other goods in comparisons between steady states.

The second effective feature of Walras's theory of investment is the recognition that the cost of investment goods will depend on the level of investment, since in the general equilibrium high levels of investment will raise the prices of the productive services needed to produce investment goods and thus the prices of the investment goods themselves. In this the Walrasian theory takes account of the distinction between the marginal efficiency of investment and the marginal efficiency of capital familiar in the Keynesian literature, as well as the modern notion of the cost of adjustment resulting from an increase in the level of investment.

The two main deficiencies of the Walrasian theory of temporary equilibrium are its lack of an analysis of the demand for assets in general in terms of the future consumption streams that the assets are expected to support and the expected utility they promise to yield, and its lack of an analysis of the demand for particular assets in terms of the distribution of their expected returns.

The neglect of future plans for consumption in determining current demand was addressed by Hicks. He did not suppose that consumers make detailed plans but that they form vague plans and expectations of future prices, which still allow some comparative statics methods to be applied in estimating the effect on current demand of changes in current or future expected prices.

Since firms are recognized explicitly in Hicks's model, they are also represented as making plans for future inputs and outputs in the light of price expectations, which in his case can be identified with the expectations of individuals who become entrepreneurs. The equilibrium of such a model in one period is a set of prices for all the goods and services traded in the market of that period such that the demand for each good or service, including any contract for future delivery that happens to be traded, equals the supply.

Hicks assumes that each consumer and each firm in its planning applies actual or expected interest rates to discount expected future prices to the present so that the problem of maximizing utility for the consumer, or present value for the firm, does not differ, in principle, from the static problem. However, he must assume that agents are risk neutral or in any case that distributions of prices may be replaced by single prices, or certainty equivalents. Thus he is no more able than Walras to analyse how the value of an asset is influenced by the distribution of its returns. But he is able to consider how changes in current prices influence expected future prices, when expected future prices do not necessarily change by the same amounts. This may be the most significant advance made by Hicks beyond Walras, together with the corollary of planning by firms and consumers for a future that involves expected prices changes.

EXPECTATIONS IN TEMPORARY EQUILIBRIUM. A natural way to generalize the Hicksian model and one which has been followed in recent years, for example, by Grandmont, is to impute to each trader an expectation function which gives a probability distribution over future prices, and perhaps over other relevant variables, both market and environmental, as functions of previous values taken by the same variables. Then assuming that each trader has a criterion by which he can choose an optimal trade plan given his expectations, he will determine an excess demand as a function of current prices. Then equilibrium is achieved if there is market clearing at the current prices. Since in the Walrasian or Hicksian model there are two kinds of traders, consumers and entrepreneurs of firms, criteria must be found for each kind of trader.

The criterion for the consumer is rather easily arrived at. It is assumed that each consumer has a von Neumann–Morgenstern utility function, so that any current trade can be evaluated in terms of the expected utility whith it makes possible. The utility in turn is derived from the utility of the various possible consumption streams multiplied by their probabilities of occurrence. Of course, these consumption streams and their probabilities logically underlie the expected utilities but they cannot be known to the consumer in detail. The probability distribution on consumption streams is induced by the probability distribution on prices and environmental variables, together with the current trade of the consumer and his plans for future trades, which are in turn contingent on the prices and environmental variables realized in the future. As Hicks points out the consumer may only try to plan levels of spending and certain large expenditures for the future. Particular price expectations will affect these plans and current spending, in total as well as on specific items. What is needed for the theory is to express consumer's demand finally as a function of current prices so that the condition of market clearing will characterize equilibrium prices. The logic of this analysis is entirely compatible with the methods of Walras, given stationary conditions for tastes, technology and resources. In simple models it can be spelled out in detail.

On the other hand, there is little agreement on an appropriate criterion for the firm. The difficulty arises that the firm is usually owned by many consumers whose preferences and probability beliefs differ. The consumer does not own capital goods directly but only stock in firms. Moreover, the firms make investment plans and plan their dividend streams in considerable independence of their owners. Walras abstracts from these difficulties in his formal development by two means. First, he treats the consumer as the owner of capital goods which are rented to the entrepreneur. Second, he values the capital goods on the assumption that prices of productive services, interest rates, depreciation rates, and insurance rates will be constant in the future. Given the prices of the productive services arbitrage in the market for capital goods results in a uniform ratio between the net rental of the capital goods, or the prices of their productive services less depreciation and insurance charges, and the prices of the capital goods. In Walras's notation $P_k = p_k/(i + \mu_k + v_k)$ where k indexes capital goods, P_k is the price of the capital goods, p_k is the price of its service, i is the interest rate per period, $\mu_k P_k$ is the depreciation change per period, and $v_k P_k$ is the insurance charge per period. In equilibrium the consumer will be indifferent between capital goods in making investments since they all promise equally attractive returns. This also applies in a similar way to investments in circulating capital or in loans.

Hicks adapts the Walrasian viewpoint to a model in which expectations are point valued but not static by imputing to the entrepreneur, who now owns the capital goods, a plan of inputs, including initial stocks, and outputs, including terminal stocks, whose values are discounted back to the present. Then the entrepreneur chooses a plan with the largest discounted value. In this case the firm achieves maximum value in the eyes of its owner. Radner (1972) adapts the Hicksian viewpoint to a model in which point estimates of future prices are not a sufficient basis for decisions. In a temporary equilibrium model his approach imputes to each firm a von Neumann–Morgenstern utility function over alternative dividend streams. This would imply an expected utility for alternative investments in the current period in the same way that the utility of alternative consumption plans implies expected utility for current spending by the consumer.

On the other hand, by use of the stock market it is possible to bring consumers into the decision making of firms. The firm's criterion is then to choose a plan of production and investment which leads to a maximum value for its shares on the stock market. It can be argued that if the firm chooses a plan which fails to maximize its value in the stock market the stock market will not be in equilibrium, since there is a profitable arbitrage opportunity for someone to buy controlling interest in the firm and revise its planning.

Existence theorems for temporary equilibrium have been proved in many special cases, particularly for trading economies where production does not enter and the number of periods is taken to be finite. Typically the method of proof parallels a method of proof for the model with complete markets, that is, appropriate continuity properties for individual, and thus market, excess demand functions are proved for the goods and services, and the future contracts, if any, which are traded in the current period. The application of a fixed point theorem completes the proof that a price system exists which results in market clearing, that is, puts each excess demand function equal to zero. However, some special problems do arise.

Consider a market at the start of period 1 when there are two periods and a second market will be held at the start of period 2. There is uncertainty about the endowment of period 2 and about the spot prices of the second market. All goods are perishable. Suppose there is trading in contracts for current delivery and in forward contracts for delivery in the second period. Let x_1^h, x_2^h be the vectors of goods and services delivered to the hth consumer in periods 1 and 2 respectively. Denote by w_1^h and w_2^h the vectors of endowments for the hth consumer in periods 1 and 2 respectively. Let $\psi^h(p_1, q_1)$ be the expectation function for the hth consumer, that is, the value of ψ^h is a probability distribution of (w_2^h, p_2), where p_1 and p_2 are the vectors of spot prices in periods 1 and 2, while q_1 is the vector of forward prices in period 1 for sure delivery in period 2. There is a finite set of goods and services in each period and a finite number of consumers each of whom holds positive initial stocks in the first period. The possible consumption sets are $X_1^h = R_+^{n_1}$ and $X_2^h = R_+^{n_2}$, the positive orthants of the respective commodity spaces.

The following assumptions are made for the consumer.

(1) There is a concave and monotone utility function u^h of von Neumann–Morgenstern type, that is, preferences over trades in the first period may be determined by taking the sum of the utilities of the resulting consumption vectors weighted by these probabilities of occurrence.

(2) The expectation function $\psi^h(p_1, q_1)$ is continuous in an appropriate sense.

(3) For every (p_1, q_1), $\psi^h(p_1, q_1)$ gives probability 1 to the set of (w_2^h, p_2) for which p_2 is positive.

(4) The support of ψ^h is independent of (p_1, q_1). The convex hull of the projection of the support of ψ^h on the second period price space has a non-empty interior Π^h.

With these assumptions a necessary and sufficient condition for the existence of competitive equilibrium is that the intersection Π of the Π^h not be empty. In other words there must be an open set of spot prices in the second period which all traders believe to have a positive probability of occurrence. Then, if the forward prices q_1 lie in Π and p_1 and q_1 are positive, excess demand is well defined. Let D be the set of (p_1, q_1) satisfying these conditions. As (p_1, q_1) converges to the boundary of D, excess demand diverges to ∞. This happens because preferences are monotone and for q_1 outside Π unlimited arbitrage becomes profitable to some trader. These results were reached by Green (1973). It should be noted that point expectations are not consistent with the assumption that Π is not empty, unless all traders expect the same prices next period. However, Π might not be needed to bound short sales if other considerations limit the commitments that will be accepted in view of the likelihood that they can be fulfilled.

MONEY IN TEMPORARY EQUILIBRIUM. There is little difficulty in introducing money into the temporary equilibrium model. It must be recognized that money serves in at least two capacities, to facilitate exchange, and as an asset with its own prospects for losing or gaining value relative to other goods. In addition it may serve as a numeraire, in terms of which prices are stated. In its capacity as an asset in a market with uncertainty, money may contribute to a diversified portfolio. On the other hand, in its capacity to facilitate exchange, money balances will affect the cost of making transactions and thus the stream of consumption

17

which is realizable from given resources. Given his context, where risks are assumed to be insurable, Walras is particularly clear in his treatment of money. If some good other than money serves as numeraire, the price of the service of availability of money is written by Walras as p_m, and the price of money itself as P_m. Then as for any asset the ratio of the net rental to the asset price is equal to the interest rate or $p_m / P_m = i$. This if money serves as the numeraire, $P_m = 1$ and $p_m = i$. Although his analysis seems somewhat artificial because uninsurable risks are absent, Walras indicates clearly how cash balances may contribute to productive efficiency and to consumer utility.

If attention is concentrated on the asset role of money, so that the transaction role is neglected, it may be shown that the assumption of static expectations may lead to the absence of equilibrium for the current period. Static expectations imply that the relative prices of present and future goods cannot be changed. Therefore, price changes leading to intertemporal substitution are prevented. Only the wealth effects of price changes have free play since price level decreases raise the value of the money stock and conversely for increases. However, as Grandmont (1983) has demonstrated, these real balance effects may be insufficient to equate supply and demand. For example, if there is excess demand for current goods, this excess demand may not be eliminated by increases in the current price level which are accompanied by equally large increases in the future price level. In a trading economy the effect of the price increases is to reduce the wealth of the traders towards the endowment point $(w(1), w(2))$ in a two period model. Suppose there is only one good, which is perishable, and money is the only store of value. Then if the marginal utility of the current endowment exceeds the marginal utility of the second period endowment for all traders, the price of the good cannot rise high enough to reduce current demand to the current endowment. The same dilemma may arise when the Hicksian elasticity of expectations is equal to one, even though expected prices do not equal current prices.

Grandmont considers a model of this type where trading in futures contracts is excluded so that point expectations do not cause difficulties. It is a trading economy in which consumers receive an endowment of perishable goods in each period of their lives and an initial money stock in the first period. In the current period they maximize a utility function of consumption over the remaining periods of life (assuming the life span to be known) subject to budget constraints of the form $p_t x_t + m_t = p_t w_t + m_{t-1}$, where future prices p_t are equal to functions ψ_t of present prices p_1. He assumes

(1) The utility function $u^h(x_1, \ldots, x_{n(h)})$ is continuous, increasing, and strictly quasi-concave for every h.

(2) The endowments w_t^h are positive for all h and t, $1 \leqslant t \leqslant n(h)$.

(3) Total money stock $M = \Sigma_h m_h$ is positive.

He then proves that the temporary monetary equilibrium exists, that is, money prices are well defined, if every agent's price expectations ψ_t^h are continuous and, for at least one agent, who will be living in the next period and who has a positive money stock, price expectations are bounded away from 0 and ∞. In Grandmont's opinion this result leaves the existence of temporary equilibrium 'somewhat problematic'.

However, it seems quite inappropriate to deal with a money which has no role to play in facilitating transactions. Grandmont and Younes (1972) have studied general equilibrium in a model similar to the model just described except that lifetimes are taken to be infinite and utility functions are separable by time period, that is $u^h(x_1,\dots) = \Sigma_{t=1}^{\infty} \delta^t u^h(t)$ for $0 < \delta < 1$. Also money is now assigned a role in transactions, that is, only part of the proceeds of sales in the current period can be used to finance purchases in this period. Thus in each period there is both a budgetary constraint as before and, in addition, a liquidity constraint, which may be written in simplest form as $p_t(x_t - w_t)^+ \leqslant m_t + kp_t(x_t - w_t)^-$, where for any vector z we write $z_i^+ = \max(z_i, 0)$ and $z_i^- = \max(-z_i, 0)$, and $0 < k < 1$. Thus the fraction k of receipts from sales can be used to buy goods in the current period. This fraction could be allowed to vary by consumer and by good. The constraint on purchases is entirely in the spirit of Walras. It is an explicit modelling of a need for liquidity that he left implicit in his account.

In order to prove that a monetary equilibrium exists an assumption to bound expected prices is made which is very similar to the previous assumption for this purpose, and also very similar to the assumption made by Green to obtain existence of temporary equilibrium in a non-monetary economy with futures trading. The assumption is that the set of expected prices, over a finite planning horizon, that result from all possible choices of current prices, which are assumed positive, lie in a compact subset of the set of positive future prices. Then if all consumers have continuous expectations which satisfy this assumption, and the assumptions of the previous model are also met, there will exist a temporary equilibrium in this case also. Indeed, the case $k = 1$, where the liquidity motive is lacking, can be allowed.

In the second model where money has a transactions role expectations are described as depending on past prices as well as current prices, which leads inelastic price expectations to be more plausible. It also gives plausibility to correct foresight in states of stationary equilibrium over sequences of periods. Grandmont and Younes (1973) prove that the stationary equilibria of the model are not Pareto optimal. However, they can be made Pareto optimal by use of a lump sum tax to reduce the quantity of money by a factor equal to the discount factor for utility. It is then proved that a continuum of such equilibria exist to sustain any Pareto optimal allocation, since the price level falls by the same factor, and it is not worthwhile to reduce a money stock, even if it is in excess of transaction requirements. Moreover, if the tax rate is set slightly too high, the consumer will always wish to increase his real balances and no stationary equilibrium will exist. Grandmont and Younes are not able to prove that an exact stationary equilibrium exists for a fixed money stock, although a near equilibrium exists if the discount factor is near 1.

In addition to proofs of existence and non-optimality for monetary equilibria, Grandmont and Younes show that the quantity theory holds between stationary equilibria, that is, if p and m_h, $h = 1,\dots,m$, provide a stationary equilibrium, then

λp and λm_h also provide one. This is the conclusion of Walras as well. On the other hand, the stationary equilibria of a monetary economy will differ from the stationary equilibria of a barter economy unless $\delta = 1$. This is apparent from the fact that the barter economy's equilibria are Pareto optimal and the monetary economy's equilibria are not, unless $\delta = 1$. Thus the simple 'classical dichotomy' does not hold.

EQUILIBRIUM OVER TIME. In addition to temporary equilibrium Hicks considered the possibility of equilibrium over time, in the sense that the expectations held by traders in one market about prices on future markets are realized when those future markets are held. However, when there is uncertainty it is not clear what is meant by the realization of expectations. If expectations take the form of a non-atomic probability measure over future prices, any vector of prices within the support of the measure is as likely as any other, that is, it has zero probability. Nor does the Hicksian trick of replacing the probability distribution by a representative price, depending on the trader, avoid the difficulty, since the representative price is not typically a statistic of the price distribution, such as the mean or the mode. Thus even if all traders held the same expectations in the sense of a probability distribution for prices, they would not have the same representative prices except by the chance that their circumstances and their risk preferences also coincide.

A way to resolve this dilemma was provided by Radner (1972). His solution is a type of perfect foresight. All traders hold the same point expectations for prices with certainty, contingent on the event in which the market is held. Only a finite number of dates are allowed and only a finite number of events may occur in each. From the viewpoint of a given market the relevant elementary events are the possible sequences of states of nature that may occur up to the horizon. For any such sequence the traders expect correctly a corresponding sequence of prices. This does not lead to a grand initial market in which all future exchanges are arranged because the set of forward commitments which are actually available in the market is a small subset of all those associated with future events. For example, it may be that most commodities are traded for sure delivery and only one commodity (money or the numeraire) is traded on a contingent basis (insurance). It should be noted that this construction does not depend on any agreement between traders on the probabilities of the alternative events. Thus the expectation functions which were introduced in the discussion of temporary equilibrium would not be likely to be the same for different traders.

In this setting the trader plans a sequence of consumptions contingent on the events in which they occur and also a sequence of trades on the markets which are open. Spot markets are open for all commodities at all dates but only a small subset of the possible markets in forward contracts may be open at any particular date. In any case since the number of dates and states of nature and thus of elementary events is finite, only finitely many prices will arise.

Let X_h be the consumption set of the hth consumer. Let M be the set of elementary date-events pairs. A consumption-trade plan for the hth consumer is a pair (x^h, z^h) where x_m^h is the consumption planned for $m \in M$ and z_m^h is the trade planned for $m \in M$. Let $\Gamma_h(p)$ be the set of feasible plans for h, given prices p. In particular, (x^h, z^h) in $\Gamma_h(p)$ implies that consumption x_m^h plus net deliveries $\bar{z}_m^h$ due at m are not greater than resource endowments w_m^h for each m and the budget constraint $p_m z_m^h$ holds at each $m \in M$.

Let $\gamma^h(p)$ be the set of plans in $\Gamma_h(p)$ which are optimal for h. An equilibrium of plans and price expectations (including current prices which are known) is given by plans (x^h, z^h) and expected prices p such that (x^h, z^h) is in $\gamma^h(p)$ for each h, that is, the plans are preferred at the expected prices, and the sum $\Sigma_h \Sigma_m^h$ of commitments at each m is non-negative, and the value of commitments $p_m \Sigma_h z_m^h = 0$ at each m, that is, Walras's Law holds. In such a purely trading economy for perishable goods with a finite set of dates and events and under assumptions of the usual kind of preferences, and positive endowments which lie in the interior of consumption sets, Radner proves that an equilibrium exists.

It is not difficult to bring production into this setting if firms are introduced with fixed production plans and with shares which are traded on a stock exchange. The ownership of a share of a firm can be equated to the ownership of a share of its output, including the end of the period capital stock. The output of a firm at any date would depend on the event, and the function relating this output to the events would be known by traders, just as future prices of goods are known, contingent on events. Now, in addition to goods prices, share prices are foreseen in each event at each date with certainty. As before the number of dates and events is finite.

A feature of this model not present in the trading model is that consumers do not own the resources of the firms as individual goods but as proportions of the batch of goods that firms hold. The consumer can buy and sell goods forward by means of long and short positions in the stock market but the trade he arranges by these means for one event at the next date determines his trade for all other events at that date. Thus spot markets still may offer useful alternatives, quite aside from the practical difficulties of physically dissolving the firm. Of course, given the presence of spot markets, dissolution of the firms is not needed if the value of the firm equals or exceeds the value of its resources.

If one tries to go further to specify how the production and trading plans are arrived at, a major problem arises of setting the objectives of the firm. Hicks solves this problem by assuming that the production plan chosen would have the maximum discounted value among those available. This value could be calculated since expectations were single-valued and interest rate, actual or expected, could be used in arriving at present values. Moreover, firms were treated like single proprietorships. In the modern literature firms have sometimes been assigned utility functions defined on the streams of profits. Another suggestion is to suppose that the firm adopts the plan that maximizes the value of its shares on the stock market. This would seem to be the approach most in accord with other parts of general equilibrium theory. However, it encounters the difficulty that the judgement of the management and the judgement of the market on the probability of different events may not coincide. If this difference of judgement exists, the market solution would be for the firm to be purchased through a takover by those who value its potential most highly and the management displaced. Markets which work in this way would correspond quite well to the original Walrasian model.

Various results on the existence of a general equilibrium have been reached with special models of production by firms. One theorem of Radner extends the existence of an equilibrium of plans and price expectations to this context. His assumptions are:

(1) Consumers satisfy the usual conditions on convexity, non-satiation, and positive endowments.

(2) Consumers own the shares of firms and each consumer owns shares in every firm.

(3) Producers have closed, convex production sets with free disposal. The total production set satisfies the condition that the negative of a producible vector of commodities is not producible.

(4) Each firm has a continuous, strictly concave utility function on profit streams.

With these assumptions he does not achieve a full existence theorem because the model is not well adapted to handle the entry and exit of forms. What may happen is that some firms show an excess supply of shares in some events and dates. Then since the firms are treated like partnerships with unlimited liability, negative share prices might be justified at this point. In any case the questions of entry and exit of firms is one that the Arrow–Debreu model also fails to deal with. The theorem proved by Radner only finds a 'pseudo-equilibrium' where the value of total excess supply (of shares) is minimized.

In the foregoing discussion it has been assumed that only a subset, possibly small, of the potential Arrow–Debreu markets is open. It is possible to justify the selection of markets which are open by postulating costs for carrying out transactions. If the markets which are open are given, the previous equilibria may be supported by assigning infinite transactions costs to the lost markets and zero costs to the open ones. Otherwise the open markets will be endogenous to the general equilibrium. In the analysis of markets with transaction activities which consume resources the same convexity or linearity assumptions have been used as for the production technology. Then it is not difficult to prove existence of equilibrium under assumptions of the usual sort.

RATIONAL EXPECTATIONS. It has been implicitly assumed in the preceding discussion of temporary equilibrium that the traders have the same information available. If this is not the case the complication arises that the equilibrium price may convey information. For example, in the market for umbrellas if some traders have the benefit of weather forecasts and some do not, a high price based on the demand of informed traders will signal to uninformed traders that rain is expected. Then all traders are informed and an equilibrium price must be consistent with fully informed demand.

A difficulty arises if it happens that the utilities of consumers depend on events in contrary ways, that is, uninformed consumers use umbrellas to ward off sun and informed traders to ward off rain. The price will be higher if rainy weather is expected by informed traders but if informed traders perceive this and become informed, the high price may not appear and a fully informed market may not show a price difference depending on the weather forecast. But then no information is transmitted so the weather forecast cannot be read out of equilibrium prices. The conclusion is that no equilibrium is possible. However, the result requires an exact balance in the effects of rain and sun on the two sets of traders, so it is unlikely to hold. More robust examples of nonexistence were given by Green (1977) and Kreps (1977). The idea of the discontinuity was first proposed by Radner (1967).

A rational expectations equilibrium is said to exist if there is a function ϕ mapping states of the world into equilibrium prices which is invertible, that is, ϕ^{-1} exists, mapping prices, from a normalized set, into states of the world. It is clear that such a function will exist if the equilibrium price which appears when all traders are fully informed is uniquely determined by the elementary event, and the relation is one to one. It is also clear, given a finite set of elementary events, that the correspondence of prices to elementary events will be one to one in all but exceptional cases. Then the equilibrium is said to be revealing. But the price function of a revealing full information equilibrium is a price function that provides a rational expectations equilibrium. This observation is due to Grossman (1981).

The situation is more complicated when the possibility is recognized that spending resources will allow more information to be gathered. The information that is disseminated free of charge by prices will discourage the use of resources to gather information and thus prevent the attainment of a Pareto optimum. In welfare terms a suboptimal amount of resources will be devoted to information activities.

AN INFINITE HORIZON. In the Arrow–Debreu model of general equilibrium there are a finite number of periods, a finite number of locations, a finite number of events, and a finite number of commodity types, so the number of distinct goods when all these grounds for distinguishing goods have been recognized is still finite. The principal objection to the restriction to a finite number of goods is that it requires a finite horizon and there is no natural way to choose the final period. Moreover, since there will be terminal stocks in the final period there is no natural way to value them without contemplating future periods in which they will be used. The finiteness of the number of locations and commodity types is achieved by making a discrete approximation to a continuum, and perhaps the finiteness of the number of states of nature can also be viewed in this light. But in the case of time, a discrete approximation by periods still leaves a denumerable infinity of dates.

There are two principal models in which an infinite number of goods appear. In one model there is a finite number of infinitely lived consumers. Such a consumer may be considered to represent a series of descendants stretching into the indefinite future, so that consumers alive in the present period have an interest in the goods of all periods. The other model has an infinite number of consumers, but only a finite number of them are alive in any period. This model is called the overlapping generations model. It was first proposed and explicitly analysed by Samuelson (1958).

A model of general competitive equilibrium with a finite number of consumers and an infinite number of commodities was first presented in rigorous form by Peleg and Yaari (1970). They assumed the number of commodities to be denumerable. This is a basic case since a noncompact but separable commodity space can be approximated arbitrarily closely with a denumerable set of commodities in the same sense that a compact commodity space can be approximated by a finite set of commodities. This assumes that a sensible neighbourhood system can be defined in the commodity space, as Debreu does for the dimensions of location and time with places and periods.

Peleg and Yaari present a trading model without production. The commodity space s is the space of all real sequences. In order to discuss continuity the space must be given a topology, in this case, the product topology. Thus a sequence of points converges if it converges in every coordinate, that is, $x^s \to x$, $s = 1, 2, \ldots$, if $x^s(i) \to x(i)$ for $i = 0, 1, \ldots$. The space is presented as a sequence of real numbers but by grouping terms it may equally well represent a sequence of vectors, for example, commodity bundles occurring in successive time periods. The hth trader has an initial stock w_h, where $w_h \in s$ and a preference relation $\succsim_h$, which is reflexive, transitive and complete on s_+, the set of non-negative sequences. Strict preferences $\succ_h$ is defined by $x \succ_h y$ if $x \succsim_h y$ and not $y \succsim_h x$.

Peleg and Yaari prove an existence theorem for this economy on the following assumptions.

(1) Desirability. If $x \geqslant y$, then $x \succsim_h y$,
(2) Strong convexity. If $x \neq y$ and $x \succsim_h y$, then $\alpha x + (1 - \alpha)y \succ_h y$ for $0 < \alpha < 1$.
(3) Continuity. The two sets $\{y \mid y \succsim_h x\}$ and $\{y \mid x \succsim_h y\}$ are closed.
(4) Positivity of total supply. Let $w = \Sigma_{h=1}^m w_h$. Then $w > 0$.

A price system is a real sequence $\pi > 0$ which satisfies $\Sigma_{i=0}^\infty \pi(i)w_h(i) < \infty$, that is, the value of the initial bundles is finite. This implies that $\pi(i)w_h(i)$ converges to 0 as $i \to \infty$. A competitive equilibrium is given by $(x_1, \ldots, x_m; \pi)$ such that π is a price system, $\Sigma_{i=0}^\infty \pi(i)x_h(i) \leqslant \Sigma_{i=0}^\infty \pi(i)w_h(i)$, for each h, and $\Sigma_{i=0}^\infty \pi(i)x(i) \leqslant \Sigma_{i=0}^\infty \pi(i)w_h(i)$ implies $x_h \succsim_h x$. Peleg and Yaari prove that a competitive equilibrium exists.

It is clear from their discussions, and it has become even clearer in subsequent work, that the use of a topology such that, in the context of an infinite horizon interpretation of the model, impatience is implied by continuity of preferences is the crucial assumption for a proof of existence. That the product topology implies impatience may be seen in the following way. If $x \succ_h y$ then by continuity there is a neighbourhood U of x such that $z \in U$ implies $z \succ_h y$. However, a neighbourhood U is defined by $|z(i) - x(i)| < \epsilon > 0$ for a finite number of coordinates where the remaining coordinates are free. Thus given $y \succ_h x$, there must exist $N > 0$ such that $z(i) = x(i)$ for $i \leqslant N$ and $z(i) = 0$ for $i > N$, and $z \succ_h y$. These conditions are met if the preference order is representable by a separable utility function which is the sum of periodwise utilities discounted back to the present at a constant rate per period, and these utilities are continuous and uniformly bounded. Such a utility function is a common way of expressing impatience.

A model of general competitive equilibrium which allows for production where there is an infinite number of commodities was first presented in a rigorous form by Bewley (1972). A preference relation $\succsim_h$ is assumed for each consumer as in Peleg and Yaari. We will describe Bewley's model for the case of a sequence of periods with an infinite horizon where N_i is the finite set of commodities available in the tth period. Then the set of all commodities is

$$M = \bigcup_{t=1}^{\infty} N_t.$$

It is assumed that $M = M_c \cup M_p$ where M_c and M_p are disjoint and M_c contains the consumption goods. Bewley confines attention to the commodity space l_∞ of bounded sequences of real numbers. Let $K_c = \{x \in l_\infty \,|\, x(i) = 0$ for not $i \in M_c$, $x(i) \geqslant 0$ for $i \in M_c\}$, and similarly for K_p. Let $\tilde{K}_c$ have the same definition as K_c except that $x(i) > \varepsilon > 0$ for all $i \in M_c$ for some given ε. Bewley's existence theorem holds for a weaker notion of continuity than that of componentwise convergence, but we will stay with the definition used by Peleg and Yaari for the sake of simplicity. Then the assumptions on the consumer sector are

(1) The consumption sets $X_h = K_c - w_h$ where w_h is the endowment of the hth consumer.

(2) The sets $\{y \,|\, y \succsim_h x\}$ and $\{y \,|\, x \succsim_h y\}$ are closed. Also $\{y \,|\, y \succsim_h x\}$ is convex.

(3) M_c is not empty and for each h, if $x \in X_h$ and $y \in \tilde{K}_c$, then $x + y \succ_h x$.

The production sector is defined by means of production sets Y_t which convert inputs belonging to N_{t-1} into outputs belong to N_t. Then $Y = \Sigma_{t=1}^{\infty} Y_t$. The assumptions on the production sector are

(4) Y is a convex closed cone with vertex at 0.

(5) If $w \in l_\infty$, then $Y + w \cap l_\infty$ is bounded.

(6) If $y \in Y$, then $y^n \in Y$ where $y_t^n = y_t$ for $t = 0, \ldots, n$, and $y_t^n = 0$ for $t > n$.

(7) $-K_p \subset Y$.

Assumption (4) means that each Y_t is a linear activities model as Walras assumed. Assumption (5) excludes unbounded production from given inputs. Assumption (6) allows production to end at any time with free disposal of the final outputs. Assumption (7) allows free disposal of all goods other than consumption goods.

In addition there is one assumption which relates the consumption sector and the production sector.

(8) For each consumer h, there exists $\bar{x}_h \in X_h$ and $\bar{y}_h \in Y$ such that $\bar{y}_h(i) - \bar{x}_h(i) > \varepsilon > 0$ for all i and some $\varepsilon > 0$.

Assumption (8) protects consumer income in the sense that the consumer is not reduced to the subsistence level in equilibrium. That is to say, there are cheaper consumption bundles within this consumption set at equilibrium prices. An equilibrium is an allocation $(x_1, \ldots, x_m, y)$ and a price sequence

$\pi = (\pi(0), \pi(1), \ldots)$ where $\pi(i)$ is non-negative for all i but different from zero for some i, which satisfy the conditions:

(I) $y \in Y$ and $\pi y = 0$, $\pi z \leqslant 0$ for all $z \in Y$. The profit condition.

(II) $x_h \in X_h$ and $\pi x_h = 0$, all h, and $z \succ_h x_h$ implies that $\pi z > \pi x_h$. The demand condition.

(III) $\Sigma_{h=1}^{m} x_h = y$. The balance condition.

On the basis of the assumptions Bewley is able to prove that an equilibrium exists where the price system $\pi \in l_1$, that is, $\Sigma_{i=0}^{\infty} \pi(i) < \infty$. This represents a generalization of the classical existence theorem in the form given by McKenzie to the case of denumerably many commodities, retaining the assumption of a finite number of consumers. The argument is stated in terms of an infinite horizon and a finite number of goods in each period, but the original theorem is more general and applies to the case of uncertainty with an infinite number of events as well as to models with a continuum of commodities. The continuum of commodities may arise from a variation in the physical properties of the goods and services.

OVERLAPPING GENERATIONS. In the overlapping generations model of general equilibrium the number of consumers as well as the number of commodities is infinite. However, at any given time the number of both is finite. While the model with a finite number of infinitely lived consumers treats the consumers who are living as if their lives were extended into the indefinite future by the lives of their descendants, in the classical overlapping generations model bequests are neglected and each generation is assumed to be interested only in its own consumption.

The first rigorous analyses of an overlapping generations model in a general equilibrium setting were done by Balasko, Cass and Shell (1980) and by Wilson (1981). They treat an exchange model in which all goods perish in each period and each consumer receives an endowment in each period. They assume that each consumer lives for two periods. However, this assumption is not essential. What is essential is that lifetimes are finite in length and some of the people alive at any date have lifetimes which overlap the lifetimes of some people who are born later than they.

The formal model makes these assumptions.

(1) In each period $t (t = 1, 2, \ldots)$ there is an arbitrary, finite number of perishable commodities $n' \geqslant 1$.

(2) Each consumer $h = 1, 2, \ldots$ lives for two periods. At the start of period t an arbitrary but finite number of consumers is born with indices $h \in G^t$.

(3) Consumption sets $X_h = R_+^{n(0)}$ for $h \in G^0$ the consumers alive when the economy begins and $X_h = R_+^{n(t)} \times R_+^{n(t+1)}$ for $h \in G^t$, $t \geqslant 1$. Write $x_h = x_h'$ for $h \in G^0$ and $x_h = (x_h(t), x_h(t+1))$ for $h \in G^t$.

(4) Each consumer has a utility function, $u_h(x(1))$ for $h \in G^0$ and $u_h(x(t), x(t+1))$ for $h \in G^t$. Utility functions u_h are continuous, quasi-concave, and without local maxima.

(5) Each consumer receives an endowment, $w_h = w_h(1)$ for $h \in G^0$ and $w_h = (w_h(t), w_h(t+1))$ for $h \in G'$. For each h, $w_h \geqslant 0$ and $w_h \neq 0$.

(6) The economy is intertemporally irreducible. Let $I(t) = \{h | h \in G^s \text{ for } 0 \leqslant s \leqslant t\}$. Then there exists a sequence $t_\mu \to \infty$ with the following property. Given any allocation $x = (x_1, x_2, \ldots)$ and $I_1(t_\mu)$ and $I_2(t_\mu) \neq \phi$, with $I_1(t_\mu) \cap I_2(t_\mu) = \phi$, and $I_1(t_\mu) \cup I_2(t_\mu) = I(t_\mu)$, there exist $y_h \geqslant 0$ for $h \in I_1(t_\mu)$ and $x_h' \geqslant 0$ for $h \in I_2(t_\mu)$ such that $\Sigma_{h \in I_1(t_\mu)} y_i(t) = 0$ when $\Sigma_{h \in I_1(t_\mu)} w_{hi}(t) = 0$, for $1 \leqslant i \leqslant n'$, $1 \leqslant t \leqslant t_\mu + 1$, and

$$\sum_{h \in I_2(t_\mu)} x_h' \leqslant \sum_{h \in I_1(t_\mu)} (w_h + y_h) + \sum_{h \in I_2(t_\mu)} w_h.$$

Moreover, $u_h(x_h') \geqslant u_h(x_h)$ for all $h \in I_2(t_\mu)$ with the strict inequality for some h.

Assumption (6) is the irreducibility assumption of McKenzie adapted to economies made up of the consumers born by the period t_μ. It says that it is always possible to increase the welfare of the second subgroup if the scale of the endowment of the first subgroup is increased.

Let $p = (p(1), p(2), \ldots)$ where $p(t) \in R^{n(t)}$. Then the pair (x, p) is a competitive equilibrium if

(I) For all h, $u_h(x_h)$ is maximal over all z_h such that $p(t)z_h(t) + (p(t+1)z_h(t+1) \leqslant p(t)w_h(t) + p(t+1)w_h(t+1)$ if $h \in G^t$, $t \geqslant 1$, and $p(1)z_h(1) \leqslant p(1)w_h(1)$ if $h \in G^0$, where $z_h \geqslant 0$.

(II) $\Sigma_h x_{hi}(t) \leqslant \Sigma_h w_{hi}(t)$ with equality if $p_i(t) > 0$, where the summation is over $h \in G^{t-1} \cup G^t$, $1 \leqslant i \leqslant M(t)$ and $t \geqslant 1$.

Condition (I) is the usual demand condition and condition (II) is the balance condition. Balasko, Cass and Shell (1980) prove that the six assumptions listed imply the existence of a competitive equilibrium. They show that the artificial assumptions on birthdates and lifetimes are irrelevant by a redefinition of the period. They also conjecture that the introduction of production and consumption sets of the usual classical type, which are closed, convex, and bounded below, would cause no major difficulties.

Wilson (1981) treats an economy which may contain both finite lived and infinite lived consumers and which may be specialized to either. He also allows intransitive preferences. He uses a somewhat simpler version of irreducibility and proves existence in an exchange economy where the number of goods in each period is finite in two circumstances (1) when the consumers are all finite lived and (2) when a finite subset of infinite lived consumers own a positive fraction of the endowment in all but a finite number of periods. If preferences are transitive and strictly convex, the competitive equilibrium is also Pareto optimal. Thus Wilson's results contain the theorems on existence of Bewley and Balasko, Shell, and Cass as special cases while also providing conditions in the model sufficient for Pareto optimality.

A striking difference between the competitive equilibria of economies where the number of consumers is finite, and the competitive equilibria of economies with overlapping generations and an infinite horizon, where the number of consumers is infinite, is that with perfect foresight the former equilibria are also Pareto optimal while the latter need not be. This is the major point emphasized by Samuelson in his initial paper. The most general theorem proving that competitive equilibria are Pareto optimal even when the number of commodities is infinite provided that the number of consumers is finite is due to Debreu (1954). Under some additional smoothness conditions on utility and boundedness conditions on prices and allocations Balasko and Shell (1980) prove that the allocation x of a competitive equilibrium is Pareto optimal if and only if $\Sigma_t(1/\|p_t\|) = \infty$. This is a condition which had already been shown to characterize efficiency in neoclassical production economies by Cass. It is clear that $\lim \inf(\|p_{t+1}\|/\|p_t\|) = r \leqslant 1$ implies that the condition for Pareto optimality is satisfied since the sums dominate $\Sigma_t(1/r^t)$ which diverges. Intuitively, for a stationary economy if the interest rates are asymptotically non-negative, the competitive equilibria will be Pareto optimal, or if the economy is growing, if the interest rates exceed the growth rate, Pareto optimality follows.

LIMITATIONS OF THE ANALYSIS. As mentioned in the beginning the claim of the theories described as general equilibrium theories to be 'general' is qualified by the set of conditions considered to be constant. Walras as well as most subsequent theorists classified the constant factors as tastes, technology, and resources, including population. However, all three of these categories have been treated by some economists as responding, in ways amenable to analysis, to market variables. These studies have usually been confined to a few variables and have usually been partial equilibrium in character, although the classical school of economists included population as a major variable in models of economic development. Their models are comprehensive but lack the market equilibrium analysis of the general equilibrium theories, whose inspiration appears to have been found in the marginal utility theory of consumer demand. Similarly, tastes have sometimes been modelled to depend on past consumption or advertising, and technology has been modelled to depend on research and development spending and on the rewards to innovation. Also natural resources, in terms of resources known to exist, are often treated as responding to prices.

From this perspective general equilibrium theory is a partial theory of economic affairs with a special set of *ceteris paribus* assumptions. The variables which are left free are chosen because they lend themselves to a particularly elegant theory in terms of consumer demand under budget constraints and producer supplies with profit conditions where these constraints and conditions are established by prices equating demand and supply. This was the vision of Walras, perhaps guided by the theory of static equilibrium of mechanical forces which he found in Poinsot.

Another direction of abstraction in general equilibrium theory in its classic expressions has been to ignore the effects of processes which do not pass through the market. In particular each consuming unit is described as interested only in its own consumption in the theory of Pareto optimality and as uninfluenced in its choices by the choices made by other households. Similarly, the production possibilities of one firm or process are treated as independent of the productive activities of other firms. Some attempts have been made to incorporate these effects in the general equilibrium models but not with complete success. In particular there is not a good theory of existence when consumer possibility sets or production sets are affected by levels of consumption and production.

The convexity assumptions which have appeared in general equilibrium models from the time of Walras are often not good approximations of reality, though they are depended on for many of the theorems of the subject, such as the theorems on existence and Pareto optimality. However, there is a theory of approximate equilibria and of limiting results as the size of the market increases relative to the participants which does something to bridge the gap between theory and fact.

Finally, the assumption that the market participants take prices as independent of their actions fails to describe many markets, and describes very few exactly. Nonetheless, this assumption may be useful for a theory that embraces all markets, whose special features cannot be described in detail. It may, that is, give a good approximation to the working of the economy as a whole. Also it is useful for its implications for optimality, a point which was perceived, albeit through a glass darkly, by Walras. The proper notion was later found by Pareto.

Just as the model does not accommodate monopoly easily, government does not fit in well. A chief difficulty arises from its compulsory features which allow it to extract resources by force rather than by voluntary agreement. Government is not easily described either as a producer selling services, or as a voluntary organization performing acts of collective consumption, though in ways it resembles both. Voluntary societies also do not fit perfectly in the scheme of producers and households though the disparity is less, since they must meet their expenses from contributions by the membership who will not contribute unless the services of the society to them are worth the dues they pay.

PROPERTIES OF GENERAL EQUILIBRIUM. Walras set the major objectives of general equilibrium theory as they have remained ever since. First, it was necessary to prove in any model of general equilibrium that the equilibrium exists. Then its optimality properties should be demonstrated. Next it should be shown how the equilibrium would be attained, that is, the stability of the equilibrium and its uniqueness should be studied. Finally, it should be shown how the equilibrium will change when conditions of demand, technology, or resources are varied, the subject now called comparative statics. He contributed to all these lines of research.

Walras's arguments for existence are not conclusive but he did contribute a basic principle, that the model should be neither underdetermined nor over-determined. That is, the number of independent equations to be satisfied and the number of variables to be determined should be equal. Some critics saw right away that this equality did not ensure a meaningful solution to the equation system, for example, that the solution to such an equation system is not guaranteed to be real. The question was not taken up seriously until the 1930s and the first rigorous treatment was given by Wald (1935, 1936b). Then in the 1950s more complete solutions on neo-classical assumptions were found by Arrow and Debreu (1954), McKenzie (1954) and Nikaido (1956).

In the discussion of models of general equilibrium that have been given above, the first requirement has been a set of assumptions from which existence could be inferred. This approach to the subject was begun in the papers of Wald and von Neumann, presented to the colloquium of Karl Menger (mathematician and son of Carl Menger, the neoclassical economist) in Vienna in the 1930s.

The optimality that Walras claimed for competitive equilibrium, under conditions of certainty, except for insurable risk, did not seem to go beyond individual maximization of utility in face of an equilibrium price system. However, Pareto gave a genuinely social definition that the allocation of goods and services in a competitive equilibrium is such that no reallocation is possible with some consumer better off unless some consumer is made worse off. In fact, Walras seemed to be groping for the same definition and his arguments may be slightly extended to establish Pareto's proposition.

As noticed in the earlier discussion of markets with certainty, Pareto optimality is implied by maximization of preference under budget constraints and von Neumann's law, or maximization of profit given the technology. The former implies that an allocation which improves one consumer's position and harms none must, given local non-satiation for all consumers, be more valuable at equilibrium prices while the latter implies that no more valuable allocation is achievable. This argument depends on the finiteness of the value of the goods in the economy. Otherwise the impossibility of a more valuable allocation is not meaningful. Thus when the horizon is infinite and the discount factor is too large, for example, equal to 1 if the economy is stationary, or in general greater than or equal to the reciprocal of the growth rate, Pareto optimality may fail in competitive equilibrium, as Samuelson showed. Also there is no reason to expect Pareto optimality, in an exact sense, when some markets are missing, a very likely eventuality when there is uncertainty and goods must be traded on every possible contingency to provide complete markets.

A second theorem on Pareto optimality asserts that any Pareto optimum can be realized as a competitive equilibrium. This theorem requires assumptions which are similar to these leading to existence, in particular, assumptions providing local non-satiation for some consumers and convexity of the preferred sets and the feasible set. Moreover, when the number of goods is infinite as in the case of an infinite horizon an additional condition is needed to give the existence of the prices. This condition may be that the sum of consumers' preferred sets has an interior or that the production set has an interior. In the case of the product topology and free disposal by consumers the preferred sets will have interiors if the periodwise utility functions are continuous and bounded (see Debreu, 1954). Finally it was shown by Arrow (1953) that in order for the Pareto optimal allocation to maximize preference over the budget set rather than only to minimize the cost of achieving a given preference level, it is useful to assume that x_i, the consumption of the ith consumer, contains a point which is cheaper than the allocation he receives, for $i = 1, \ldots m$.

The stability theory for general equilibrium has been largely devoted to the stability of the Walrasian tâtonnement, or process of groping for equilibrium prices through a process of price revision according to excess demand. That is, prices rise or fall depending on whether excess demand is positive or negative. In the tâtonnement there is no trading until equilibrium prices have been reached. The most convincing theorems concern local stability and the dominant assumption leading to local stability is that the market excess demand function satisfies the weak axiom of revealed preference between the equilibrium price and any other price in a sufficiently small neighbourhood of the equilibrium price. That is, if $\bar{p}$ is an equilibrium price and e is the excess demand function, $p \cdot e(\bar{p}) - p \cdot e(p) \leqslant 0$ implies $\bar{p} \cdot e(\bar{p}) - \bar{p} \cdot e(p) < 0$. Since $\bar{p}$ is an equilibrium price, $e(\bar{p}) = 0$, and $p \cdot e(p) = 0$ by Walras's Law. Therefore, the condition holds and we may conclude that $\bar{p} \cdot e(p) > 0$. The weak axiom for the market may be expected to hold if the net income effect of price changes is small.

Consider the price revision process given by $dp_i/dt = \dot{p}_i = e_i(p)$, $i = 1, \ldots, n-1$, where the nth good is numeraire so $\dot{p}_n \equiv 0$. Then consider the function $|p(t) - \bar{p}|^2$, the square of the distance from the equilibrium price vector to the price vector at time t. We derive

$$\mathrm{d}/\mathrm{d}t(|p(t) - \bar{p}|)^2 = 2\sum_1^n (p_i - \bar{p}_i)\dot{p}_i = 2\sum_1^n (p_i - \bar{p}_i)e_i < 0,$$

using the weak axiom of revealed preference and Walras's Law. Thus the distance of $p(t)$ from $\bar{p}$ constantly falls, or $p(t) \to \bar{p}$ as $t \to \infty$. Since locally the rate of price change can be equated to excess demand for any continuous tâtonnement by choice of units, this is a general argument. Since the assumption of gross substitutes ($e_{ij} < 0$ for $i \neq j$ and $e_{ij} - \partial e_i(p)/\partial p_j$) implies the weak axiom, and the assumption of a negative definite Jacobian $[e_{ij}]$, $i, j = 1, \ldots, n-1$, at equilibrium is equivalent to the weak axiom locally, the weak axiom is a dominant condition for local stability. All global stability results are very special and relatively unconvincing.

A rigorous treatment of the stability problem for the tâtonnement was given by Arrow and Hurwicz (1958) and Arrow, Block and Hurwicz (1959). A stability theory which allows for trading was given by Hahn and Negishi (1962). These theories do not allow for speculative trading although profitable arbitrage opportunities would be likely to exist for any speculator who correctly inferred what the price revision process was. The stability of the tâtonnement was conjectured by Walras to be the normal case for economies with many goods, and essentially correct arguments were given by Walras for the case of exchange economies with two goods. He recognized and illustrated the case of locally unstable equilibria in the two good case.

Finally, as Walras saw, it may be possible through a general equilibrium analysis to determine the effect of changes in the exogenous factors, resources, technology, or tastes, on the economic variables in equilibrium. This is analogous to the effect of a change in the constraints on the equilibrium of mechanical forces, an analogy with which Walras would have been familiar from the book of Poinsot. In the case of the exchange of two commodities Walras derives some simple and correct results for comparative statics just as he does for stability. He observes that an increase in the marginal utility of a good or a reduction in its supply will raise its price. In drawing this inference form his demand and offer curves he confines himself to stable equilibria as the only equilibria of interest.

Hicks used the comparative static result of Walras in a market with many goods to define stability of equilibrium. Samuelson (1947) pointed out that stability of equilibrium, where stability is given a dynamic interpretation as in a continuous tâtonnement, may imply comparative static results as a general principle. However, the straightforward generalization of Walras is the use of conditions which are sufficient to imply stability as a basis for deriving theorems on comparative statics. The most interesting theorem may be that derived from the revealed preference assumption at equilibrium.

Suppose that $e(\bar{p}) = 0$ but excess demand changes so that the new excess demand function $e_i'(\bar{p}) = e_i(\bar{p})$ for $i \neq 1$ or n and $e_1'(\bar{p}) = \delta_1 < 0$ while $e_n'(\bar{p}) = \delta_n > 0$. Let n be numeraire. This change can be arranged by taking δ_n of the nth good from some holder and compensating him with $\delta_1 = \delta_n/\bar{p}_1$ of the first good. Suppose that the new equilibrium price is p, or $e'(p) = 0$. By Walras's Law $\bar{p} \cdot e(\bar{p}) = 0$ and by the assumption of revealed preference $p \cdot e'(\bar{p}) > 0$. Thus $(\bar{p} - p) \cdot e'(\bar{p}) < 0$, or $(\bar{p}_1 - p_1)\delta_1 < 0$, or $\bar{p}_1 - p_1 > 0$. Any good falls in price when the excess demand for the numeraire rises at the expense of that good (see Allingham, 1975).

A type of stability has been proved for competitive equilibrium over time which concerns the path of equilibrium prices over real time rather than the path of disequilibrium prices over virtual time, that is, the time of the tâtonnement. It was shown by Negishi (1960) that there is a social welfare function associated with a competitive equilibrium which is maximized in the equilibrium over feasible allocations. Suppose each consumer has a concave utility function which is given by a discounted sum of periodwise utilities. Then the social welfare function which is maximized is also a discounted sum of periodwise utilities equal to a weighted sum of the individual utilities. Then using results from turnpike theory for optimal capital accumulation it has been shown by Bewley (1982) that the competitive equilibrium allocations converge over time to the allocations of a stationary competitive equilibrium whose capital stocks and allocations are the same as those of the unique optimal stationary path of capital accumulation given the social welfare function. The utility functions and the production functions are assumed to be strictly concave and the discount factors are the same for all consumers and sufficiently near 1. However, these conditions may be relaxed.

Comparative static and comparative dynamic results have been derived from stability conditions in the context of optimal capital accumulation, which is equivalent to competitive equilibrium over time with a representative consumer. We may say that an optimal stationary path of capital is regular if an increase in the discount factor implies an increase in the value of capital stocks at initial prices. Then there are sufficient conditions for local stability of the optimal stationary path which imply that the path is regular. Similar dynamic results may be achieved for non-stationary paths as well (see Araujo and Scheinkman, 1979). It may be possible to extend these results to Bewley type economies.

BIBLIOGRAPHY

Allingham, M. 1975. *General Equilibrium*. New York: Wiley.

Araujo, A.P. de and Scheinkman, J.A. 1979. Notes on comparative dynamics. In *General Equilibrium, Growth, and Trade*, ed. J.R. Green and J.A. Scheinkman, New York: Academic Press.

Arrow, K.J. 1951. An extension of the basic theorems of classical welfare economics. In *Proceedings of the Second Berkeley Symposium*, ed. J. Neyman, Berkeley: University of California Press.

Arrow, K.J. 1953. Le rôle des valeurs boursières pour la répartition la meilleure des risques. *Econométrie*, Paris: Centre National de la Recherche Scientifique. Trans. as 'The role of securities in the optimal allocation of risk-bearing', *Review of Economic Studies* 31, (1964), 91–6.

Arrow, K.J. and Debreu, G. 1954. Existence of an equilibrium for a competitive economy. *Econometrica* 22, 265–90.

Arrow, K.J. and Hurwicz, L. 1958. On the stability of the competitive equilibrium I. *Econometrica* 26, 522–52.

Arrow, K.J., Block, H. D. and Hurwicz, L. 1959. On the stability of the competitive equilibrium II. *Econometrica* 27, 82–109.

Balasko, Y. and Shell, K. 1980. The overlapping generations model, I: the case of pure exchange without money. *Journal of Economic Theory* 23, 281–306.

Balasko, Y., Cass, D. and Shell, K. 1980. Existence of competitive equilibrium in a general overlapping generations model. *Journal of Economic Theory* 23, 307–22.

Bewley, T.F. 1972. Existence of equilibria in economies with infinitely many commodities. *Journal of Economic Theory* 4, 514–40.

Bewley, T.F. 1982. An integration of equilibrium theory and turnpike theory. *Journal of Mathematical Economics* 10, 233–68.

Cassel, G. 1918. *Theoretische Sozialökonomie*. 5th German edn, trans. as *The Theory of Social Economy*, New York: Harcourt Brace, 1932.

Cournot, A. 1838. *Recherches sur les principles mathématiques de la théorie des richesses*. Paris: Hachette. Trans. as *Researchs into the Mathematical Principles of the Theory of Wealth*, New York: Kelley, 1960.

Debreu, G. 1954. Valuation equilibrium and Pareto optimum. *Proceedings of the National Academy of Sciences* 40, 588–92.

Debreu, G. 1959. *Theory of Value*. New York: Wiley.

Debreu, G. 1962. New concepts and techniques for equilibrium analysis. *International Economic Review* 3, 257–73.

Gossen, H. 1854. *Entwicklung der Gesetze des menschlichen Verkehrs*. 3rd edn, Berlin: Prager, 1927.

Grandmont, J.M. 1973. On the efficiency of a monetary equilibrium. *Review of Economic Studies* 40, 149–65.

Grandmont, J.M. 1977. Temporary general equilibrium theory. *Econometrica* 45, 535–72.

Grandmont, J.M. 1983. *Money and Value*. New York: Cambridge University Press.

Grandmont, J.M. and Younes, Y. 1972. On the role of money and the existence of a monetary equilibrium. *Review of Economic Studies* 39, 355–72.

Green, J.R. 1973. Temporary general equilibrium in a sequential trading model with spot and future transactions. *Econometrica* 41, 1103–23.

Green, J.R. 1977. The nonexistence of informational equilibria.. *Review of Economic Studies* 44, 451–63.

Grossman, S.J. 1981: An introduction to the theory of rational expectations under asymmetric information. *Review of Economic Studies* 48, 541–60.

Hahn, F.H. and Negishi, T. 1962. A theorem of non-tâtonnement stability. *Econometrica* 30, 463–9.

Hicks, J.R. 1939. *Value and Capital*, Oxford: Clarendon Press; 2nd edn, New York: Oxford University Press, 1946.

Jevons, W.S. 1871. *The Theory of Political Economy*. London: Macmillan; 5th edn, New York: Kelley and Millman, 1957.

Koopmans, T.C. 1951. Analysis of production as an efficient combination of activities. In *Activity Analysis of Production and Allocation*, ed. T.C. Koopmans, Wiley: New York.

Kreps, D.M. 1977. A note on fulfilled expectations equilibria. *Journal of Economic Theory* 14, 32–43.

McKenzie, L.W. 1954. On equilibrium in Graham's model of world trade and other competitive systems. *Econometrica* 22, 147–61.

McKenzie, L.W. 1959. On the existence of general equilibrium for a competitive market. *Econometrica* 27, 54–71.

McKenzie, L.W. 1981. The classical theorem on existence of competitive equilibrium. *Econometrica* 49, 819–41.

Marshall, A. 1980. *Principles of Economics*. 8th edn, London: Macmillan, 1920; New York: Macmillan, 1948.

Menger, C. 1871. *Grundsätze der Volkwirtshaftslehre*. Vienna. Trans. as *Principles of Economics*, Glencoe, Ill.: Free Press, 1950.

Mill, J.S. 1848. *Principles of Political Economy*. London: Parker. New edn, London: Longmans, 1909; 9th edn, New York: Longmans, 1923.

Negishi, Y. 1960. Welfare economics and existence of an equilibrium for a competitive economy. *Metroeconomica* 12, 92–7.

Neumann, J. von. 1937. Über ein Ökonomisches Gleichungssystem und eine Verallgemeinerung des Brouwerschen Fixpunksatzes. *Ergebnisse eines mathematischen Kolloquiums* 8, 73–83. Trans. in *Review of Economic Studies* 13, (1945) 1–9.

Nikaido, H. 1956. On the classical multilateral exchange problem. *Metroeconomica* 8, 135–45.

Novshek, W. and Sonnenschein, H. 1980. Small efficient scale as a foundation for Walrasian equilibrium. *Journal of Economic Theory* 22, 243–55.

Pareto, V. 1909. *Manuel d'économie politique*. Paris. Trans. from 1927 edn as *Manual of Political Economy*, New York: Kelley, 1971.

Peleg, B. and Yaari, M.E. 1970. Markets with countably many commodities. *International Economic Review* 11, 369–77.

Poinsot, L. 1803. *Eléments de statique*. 8th edn, Paris, 1842.

Radner, R. 1967. Equilibre des marchés à terme et au comptant en cas d'incertitude. *Cahiers d'Econométrie*, Paris: CNRS, 4, 35–52.

Radner, R. 1972. Existence of equilibrium of plans, prices and price expectations in a sequence of markets. *Econometrica* 40, 289–303.

Samuelson, P.A. 1947. *Foundations of Economic Analysis*. Cambridge, Mass.: Harvard University Press.

Samuelson, P.A. 1958. An exact consumption – loan model of interest with or without the social contrivance of money. *Journal of Political Economy* 66, 467–82.

Scarf, H.F. (With T. Hansen) 1973. *The Computation of Economic Equilibria.* New Haven: Yale University Press.

Smith, A. 1776. *An Inquiry into the Nature and Causes of the Wealth of Nations.* 5th edn, ed. E. Cannan, London: Methuen, 1906; Chicago: University of Chicago Press, 1976.

Wald, A. 1935. Über die eindeutige positive Losbarkeit der neuen Produktionsgleichungen. *Ergebnisse eines mathematischen Kolloquiums* 6, 12–20.

Wald, A. 1936a. Über die Produkionsgleichungen der Ökonomischen Wertlehre. *Ergebnisse eines mathematischen Kolloquiums* 7, 1–6.

Wald, A. 1936b. Über einige Gleichungssysteme der mathematischen Ökonomie. *Zeitschrift für Nationalökonomie* 7, 637–70. Trans. as 'On some systems of equations of mathematical economics', *Econometrica* 19, 1951, 368–403.

Walras, L. 1874–7. *Elements d'économie politique pure.* Lausanne: Corbaz. Trans. by W. Jaffé as *Elements of Pure Economics*, London: George Allen & Unwin, from the 1926 definitive edition, 1954; New York: Orion.

Weintraub, E.R. 1983. On the existence of a competitive equilibrium: 1930–1954. *Journal of Economic Literature* 21, 1–39.

Wilson, C.A. 1981. Equilibrium in dynamic models with an infinity of agents. *Journal of Economic Theory* 24, 95–111.

Adjustment Processes and Stability

FRANKLIN M. FISHER

Economic theory is pre-eminently a matter of equilibrium analysis. In particular, the centrepiece of the subject – general equilibrium theory – deals with the existence and efficiency properties of competitive equilibrium. Nor is this only an abstract matter. The principal policy insight of economics – that a competitive price system produces desirable results and that government interference will generally lead to an inefficient allocation of resources – rests on the intimate connections between competitive equilibrium and Pareto efficiency.

Yet the very power and elegance of equilibrium analysis often obscures the fact that it rests on a very uncertain foundation. We have no similarly elegant theory of what happens *out* of equilibrium, of how agents behave when their plans are frustrated. As a result, we have no rigorous basis for believing that equilibria can be achieved or maintained if disturbed. Unless one robs words of their meaning and defines every state of the world as an 'equilibrium' in the sense that agents do what they do instead of doing something else, there is no disguising the fact that this is a major lacuna in economic analysis.

Nor is that lacuna only important in microeconomics. For example, the Keynesian question of whether an economy can become trapped in a situation of underemployment is not merely a question of whether underemployment equilibria exist. It is also a question of whether such equilibria are stable. As such, its answer depends on the properties of the general (dis)equilibrium system which macroeconomic analysis attempts to summarize. Not surprisingly, modern attempts to deal with such systems have been increasingly forced to treat such familiar macroeconomic issues as the role of money.

We do, of course, have some idea as to how disequilibrium adjustment takes place. From Adam Smith's discussion of the 'Invisible Hand' to the standard elementary textbook's treatment of the 'Law of Supply and Demand', economists have stressed how the perception of profit opportunities leads agents to act. What remains unclear is whether (as most economists believe) the pursuit of such profit opportunities in fact leads to equilibrium – more particularly, to a competitive equilibrium where such opportunities no longer exist. If one thinks of a competitive economy as a dynamic system driven by the self-seeking actions of individual agents, does that system have competitive equilibria as stable rest points? If so, are such equilibria attained so quickly that the system can be studied without attention to its disequilibrium behaviour? The answers to these crucial questions remain unclear.

A primary reason for that lack of clarity is the lack of a satisfactory theory about the disequilibrium behaviour of agents. A central example of the problem can be stated as follows. In perfect competition, all agents take prices as given. Then how can prices ever change? In a single market, for example, every firm believes that it will lose all its customers if it raises its price. Then who decides to go first when demand or cost increases? We are certain that such decisions are taken, but, at the level of satisfactory formal analysis, we do not know how.

While these issues arise in partial as well as general models, most of the literature on adjustment and stability has been at the general equilibrium level. (Search theory can be considered a partial modern-day exception.) Not surprisingly, that literature has largely begged the price-adjustment question, simply assuming that price somehow changes in the direction suggested by excess demand: $dp_i/dt = H^i(Z_i(p))$, where p is the vector of prices, $Z_i(p)$, the excess demand for the ith commodity, and $H^i(\cdot)$ a sign-preserving continuous function.

The question of who adjusts prices in this way is typically left unanswered or put aside with a reference to a fictitious Walrasian 'auctioneer'. That character does not appear in Walras (who did have prices adjusting to excess demands) but may have been invented by Schumpeter in lectures and introduced into the literature by Samuelson (who certainly did introduce the mathematical statement of price adjustment just given). Interestingly, however, the need for some such construct can reasonably be said to originate with Edgeworth, who wrote:

> You might suppose each dealer to write down his demand, how much of an article he would take at each price, without attempting to conceal his requirements; and these data having been furnished to a sort of market-machine, the price to be passionlessly evaluated (1881, p. 30).

There has been only moderate progress since Edgeworth's day in explaining just what one is to suppose in considering anonymous price adjustment in competitive markets.

General equilibrium theory has taken its most analytically satisfactory form in the Arrow–Debreu world where all markets for present and future commodities open and close before any other economic activity actually takes place. Despite the lack of realism, this made it natural to consider adjustment processes in which only prices move (in the way described above) and trade, production, and consumption only occur after equilibrium is reached. Such a dynamic process is called 'tâtonnement', and the study of tâtonnement models dominated the stability literature until 1960. In that year, the publication of Herbert Scarf's

37

counterexample (Scarf, 1960) put an end to the hope that such models would turn out generally stable given only the ordinary assumptions of microeconomics. Tâtonnement stability requires extremely strong special assumptions.

This has extremely important implications. Indeed, it is not too strong to say that the entire theory of value is at stake. If stability requires trading (or production and consumption) to take place before equilibrium is reached, then the adjustment process itself changes the givens of the equilibrium problem (the endowments of agents, for example). This makes the set of equilibria also change in the course of adjustment, so that the equilibrium finally reached (assuming stability) differs from that computed by algorithms taking the initial situation as fixed. Moreover, comparative static analysis, that major tool of theory, will miscompute the effects of a displacement of equilibrium, for the equilibrium reached will depend on the adjustment process and not merely on the displacement itself. While such effects may be small, they are certainly not known to be small. The argument that they are likely to be negligible because prices adjust much faster than quantities is unconvincing. The limiting case of such relative speeds of adjustment is tâtonnement and is known to lack general convergence properties.

The failure of tâtonnement was by no means the end of the stability literature, however. The early 1960s were marked by two important insights. These were: first, that considerable gains might be achieved by restricting the adjustment process itself rather than the excess demand functions of agents (Hahn, 1961); second, that consideration of how trade takes place might lead to sensible restrictions. While logically separte, these two insights developed together in the study of 'non-tâtonnemet processes', which are better called 'trading processes'.

In a pure-exchange trading process, prices continue to adjust as indicated by excess demands, but trade also takes place (consumption, however, still being postponed to equilibrium). The crucial question is how such trades should naturally be restricted, and here there are two leading candidates.

The first of these is the 'Edgeworth Process' (Uzawa, 1962; Hahn, 1962). Here the basic assumption is that trade takes place if and only if there is a group of agents, all of whom can gain in utility by trading among themselves at the current prices. With some complications due to the possibility that no such trades can be made at the initial configuration of prices, this assumption can be shown to generate a stable adjustment process. The crucial feature of the proof is that the sum of the utilities that would be achieved if trade ceases is increasing out of equilibrium, making that sum suitable for use as a Lyapunov function.

The basic assumption of the Edgeworth Process certainly seems attractive. Trade takes place because the agents participating make themselves better off thereby. Unfortunately, such attractiveness is somewhat superficial. First, the assumption places very large information requirements on the system. It is easy to construct examples where the only Pareto-improving trades require the participation of vast numbers of agents. While, as in the case of coalition formation in the theory of the core, the number of agents required cannot exceed the number of commodities, this is not a helpful limit when all future commodities are being traded. The assumption that trade readily takes place in such circumstances is not an easy one.

Second (and perhaps more important), the assumption that trade only takes place when participants each immediately gain in utility is only attractive when agents are supposed stupidly to expect prices constant and transactions to be completed. Once agents are allowed to become conscious of disequilibrium, transactions need not bring immediate utility gain; some transactions will be undertaken for speculative purposes, in the hopes that later transactions at profitable prices will materialize. While no rational agent ever trades without expecting to gain thereby, the basic assumption of the Edgeworth Process requires that every leg of a transaction bring a utility gain. It is crucial that the sum of the utilities agents would receive if trading ceased should always be increasing out of equilibrium. This is not true when arbitrage is involved – particularly when trade takes place for money. It is an open question whether the Edgeworth Process models can be adapted to allow more interesting behaviour.

The second major trading process model is the 'Hahn Process' (Hahn and Negishi, 1962). Its basic assumption (sometimes known as the 'Orderly Markets Assumption') is as follows. After trade, there may be unsatisfied demanders of a particular commodity, say apples, or there may be unsatisfied suppliers of that commodity, but if markets are sufficiently well organized there will not be both. The Hahn Process assumes that potential apple buyers and potential apple sellers can find each other. Indeed, it might be said that this is what we mean when we speak of such buyers and sellers as being in the same 'market'. As a result, we assume that – after trade – any agent with a non-zero excess demand for some commodity finds that his or her excess demand for that commodity is of the same sign as that commodity's aggregate excess demand.

This has a powerful consequence. Since prices move in the same direction as aggregate excess demand, any agent who cannot complete all planned transactions finds that the goods he or she would like to sell are falling in price, while the goods he or she would like to buy are becoming more expensive. The agent's target utility – the utility he or she would achieve if all transactions could be completed – is falling. As a result, out of equilibrium the sum of all target utilities falls and so can serve as a Lyapunov function. In effect, agents begin with unrealistically optimistic expectations and revise them downward until equilibrium is reached and expectations become mutually compatible. With some additional, relatively minor assumptions, the Hahn Process can be shown to be globally stable.

In fact, things are not so simple, for the assumption that buyers and sellers can find each other does not guarantee that unsatisfied excess demands for a given commodity will all have the same sign. This is because of the possibility that buyers will have nothing to offer that sellers are willing to accept. This problem cries out for the introduction of money as a medium of exchange (cf. Clower, 1965). That introduction was accomplished by Arrow and Hahn (1971) who assumed that offers to buy must be backed up with money in order to be active and that prices are affected only by active, rather than target excess demands. Applying the Hahn Process assumption to active excess demands, the same global stability results can be obtained – provided one assumes that agents never run out of money. This 'Positive Cash Assumption' is very difficult to justify from more primitive ones in the context of naïve expectations.

The introduction of money raises other problems. In particular, unless money is included in the utility function, it is hard to see why agents plan to hold it in equilibrium. Nevertheless, such introduction is essential, particularly if firms are to be included. Without a common medium of exchange in which profits are measured, firms producing an oversupply of some good, say toothpaste, will have no incentive to sell it, reckoning profits in toothpaste rather than in dollars.

With money, however, the inclusion of firms in the Hahn Process model is fairly easy (Fisher, 1974). Firms are assumed to sell promises to deliver outputs and acquire contracts to supply inputs, acting so as to maximize profits subject to ultimate production being feasible. Production itself is postponed until equilibrium (as is consumption in the pure exchange version). Again assuming that no household or firm ever runs out of cash, the target profits of firms decline if they cannot complete their planned transactions. Given that, the target utilities of the firms' owners – the households – also decline, and the stability result goes through much as before.

Despite its elegance, this is not a truly satifactory result if one is interested in justifying the use of equilibrium economics. Apart from other difficulties, the equilibrium reached is one in which all trading opportunities have been exhausted. This is the consequence of working in an Arrow–Debreu framework, but it is not very satisfactory, and remains so even when some attempt is made to introduce production and consumption out of equilibrium (Fisher, 1976). One would rather expect equilibrium to involve the carrying out of planned trades at correctly foreseen prices.

Further, the agents in trading-process models are remarkably stupid, always expecting prices to remain constant and transactions to be completed, when their constant experience tells them that this is not so. A model that hopes to explain how arbitraging agents drive a competitive economy to equilibrium can hardly afford to assume that agents do not perceive the very arbitrage opportunities that characterize disequilibrium.

An ambitious, though not altogether successful attempt to deal with these problems was made in the disequilibrium model of Fisher (1983). Agents have point expectations and are allowed to expect price changes. They take advantage of arbitrage opportunities, limited only by rules as to short sales and credit availability. Households maximize utility and firms profits, planning and engaging in consumption and production, respectively, in real time. Trade in firms' shares takes place both because of differing price expectations and because households purchase expected dividend streams as a way of transferring liquidity across time periods.

Agents also realize that they are restricted as to the size of their transactions. They make price offers to get around such constraints. Thus each seller believes he or she faces a declining demand curve and has some monopoly power (similarly for buyers). The question of whether such perceptions disappear in equilibrium is the question of whether the equilibrium is Walrasian. In one form, it is also the question of whether there is equilibrium underemployment of resources. The answer turns out to be closely related to the extent to which the liquidity constraints are binding in equilibrium.

As this suggests, money plays a central role. The transactions demand for money does not disappear in equilibrium, which now involves the carrying out of previously planned transactions at the expected prices. On the other hand, 'money' in this model consists of very short-term bonds, bearing the same interest as all other assets in equilibrium. There is still no satisfactory theory in which agents hold non-interest-bearing bank notes in equilibrium.

Once one leaves equilibrium and leaves the theory of how the individual agent plans, matters become less satisfactory. This is largely because one has to deal with the behaviour of agents whose expectations are disappointed. The model handles this issue by making an extremely strong assumption called 'No Favourable Surprise'. This states that new, unexpected, favourable opportunities cease appearing. In effect, the kinds of shocks emphasized by Schumpeter (1911) – discovery of new products or processes, new ways of marketing, new sources of raw materials, and so forth – are ruled out if they are totally unforeseen. As in the Hahn Process, agents find that unexpected change makes them worse off as old opportunities disappear. With some technical complications, this ensures convergence to some equilibrium, although that equilibrium need not be Walrasian.

The problem is that 'No Favourable Surprise' is not a primitive assumption. One cannot hope to prove stability in a world constantly bombarded with exogenous Schumpeterian shocks. 'No Favourable Surprise', however, rules out the appearance of any unexpected opportunities, even those which arise in the course of adjustment to previous exogenous shocks. The Hahn Process model is a special case of this. So is the assumption of rational expectations. In a model with point expectations, however, rational expectations amounts to perfect foresight, and this begs the question of disequilibrium adjustment. It is unclear what happens under uncertainty and also unclear whether 'No Favourable Surprise' can be derived from other underlying premises.

Further, the very generality of the 'No Favourable Surprise' stability result has both satisfactory and unsatisfactory aspects. On the one hand, the price-adjustment mechanism left over from tâtonnement days can be dispensed with and individuals allowed to make price offers. On the other hand, just how those offers get made (or accepted) remains a mystery within the general confines of the 'No Favourable Surprise' assumption. We know that this depends on developing perceptions of demand and supply curves – of individual monopoly or monopsony power – but we do not know how those perceptions develop. As a consequence, the stability results give little insight into whether the system approaches a Walrasian or a non-Walrasian, quantity-constrained equilibrium. Similarly, we do not know the extent to which the adjustment process shifts the ultimate equilibrium or anything about adjustment speeds.

These remain questions of crucial importance for the under-pinnings of equilibrium analysis and, possibly, for the study of actual economies. They will remain unanswered without detailed analysis of how disequilibrium adjustment takes place when plans are frustrated. Equilibrium techniques will not succeed here, and new modes of analysis are needed if equilibrium economic theory is to have a satisfactory foundation.

BIBLIOGRAPHY

Arrow, K.J. and F.H. Hahn. 1971. *General Competitive Analysis.* San Francisco: Holden-Day; Edinburgh: Oliver & Boyd.

Clower, R.W. 1965. The Keynesian counterrevolution: a theoretical appraisal. In *The Theory of Interest Rates*, ed. F.H. Hahn and F.P.R. Brechling, London: Macmillan; New York: St. Martin's Press.

Edgeworth, F.Y. 1881. *Mathematical Psychics.* Reprinted, New York: Augustus M. Kelley, 1967.

Fisher, F.M. 1974. The Hahn process with firms but no production. *Econometrica* 42, May, 471–86.

Fisher, F.M. 1976. A non-tâtonnement model with production and consumption. *Econometrica* 44, September, 907–38.

Fisher, F.M. 1983. *Disequilibrium Foundations of Equilibrium Economics.* Cambridge: Cambridge University Press.

Hahn, F.H. 1961. A stable adjustment process for a competitive economy. *Review of Economic Studies* 29, October, 62–5.

Hahn, F.H. 1962. On the stability of pure exchange equilibrium. *International Economic Review* 3, May, 206–14.

Hahn, F.H. and Negishi, T. 1962. A theorem on non-tâtonnement stability. *Econometrica* 30, July, 463–9.

Scarf, H. 1960. Some examples of global instability of the competitive equilibrium. *International Economic Review* 1, September, 157–72.

Schumpeter, J. 1911. *The Theory of Economic Development.* 4th printing of English trans, Cambridge, Mass.: Harvard University Press, 1951.

Uzawa, H. 1962. On the stability of Edgeworth's barter process. *International Economic Review* 3, May, 218–32.

Arrow–Debreu Model of General Equilibrium

JOHN GEANAKOPLOS

I. INTRODUCTION

It is not easy to separate the significance and influence of the Arrow–Debreu model of general equilibrium from that of mathematical economics itself. In an extraordinary series of papers (Arrow, 1951; Debreu, 1951; Arrow–Debreu, 1954), two of the oldest and most important questions of neoclassical economics, the viability and efficiency of the market system, were shown to be susceptible to analysis in a model completely faithful to the neoclassical methodological premises of individual rationality, market clearing, and rational expectations, through arguments at least as elegant as any in economic theory, using the two techniques (convexity and fixed point theory) that are still, after thirty years, the most important mathematical devices in mathematical economics. Fifteen years after its birth (e.g. Arrow, 1969), the model was still being reinterpreted to yield fresh economic insights, and twenty years later the same model was still capable of yielding new and fundamental mathematical properties (e.g. Debreu, 1970, 1974). When we consider that the same two men who derived the most fundamental properties of the model (along with McKenzie, 1954) also provided the most significant economic interpretations, it is no wonder that its invention has helped earn for each of its creators, in different years, the Nobel Prize for economics.

In the next few pages I shall try to summarize the primitive mathematical concepts, and their economic interpretations, that define the model. I give a hint of the arguments used to establish the model's conclusions. Finally, on the theory that a model is equally well described by what it cannot explain, I list several phenomena that the model is not equipped to handle.

II. THE MODEL

Commodities and Arrow–Debreu Commodities (A.1) Let there be L commodities, $l = 1, \ldots, L$. The amount of a commodity is described by a real number. A list of quantities of all commodities is given by a vector in $\mathbb{R}^L$.

43

The notion of commodity is the fundamental primitive concept in economic theory. Each commodity is assumed to have an objective, quantifiable, and universally agreed upon (i.e. measurable) description. Of course, in reality this description is somewhat ambiguous (should two apples of different sizes by considered two units of the same commodity, or two different commodities?) but the essential quantitative aspect of commodity cannot be doubted. Production and consumption are defined in terms of transformations of commodities that they cause. Conversely, the set of commodities is the minimum collection of objects necessary to describe production and consumption. Other objects, such as financial assets, may be traded, but they are not commodities. General equilibrium theory is concerned with the allocation of commodities (between nations, or individuals, across time, or under uncertainty etc.). The Arrow–Debreu model studies those allocations which can be achieved through the exchange of commodities at one moment in time.

It is easy to see that it is often important to the agents in an economy to have precise physical descriptions of commodities, as for example when placing an order for a particular grade of steel or oil. The less crude the categorization of commodities becomes, the more scope there is for agents to trade, and the greater is the set of imaginable allocations. Two agents may each have apples and oranges. There is no point in exchanging one man's fruit for the other man's fruit, but both might be made better off if one could exchange his apples for the other's oranges. Of course there need not be any end to the distinctions which in principle could be drawn between commodities, but presumably finer details become less and less important. When the descriptions are so precise that further refinements cannot yield imaginable allocations which increase the satisfaction of the agents in the economy, then the commodities are called Arrow–Debreu commodities.

A field is better allocated to one productive use than another depending upon how much rain has fallen on it; but it is also better allocated depending on how much rain has fallen on other fields. This illustrates the apparently paradoxical usefulness of including in the description of an Arrow–Debreu commodity characteristics of the world, for example the commodity's geographic location, its temporal location (Hicks, 1939), its state of nature (Arrow, 1953; Debreu, 1959; Radner, 1968), and perhaps even the name of its final consumer (Arrow, 1969), which at first glance do not seem intrinsically connected with the object itself (but which are in principle observable).

Hicks, perhaps anticipated by Fisher and Hayek, was the first to suggest an elaborate notion of commodity; this idea has been developed by others, especially Arrow in connection with uncertainty. Hicks was also the first to understand apparently complicated transactions, perhaps involving the exchange of paper assets or other noncommodities, over many time periods, in terms of commodity trade at one moment in time. Thus saving, or the lending of money, might be thought of as the purchase today of a particular future dated commodity. The second welfare theorem, which we shall shortly discuss, shows that an 'optimal' series of transactions can always be so regarded. By making the distinction between the same physical object depending, for example, on the state of nature, the general equilibrium theory of the supply and demand of commodities at one moment in time can incorporate the analysis of the optimal allocation of risk (a concept which appears far removed from the mundane qualities of fresh fruit) with exactly the same apparatus used to analyse the exchange of apples and oranges. Classifying physical objects according to their location likewise allows transportation costs to be handled in the same framework. Distinguishing commodities by who ultimately consumes them could allow general equilibrium analysis to systematically include externalities and public goods as special cases, though this has not been much pursued.

In reality, it is very rare to find a market for a pure Arrow–Debreu commodity. The more finely the commodities are described, the less likely are the commodity markets to have many buyers and sellers (i.e. to be competitive). More commonly, many groups of Arrow–Debreu commodities are traded together, in unbreakable bundles, at many moments in time, in 'second best' transactions. Nevertheless, this understanding of the limitations of real world markets, based on the concept of the Arrow–Debreu commodity, is one of the most powerful analytical tools of systematic accounting available to the general equilibrium theorist. Similarly, the model of Arrow–Debreu, with its idealization of a separate market for each Arrow–Debreu commodity, all simultaneously meeting, is the benchmark against which the real economy can be measured.

Consumers. (A.1) Let there be H consumers, $h = 1, \ldots, H$. □

Each consumer h can imagine consumption plans $x \in \mathbb{R}^L$ lying in some consumption set X^h. (A.2) X^h is a closed subset in $\mathbb{R}^L$ which is bounded from below. □

Each consumer h also has well defined preferences $\succcurlyeq h$ over every pair $(x, y) \in X^h \times X^h$, where $x \succcurlyeq y$ means x is at least as desirable as y. Typically it is assumed that (A.3) $\succcurlyeq$ is a complete, transitive, continuous ordering. □

Notice that in general equilibrium consumers make choices between entire consumption plans, not between individual commodities. A single commodity has significance to the consumer only in relation to the other commodities he has consumed, or plans to consumer. Together with transitivity and completeness, this hypothesis about consumer preferences embodies the neoclassical ideal of rational choice.

Rationality has not always been a primitive hypothesis in neoclassical economics. It was customary (e.g. for Bentham, Jevons, Menger, Walras) to regard satisfaction, or utility, as a measurable primitive; rational choice, when it was thought to occur at all, was the consequence of the maximization of utility. And since utility was often thought to be instantaneously produced, sequential consumer choice on the basis of sequential instantaneous utility maximization was sometimes explicitly discussed as irrational (see e.g. Böhm-Bawerk on saving and the reasons why the rate of interest is always positive).

Once utility is taken to be a function not of instantaneous consumption, but of the entire consumption plan, then rational choice is equivalent to utility maximization. Debreu (1951) proved that any preference ordering $\succcurlyeq_h$ defined on $X^h \times X^h$ satisfies (A.1)–(A.3) if and only if there is a utility function $u^h: X^h \to \mathbb{R}$ such that $x \succcurlyeq_h y$ exactly when $u^h(x) \geqq u^h(y)$.

Under the influence of Pareto (1909), Hicks (1939) and Samuelson (1947), neoclassical economics has come to take rationality as primitive, and utility maximization as a logical consequence. This has had a profound effect on welfare economics, and perhaps on the scope of economic theory as well. In the first place, if utility is not directly measurable, then it can only be deduced from observable choices, as in the proof of Debreu. But at best this will give an 'ordinal' utility, since if $f: \mathbb{R} \to \mathbb{R}$ is any strictly increasing function, then u^h represents $\succcurlyeq_h$ if and only if $v^h \equiv f \circ u^h$ represents $\succcurlyeq_h$. Hence there can be no meaning to interpersonal utility comparisons; the Benthamite sum $\Sigma_{h=1}^H u^h$ is very different from the Benthamite sum $\Sigma_{h=1}^H f^{h \circ} u^h$. In the second place, the ideal of rational choice or preference, freed from the need for measurement, is much more easily extended to domains not directly connected to the market and commodities such as political candidates or platforms, or 'social states'. The elaboration of the nature of the primitive concepts of commodity and rational choice, developed as the basis of the theory of market equilibrium, prepared the way for the methodological principles of neoclassical economics (rational choice and equilibrium) to be applied to questions far beyond those of the market.

Although the rationality principle is in some respects a weakening of the hypothesis of measurable utility and instantaneous utility maximization, when coupled with the notion of consumption plan it is also a strengthening of this hypothesis, and a very strong assumption indeed. For example there is not room in the theory for the Freudian split psyche (or self-deception), or for Odysseus-like changes of heart. Perhaps more importantly, a consumers's preferences (for example how thrifty he is) do not change according to the role he plays in the process of production (e.g. on whether he is a capitalist or landowner), nor do they change depending on other consumers' preferences, or the supply of commodities. As an instance of this last case, note that it follows from the rationality hypothesis that the surge in the microcomputer industry influenced consumer choice between typewriters and word processors only through availability (via the price), and not through any learning effect. (Consumers can 'learn' in the Arrow–Debreu model, e.g. their marginal rates of substitution can depend on the state of nature, but the rate at which they learn is independent of production or consumption – it depends on the exogenous realization of the state. We shall come back to this when we consider information.) If for no other reason, the burden of calculation and attention which rational choice over consumption plans imposes on the individual is so large that one expects rationality to give way to some kind of bounded rationality in some future general equilibrium models.

Two more assumptions on preferences made in the model of Arrow–Debreu are nonsatiation and convexity:

(A.4) For each $x \in X^h$, there is a $y \in X^h$ with $y \succ_h x$, i.e. such that $y \succcurlyeq_h x$ and not $x \succcurlyeq_h y$. $\qquad\qquad\square$

(A.5) X^h is a convex set, and $\succcurlyeq_h$ is convex, i.e., if $y \succ_h x$ and $0 < t \leqslant 1$, then $[ty + (1 - t)x] \succ_h x$. $\qquad\square$

The nonsatiation hypothesis seems entirely in accordance with human nature. The convexity hypothesis implies that commodities are infinitely divisible, and that mixtures are at least as good as extremes. When commodities are distinguished very finely according to dates, so that they must be thought of as flows, then the convexity hypothesis is untenable. In a standard example, a man may be indifferent between drinking a glass of gin or scotch at a particular moment, but he would be much worse off if he had to drink a glass of half gin–half scotch. On the other hand, if the commodities were not so finely dated, then they would be more analogous to stocks, and a consumer might well be better off with a litre of gin and a litre of scotch, than two litres of either one. In any case, as we shall remark later, if every agent is small relative to the market (i.e. if there are many agents) then the nonconvexities in preferences are relatively unimportant.

Each agent h is also characterized by a vector of initial endowments

(A.6) $e^h \in X^h \subset \mathbb{R}^L$ $\qquad$ for all $h = 1, \ldots, H$. $\qquad\square$

The endowment vector e^h represents the claims that the consumer has on all commodities, not necessarily commodities in his physical possession. The fact that $e^h \in X^h$ means that the consumer can ensure his own survival even if he is deprived of all opportunity to trade. This is a somewhat strange hypothesis for the modern world, in which individuals often have labour but few other endowments, e.g. land. Doubtless the hypothesis could be relaxed; in any case, survival is not an issue that is addressed in the Arrow–Debreu model.

Each individual h is also endowed with an ownership share of each of the firms $j = 1, \ldots, J$.

(A.7) For all $h = 1, \ldots, H$, $j = 1, \ldots, J$, $d_{hj} \geqslant 0$,
$\qquad$ and for all $j = 1, \ldots, J$, $\Sigma_{h=1}^H d_{hj} = 1$. $\qquad\square$

Firms. (A.8) Let there be J firms, $j = 1, \ldots, J$. $\qquad\square$

The firm in Arrow–Debreu is characterized by its initial distribution of owners, and by its technological capacity $Y_j \subset \mathbb{R}^L$ to transform commodities. Any production plan $y \in \mathbb{R}^L$, where negative components of y refer to inputs and positive components denote outputs, is feasible for firm j if $y \in Y_j$. A customary assumption made in the Arrow–Debreu model is free disposal: if $l = 1, \ldots, L$ is any commodity, and v_l is the unit vector in $\mathbb{R}^L$, with one in the lth coordinate and zero elsewhere, then

(A.9) For all $l = 1, \ldots, L$ and $k > 0$, $-kv_l \in Y_j$, for some $j = 1, \ldots, J$. $\qquad\square$

Although it is strange, when thinking of nuclear waste etc., to think that any commodity can be disposed without cost (i.e. without the use of any other inputs), as we shall remark later, this assumption can be relaxed, if negative prices are introduced (or if weak monotonicity is assumed).

47

The empirically most vulnerable assumption to the Arrow–Debreu model, and one crucial to its logic, is:

(A.10) For each j, Y_j is a closed, convex set containing 0. □

This convexity assumption rules out indivisibilities in production (e.g. half a tunnel), increasing returns to scale, gains from specialization, etc. As with consumption, if the indivisibilities of production are small relative to the size of the whole economy, then the conclusions we shall shortly present are not much affected. But when they are large, or when there are significant increasing returns to scale, the model of competitive equilibrium that we are about to examine is simply not applicable. Nevertheless, convexity is consistent with the traditionally important cases of decreasing and constant returns to scale in production.

We conclude by presenting three final assumptions used in the Arrow–Debreu model.

(A.11) Let $e = \Sigma_{h=1}^{H} e^h$,
   let $F = \{ y \in \mathbb{R}^L | y = \Sigma_{j=1}^{J} y_j, y_j \in Y^j, j = 1, \ldots, J \}$,
   let $\bar{F} = \{ y \in F | y + e \geq 0 \}$, and
   let $K = \{ (y_1, \ldots, y_J) \in Y_1 \times \cdots \times Y_J | \equiv y \Sigma_{j=1}^{J} y^j \in \bar{F} \}$.
Then $\bar{F} \cap \mathbb{R}^L_{++} \neq \phi$, and K is compact. □

Assumption (A.11) requires that the level of productive activity that is possible even if the productive sector appropriates all the resources of the consuming sector is bounded (as well as closed).

Notice that these assumptions are consistent with firms owning initial resources, as well as individuals. In the original Arrow–Debreu model (1954), the firms were prohibited from owning initial resources (they were assigned to the firm owners: with complete markets there is little difference, but with incomplete markets the earlier assumption is restrictive).

(A.12) The economy is irreducible. □

We shall not elaborate this assumption here. It means that for any two agents h and h', the endowment e^h of agent h is positive in some commodity l, which (taking into account the possibilities of production) agent h' could use to make himself strictly better off. It certainly seems reasonable that each agent's labour power could be used to make another agent better off.

Lastly, we assume that

(A.13) The commodities are not distinguished according to which firm produces them, or who consumes them. □

Assumption (A.13) is made simply for the purposes of interpretation. When put together with the definition of competitive equilibrium, it implies that there are no externalities to production or consumption, no public goods, etc. Mathematically, however, (A.13) has no content. In other words, if we dropped assumption (A.13), the Arrow–Debreu notion of competitive equilibrium would still make sense (even in the presence of externalities and public goods) and it would still have the optimality properties we shall elaborate in Section III, but it would require an entirely different interpretation. Consumers, for example, would be charged different prices for the same physical commodities (same, that is, according, to date, location and state of nature). In more technical language, a Lindahl equilibrium is a special case of an (A.1)–(A.12) Arrow–Debreu equilibrium, with the commodity space suitably expanded and interpreted. Thus each physical unit of a public good is replaced by H goods, one unit for the public good indexed by which agent consumes it. Also the physical technology set describing the production of the public good is replaced by a different set in the Arrow–Debreu model, lying in a higher dimensional space, where the output of the one physical public good is replaced by the joint output of the same amount of H goods. In an Arrow–Debreu equilibrium, consumers will likely pay different prices for these H goods, i.e. for what in reality represents the same physical public good. Hence the differential pay principle for the optimal provision of public goods elucidated by Samuelson, which appeared to point to a qualitative difference between the analytical apparatus needed to describe optimality in public goods and private goods economies, is thus shown to be explicable by exactly the same apparatus used for private goods economies, simply by multiplying the number of commodities. The same device can also be used for analysing the optimal provision of goods when there are externalities, provided that negative prices are allowed. Assumption (A.13) thus seriously limits the normative conclusions that can be drawn from the model. From a descriptive point of view, however, rationality and the price taking behaviour which equilibrium implies, make (A.13) necessary.

III. EQUILIBRIUM

Price is the final primitive concept in the Arrow–Debreu model. Like commodity it is quantifiable and directly measurable. As Debreu has remarked, the fundamental role which mathematics plays in economics is partly owing to the quantifiable nature of these two primitive concepts, and to the rich mathematical relationship of dual vector spaces, into which it is natural to classify the collections of price values and commodity quantities. Properly speaking, price is only sensible (and measurable) as a relationship between two commodities, i.e. as relative price. Hence there should be $L^2 - L$ relative prices in the Arrow–Debreu model. But the definition of Arrow–Debreu equilibrium immediately implies that it suffices to give $L - 1$ of these ratios, and all the rest are determined.

For mathematical convenience (namely to treat prices and quantities as dual vectors), one price is specified for each unit quantity of each commodity. The relative price of two commodities can be obtained by taking the ratio of the Arrow–Debreu prices of these commodities.

I shall proceed by specifying the definition of Arrow–Debreu equilibrium, and then I make a number of remarks emphasizing some of the salient characteristics of the definition. The longest remark concerns the differences between the historical development of general equilibrium, up until the time of Hicks and Samuelson and the particular Arrow–Debreu model of general equilibrium.

An Arrow–Debreu economy E is an array $E = \{L, H, J(X^h, e^h, \succcurlyeq_h), (Y^j), (d^{hj}), h = 1, \ldots, H, j = 1, \ldots, J\}$ satisfying assumptions (A.1)–(A.13). An Arrow–Debreu equilibrium is an array $[(\bar{p}_l), (\bar{x}_l^h), (\bar{y}_l^j), l = 1, \ldots, L, h = 1, \ldots, H, j = 1, \ldots, J]$ satisfying:

For all $j = 1, \ldots, J, \bar{y}_J \in$

$$\arg\max \left\{ \sum_{l=1}^{L} \bar{p}_l y_l \,|\, (y = y_1, \ldots, y_L) \in Y^j \right\} \tag{1}$$

For all $h = 1, \ldots, H, \bar{x}^h \in B^h(\bar{p})$, where $B^h(\bar{p})$

$$\equiv \left\{ x \in X^h \,|\, \sum_{l=1}^{L} \bar{p}_l x_l \leq \sum_{l=1}^{L} \bar{p}_l e_l^h + \sum_{j=1}^{J} d^{hj} \sum_{l=1}^{L} \bar{p}_l \bar{y}_l^j \right\} \tag{2}$$

and if $x \in B^h(\bar{p})$, then not $x \succ_h \bar{x}^h$,

For all $l = 1, \ldots, L, \ \sum_{h=1}^{H} \bar{x}_l^h = \sum_{h=1}^{H} e_l^h + \sum_{j=1}^{J} \bar{y}_l^j. \tag{3}$

The most striking feature of general equilibrium is the juxtaposition of the great diversity in goals and resources it allows, together with the supreme coordination it requires. Every desire of each consumer, no matter how whimsical, is met precisely by the voluntary supply of some producer. And this is true for all markets and consumers simultaneously.

There is a symmetry to the general equilibrium model, in the way that all agents enter the model individually motivated by self-interest (not as members of distinct classes motivated by class interests), and simultaneously, so that no agent acts prior to any other on a given market (e.g. by setting prices). If workers' subsistence were not assumed, for example, that would break the symmetry; workers income could have to be guaranteed first, otherwise demand would (discontinuously) collapse. As it is, at the aggregate level, supply and demand equally and simultaneously determine price; in equilibrium, both the consumers' marginal rates of substitution and the producers' marginal rates of transformation are equal to relative prices (assuming differentiability and interiority). There are gains to trade both through exchange and through production. This point of view represents a significant break with the classical tradition of Ricardo and Marx. We shall come to the main difference between the classical and neoclassical approaches shortly. Another difference is that there need not be fixed coefficients of production in the Arrow–Debreu model – the sets Y are much more general. Also in an Arrow–Debreu equilibrium, there is no reason for there to be a uniform rate of profit. There is none the less one aspect of the model which these authors would have greatly approved, namely the shares d^{hj} which allow the owners of firms to collect profits even though they have contributed nothing to production.

Notice that in general equilibrium each agent need only concern himself with his own goals (preferences or profits) and the prices. The implicit assumption that every agent 'knows' all the prices is highly non-trivial. It means that at each date each agent is capable of forecasting perfectly all future prices until the end of time. It is in this sense that the Arrow–Debreu model depends on 'rational expectations'. Each agent must also be informed of the 'price' q_j of each firm j, where $q_j = \Sigma_{l=1}^{L} \bar{p}_l \bar{y}_l^j$. (Firms that produce under constant returns to scale must also discover the level of production, which cannot be deduced from the prices alone.) Assuming that the 'man on the spot' (Hayek's expression) knows much better than anyone else what he wants, or best how his changing environment is suited to producing his product, decentralized decision making would seem to be highly desirable, if it is not incompatible with coordination. Indeed, harmony through diversity is one of the sacred doctrines of the liberal tradition.

The greatest triumph of the Arrow–Debreu model was to lay out explicitly the conditions (roughly (A.1)–(A.13)) under which it is possible to claim that a properly chosen price system must always exist that, like the invisible hand, can guide diverse and independent agents to make mutually compatible choices. The idea of general equilibrium had gradually developed since the time of Adam Smith, mostly through the pioneering work of Walras (1874), Von Neumann (1937), Wald (1932). Hicks (1939) and Samuelson (1947). By the late 1940s the definition of equilibrium, including ownership shares in the firms, was well-established. But it was Arrow–Debreu (1954) that spelled out precise microeconomic assumptions at the level of the individual agents that could be used to show the model was consistent..

The axiomatic and rigorous approach that characterized the formulation of general equilibrium by Arrow–Debreu has been enormously influential. It is now taken for granted that a model is not properly defined unless it has been proved to be logically consistent. Much of the clamour for 'microeconomic foundations to macroeconomics', for example, is a desire to see an axiomatic clarity similar to that of the Arrow–Debreu model applied to other areas of economics. Of course, there were other earlier economic models that were similarly axiomatic and rigorous; one thinks especially of Von Neumann–Morgenstern's *Theory of Games* (1944). But game theory was, at the time, on the periphery of economics. Competitive equilibrium is at its heart.

The central mathematical techniques, convexity theory (separating hyperplane theorem) and Brouwer's (Kakutani's) fixed point theorem, used in Arrow–Debreu are, thirty years later, still the most important tools used in mathematical economics. Both elements had played a (hidden) role in Von Neumann's work. Convexity had been prominent in the work of Koopmans (1951) on activity analysis, in the work of Kuhn and Tucker (1951) on optimization, and in the papers of Arrow (1951) and Debreu (1951) on optimality. Fixed point theorems had been used by Von Neumann (1937), by Nash (1950) and especially by McKenzie (1954), who one month earlier than Arrow–Debreu had published a proof of general equilibrium using Kakutani's theorem, albeit in a model where the primitive assumptions were made on demand functions, rather than preferences. McKenzie (1959) also made an early contribution to the notion of an irreducible economy (assumption (A.9)).

The first fruit of the more precise formulation of equilibrium that began to emerge in the early 1950s was the transparent demonstration of the first and second welfare theorems that Arrow and Debreu simultaneously gave in 1951. Particularly noteworthy is the proof that every equilibrium is Pareto optimal. So simple and illuminating is this demonstration that it is no exaggeration to call it the most frequently imitated argument in all of neoclassical economic theory.

Among the confusions that were cleared away by the careful axiomatic treatment of equilibrium was the reliance of the discussions by Hicks and Samuelson on interior solutions and differentiability. When discussing the optimal allocation of housing, for example, it is evident that most agents will consume nothing of most houses, but this does not affect the Pareto optimality of a free (and complete) market allocation of housing. Similarly, it is not necessary to either the existence of Arrow–Debreu equilibrium, nor to the first and second welfare theorems, that preferences or production sets be either differentiable or strictly convex. In particular, it is possible to incorporate the 'neoclassical production function' with constant returns to scale with variable inputs, the classical fixed coefficients methods of production, and the strictly concave production functions of the Hicks–Samuelson vintage, all in the same framework.

This is not to say that differentiability has no role to play in the Arrow–Debreu model. In his seminal paper (1970), Debreu resurrected the role of differentiability by showing, via the methods of transversality theory (a branch of differential topology) that almost every differentiable economy is regular, in the sense that small perturbations to the economic data (e.g. the endowments) make small changes in all the equilibrium prices Before Debreu, comparative statics could be handled only under specialized hypothesis, for example, the invertibility of excess demand at all prices, etc. We shall give a fuller discussion of the three crucial mathematical results of the Arrow–Debreu model – existence, optimality and local uniqueness – in the next section.

Observe finally, that although the commodities may include physical goods dated over many time periods, there is only one budget constraint in an Arrow–Debreu equilibrium. The income that could be obtained from the sale of an endowed commodity, dated from the last period, is available already in the first period.

IV. PARETO OPTIMALITY

The first theorem of welfare economics states that any Arrow–Debreu equilibrium allocation $\bar{x} = (\bar{x}^h)$, $h = 1, \ldots, H$ is Pareto optimal in the sense that if $[(x^h),(y^j)]$ satisfies $y^j \in Y^j$, $\Sigma_{h=1}^{H} x^h = \Sigma_{j=1}^{J} y_n^j + e$, then it cannot be the case that $x^h \succ_h \bar{x}^h$ for all h. The second theorem of welfare analysis states the converse, namely that any Pareto optimal allocation for an Arrow–Debreu economy E is a competitive equilibrium allocation for an Arrow–Debreu economy $\hat{E}$ obtained from E by rearranging the initial endowments of commodities and ownership shares.

The first welfare theorem expresses the efficiency of the ideal market system, although it makes no claim as to the justice of the initial distribution of resources.

The second welfare theorem implies that any income redistribution is best effected through a lump sum transfer, rather than through manipulating the market, e.g. through rent control, etc.

The connection between competitive equilibrium and Pareto optimality has been perceived for a long time, but until 1951 there was a general confusion between the necessity and sufficiency part of the arguments. The old proof of Pareto optimality (see Lange, 1942) assumed differentiable utilities of production sets, and a strictly positive allocation $\bar{x}$. It noted the first order conditions to the problem of maximizing the ith consumer's utility, subject to maintaining all the others at least as high as they got under $\bar{x}$, and feasibility, are satisfied at $\bar{x}$, if and only if $\bar{x}$ is a competitive equilibrium allocation for a 'rearranged' economy $\hat{E}$. This first order, or infinitesimal, proof of equivalence between competitive equilibrium and Pareto optimality could have been made global by postulating in addition that preferences and production sets are convex.

The Arrow and Debreu (1954) proofs of the equivalence between competitive equilibrium and Pareto optimality, under global changes, do not require differentiability, nor do they require that all agents consume a strictly positive amount of every good. In fact the proof of the first welfare theorem, that each competitive equilibrium is Pareto optimal, does not even use convexity.

The only requirement is local nonsatiation, so that every agent spends all his income in equilibrium. If (x, y) Pareto dominates the equilibrium allocation $(\bar{p}, \bar{x}, \bar{y})$, then for all h, $\bar{p} \cdot x^h < \bar{p} \cdot \bar{x}^h$. Since profit maximization implies that for all j, $\bar{p} \cdot \bar{y}^j \geqq \bar{p} \cdot y^j$, it follows that $\bar{p}(\Sigma_h x^h - \Sigma_j y^j) > \bar{p} \cdot (\Sigma_h \bar{x}^h - \Sigma_j \bar{y}^j)$, contradicting feasibility.

The proof of the second welfare theorem, on the other hand, does require convexity of the preferences and production sets (though not their differentiability, nor the interiority of the candidate allocation $\bar{x}$). Essentially it depends on Minkowski's theorem, which asserts that between any two disjoint convex sets in $\mathbb{R}^L$ there must be a separating hyperplane.

In this connection let us mention one more remarkable mathematical property of the Arrow–Debreu model. Let us suppose that all production takes place under constant returns to scale: if $y \in Y^j$, then so is λy, for $\lambda \geqslant 0$. We say that a feasible allocation $\bar{x}$ for the economy E is in the core if there is no coalition of consumers $S \subset \{1, \ldots, H\}$ such that using only their initial endowments of resources, as well as access to all the production technologies, they cannot achieve an allocation for themselves which they all prefer to $\bar{x}$. The core is meant to reflect those allocations which could be maintained when bargaining (the formation of coalitions) is costless. In a status quo core allocation, any labour union or cartel of owners that threatens to withhold its goods from the market knows that another coalition could form and by withholding its goods, prevent some members of the original coalition from being better off than they were under the status quo. It is easy to see that any competitive equilibrium is in the core. Debreu–Scarf (1963), building on earlier work of Scarf, showed by using the separating hyperplane theorem, that if agents are small relative to the market, in the sense they made precise through the notion of replication, then the core consists only of competitive allocations. Such a theorem can also be proved even if there are small nonconvexities in preferences (see Aumann (1964) for a different formulation of the small agent).

EXISTENCE OF EQUILIBRIUM. Suppose that agents' preferences and firms' production sets are strictly convex, and that agents strictly prefer more of any commodity to less (strict monotonicity) and that they all have strictly positive endowments. Let Δ be the set of L-price vectors, all non-negative, summing to one. Let $f^h(p)$ be the commodity bundle most preferred by agent h, given the strictly positive prices $p \in \Delta_{++}$. Similarly let $g^i(p)$ be the profit maximizing choice of firm j, given prices $p \in \Delta_{++}$. Finally, let $f(p) = \Sigma_{h=1}^{H} f^h(p) - \Sigma_{j=1}^{j} g^j(p) - e$. It is easy to show that f is a continuous function at all $p \in \Delta_{++}$. A price $\bar{p} \in \Delta_{++}$ is an Arrow–Debreu equilibrium price if and only if $f(\bar{p}) = 0$.

In general there is no reason to expect a continuous function to have a zero. Thus Wald could prove only with great difficulty in a special case that an equilibrium necessarily exists. Now observe that the function must satisfy Walras's Law, $p \cdot f(p) = 0$, for all p. So f is not arbitrary.

Consider the convex, compact set Δ_ε of prices $p \in \Delta$ with $p_l \geq \varepsilon > 0$, for all l. Consider also the continuous function $\phi: \Delta_\varepsilon \to \Delta_\varepsilon$ mapping p to the closest point $\hat{p}$ in Δ_ε to $f(p) + p$. By Brouwer's fixed point theorem, there must be some $\bar{p}$ with $\phi(\bar{p}) = \bar{p}$. From strict monotonicity, it follows that $\bar{p}$ cannot be on the boundary of Δ_ε, if ε is chosen sufficiently small. From Walras's Law it follows that if $\bar{p}$ is the interior of Δ_ε, then $f(\bar{p}) = 0$. The demonstration of the existence of equilibrium by Arrow and Debreu, as modified later by Debreu (1959), followed a similar logic.

Note the essential role of convexity in two parts of the above proof. It was used with respect to agents' characteristics to guarantee that their optimizing behaviour is continuous. And it was also used to ensure that the space Δ_ε has the fixed point property. Smale (1976) has given a path-following proof (related to Scarf's (1973) algorithm) that on closer inspection does not require convexity of the price space. (Dierker (1974) and Balasko (1986) have given homotopy proofs.) This is not only of computational importance. It appears that there may be economic problems, dealing with general equilibrium with incomplete markets, in which the price space is intrinsically nonconvex, and in which the existence of equilibrium can only be proved using path-following methods (see Duffie-Shaffer, 1985).

To weaken the assumption of strict convexity, in the above proof, one can replace Brouwer's fixed point theorem with Kakutani's. An important conceptual point arises in connection with strict montonicity. If that is dropped, and the production sets do not have free disposal, then in order to guarantee the existence of equilibrium, the definition must be revised to require either $f_l(\bar{p}) = 0$, or $f_l(\bar{p}) < 0$ and $\bar{p}_l = 0$. There may be free goods, like air, in excess supply. One cannot drop monotonicity and free disposal without allowing for negative prices.

Finally, it can be shown that if there are small nonconvexities in either preference or production, and if all the agents are small relative to the market (either in the replication sense of Debreu–Scarf, or the measure zero sense of Aumann), then there will be prices at which the markets nearly clear. On the other hand, increasing returns to scale over a broad range is definitely incompatible with equilibrium.

LOCAL UNIQUENESS AND COMPARATIVE STATICS. Another property of the excess demand function $f(p)$ is that it is homogeneous of degree zero. So instead of taking $p \in \Delta$, let us fix $p_l = 1$. Similarly, let $F(p)$ be the $L - 1$ vector of excess demands for goods $l = 2, \ldots, L$. If $F(p) = 0$, then by Walras's Law, $f(p) = 0$.

Suppose furthermore that agent characteristics are smooth. Then $F(P)$ is a differentiable function. If $D_p F(\bar{p})$ has full rank at an equilibrium $\bar{p}$, then $\bar{p}$ is locally unique. Moreover, the equilibrium $\bar{p}$ will move continuously, given continuous, small changes in the agents' characteristics, such as their endowments e. If $D_p F(\bar{p})$ has full rank at all equilibria $\bar{p}$, then there are only a finite number of equilibria. Debreu (1970) called an economy E regular if $D_p F(\bar{p})$ has full rank at all equilibrium $\bar{p}$ of E.

The problem of trying to give sufficient conditions on preferences etc. to guarantee that $D_p F$ has full rank in equilibrium has proved intractable (except for restrictive, special cases). But Debreu (1970) solved the problem in classic style, appealing to the transversality theorem of differential topology (or Sard's theorem), to show that if one were content with regularity for 'almost all' economies, then the problem is simple. He proved that for almost all economies, $D_p F$ has full rank at every equilibrium. Hence, in almost all economies comparative statics (the change in equilibrium, given exogenous changes to the economy) is well defined.

Observe that excess demand F depends on the agents' characteristics, including their endowments, so we could write $F(e, p)$. Now the transversality theorem says that (given some technical conditions) if $D_e F(e, \bar{p})$ has full rank at all equilibria $\bar{p}$ for the economy $E(e)$ with endowments e, for all e, then for 'almost all' e, $D_p F(e, \bar{p})$ has full rank at all equilibrium $\bar{p}$ of $E(e)$. But it is easy to show that $D_e F(e, p)$ always has full rank. Along similar lines, Debreu proved the 'generic regularity' of equilibrium.

There is one unfortunate side to this comparative statics story. One would like to show not only that comparative statics are well defined, but also that they have a definite form. In a concave programming problem, for example, a small increase in an input results in a decrease in that input's shadow price, and an increase in output approximately equal to the size of the input increase multiplied by its original shadow price. Given the strong rationality hypothesis of the Arrow–Debreu model, one would hope for some sort of analogous result. Following a conjecture of Sonnenschein, Debreu proved in 1974 that given any function $f(p)$ on Δ_ε satisfying Walras's Law, he could find an Arrow–Debreu economy such that $f(p)$ is its aggregate excess demand on Δ_ε. Thus assumptions (A.1)–(A.13) do not permit any *a priori* predictions about the changes that must occur in equilibrium given exogenous changes to the economy. An increase in the aggregate endowment of a particular good, for example, might cause its equilibrium price to rise. The possibility of such pathologies is disappointing. It means that to make even qualitative predictions, the economist needs detailed data on the excess demands F.

V. WHAT THE MODEL DOESN'T EXPLAIN

We have already discussed the implications of the notion of Arrow–Debreu commodities and the second welfare theorem for insurance, namely that since every Pareto optimal allocation is supportable as an Arrow–Debreu equilibrium, every optimal allocation of risk bearing can be accomplished by the production and trade of Arrow–Debreu commodities, i.e. without recourse to additional kinds of insurance markets specializing in risks. Every Arrow–Debreu commodity is as much a diversifier in location, or time, or physical quality as it is for risk. This leads to a great simplification and economy of analysis. But it also means, that from the positive point of view, the Arrow–Debreu economy cannot directly provide an analysis of insurance markets (except as a benchmark case). In this section I shall try to point out a few of the other phenomena which recede into the background in the Arrow–Debreu model but which would emerge if the assumption of a finite, but complete set of Arrow–Debreu commodities, and consumers was dropped.

There are four currently active lines of research which attempt to come to grips in a general equilibrium framework with some of these phenomena, while preserving the fundamental neoclassical Arrow–Debreu principles of agent optimization, market clearing, and rational expectations, that I think are particularly worthy of attention. They are the theory of general equilibrium with incomplete asset markets which can be traced back to Arrow's (1953) seminal paper on securities; overlapping generations economies, whose study was initiated by Samuelson (1958) in his classic consumption loan model; the Cournot theory of market exchange with few traders, first adapted to general equilibrium by Shapley–Shubik (1977), and the model of rational expectations equilibrium, pioneered by Lucas (1972).

Let us note first of all that in Arrow–Debreu equilibrium there is no trade in shares of firms. A stock certificate is not an Arrow–Debreu commodity, for its possession entitles the owner to additional commodities which he need not obtain through exchange. Note also that in Arrow–Debreu equilibrium, the hypothesis that all prices will remain the same, no matter how an individual firm changes its production plan, guarantees that firm owners unanimously agree on the firm objective, to maximize profit. If there were a market for firm shares, there would not be any trade anyway, since ownership of the firm and the income necessary to purchase it would be perfect substitutes. In an incomplete markets equilibrium, different sources of revenue are not necessarily perfect substitutes. There could be active trade on the stock market. Of course, such a model would have to specify the firm objectives, since one would not expect unanimity. The theory of stock market equilibrium is still in its infancy, although some important work has already been done. (See Dreze, 1974, and Grossman–Hart, 1979.)

Bankruptcy is not allowed in an Arrow–Debreu equilibrium. That follows from the fact that all agents must meet their budget constraints. In a game theoretic formulation of equilibrium (such as I shall discuss shortly), it is achieved by imposing an infinite bankruptcy penalty. Since every Arrow–Debreu equilibrium is Pareto optimal, there would be no benefit in reducing the bankruptcy penalty to the point where someone might choose to go bankrupt. But with incomplete markets, such a policy might be Pareto improving, even allowing for the deadweight loss of imposing the penalties.

Money does not appear in the Arrow–Debreu model. Of course, all of the reasons for its real life existence: transactions demand, precautionary demand, store of value, unit of account, etc. are already taken care of in the Arrow–Debreu model. One could imagine money in the model: at data zero every agent could borrow money from the central bank. At every date afterwards he would be required to finance his purchases out of his stock of money, adding to that stock from his sales. At the last date he would be required to return to the bank exactly what he borrowed (or else face an infinite brankruptcy penalty). In such a model the Arrow–Debreu prices would appear as money prices. The absolute level of money prices and the aggregate amount of borrowing would not be determined, but the allocations of commodities would be the same as in Arrow–Debreu. There is no point in making the role of money explicit in the Arrow–Debreu model, since it has no effect on the real allocations. However, if one considers the same model with incomplete asset markets, the presence of explicitly financial securities can be of great significance to the real allocations.

In the Arrow–Debreu model, all trade takes place at the beginning of time. If markets were reopened at later dates for the same Arrow–Debreu commodities, then no additional trade would take place anyway. At the other extreme, one might consider a model in which at every date and state of nature only those Arrow–Debreu commodities could be traded which were indexed by the corresponding (date, state) pair. An intermediate case would also permit the trade of some (but not all) differently indexed Arrow–Debreu commodities. Now the Arrow–Debreu proofs of the existence and Pareto optimality of equilibrium do not apply to such an incomplete markets economy, as Hart (1975) first pointed out. We have already noted the existence problem. As for efficiency, the Pareto optimality of Arrow–Debreu equilibria might suggest the presumption that, though there might be a loss to eliminating markets, trade on the remaining markets would be as efficient as possible. In fact, it can be shown (generically) that equilibrium trades do not make efficient use of the existing markets.

The Arrow–Debreu model of general equilibrium is relentlessly neoclassical; in fact it has become the paradigm of the neoclassical approach. This stems in part from its individualistic hypothesis, and its celebrated conclusions about the potential efficacy of unencumbered markets. (Although Arrow, for example, has always maintained that a proper understanding of Arrow–Debreu commodities is also useful to showing how inefficient is the limited real world market system.) But still more telling is the fact that the assumption of a finite number of commodities (and hence of dates) forces upon the model the interpretation of the economic process as a one-way activity of converting given primary resources into final consumption goods. If there is universal agreement about when the world will end, there can be no question about the reproduction of the capital stock. In equilibrium it will be run down to zero. Similarly when the world has a definite beginning, so that the first market transaction takes place after the ownership of all resources and techniques of production, and the preferences of all individuals have been determined, one cannot study the evolution of the social norms of consumption in terms of the historical development of the relations of production. One certainly cannot speak about the production of all commodities by commodities (Sraffa, 1960) (since at date zero there must be commodities which have not been produced by commodities, i.e. by physical objects which are traded).

It seems natural to suppose that as L becomes very large, so that the end of the world is put off until the distant future, that this event cannot be of much significance to behaviour now. But let us not forget the rationality imposed on the agents. Far off as the end of the world might be, it is perfectly taken into account. Thus, for example, social security (funded as it is in the US by taxes on the young) could not exist if rational agents agreed on a final stopping time to transactions.

Consider a model satisfying all the assumptions (A.1)–(A.13), except that L and H are allowed to be infinite, such as the overlapping generations model. It can be shown that there is a robust collection of economies which have a continuum of equilibria, most of which are Pareto sub-optimal, which differ enormously in time 0 behaviour. Thus in a model where time does not have a definite end, the optimality and comparative statics properties of equilibria are radically different. (For example, there may be a continuum of equilibria, indexed by the level of period 0 real wages (inversely related to the rate of profit) or the level of output or employment. The interested reader can consult the entry on OVERLAPPING GENERATIONS MODELS. A systematic study of economies where only L is allowed to be infinite was begun by Bewley (1972). Such economies tend to have properties similar to those of Arrow–Debreu.)

There is no place in the Arrow–Debreu model for asymmetric information. The second welfare theorem, for example, relies on lump sum redistributions, i.e. redistributions that occur in advance of the market interactions. But if agents cannot be distinguished except through their market behaviour, then the redistribution must be a function of market behaviour. Rational agents, anticipating this, will distort their behaviour and the optimality of the redistribution will be lost.

Similarly, in the definition of equilibrium no agent takes into account what other agents know, for example about the state of nature. Thus it is quite possible in an Arrow–Debreu equilibrium for some ignorant agents to exchange valuable commodities for commodities indexed by states that other agents know will not occur. This problem received enormous attention in the finance literature, and some claim (see Grossman 1981) that it has been solved by extending the Arrow–Debreu definition of equilibrium to a 'rational expectations equilibrium'

(Lucas, 1972; see also Radner, 1979). But this definition is itself suspect; in particular, it may not be implementable.

Even if rational expectations equilibrium (REE) were accepted as a viable notion of equilibrium, it could not come to grips with the most fundamental problems of asymmetric information. For like Arrow–Debreu equilibrium, in REE all trade is conducted anonymously through the market at given prices. Implicit in this definition is the assumption of large numbers of traders on both sides of every market. But what has come to be called the incentive problem in economics revolves around individual or firm specific uncertainty, i.e. trade in commodities indexed by the names of the traders, which by definition involves few traders.

This brings us to another major riddle: how are agents supposed to get to equilibrium in the Arrow–Debreu model? The pioneers of general equilibrium never imagined that the economy was necessarily in equilibrium; Walras, for example, proposed an explicit tâtonnement procedure which he conjectured converged to equilibrium. But that idea is flawed in two respects: in general, it can be shown not to converge, and more importantly, it is an imaginary process in which no exchange is permitted until equilibrium is reached. This illustrates a grave shortcoming of any equilibrium theory, namely that it cannot begin to specify outcomes out of equilibrium. The major crisis of labour market clearing in the 1930s, and again recently, argues strongly that there are limits to the applicability of equilibrium analysis.

One is led naturally to consider market games, in which the outcomes are well-specified even when agents do not make their equilibrium moves. The most famous market game is Cournot's doupoly model, which has been extended to general equilibrium by Shapley–Shubik (1977). When there are a large number of agents of each type, the Nash equilibria of the Shapley–Shubik game give nearly identical allocations to the competitive allocations of Arrow–Debreu. This justifies (to first approximation) the price taking behaviour of the Arrow–Debreu agents. But note that the informational requirements of Nash equilibrium are at least twice that of Arrow–Debreu competitive equilibrium (each agent must know the aggregates of bids and offers on each market). It is also extremely interesting that trade takes place in the Shapley–Shubik game even if there is only one trader on each side of the market. Hence many problems in asymmetric information which have no place in the Arrow–Debreu model, because they involve too fine a specification of the commodities to be consistent with price taking, might be sensible in a market game context. Finally, it can be shown that REE is not consistent with the Shapley–Shubik game, or indeed with any continuous game.

We have indicated some of the ways in which it is possible to extend general equilibrium analysis to phenomena outside the scope of the Arrow–Debreu model, while at the same time preserving the neoclassical methodological premises of agent optimization, rational expectations, and equilibrium. It is important to note that these variations have extended the definition of equilibrium as well;

this is most obvious in the case of market games, where Nash equilibrium replaces competitive equilibrium. All of the models have retained, on the other hand, more or less the same notion of rationality, sometimes at the cost of increasing the demands on the rationality of expectations. A great challenge for future general equilibrium models is how to formulate a sensible notion of bounded rationality, without destroying the possibility of drawing normative conclusions.

BIBLIOGRAPHY

Arrow, K.J. 1951. An extension of the basic theorems of classical welfare economics. *Proceedings of the Second Berkeley Symposium on Mathematical Statistics and Probability*, ed. J. Neyman, University of California Press, 507–532.

Arrow, K.J. 1953. Le rôle des valeurs boursières pour la répartition la meilleure des risques. *Économétrie*, Paris: Centre National de la Récherche Scientifique, 41–8.

Arrow, K.J. 1969. The organization of economic activity: issues pertinent to the choice of market vs nonmarket allocation, reprinted in *Collected Papers of Kenneth Arrow*, Cambridge, Mass.: Belknap Press, Vol. II, 133–55.

Arrow, K.J. and Debreu, G. 1954. Existence of an equilibrium for a competitive economy. *Econometrica* 22, 265–90.

Aumann, R.J. 1964. Markets with a continuum of traders. *Econometrica* 32, 39–50.

Balasko, Y. 1986. *Foundations of the Theory of General Equilibrium*. New York: Academic Press.

Bewley, T. 1972. Existence of equilibria in economies with infinitely many commodities. *Journal of Economic Theory* 4, 514–40.

Cournot, A. 1838. *Recherches sur les principes mathématiques de la théorie des richesses*. Paris: L. Hachette.

Debreu, G. 1951. The coefficient of resource utilization. *Econometrica* 19, 273–92.

Debreu, G. 1959. *Theory of Value, An Axiomatic Analysis of Economic Equilibrium*. New York: Wiley.

Debreu, G. 1970. Economies with a finite set of equilibria. *Econometrica* 38, 387–92.

Debreu, G. 1974. Excess demand function. *Journal of Mathematical Economics* 1, 15–21.

Debreu, G. and Scarf, H. 1963. A limit theorem on the core of an economy. *International Economic Review* 4, 235–46.

Dierker, E. 1974. *Topological Methods in Walrasian Economics*. Berlin: Springer.

Drèze, J. 1974. Investment under private ownership: optimality, equilibrium, and stability. In *Allocation under Uncertainty*, ed. J. Drèze, New York: Macmillan.

Duffie, D. and Shafer, W. 1985. Equilibrium in incomplete markets: I–A basic model of generic existence. *Journal of Mathematical Economics* 14(3), 285–300.

Geanakoplos, J.D. and Polemarchakis, H.M. 1987. Existence, regularity, and constrained suboptimality of equilibrium with incomplete asset markets. In *Essays in Honor of Kenneth J. Arrow*, New York: Cambridge University Press.

Grossman, S. 1981. An introduction to the theory of rational expectations under asymmetric information. *Review of Economic Studies* 48, 541–60.

Grossman, S. and Hart, O. 1979. A theory of competitive equilibrium in stock market economies. *Econometrica* 47, 293–329.

Hart, O. 1975. On the optimality of equilibrium when the market structure is incomplete. *Journal of Economic Theory* 11(3), 418–33.

Hicks, J.R. 1939. *Value and Capital*. Oxford: Clarendon Press; 2nd edn, New York: Oxford University Press, 1946.

Koopmans, T.C. (ed.) 1951. *Activity Analysis of Production and Allocation.* New York: Wiley.

Kuhn, H.W. and Tucker, A.W. 1951. Nonlinear programming. *Proceedings of the Second Berkeley Symposium on Mathematical Statistics and Probability,* 481–92.

Lucas, R.E. 1972. Expectations and the neutrality of money. *Journal of Economic Theory* 4, 103–124.

McKenzie, L.W. 1954. On equilibrium in Graham's model of world trade and other competitive systems. *Econometrica* 22, 147–61.

McKenzie, L.W. 1959. On the existence of general equilibrium for a competitive market. *Econometrica* 27, 54–71.

Nash, J.F. 1950. Equilibrium points in n-person games. *Proceedings of the National Academy of Sciences of the USA* 36, 48–9.

Neumann, J. von. 1928. Zur theorie der Gesellschaftsspiele. *Mathematische Annalen* 100, 295–320.

Neumann, J. von. 1937. Uber ein ökonomisches Gleichungssystem und eine Verallgemeinerung des Brouwerschen Fixpunktsatzes. *Ergebnisse eines mathematischen Kolloquiums* 8, 73–83.

Neumann, J. von and Morgenstern, O. 1944. *Theory of Games and Economic Behavior.* Princeton: Princeton University Press.

Pareto, V. 1909. *Manuel d'économie politique.* Paris: Giard. Trans. as *Manual of Political Economy,* New York: Augustus M. Kelley, 1971.

Radner, R. 1968. Competitive equilibrium under uncertainty. *Econometrica* 36(1), 31–58.

Radner, R. 1979. Rational expectations equilibrium: generic existence and the information revealed by prices. *Econometrica* 17, 655–78.

Samuelson, P.A. 1947. *Foundations of Economic Analysis.* Cambridge, Mass.: Harvard University Press.

Samuelson, P.A. 1958. An exact consumption-loan model of interest with or without the social contrivance of money. *Journal of Political Economy* 66, 467–82.

Scarf, H. (with the collaboration of T. Hansen.) 1973. *The Computation of Economic Equilibria.* New Haven: Yale University Press.

Shapley, L. and Shubik, M. 1977. Trade using one commodity as a means of payment. *Journal of Political Economy* 85, 937–68.

Smale, S. 1976. A convergent process of price adjustment and global Newton methods. *Journal of Mathematical Economics* 3, 107–120.

Sonnenschein, H. 1973. Do Walras' identity and continuity characterize the class of community excess demand functions? *Journal of Economic Theory* 6, 345–54.

Sraffa, P. 1960. *Production of Commodities by Means of Commodities.* Cambridge: Cambridge University Press.

Walras, L. 1874–7. *Eléments d'économie politique pure.* Lausanne: L. Corbaz. Trans. by W. Jaffé as *Elements of Pure Economics,* New York: Orion, 1954.

Auctioneer

F.H. HAHN

Walras (1874) introduced the idea of a tâtonnement to provide a theoretical account of the formation of equilibrium prices. This account was not meant to be taken descriptively but rather as a 'Gedanken Experiment'. It was hoped that its study would provide insights into the actual *modus operandi* of the price mechanism.

Consider an economy of H households, F firms and n goods. Let $p \in \Delta \subset R^n_+$, where p is a price vector and Δ the simplex. Given the endowments of households $(e^h \in R^n_+)$, $x^h - e^h$ is the net trade vector of household h where $x^h \in R^n_+$ is the vector of demand of household h. Assume that

$$x^h - e^h = \xi_h(p)$$

where $\xi_h(p)$ is a continuous function from Δ to R^n. Let $y^f \in R^n$ be an activity of firm f, where $y^f_i > 0$ is interpreted as 'the firm supplies good i' and $y^f_i < 0$ is interpreted as 'the firm demands good i as an input'. Let $y = \Sigma_f y^f$ and assume that

$$y = \eta(p)$$

is a continuous function from Δ to R^n. Then define

$$z = \sum (x^h - e^h) - y$$

which by our assumptions can be written as, say

$$z = \sum_h \xi_h(p) - \eta(p) = \theta(p).$$

It is known that addition of budget constraints implies

$$p \cdot z = 0 \qquad \text{all } p \in \Delta.$$

(Walras's Law). An equilibrium of the economy is $p^* \in \Delta$ such that

$$\theta(p^*) \leqslant 0.$$

It should be added that the net trades $\xi_h(p)$ are assumed to be utility maximizing for each household under the budget constraint:

$$p \cdot \xi_h(p) \leqslant \sum_f \lambda_{hf}(p \cdot y^f)$$

where $1 \geqslant \lambda_{hf} \geqslant 0$, $\Sigma_h \lambda_{hf} = 1$, is the share of h in the profits of firm f. Similarly $\eta^f(p) = y^f$ satisfies for all f:

$$p \cdot \eta^f(p) \geqslant p \cdot y^f \qquad \text{all } y \text{ which the firm can choose amongst.}$$

A tâtonnement is now described as follows. A fictitious agent called the *auctioneer* announces $p \in \Delta$. Households now report to this auctioneer their desired net trades $[\xi_h(p)]$ and firms report to him their desired activities $[\eta^f(p)]$. From these reports the auctioneer can deduce $\theta(p)$. In its light he calculates a new price vector p' as follows:

$$\frac{p'_1}{\sum p'_i} = \frac{p_i}{\sum p_i} \qquad \text{if } \theta_i(p) = 0 \text{ or if } \theta_i(p) < 0 \text{ and } p = 0$$

$$\frac{p'_i}{\sum p'_i} > \frac{p_i}{\sum p_i} \qquad \text{if } \theta_i(p) > 0$$

$$\frac{p'_i}{\sum p'_i} < \frac{p_i}{\sum p_i} \qquad \text{if } \theta_i(p) < 0.$$

He announces p' and agents send back messages which allow him to calculate $\theta(p')$. The process continues until and if the rule for calculating a new price vector yields the preceding price vector. *No actual trading occurs* during this process.

The rule which we have supposed the auctioneer follows in changing his price announcement is only one of a number of possible ones. Indeed, it is not the one proposed by Walras. He supposed the auctioneer to concentrate on one market at a time, specifically he changes only one price. Suppose he changes the ith price. Then he changes it until, given all other prices which are held constant, the ith market is in equilibrium. (He assumed that there always is such a price and that it is unique.) Thereafter he moves on to the next market. Of course, this process may never terminate in an equilibrium.

In all of this one ought to specify what it is that the auctioneer knows. So far we have assumed that he does not know the function $\theta(p)$. If, however, he does know this function we may think of the auctioneer as being concerned to find a solution to $\theta(p) \leqslant 0$ for $p \in \Delta$. He is then no more than a programmer. In this case, for instance, he may adopt Newton's method (Arrow and Hahn, 1971; Smale, 1976). That is he proceeds as follows: Let $J(p)$ be the $(n-1) \times (n-1)$ Jacobian of the first $(n-1)$ excess demand functions $[\hat{\theta} = \theta_1(p) \dots \theta_{n-1}(p)]$. The price of the nth good is set identically equal to unity (it is the numeraire). Then define $\hat{p} = (p_1, \dots, p_{n-1})$ and let $\hat{q} = (q_1, \dots, q_{n-1})$ solve:

$$\hat{\theta}(\hat{p}) - J(\hat{p})(\hat{q} - \hat{p}) = 0$$

where it is assumed that a solution exists:

$$(\hat{q} - \hat{p}) = J(\hat{p})^{-1}\hat{\theta}(\hat{p}).$$

The auctioneer now follows the rule: raise p_i if $q_i - p_i > 0$, lower p_i if $q_i - p_i < 0$ and $p_i > 0$ and leave p_i unchanged if either $q_i = p_i$ or $q_i < p_i$ and $p_i = 0$. Under certain technical assumptions this way of calculating will lead the auctioneer to an equilibrium (see Arrow and Hahn, 1971).

This example demonstrates that it is possible to think of a tâtonnement as a kind of computer program. If one adopts this view, however, one will certainly not be mimicking the invisible hand. For instance, in the Newton method the price change in any one market depends on the excess demand functions in all markets and that is not what any version of 'the law of supply and demand' stipulates. Moreover the proposal violates the supposed economy in information of decentralized economies – that is much more is known to the auctioneer than can be known to any one agent. From the point of view of positive theory, therefore, this second interpretation of the auctioneer is not helpful, although it has found application in the theory of planning (e.g. Heal, 1973).

Assuming that the auctioneer only knows aggregate excess demands at the announced p, it has been customary ever since a famous paper by Samuelson (1941, 1942) on Hicksian stability to formulate the rule followed by the auctioneer dynamically. For instance:

$$\frac{\mathrm{d}p_i}{\mathrm{d}t} = 0 \qquad\qquad \text{if } \theta_i(p) < 0 \text{ and } p_i = 0$$

$$\frac{\mathrm{d}p_i}{\mathrm{d}t} = k_i\theta_i(p) \qquad\qquad \text{otherwise with } k_i > 0.$$

Even if this process leads to p^* it will do so only as $t \to \infty$. This is awkward since no one is allowed to trade while the process is still in motion. Some economists have by-passed this by saying that the time here involved is not calendar, but 'model-time'. On reflection it is not clear what that means unless it is 'computer time' which is meant and, if it is, one must again ask whether the construction will then have anything to do with any actual price mechanism.

Arrow (1959) has suggested an alternative interpretation which, however, much restricts the applicability of the tâtonnement. Suppose we think of time as divided into trading periods and let the auctioneer follow the rule:

$$p_i(t) = p_i(t-1) + k_i\theta_i[p(t-1)] \qquad k_i > 0$$

(with the usual boundary condition to avoid negative prices). Now suppose (a) that one is concerned with a pure exchange economy and (b) that all goods last for only one period so that agents in each period receive new endowments (identical for each period). Then we can allow the agents to trade during the process *without the trade in any one period* affecting the excess demand at any p in a subsequent period. So now (a) we think of the process in real time and

(b) even if it converges to $p*$ only as $t \to \infty$ or does not converge at all, agents can trade.

This very restrictive case clarifies the reason why in general the tâtonnement prohibits trade out of equilibrium. Let $\hat{e} = (e^1, \ldots, e^H)$, the endowment matrix of a pure exchange economy in which goods are durable. Let us now take explicit note of $\hat{e}$ in this excess demand function (since it was constant it was omitted hitherto) and write

$$\sum_h (x^h - e^h) = \hat{\theta}(p, \hat{e}).$$

Assuming that $\hat{\theta}(p, \hat{e}) = 0$ has a unique solution, the latter will depend on $\hat{e}$ and may be written as $p*(\hat{e})$. If now trading takes place out of equilibrium, $\hat{e}$ will be changing and so therefore will $p*(\hat{e})$. Thus when there is such out of equilibrium trading, the equilibrium which the tâtonnement is groping for will depend on the manner of the groping. To exclude this dependence was the purpose of excluding out of equilibrium trade. But there was another reason, namely the lack of any clear theory of how trade would proceed when either some prospective buyers or sellers could not carry out their trading intentions.

The fictitious auctioneer is also a consequence of theoretical lacunae and indeed of a certain logical difficulty. If prices are to be changed by the economic agents of the theory, that is either by households or firms or both then it is not easy to see how those same agents are also to treat prices as given exogenously as is required by the postulate of perfect competition. This difficulty was first noted by Arrow (1959) who argued that out of equilibrium price changes not brought about by an auctioneer require a departure from the perfect competition assumption if they are to be understood. Take for instance a situation for which $\hat{\theta}_i(p, \hat{e}) > 0$. Then at p there will be unsatisfied buyers. But that means that any firm raising its price for good i by a little will not, as in the usual perfect competition setting, lose all its customers. The reason is that buyers cannot be sure of obtaining the good from any of the other firms which have not yet raised their price. Hence the demand curve for good i facing a producer of that good is not perfectly elastic. (On the other hand, in equilibrium it well might be.) The postulate of the auctioneer sidesteps these problems at the cost of an understanding of how prices are actually changed. It has enabled theorists to ignore the role of monopolistic competition in the process of price formation – a circumstance which until recently has left the whole matter without proper theoretical foundations.

But it must also be admitted that there are formidable theoretical difficulties to be faced in banishing the auctioneer. Whether we think of prices as formed by a bargaining process or by monopolistic competition or in some form of auction process, strategic considerations, that is to say, game theoretic tools, will be required. In addition, careful attention will have to be given to the information available to each of the agents involved in the process. Some progress has been made (e.g. Roth, 1979; Schmeidler, 1980; Rubinstein and Wolinsky, 1985) but there is a very long way to go. (Some economists have banished the auctioneer without considering these matters by the simple device of treating it as axiomatic that at all times the economy is in competitive equilibrium. There is nothing favourable to be said for this move.)

There is now also a somewhat subtler point to consider: the behaviour postulated for the auctioneer will implicitly define what we are to mean by an equilibrium: that state of affairs when the rules tell the auctioneer to leave prices where they are. But the auctioneer's pricing rules are not derived from any consideration of the rational actions of agents on which the theory is supposed to rest. Thus the equilibrium notion becomes arbitrary and unfounded. If, on the other hand, we had a theory of price formation based on the rational calculations of rational agents then the equilibrium notion would be a natural corollary of such a theory. For instance, one might then be led to describe a situation in which there is unemployment as one of equilibrium because neither firms nor workers, given their information and beliefs, find it advantageous to change the wage.

This line of reasoning leads one to a central objection to the auctioneer and indeed the tâtonnement: it sidesteps the important question of the co-ordinating power of the price mechanism. Here is an example. In an oligopolistic industry with excess supply it may not be advantagous for any one firm to reduce its price given its beliefs as to the strategies of its competitors. Yet it may be to all of the firms' advantage to have the price reduced: there is a co-operative solution which dominates the competitive one. Put another way, there are significant externalities in price-signalling. To leave these unstudied is to leave very important matters in darkness. The auctioneer is a co-ordinator *deus ex machina* and hides what is central.

These considerations are most striking in the context of Keynesian theory. As long as the auctioneer is in the picture no state of the economy in which there is involuntary unemployment can qualify as an equilibrium – the auctioneer would be reducing wages. But without the auctioneer the observation that a worker would prefer to work at the going real wage to being idle does not logically entail the proposition that the wage will be reduced. That proposition would require a greal deal of further theoretical underpinning turning on the beliefs of workers, the strategies of other workers and the strategies of employers. It would also turn on the information available to agents. For instance, if lowering one's wage is regarded as a signal of lower quality of work then one may be reluctant to offer to work at a lower wage. The fictitious auctioneer makes sure that none of these matters is studied or understood. The use of this fiction encourages the view that all Pareto-improving moves will, in a competitive economy, be undertaken. This view, however, lacks any foundations other than the auctioneer himself.

One might just about convince oneself that notwithstanding all these objections, the tâtonnement and its auctioneer are worthwhile, if it were the case that it provided one story which showed how equilibrium was brought about. Unfortunately, however, it does not do this for there are only a few special cases for which the auctioneer process leads the economy to an equilibrium. In many others it will not do so. Indeed, in so far as one holds the view that an equilibrium is the normal state of an economy one should not be tempted to understand this circumstance by means of a tâtonnement.

BIBLIOGRAPHY

Arrow, K.J. 1959. Towards a theory of price adjustment. In *The Allocation of Economic Resources*, ed. M. Abramovitz et al., Stanford: Stanford University Press, 41–51.

Arrow, K.J. and Hahn, F.H. 1971. *General Competitive Analysis.* San Francisco: Holden-Day; Edinburgh: Oliver & Boyd.

Heal, G.M. 1973. *The Theory of Economic Planning.* Amsterdam, London: North-Holland.

Roth, A.E. 1979. *Axiomatic Models of Bargaining.* Lecture Notes in Economics 170, Berlin: Springer-Verlag.

Rubinstein, A. and Wolinsky, A. 1985. Equilibrium in a market with sequential bargaining. *Econometrica* 53(4), 1133–50.

Samuelson, P.A. 1941, 1942. The stability of equilibrium. *Econometrica* 9, 97–120; 10, 1–25. Reprinted in Samuelson (1966), Vol. I, 539–62, 565–89.

Samuelson, P.A. 1966. *The Collected Scientific Papers of Paul A. Samuelson.* Ed. Joseph E. Stiglitz, Cambridge, Mass.: MIT Press.

Schmeidler, D. 1980. Walrasian analysis via strategic outcome functions. *Econometrica* 48, 1585–93.

Smale, S. 1976. A convergent process of price adjustment and global Newton methods. *Journal of Mathematical Economics* 3(2), 107–20.

Walras, L. 1874–7. *Eléments d'économie politique pure.* Definitive edn, Lausanne, 1926. Trans. by W. Jaffé as *Elements of Pure Economics*, London: George Allen & Unwin, 1954; New York: Orion, 1954.

Catastrophe Theory

Y. BALASKO

The theory of general equilibrium defines equilibrium prices p as the solutions in the commodity space of the vector equation defined by equality of supply and demand, namely $z(p) = 0$, where z denotes aggregate excess demand. This formulation leads to a purely mathematical problem, namely the study of the properties of the solutions of the equation $z(p) = 0$. The first problem to come into the picture is that of existence. Its positive solution leads to new issues such as the determinateness of the solutions or their number. The fact that these problems cannot be solved uniformly with exactly the same answer for every economy necessitates the introduction of suitable parameters in terms of which the properties of the solutions of the equilibrium equation can be properly described. Let ω denote this parameter chosen in some suitable vector space Ω. This means that the aggregate demand function z can be viewed as depending on $\omega \in \Omega$ which we now denote by $z(\cdot, \omega)$ and the goal of equilibrium theory becomes one of relating the properties of the solutions to $z(p, \omega) = 0$ with the parameter ω. In practice, one chooses for ω the initial endowments of every consumer, the equilibrium model simply describing a pure exchange economy.

This way of handling problems by parameterizing them had been introduced by Poincaré, who called it the continuation method. It has also been extensively used by engineers dealing with applied issues involving solving equations dependent on parameters. The topic popularized by Thom under the name catastrophe theory consists simply in combining Poincaré's continuity method with the tools of singularity theory. As a first approximation, a singularity is just another word for a multiple root of the equation $z(p, \omega) = 0$ where the unknown is the vector p. One easily sees, at least intuitively, that multiple roots, and especially double roots, correspond to borderline cases associated with changes in the number of solutions, the standard picture being that solutions appear or disappear in pairs at these double roots. Clearly enough, this may entail discontinuous behaviour of the equilibrium solution despite the fact every other feature of the model is continuous or even smooth. Catastrophe theory has often been unduly identified to this discontinuity property.

68

In a pure exchange economy consisting of l commodities and m consumers, the parameter space Ω, namely the set of initial endowments, can be identified to $(\mathbb{R}^l)^m$. Prices can conveniently be normalized, for example, with the help of the numeraire convention, so that the price space can be identified to $S = \mathbb{R}^{l-1}_{++}$. Then, the problem is to describe the set E of solutions (p, ω) to $z(p, \omega) = 0$, i.e., $E = \{(p, \omega) \in S \times \Omega / z(p, \omega) = 0\}$ (global approach), and the solutions $(p, \omega) \in E$ when ω varies (local approach). The main results are the following ones:

(1) Under smoothness assumptions for preferences, E is a smooth submanifold of $S \times \Omega$ diffeomorphic to Ω. Furthermore, the natural projection $\pi: E \to \Omega$ defined by the formula $(p, \omega) \to \omega$ is proper (and smooth).

(2) The set Σ consisting of $\omega \in \Omega$ for which the equilibrium equation possesses a multiple root is closed with Lebesgue measure zero.

(3) Let P be the set of Pareto optima. This subset does not intersect Σ. Furthermore, there is uniqueness of equilibrium when ω describes the connected component containing the set of Pareto optima P in the complement of the set Σ in Ω.

This latter result implies that, for an economy where the trade vector remains small to some extent, equilibrium is unique and depends smoothly on the parameters defining the economy. On the other hand, when this trade vector is large, the economy is likely to have multiple equilibria so that, when the parameter vector ω varies, 'catastrophic' changes of the equilibrium prices and allocations are susceptible of being observed.

These relationships between the properties of equilibria and their number are special cases of a far more general property of the general equilibrium model. We state it as follows. Let $N(\omega)$ denotes the number of solutions of the equilibrium equation $z(p, \omega) - 0$, with $p \in S$. Then, assume that N is given (i.e., the number of solutions of the equilibrium equation is known for every $\omega \in \Omega$). Furthermore, assume there exists an economy ω with at least two equilibria, i.e., $N(\omega) \geqslant 2$. Then, there is enough information to determine all the equilibrium prices associated with every economy $\omega \in \Omega$. In other words, the economic model possesses the quite remarkable property that knowing the number of solutions suffices to determine the precise value of these solutions (provided there is an economy with multiple equilibria). If there is uniqueness of equilibrium, the above statement does not hold true any more. In that case, one finds that this unique equilibrium price vector is constant, i.e., does not depend on the economy $\omega \in \Omega$.

Circular Flow

GIORGIO GILBERT

The analysis of the social process of production and consumption must start from some notion of commodity circulation. Consideration of the simple cycle of agricultural production suggests that production is an essentially circular process, in the sense that the same goods appear both among the products and among the means of production. From this viewpoint, commodity (as well as money) circulation is a triviality, whose discovery cannot really be attributed to any particular economist.

It has been suggested that the notion was originally developed by François Quesnay, a surgeon, by analogy with the circulation of the blood. However the popular analogy between money and blood is much older (see for instance 'Money is for the state what blood is for the human body', *Etats généraux*, 1484); and the process of money and commodity circulation among different classes (landlords, labourers, merchants) and areas (town and country) was clearly described by Boisguillebert and Cantillon several decades before the physiocrats.

What is truly novel with Quesnay is the idea that the essential task of economic science is the investigation of the technical and social conditions which allow the repetition of the circular process of production. This approach (at least in the extreme form given it by the physiocrats), and the peculiar model building activity that sprang from it, was later abandoned by economists. More than a century had to pass before the theme could be resumed, following the publication of Marx's own *tableaux* in the second volume of *Capital* (1885), but merely within the rather limited and isolated group of the German and Russian theoretical economists.

Tugan-Baranowsky considered circularity as the essential feature of capitalist economy, in which production was the end of consumption rather than the other way round; in his view, the economists were unable to understand this 'paradox' because (with the remarkable exception of Marx) they had strayed from the way opened up by Quesnay. The young Schumpeter, in a justly celebrated essay, dated the birth of economics as a science from the physiocratic analysis of the circular flow. And Leontief (1928) wrote in a similar vein, arguing in favour of the substitution of the principle of circular flow (the 'reproducibility viewpoint') for that of *homo oeconomicus* (the 'scarcity viewpoint') as the cornerstone of economic theory.

The reproducibility viewpoint is shared by the whole classical tradition of political economy. However, within this broad theoretical tradition, we can single out a radical strand which considers the economic behaviour of every individual as completely determined by the reproduction requirements of the system. This peculiar approach characterizes the pure theorists of the circular flow, with whom we will now briefly deal. Not surprisingly, this theoretical approach is often associated with a practical attitude in favour of some sort of central planning (as a consequence of the distrust for the 'anarchy' of the market).

The *Tableau économique* depicts all the transactions taking place during the year among the three basic classes of society: the class of landowners (L), the 'productive' class of farmers (P_a), and the 'sterile' class of manufacturers (P_m). These transactions can be summarized by a graph, where three points – one for each class – are connected by lines, representing the transactions; the lines are oriented according to the direction of the money flows, whose value is shown by numbers (thousand millions of *livres*). Figure 1 is drawn on the data of Quesnay (1766); since the sum of the money flows leaving each point equals that of those coming in, the system is reproducible.

Marx's (simple) reproduction scheme can also be easily adapted to the same type of three-point graph, once capitalists are substituted for landowners,

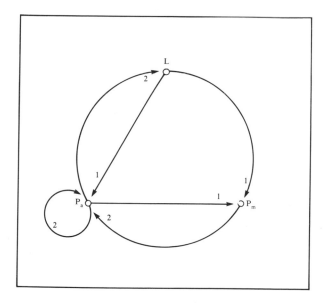

Figure 1

and the two industries producing intermediate goods ('constant' capital) and consumption goods ('variable' capital and luxuries) are substituted for the two classes of manufacturers and farmers respectively. It should be noted that, while Quesnay's *tableaux* are inherently static, Marx does also consider expanded reproduction: in his own words, the picture shifts from a circle to a spiral. A modern example of a circular representation of an expanding economy is the well-known von Neumann model, which, from this point of view, can be considered as the most sophisticated heir to the Marxian schemes.

Quesnay's and Marx's *tableaux* were offered in value terms; but there is no conceptual difficulty in imagining analogous schemes in physical terms. Now, if all the physical transactions taking place among all the agents of the economy are known, there is a unique set of relative prices which makes it possible for the process to be repeated.

Let us consider an economy in which n producers produce n goods. If we know all the physical amounts x_{ij} of the various goods consumed by the different producers, and if the economy is closed (i.e. production equals consumption for each good), relative prices p_i are determined by the following linear homogeneous equations:

$$\sum_i x_{ij} p_i = p_j \sum_h x_{jh}. \tag{1}$$

This theory of prices has now come to be associated with the closed Leontief model (1941), but it was originally formulated in the late 18th century by Achille Isnard. He considered a simple example with three producers and consistently computed the corresponding prices.

His example is illustrated by the graph in Figure 2: three points, one for each producer, are connected by lines, corresponding to the amounts exchanged; the lines are now oriented according to the physical commodity flows. Relative prices have to be such as to equalize the value of the flows leaving each point with that of the flows coming in; the loops at the vertices (self-consumption) are not relevant to our problem.

When Leontief, a century and a half later, rediscovered the theory, he recognized in it the 'objective' theory of value. One year later, the German mathematician Robert Remak interpreted system (1) as determining the rational prices for an economy in which the individual standards of living are fixed by a central authority. He showed that the system has in general meaningful solutions; and maintained that these prices could be practically computed and implemented.

Until now, we have considered only closed systems, in which all transactions are assumed as known irrespective of their nature (technical inputs or human 'final' uses). We can now open the model, by considering as given only those transactions which are dictated by the technology in use (including workers' subsistence) and leaving undetermined the final utilization of the surplus thus appearing.

There is now room for an additional relation, stating the way in which the surplus is distributed. If we assume that it is entirely appropriated by profit-earners

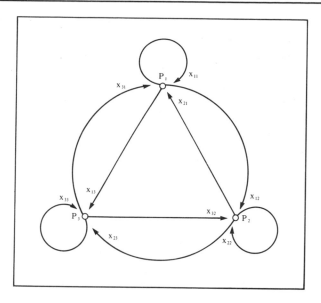

Figure 2

in proportion to the capital advanced, we land on the familiar ground of the classical theory of production prices.

The case can be illustrated by a simple numerical example supplied by Sraffa: there are only two industries, producing wheat (P_a) and iron (P_m) respectively; the class of capitalists (C) gets the entire surplus, consisting only of wheat. In Figure 3 the numbers on the oriented graph refer to the physical quantities (quarters and tons) in the example.

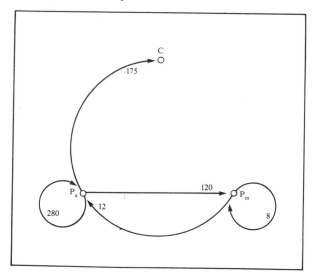

Figure 3

The uniform profit rate has to be such as to equalize the value of the surplus bought by capitalists to the profits accruing to them; and the exchange value between the two commodities has to be such as to enable each industry to replace its advances and to distribute profits in proportion to their value. Loops are now relevant.

The system is then reproducible when the money flows leaving each point are equal to those coming in; the situation is illustrated in Figure 4, and corresponds to a price of iron in terms of wheat equal to 15 and to a common profit rate equal to 25 per cent.

Finally, if we allow the wage earners to share the surplus with the capitalists, we generate the pure theory developed by Piero Sraffa (1960).

We are now able to interpret the abstract transition from our original circular theory to the classical theory of production prices, and eventually to its modern Sraffa version, as successive steps in a gradual opening of the model. From an initial system in which the economic behaviour of every individual is assumed to be rigidly determined by reproduction requirements, we have passed to a system in which capitalists (and rentiers) are assumed to be free in determining their final demand; and finally we have also granted some degree of freedom to the workers.

The term 'free' means here only that the composition of final demand is an issue which lies outside the domain of the pure theory of prices; of course, it can be the object of a distinct section of economic theory. In this perspective, we could say that the neoclassical theory of prices corresponds to a vision of the

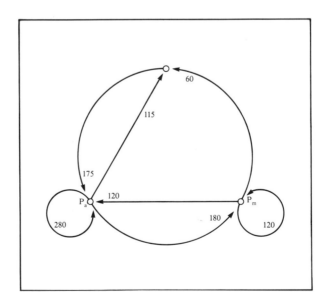

Figure 4

economy in which the individuals are supposed to be undifferentiated (i.e. there are no classes) and all equally free (the reproduction requirements do not play any essential role in determining prices).

BIBLIOGRAPHY

Boisguillebert, P. de 1707. *Dissertation de la nature des richesses*. In *Oeuvres manuscrites et imprimées*, Paris: INED, 1966.

Cantillon, R. 1755. *Essai sur la nature du commerce en général*. Paris: INED, 1952.

Isnard, A.N. 1781. *Traité des richesses*. Lausanne: Grasset.

Leontief, W. 1928. Die Wirtschaft als Kreislauf. *Archiv für Sozialwissenschaft und Sozialpolitik* 3.

Leontief, W. 1941. *The Structure of American Economy*. Oxford and New York: Oxford University Press.

Marx, K. 1885. *Das Kapital*, Vol. II. Hamburg: Meissner.

Neumann, J. von. 1937. Über ein ökonomisches Gleichungssystem und eine Verallgemeinerung des Brouwerschen Fixpunktsatzes. *Ergebnisse eines mathematischen Kolloquiums* VIII.

Peter, H. 1954. *Mathematische Strukturlehre des Wirtschaftskreislaufes*. Göttingen: Schwartz.

Quesnay, F. 1766. *Analyse de la formule arithmétique du Tableau économique*. In *Textes annotés*, Paris: INED, 1958.

Remak, R. 1929. Kann die Volkswirtschaftslehre eine exakte Wissenschaft werden? *Jahrbücher für Nationalökonomie und Statistik* 76.

Remak, R. 1933. Können superponierte Preissysteme praktisch berechnet werden? *Jahrbücher für Nationalökonomie und Statistik* 80.

Schumpeter, J. 1914. *Epochen der Dogmen und Methodengeschichte*. In *Grundriss der Sozialökonomik*, Tübingen: Mohr, Trans. by R. Aris as *Economic Doctrine and Method: an historical sketch*, Oxford: Philip Allen, 1954; New York: Oxford University Press.

Sraffa, P. 1960. *Production of Commodities by Means of Commodities*. Cambridge: Cambridge University Press.

Tugan-Baranowsky, M. 1894. *Les crises industrielles en Angleterre*. French trans., Paris: Giard, 1913.

Comparative Statics

TIMOTHY J. KEHOE

Comparative statics is the method of analysing the impact of a change in the parameters of a model by comparing the equilibrium that results from the change with the original equilibrium. The term 'statics' is not usually meant to have descriptive content: although terms like 'comparative dynamics' and 'comparative steady states' are sometimes used, comparative statics analysis can be performed on dynamic economic models. The restrictive aspects of this analysis are that there is no analysis of the historical forces that have brought about the original equilibrium position and no analysis of the transitional process involved in the adjustment from one equilibrium position to another. The use of comparative statics, of comparing one equilibrium with another, is as old as economics itself. It was, for example, the method used by Hume (1752) in his analysis of an increase in the stock of gold on prices in an economy.

The neoclassical method of comparative statics analysis was formalized by Hicks (1939) and, most clearly, by Samuelson (1947). This method makes heavy use of differential calculus to analyse the impact of small (infinitesimal) changes in the parameters of model on its equilibrium. Samuelson considered a system of equations involving endogenous variables and exogenous variables, or parameters, of the form:

$$f_1(p_1,\ldots,p_n,\alpha_1,\ldots,\alpha_m) = 0$$
$$\vdots$$
$$f_n(p_1,\ldots,p_n,\alpha_1,\ldots,\alpha_m) = 0.$$

Here $(\alpha_1,\ldots,\alpha_m)$ is a vector of parameters that specifies the economic environment. It may include the government policy parameters such as tax rates; it may also include completely exogenous factors such as variables describing the state of the weather or consumers' tastes and preferences. The vector $(p_1,\ldots,p_n)$ is a vector of endogenous variables that specifies the state of the economic system. It may include production levels and allocation levels for different goods. For the neoclassical economist, however, the typical endogenous variable is the price of a good. The equations themselves are the equilibrium conditions. A solution to them is taken to specify completely the state of the economic system.

Samuelson's type of model can be written out compactly in vector notation as

$$f(p, \alpha) = 0$$

where $f: P \times A \to R^n$, $P \subset R^n$, and $A \subset R^m$. The important thing to notice is that the number of endogenous variables and the number of equilibrium conditions are equal. Assume that (p^0, α^0) is a solution to this system of equations, that the function f is continuously differentiable, and that the $n \times n$ matrix of partial derivatives

$$\begin{bmatrix} \dfrac{\partial f_1}{\partial p_1}(p^0, \alpha^0) \ldots \dfrac{\partial f_1}{\partial p_n}(p^0, \alpha^0) \\ \vdots \qquad\qquad \vdots \\ \dfrac{\partial f_n}{\partial p_1}(p^0, \alpha^0) \ldots \dfrac{\partial f_n}{\partial p_n}(p^0, \alpha^0) \end{bmatrix}$$

is invertible. Then the inverse function theorem of differential calculus says that, in a small neighbourhood of p^0 in P, this implies that $p^0 = f^{-1}(0, \alpha^0)$ is the locally unique solution to the equilibrium conditions. Furthermore, under the same assumptions, the implicit function theorem says that the locally unique vector p that satisfies $f(p, \alpha) = 0$ varies continuously with α near α^0. In other words, there exists a continuous function $p(\alpha)$ such that

$$f[p(\alpha), \alpha] = 0.$$

To calculate the impact of small changes in α on p we differentiate with respect to α using the chain rule:

$$Df_p[p(\alpha), \alpha]Dp(\alpha) + Df_\alpha[p(\alpha), \alpha] \equiv 0$$

$$Df_p(p^0, \alpha^0)Dp(\alpha^0) + Df_\alpha(p^0, \alpha^0) = 0$$

$$Dp(\alpha^0) = -Df_p(p^0, \alpha^0)^{-1}Df_\alpha(p^0, \alpha^0).$$

The elements of the $n \times m$ matrix

$$Dp(\alpha^0) = \begin{bmatrix} \dfrac{\partial p_1}{\partial \alpha_1}(\alpha^0) \ldots \dfrac{\partial p_1}{\partial \alpha_m}(\alpha^0) \\ \vdots \qquad\qquad \vdots \\ \dfrac{\partial p_n}{\partial \alpha_1}(\alpha^0) \ldots \dfrac{\partial p_n}{\partial \alpha_m}(\alpha^0) \end{bmatrix}$$

are called the comparative statics-multipliers: for example, when the first parameter changes from α_1^0 to α_1, the equilibrium value of the second endogenous variable changes from p_2^0 to approximately

$$p_2^0 + \frac{\partial p_2}{\partial \alpha_1}(\alpha^0)(\alpha_1 - \alpha_1^0),$$

at least if $\alpha_1 - \alpha_1^0$ is small enough.

The prototypical model to which Samuelson applied such comparative statics analysis was Walras's (1874) model of economic equilibrium. Here the endogenous variables are the prices of the n goods in the economy and the equilibrium conditions are requirements that excess demands (demand minus supply) for these goods be equal to zero. Since the number of endogenous variables and the number of equilibrium conditions are both equal to n, it would seem that the method of analysis described above is immediately applicable. Walras realized, however, that there were two offsetting complications. First, multiplying all prices by any positive constant leaves excess demands unchanged, that is, excess demands are homogeneous of degree zero, since this is merely a change in accounting units. Second, the total value of all demands equals the value of all supplies since all income is spent on goods. This second requirement, known as Walras's Law, can be written out as

$$\sum_{i=1}^{n} p_i f_i(p, \alpha) \equiv 0.$$

Walras considered an economy in which all prices were strictly positive. He used the homogeneity condition to reduce the numbers of endogenous variables by one, setting $p_1 = 1$ as numeraire. He used Walras's Law to reduce the number of equilibrium conditions by one, ignoring the first one since

$$f_1(p, \alpha) \equiv -\sum_{i=2}^{n} p_i f_i(p, \alpha).$$

Walras gave two arguments for the existence of equilibrium. The first involved the counting of equations and unknowns given above. The second involved a transitional process for adjusting prices when not in equilibrium, which he called *tâtonnement*. Samuelson formalized this process in a system of differential equations:

$$\frac{dp_1}{dt} = f_i(p, \alpha), \qquad i = 1, \ldots, n.$$

Near an equilibrium p^0 this system can be linearized as

$$Dp(t) = Df_p(p^0, \alpha)[p(t) - p^0].$$

The requirement that the equilibrium p^0 be locally stable involves restrictions on the eigenvalues of the matrix $Df_p(p^0, \alpha)$. This is the same matrix whose inverse plays the crucial role in determining the comparative statics multipliers. Samuelson's view was that, by making assumptions on the sign pattern of the elements of $Df_\alpha(p^0, \alpha)$, the responses of excess demands to changes in the parameters, and by imposing the requirement of local stability on $Df_p(p^0, \alpha)$, 'meaningful theorems' about the signs of the comparative statics multipliers $Dp(\alpha)$ could be derived. He called this methodology 'The Correspondence Principle'. Unfortunately, however, except for very low dimensional cases ($n = 2, 3$) very few such theorems seem available. The *tâtonnement* process itself is unattractive because it offers no real time interpretation: an auctioneer calls out prices and agents announce their excess demands. The auctioneer then adjusts prices until excess demands equal zero. Until this point is reached no production or consumption takes place; once it is reached all production and consumption take place, and the economy shuts down.

In the 1950s attention turned away from derivation of the comparative statics properties of a model to proofs of the existence of equilibrium. Wald (1936) had pointed out the inadequacy of Walras' existence arguments and had provided existence proofs. The role of differential calculus in providing the mathematical tools was assumed by topology and convexity theory. Using these tools, Arrow and Debreu (1954) and others were able to provide proofs of the existence of equilibrium for very general models. The principal mathematical tool employed was Brouwer's fixed point theorem, which says that any continuous mapping g of a non-empty, compact, convex set into itself has a point that stays fixed under the mapping, that is, where $p^* = g(p^*)$. This theorem is illustrated in Figure 1, where the non-empty, compact convex set is the interval $(0, 1)$. Notice that there are three fixed points.

To use Brouwer's fixed point theorem it is necessary to convert equilibrium conditions of the form $f(p, \alpha) = 0$ into the form $p - g(p, \alpha) = 0$, where the mapping g has the right properties. The price domain is often taken to be the simplex

$$S = \left\{ p \in R^n \mid \sum_{i=1}^{n} p_i = 1, p_i \geqslant 0 \right\},$$

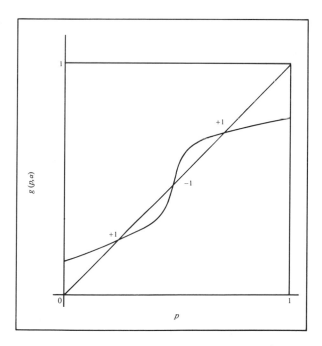

Figure 1

which is a non-empty, compact, convex set. The mapping g is constructed by manipulating $p + f(p, \alpha)$ until it only takes on values in S.

Scarf (1973) developed a computational algorithm for finding the fixed points of mappings that satisfy the conditions of Brouwer's fixed point theorem. As our discussion above indicates, this algorithm can be used to compute equilibria of economic models. Following this development, a number of economists have employed large-scale numerical general equilibrium models to analyse the impact of policy changes such as changes in tax systems and tariff rates on individual countries or groups of countries. The methodology is that of comparative statics: The parameters of the model are calibrated or econometrically estimated to match a historically given state of the economy. A change in some of the parameters is then introduced and a new equilibrium position is calculated. Finally, the new equilibrium is compared with the original equilibrium. Such models have been developed to incorporate such phenomena as fixed prices, rationing, government intervention, and simple dynamic considerations. Shoven and Whalley (1984) offer a survey. An earlier tradition in large-scale use of comparative statics started with the work of Johansen (1960), who used calculus techniques to analyse the impact of small changes in parameters.

Proofs of the existence of an equilibrium leave many important questions unanswered: for example, is the equilibrium price vector unique? If not, is it locally unique? Does it vary continuously with the parameters of the model? Answers to such questions are essential in any application of comparative statics analysis. To answer such questions, economists have made heavy use of the tools of differential topology, which combines those of calculus and topology (see Mas-Colell, 1985). Debreu (1970) developed the concept of a regular economy to answer the questions of local uniqueness and continuity. A regular economy is one for which the matrix of partial derivatives of $p - g(p, \alpha)$ with respect to p, $I - Dg_p(p, \alpha)$, where I is $n \times n$ identity matrix, is invertible at every equilibrium p^*. Not surprisingly, this turns out to be equivalent to the condition that the $(n-1) \times (n-1)$ matrix formed by deleting the first row and column from $Df_p(p, \alpha)$ is invertible. That this latter matrix is invertible is, of course, what is meant by the claim that the equilibrium conditions involve equal numbers of independent equations and unknowns once one price has been fixed as numeraire and one equation deleted. Debreu proved that almost all models, in a strict mathematical sense, are regular. This result provides some justification for Samuelson's comparative statics methodology. It is illustrated in Figure 2, where small perturbations to a model that is not regular result in it becoming a regular economy.

Dierker (1972) and Varian (1975) realized that the tools of differential topology could also be used to answer the uniqueness question. Consider again the illustration of Brouwer's fixed point theorem in Figure 1. Suppose that neither 0 or 1 is a fixed point of g and that the graph of g never becomes tangent to the diagonal. Then the graph of g must cross the diagonal one more time from above than it does from below. Associate an index $+1$ with a fixed point p^* if the graph of g crosses the diagonal from above and an index -1 if it crosses from

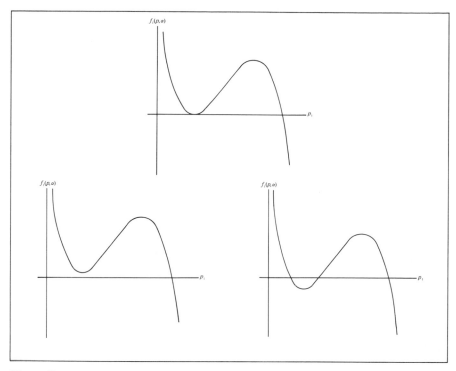

Figure 2

below. This index can be computed by finding the sign of the expression $1 - (\partial g/\partial p)(p^*, \alpha)$. The sum of the indices of all fixed points is $+1$. Consequently, if index $(p^*) = +1$ at every equilibrium, then there is only one equilibrium, but, if index $(p^*) = -1$ at any equilibrium, there must be multiple equilibria. The fixed point index theorem says that these results hold in higher dimensions when the index of a fixed point is computed by finding the sign of the expression $\det[I - Dg_p(p^*, \alpha)]$. We have already seen that, if this expression is non-zero, then the equilibrium p^* is unique and varies continuously with α. The fixed point index theorem says that this expression is also crucial for conditions that guarantee uniqueness of equilibrium.

Unfortunately such conditions appear to be extremely restrictive. For Walrasian models with production, for example, Kehoe (1985b) argued that the only two such conditions with economic interpretations are (i) that the consumer side of the economy behaves as though there were only one consumer, and (ii) that the conditions of the non-substitution theorem are met, so that prices are determined by production conditions alone. In applied models where taxes and other distortions play significant roles not even these conditions suffice (see Kehoe, 1985a). In the presence of multiple equilibria, the value of comparative

81

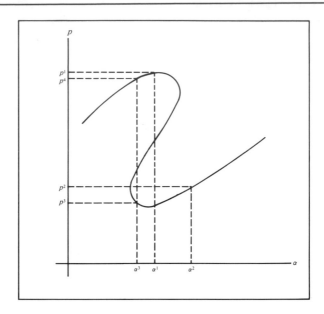

Figure 3

statics analysis becomes problematical. We must pay attention to the historical forces that have brought about the original equilibrium position and to the transitional process involved in the adjustment from one equilibrium position to another. Even if we start with a historically given equilibrium that is locally stable with respect to some adjustment process, we can run into problems in the face of mathematical catastrophes of the sort depicted in Figure 3. Here the change in the value of the parameter α from α^1 to α^2 brings about a discontinuous jump from p^1 to p^2. Another danger that non-uniqueness presents is the possibility that a researcher might compute p^4 as the new equilibrium after changing the parameter from α^1 to α^3, without even knowing that p^4 exists.

The problem of non-uniqueness of equilibrium is even more acute in dynamic models (such as Samuelson's, 1958 overlapping generations model) that involve an infinite number of consumers and goods. Such models need not have even locally unique equilibria, and no current version of comparative statics analysis seems to be applicable (see Kehoe and Levine, 1985).

BIBLIOGRAPHY

Arrow, K.J. and Debreu, G. 1954. Existence of an equilibrium for a competitive economy. *Econometrica* 22, 265–90.

Debreu, G. 1970. Economics with a finite set equilibria. *Econometrica* 38, 387–93.

Dierker, E. 1972. Two remarks on the number of equilibria of an economy. *Econometrica* 40, 951–3.

Hicks, J.R. 1939. *Value and Capital*. Oxford: Clarendon Press; 2nd edn, New York: Oxford University Press, 1946.

Hume, D. 1752. Of the balance of trade. In *Essays, Moral, Political and Literary*, London: Longmans Green, 1898.

Johansen, L. 1960. *A Multi-Sectoral Study of Economic Growth*. Amsterdam: North-Holland.

Kehoe, T.J. 1985a. The comparative statics properties of tax models. *Canadian Journal of Economics* 18, 314–34.

Kehoe, T.J. 1985b. Multiplicity of equilibria and comparative statics. *Quarterly Journal of Economics* 100, 119–47.

Kehoe, T.J. and Levine, D.K. 1985. Comparative statics and perfect foresight in infinite horizon economics. *Econometrica* 53, 433–53.

Mas-Colell, A. 1985. *The Theory of General Economic Equilibrium: A Differentiable Approach*. Cambridge: Cambridge University Press.

Samuelson, P.A. 1947. *Foundations of Economic Analysis*. Cambridge, Massachusetts: Harvard University Press.

Samuelson, P.A. 1958. An exact consumption-loan model of interest with or without the social contrivance of money. *Journal of Political Economy* 66, 467–82.

Scarf, H.E. 1973. *The Computation of Economic Equilibria*. New Haven: Yale University Press.

Shoven, J.B. and Whalley, J. 1984. Applied general equilibrium models of taxation and international trade. *Journal of Economic Literature* 22, 1007–51.

Varian, H.R. 1975. A third remark on the number of equilibria of an economy. *Econometrica* 43, 985–6.

Wald, A. 1936. Über einige Gleichungssysteme der mathematischen Ökonomie. *Zeitschrift für Nationalökonomie* 7, 637–70. Translated as 'On some systems of equations in mathematical economics', *Econometrica* 19, (1951), 368–403.

Walras, L. 1874–7. *Eléments d'économie politique pure*. Lausanne: Corbaz. Translated by W. Jaffé as *Elements of Pure Economics*, London: Allen & Unwin, 1954; New York: Orion, 1954.

Computation of General Equilibria

HERBERT E. SCARF

The general equilibrium model, as elaborated by Walras and his successors, is one of the most comprehensive and ambitious formulations in the current body of economic theory. The basic ingredients with which the Walrasian model is constructed are remarkably spare: a specification of the asset ownership and preferences for goods and services of the consuming units in the economy, and a description of the current state of productive knowledge possessed by each of the firms engaged in manufacturing or in the provision of services. The model then yields a complete determination of the course of prices and interest rates over time, levels of output and the choice of techniques by each firm, and the distribution of income and patterns of saving for each consumer.

The Walrasian model is essentially a generalization, to the entire economy and to all markets simultaneously, of the ancient and elementary notion that prices move to levels which equilibrate supply and demand. No intellectual construction of this scope, designed to address basic questions in a subject as complex and elusive as economics, can be described as simply true or false – in the sense in which these terms are used in mathematics or perhaps in the physical sciences. The assertions of economic theory are not susceptible to crisp and immediate experimental verification. Moreover, the Walrasian model disregards obvious aspects of human motivation which are of the greatest economic significance and which cannot be addressed in the language of our subject: economic theory is mute about our affective lives, about our opposing needs for community and individual assertion, and about the non-pecuniary determinants of entrepreneurial energy.

There are, in addition, aspects of economic reality which are capable of being described in the framework of the Walrasian model but which must be assumed away in order for the model to yield a determinate outcome. Uncertainty about the future is an ever-present fact of economic life, and yet the complete set of markets for contingent commodities required by the Arrow–Debreu treatment of uncertainty is not available in practice. Economies of scale in production are a central feature in the rise of the large manufacturing entities which dominate modern economic activity; their incorporation into the Walrasian model requires the introduction of non-convex production possibility sets for which the competitive equilibrium will typically fail to exist.

In spite of its many shortcomings, the Walrasian model – if used with tact and circumspection – is an important conceptual framework for evaluating the consequence of changes in economic policy or in the environment in which the economy finds itself. The effects of a major shock to the economy of the United States – such as the four-fold increase in the price of imported oil which occurred in late 1973 – can be studied by constrasting equilibrium prices, real wages and the choice of productive techniques both before and after the event in question. Generations of economists have used the Walrasian model to analyse the terms of trade, the impact of customs unions, changes in tariffs and a variety of other issues in the theory of International Trade. And much of the literature in the field of Public Finance is based on the assumption that the competitive model is an adequate description of economic reality.

In these discussions the analysis is frequently conducted in terms of simple geometrical diagrams whose use places a severe restriction on the number of consumers, commodities and productive sectors that can be considered. This is in contrast to formal mathematical treatments of the Walrasian model, which permit an extraordinary generality in the elaboration of the model at the expense of immediate geometrical visualization. Unfortunately, however, it is only under the most severe assumptions that mathematical analysis will be capable of providing unambiguous answers concerning the direction and magnitude of the changes in significant economic variables, when the system is perturbed in a substantial fashion. In order for a comparative analysis to be carried out in a multi-sector framework it is necessary to employ computational techniques for the explicit numerical solution of the highly non-linear system of equations and inequalities which represent the general Walrasian model.

THE USE OF FIXED-POINT THEOREMS IN EQUILIBRIUM ANALYSIS

One of the triumphs of mathematical reasoning in economic theory has been the demonstration of the existence of a solution for the general equilibrium model of an economy, under relatively mild assumptions on the preferences of consumers and the nature of production possibility sets (see Debreu, 1982). The arguments for the existence of equilibrium prices inevitably make use of Brouwer's Fixed-Point Theorem, or one of its many variants, and any effective numerical procedure for the computation of equilibrium prices must therefore be capable of computing the fixed points whose existence is asserted by this mathematical statement.

Brouwer's Fixed-Point Theorem, enunciated by the distinguished Dutch mathematician L.E.J. Brouwer in 1912, is the generalization to higher dimensions of the elementary observation that a continuous function of a single variable which has two distinct signs at the two endpoints of the unit interval, must vanish at some intermediary point. In Brouwer's theorem the unit interval is replaced by an arbitrary closed, bounded convex set S in R^n, and the continuous function is replaced by a continuous mapping of the set S into itself: $x \to g(x)$. Brouwer's Theorem then asserts the existence of at least one point x which is mapped into itself under the mapping; that is, a point x for which $x = g(x)$. To see how this conclusion is used in solving the existence problem let us begin by specifying, in mathematical form, the basic ingredients of the Walrasian model.

The typical consumer is assumed to have a preference order for, say, the non-negative commodity bundles $x = (x_1, x_2, \ldots, x_n)$ in R^n; the preference ordering is described either by a specific utility function $u(x_1, x_2, \ldots, x_n)$ or by means of an abstract representation of preferences. The consumer will also possess, prior to production and trade, a vector of initial assets $w = (w_1, w_2, \ldots, w_n)$. When a non-negative price vector $p = (p_1, p_2, \ldots, p_n)$ is announced the consumer's income will be $I = p \cdot w$ and his demands will be obtained by maximizing preferences subject to the budget constraint $p \cdot x \leqslant p \cdot w$. If the preferences satisfy sufficient regularity assumptions, the consumer's demand functions $x(p)$ will be single-valued functions of p, continuous (except possibly when some of the individual prices are zero), homogeneous of degree zero and will satisfy the budget constraint $p \cdot x(p) = p \cdot w$.

The market demands are obtained by aggregating over individual demand functions and, as such, will inherit the properties described above. The market *excess* demand functions, which I shall denote by $f(p)$, arise by subtracting the supply of assets owned by all consumers from the demand functions themselves. It is these functions which are required for a complete specification of the consumer side of the economy in the general equilibrium model: they may be obtained either by the aggregation of individual demand functions – as we have

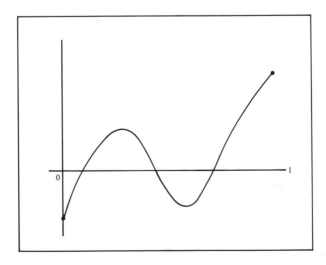

Figure 1

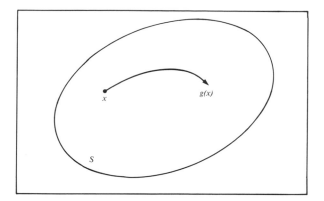

Figure 2

just described – or they may be directly estimated from econometric data. The following properties will hold, either as a logical conclusion or by assumption:

1. $f(p)$ is homogenous of degree zero.
2. $f(p)$ is continuous in the interior of the positive orthant.
3. $f(p)$ satisfies the Walras Law $p \cdot f(p) = 0$.

The first of these properties permits us to normalize prices in any one of several ways; for example, $\Sigma p_j = 1$ or $\Sigma p_j^2 = 1$. Given either of these normalizations, I personally do not find it offensive to extend the property of continuity to the boundary, even though there are elementary examples of utility functions, such as the Cobb-Douglas function, for which this would not be correct.

The production side of the economy requires for its description a complete specification of the current state of technical knowledge about the methods of transforming inputs into outputs – with commodities differentiated according to their location and the time of their availability. This can be done by means of production functions, an input/output table with substitution possibilities and several scarce factors rather than labour alone, or by a general activity analysis model:

$$
A = \begin{bmatrix}
-1 & 0 & \cdots & 0 & a_{1,n+1} & \cdots & a_{1,k} \\
0 & -1 & & 0 & a_{2,n+1} & & a_{2,k} \\
\vdots & \vdots & & \vdots & \vdots & & \vdots \\
0 & 0 & & -1 & a_{n,n+1} & & a_{n,k}
\end{bmatrix}
$$

Each column of A describes a particular productive process, with inputs represented by non-negative entries and outputs by positive entries. The activities are assumed capable of being used simultaneously and at arbitrary non-negative levels $x = (x_1, x_2, \ldots, x_k)$; the net production plan is then $y = Ax$.

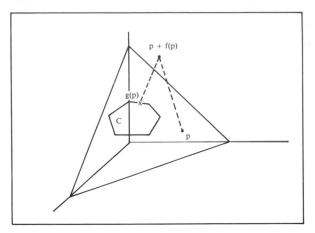

Figure 3 The Equilibrium Model as a Tool for Policy Evaluation

With this formulation, a competitive equilibrium is defined by a non-negative vector of prices $p = (p_1, p_2, \ldots, p_n)$ and a non-negative vector of activity levels $x = (x_1, x_2, \ldots, x_k)$ satisfying the following conditions:

1. $f(p) = Ax$,
2. $pA \leqslant 0$.

The first condition states that supply and demand are equal in all markets, and the second that there are not opportunities for positive profits when the profitability of each activity is evaluated at the equilibrium prices. Taken in conjunction with the Walras's Law, these conditions imply that those activities which are used at a positive level in the equilibrium solution make a profit of zero.

Given the assumption of continuous and single-valued excess demand functions and the description of the production possibility set by means of an activity analysis model, the following rather direct application of Brouwer's Theorem is sufficient to demonstrate the existence of a equilibrium solution. Under weaker assumptions on the model, variants such as Kakutani's Fixed-Point Theorem may be required.

Let prices be normalized so as to lie on the unit simplex $S = \{p = (p_1, p_2, \ldots, p_n) | p_i \geqslant 0, \Sigma p_i = 1\}$. The set of prices p for which $pA \leqslant 0$ is termed the *dual cone* of the production possibility set generated by the activity analysis matrix A. Its intersection with the unit simplex is a convex polyhedron C consisting of those normalized prices which yield a profit less than or equal to zero for all activities.

We construct a continuous mapping of S into itself as follows: for each p in S consider the point $p + f(p)$; a point which is generally not on the unit simplex itself. We then define $g(p)$ – the image of p under the mapping – to be that point in C which is closest, in the sense of Euclidean distance, to $p + f(p)$. It is then an elementary application of the Kuhn–Tucker Theorem to show that a fixed point of this mapping is, indeed, an equilibrium price vector.

Brouwer's original proof of his theorem was not only difficult mathematically, but it was decidedly non-constructive; it offered no method for effectively computing a fixed point of the mapping. Brouwer did, in fact, reject his own argument during the later 'intuitionist' phase of his career, in which he proclaimed the acceptability of only those mathematical conclusions obtained by constructive procedures. In spite of the many simplifications in the proof of Brouwer's Theorem offered during the subsequent half-century, it was not until the mid-1960s that constructive methods for approximating fixed points of a continuous mapping finally made their appearance on the scene (Scarf, 1967) – aided by the development of the modern electronic computer and by the rapid methodological advances in the discipline of operations research.

In the early decades of this century, the question of the explicit numerical solution of the general equilibrium model was an active topic of discussion – not by numerical analysts – but rather by economists concerned with the techniques of economic planning in a socialist economy. The issue was raised in the remarkable paper published by Enrico Barone in 1908, entitled 'The Ministry of Production in a Socialist Economy'. Barone, and subsequently Oskar Lange (1936), accepted the Walrasian model – with suitable transfers of income – as an adequate description of ideal economic activity in an economy in which the means of production were collectively owned. In the absence of markets, prices, levels of output and the choice of productive techniques were to be obtained by an explicit numerical solution of the Walrasian system. A key feature of Barone's analysis was the concept of the 'technical coefficients of production' – the input/output coefficients associated with those activities in use at equilibrium. Barone's contention was that the equilibrium could be found – by an extremely laborious calculation which might indeed claim a significant share of the national product – only if the correct activities were known in advance. For Barone, rational economic calculation in a socialist economy was defeated by the many opportunities for substitution in production: the particular activities in use at equilibrium would be impossible to determine by a prior computation. It is instructive to quote Barone on this point.

The determination of the coefficients economically most advantageous can only be done in an *experimental* way: and not on a *small* scale, as could be done in a laboratory; but with experiments on a *very large scale*, because often the advantage of the variation has its origin precisely in a new and greater dimension of the undertaking. Experiments may be successful in the sense that they may lead to a lower cost combination of factors; or they may be unsuccessful, in which case the particular organization may not be copied and repeated and others will be preferred, which *experimentally* have given a better result.

The Ministry of Production could not do without these experiments for the determination of the *economically* most advantageous technical coefficients if it would realize the condition of the minimum cost of production which is *essential* for the attainment of the maximum collective welfare.

It is on this account that the equations of the equilibrium with the maximum collective welfare are not soluble *a priori*, on paper.

AN ELEMENTARY ALGORITHM

Barone's negative conclusion is certainly valid if the full production possibility set, including all of the possibilities for substitution in production, is not known to the central planner. In this event, numerical calculation is impossible, and Lange's suggestion, made some 20 years later, may be appropriate: the problem can be turned on its head and the market, itself, can be used as a mechanism of discovery as well as a giant analogue computer. But if the production possibility set can be explicitly constructed, substitution – in and of itself – does not seem to me to be a severe impediment to numerical computation.

At the present moment, some 20 years after the introduction and continued refinement of fixed-point computational techniques, I have in my possession a small floppy disk with a computer program which will routinely solve – on a personal computer – for equilibrium prices and activity levels in a Walrasian model in which the number of variables is on the order of 100. (The authors of the program suggests that examples with 300 variables can be accommodated on a mainframe computer.) Substantial possibilities of substitution, if known in advance, offer no difficulty to the successful functioning of this algorithm. In my opinion, the modern restatement of Barone's problem is rather that even 300 variables are extremely small in number in contrast to the millions of prices and activity levels implicit in his account. The computer, while expanding our capabilities immeasurably, has taught us a severe lesson about the role of mathematical reasoning in economic practice and forced us to shift our point of view dramatically from that held by our predecessors. We realize that our preoccupations are not with universal laws which describe economic phenomena with full and complete generality, but rather with intellectual formulations which are an imperfect representation of a complex and elusive reality. The application of general equilibrium theory to economic planning, and more generally to the evaluation of the consequences of changes in economic policy, must be based on highly aggregated models whose conclusions are at best tentative guides to action.

An exercise in comparative statics is begun by constructing a general equilibrium model whose solution reflects the economic situation existing prior to the proposed policy change. The number of parameters required to describe demand functions, initial endowments and the production possibility set is considerable, and in practice the constraint of reproducing the current equilibrium must be augmented by a variety of additional statistical estimates in order to specify the model. The limitations of data in the form required by the Walrasian model inevitably make this estimation procedure less than fully satisfactory.

The second step in the exercise is to calculate the solution after the proposed

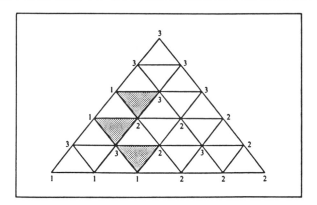

Figure 4

policy changes are explicitly introduced into the model. In some cases the policy variables being studied can be directly incorporated as parameters in the equations whose solution yields the equilibrium values; if the changes are small, their effects on the solution may be obtained by differentiating these equations and solving the resulting linear system for the corresponding changes in the equilibrium values themselves. This approach was adopted by Leif Johansen (1960) and by Arnold Harberger (1962) in his study of the incidence of a tax on corporate profits. The use of this method in policy analysis continues in Norway, and it forms the basis of the ambitious programme carried out by Peter Dixon and his collaborators in Australia (1982). If, on the other hand, the policy changes are large, the equilibrium position may be shifted substantially, and its determination may require the use of more sophisticated computational methods.

Fixed-point algorithms can be divided into two major classes: those based on the elements of differential topology, surveyed by Smale (1981), and those which are combinatorial in nature. The most elementary of the combinatorial algorithms for approximating a fixed point of a continuous mapping of the unit simplex $S = \{x = (x_1, x_2, \ldots, x_n) | x_i \geq 0, \Sigma x_i = 1\}$ begins by dividing the simplex into a large number of small subsimplices as illustrated in Figure 4. In our notation the simplex is of dimension $n - 1$ and has faces of dimension $n - 2, \ldots, 1$. It is a requirement of the subdivision that the intersection of any two of the subsimplices is either empty or a full lower dimensional face of both of them.

Each vertex of the subdivision will have associated with it an integer label selected from the set $(1, 2, \ldots, n)$. When the method is applied to the determination of a fixed point of a particular mapping, the labels associated with a vertex will depend on the mapping evaluated at that point. For the moment, however, the association will be arbitrary aside from the requirement that a vertex on the boundary of the simplex will have a label i only if the ith coordinate of that vertex is positive.

The remarkable combinatorial lemma demonstrated by Emanuel Sperner

(1928) in his doctoral thesis is that at least one subsimplex must have all of its vertices differently labelled. Assuming this result to be correct, let us consider a mapping of the simplex in which the image of the vector $x = (x_1, \ldots, x_n)$ is $f(x) = [f_1(x), \ldots, f_n(x)]$. The requirement that the image on the simplex implies that $f_i(x) \geqslant 0$ and that $\Sigma f_i(x) = 1$. It follows that for every vertex of the subdivision of v, unless v is a fixed point of the mapping, there will be at least one index i for which $f_i(v) - v_i < 0$. If we select such an index to be the label associated with the vertex v, then the assumptions of Sperner's Lemma are clearly satisfied, and the conclusion asserts the existence of a simplex whose vertices are distinctly labelled.

If the simplicial subdivision is very fine, the vertices of this subsimplex are all close together; at each vertex a different coordinate is decreasing under the mapping, and by continuity every point in the small subsimplex will have the property that each coordinate is not increasing very much under the mapping. Since the sum of the coordinate changes is by definition zero, the image of any point in the completely labelled subsimplex will be close to itself, and such a point will therefore serve as an approximate fixed point of the mapping. A formal proof of Brouwer's Theorem requires us to construct a sequence of finer and finer subdivisions, to find, for each subdivision, a completely labelled simplex, and to select a convergent sequence of these simplices tending to a fixed point of the mapping.

Sperner's Lemma may be applied to the equilibrium problem directly. For simplicity, consider the model of exchange in which the market excess demand functions are given by $g(p)$, with p on the unit price simplex. As before, we subdivide the simplex and associate an integer label from the set $(1, \ldots, n)$ with each vertex v of the subdivision, according to the following rule: the label i is to be selected from the set of those indices of which $g_i(p) \leqslant 0$. It is an elementary consequence of Walras's Law that a selection can be made which is consistent with the assumptions of Sperner's Lemma, and there will therefore be a subsimplex all of whose vertices bear distinct labels. By virtue of the particular labelling rule, any point in such a completely labelled simplex will be an approximate equilibrium price vector in the sense that all excess demands, at this price, will be either negative or, if positive, very small.

Sperner's original proof of his combinatorial lemma was not constructive; it was based on an inductive argument which required a complete enumeration of all completely labelled simplices for a series of lower dimensional problems. In order to develop an effective numerical algorithm for the determination of such a simplex let us begin by embedding the unit simplex, and its subsimplices, in a larger simplex T, as in Figure 5. The larger simplex is subdivided by joining its n new vertices to those vertices of the original subdivision lying on the boundary of the unit simplex. The assumptions of Sperner's Lemma permit the new vertices to be given distinct labels from the set $(1, \ldots, n)$, in such a way that no additional completely labelled simplices are generated. For concreteness, let the new vertex receiving the label i be denoted by v^i.

We begin our search for a completed labelled simplex by considering the

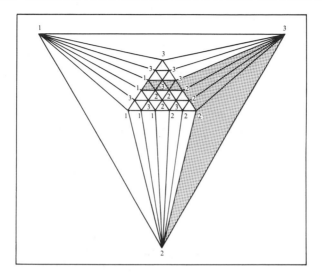

Figure 5

simplex with vertices $v^2, \ldots, v^n$ and one additional vertex, say v^*. If v^* has the label 1, this simplex is completely labelled and our search terminates; otherwise we move to an adjacent simplex by removing the vertex whose label agrees with that of v^* and replacing it with that unique other vertex yielding a simplex in the subdivision. As the process continues, we are, at each step, at a simplex whose vertices bear the labels $2, \ldots, n$, with a single one of these labels appearing on a pair of vertices. Precisely two $n-2$ dimensional faces have a complete set of labels $2, \ldots, n$. The simplex has been entered through one of these faces; the algorithm proceeds by exiting through the other such face.

The argument first introduced by Lemke (1965) in his study of two person non-zero sum games was carried over by Scarf (1967) to show that the above algorithm never returns to a simplex previously visited and never requires a move outside of T. Since the number of simplices is finite, the algorithm must terminate, and termination can only occur when a completely labelled simplex is reached.

IMPROVEMENTS IN THE ALGORITHM

The algorithm can easily be programmed for a computer, and it provides the most elementary numerical procedure for approximating fixed points of a continuous mapping and equilibrium prices for the Walrasian model. Since its introduction in 1967, the algorithm, in this particular form, has been applied to a great number of examples of moderate size, and it performs sufficiently well in practice to conclude that the numerical determination of equilibrium prices is a feasible undertaking. The algorithm does, however, have some obvious drawbacks which must be overcome to make it available for problems of significant size. For example, the information which yields the labelling of the vertices, and therefore the path taken by the algorithm, is simply the index of a coordinate which happens to be decreasing when the mapping is evaluated at the vertex. More recent algorithms make use of the full set of coordinates of the image of the vertex instead of a single summary statistic.

Second, this primitive algorithm is always initiated at the boundary of the simplex. If the approximation is not sufficiently good, the grid size must be refined, and a recalculation, which makes no use of previous information, must be performed. It is of the greatest importance to be able to initiate the algorithm at an arbitrary interior point of the simplex selected as our best *a priori* estimate of the answer.

The following geometrical setting (Eaves and Scarf, 1976) for the elementary algorithm suggests the form these improvements can take. Let us construct a piecewise linear mapping, $h(x)$, of T into itself as follows: for each vertex v in the subdivision let $h(v) = v^i$, where i is the label associated with v. We then complete the mapping by requiring h to be linear in each simplex of the subdivision. The mapping is clearly continuous on T and maps every boundary point of T into itself. Moreover, every subsimplex in the subdivision whose vertices are not completely labelled is mapped, by h, into the boundary of T. If none of the simplices were completely labelled, this construction would yield a most improbable conclusion: a continuous mapping of T into itself which is the identity on the boundary and which maps the entire simplex into the boundary. That such a mapping cannot exist is known as the Non-Retraction Theorem, an assertion which is, in fact, equivalent to Brouwer's Theorem. The impossibility of such a mapping reinforces our conclusion that a completely labelled simplex does not exist.

Select a point c interior to one of the boundary faces of T and consider the set of points which map into c; that is, the set of x for which $h(x) = c$. As Figure 6 indicates, this set contains a piecewise linear path beginning at the point c, and transversing precisely those simplices encountered in our elementary algorithm. There are however, other parts of the set $\{x | h(x) = c\}$: closed loops which do not touch the boundary of T and other piecewise linear paths connecting a pair of completely labelled simplices. Stated somewhat informally, the general conclusion, of which this is an example, is that the inverse image of a particular point, under a piecewise linear mapping from an n dimensional set to an $n-1$ dimensional set, consists of a finite union of interior loops, and paths which join two boundary points, (see Milnor, 1965, for the differentiable version).

To see how this observation can be used, consider the product of the unit simplex S and the closed unit interval $[0, 1]$; that is, the set of points (x, t) with x in S and $0 \leqslant t \leqslant 1$, as in Figure 7. Extend the mapping from the unit simplex to this large set by defining $F(x, t) = (1 - t)f(x) + tx^*$, with x^* a preselected point on the simplex, taken to be an estimate of the true fixed point. The set of points for which $F(x, t) - x = 0$ is, by our general conclusion, a finite union of paths and loops. Precisely one of these paths intersects the upper boundary of the enlarged set. If the path is followed, its other endpoint must lie in the face $t = 0$ and yield a fixed point of the original mapping.

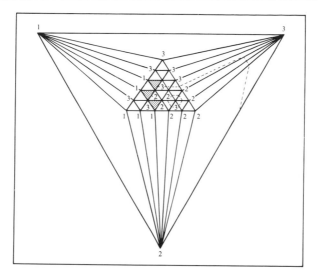

Figure 6

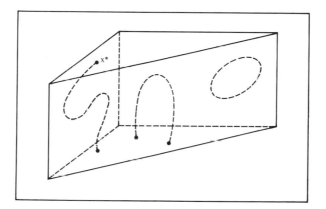

Figure 7

The path leading to the fixed point can be followed on the computer in several ways. We can, for example, introduce a simplicial decomposition of the set $S \times [0, 1]$ and approximate F by a piecewise linear mapping agreeing with F on the vertices of the subdivision. Following the path then involves the same type of calculation we have become accustomed to in carrying out linear programming pivot steps. There are a great many variations in the mode of simplicial subdivision leading to substantial improvements in the efficiency of our original fixed-point algorithm (Eaves, 1972; Merrill, 1972; van der Laan and Talman, 1979).

An alternative procedure, adopted by Kellogg, Li and Yorke (1976) and Smale (1976), is to impose sufficient regularity conditions on the underlying mapping so that differentiation of $F(x, t) - x = 0$ yields a set of differential equations for

95

the path joining x^* to the fixed point on $t = 0$. This leads to a variant of Newton's method which is global in the sense that it need not be initiated in the vicinity of the correct answer. But whichever of these alternatives we select, the numerical difficulties in computing equilibrium prices can be overcome for all problems of reasonable size.

APPLIED GENERAL EQUILIBRIUM ANALYSIS

During the last 15 years, the field of Applied General Equilibrium Analysis has grown considerably; instead of the few tentative examples illustrating our ability to solve general equilibrium problems, we have seen the construction of a large number of models of substantial size designed to illuminate specific policy issues. The number of books and papers which have appeared in the field is far too large for a complete enumeration in this essay, and I shall mention only a few publications which may be consulted to obtain an indication of the diversity of this activity. The paper by Shoven and Whalley (1984) in the *Journal of Economic Literature* is a survey of applied general equilibrium models in the fields of taxation and international trade constructed by these authors and their colleagues. The volume by Adelman and Robinson (1978) is concerned with the application of general equilibrium analysis to problems of economic development. Whalley (1985) has written on trade liberalization, and Ballard, Fullerton, Shoven and Whalley (1985) on the evaluation of tax policy. Jorgenson (Hudson and Jorgenson, 1974) and Manne (1976) have made extensive applications of this methodology to energy policy, and Ginsburg and Waelbroeck (1981) provide a refreshing discussion of alternative computational procedures applied to a model of international trade involving over 200 commodities. The volume edited by Scarf and Shoven (1985) contains a collection of papers presented at one of an annual series of workshops in which both applied and theoretical topics of interest to researchers in the field of Applied General Equilibrium Analysis are discussed.

BIBLIOGRAPHY

Adelman, I. and Robinson, S. 1978. *Income Distribution Policy in Developing Countries: A Case Study of Korea.* Stanford: Stanford University Press.

Ballard, C.L., Fullerton, D., Shoven, J.B. and Whalley, J. 1985. *A General Equilibrium Model for Tax Policy Evaluation.* Chicago: University of Chicago Press.

Barone, E. 1908. Il Ministerio della Produzione nello stato colletivista. *Giornale degli Economisti e Revista di Statistica.* Trans. as 'The Ministry of Production in the Collectivist State', in *Collectivist Economic Planning*, ed. F.A. Hayek, London: G. Routledge & Sons, 1935.

Brouwer, L.E.J. 1912. Über Abbildungen von Mannigfaltigkeiten. *Mathematische Annalen* 71, 97–115.

Debreu, G. 1982. Existence of competitive equilibrium. In *Handbook of Mathematical Economics*, ed. K.J. Arrow and M. Intriligator, Amsterdam: North-Holland.

Dixon, P.B., Parmenter, B.R., Sutton, J. and Vincent D.P. 1982. *ORANI: A Multisectoral Model of the Australian Economy.* Amsterdam: North-Holland.

Eaves, B.C. 1972. Homotopies for the computation of fixed points. *Mathematical Programming* 3, 1–22.

Eaves, B.C. and Scarf, H. 1976. The solution of systems of piecewise linear equations. *Mathematics of Operations Research* 1, 1–27.

Ginsburg, V.A. and Waelbroeck, J.L. 1981. *Activity Analysis and General Equilibrium Modelling*. Amsterdam: North-Holland.

Harberger, A. 1962. The incidence of the corporation income tax. *Journal of Political Economics* 70, 215–40.

Hudson, E.A. and Jorgenson, D.W. 1974. U.S. Energy policy and economic growth. *Bell Journal of Economics and Management Science* 5, 461–514.

Johansen, L. 1960. *A Multi-Sectoral Study of Economic Growth*. Amsterdam: North-Holland.

Kellogg, R.B., Li, T.Y. and Yorke, J. 1976. A constructive proof of the Brouwer Fixed Point Theorem and computational results. *SIAM Journal of Numerical Analysis* 13, 473–83.

Kuhn, H.W. 1968. Simplicial approximation of fixed points. *Proceedings of the National Academy of Sciences* 61, 1238–42.

Lange, O. 1936. On the economic theory of socialism. *Review of Economic Studies* 4, 53–71, 123–42.

Lemke, C.E. 1965. Bimatrix equilibrium points and mathematical programming. *Management Science* 11, 681–9.

Manne, A.S. 1976. ETA: a model of energy technology assessment. *Bell Journal of Economics and Management Science* 7, 379–406.

Merrill, O.H. 1971. Applications and extensions of an algorithm that computes fixed points of certain non-empty convex upper semicontinuous point to set mappings. Technical Report 71–7, University of Michigan.

Milnor, J. 1965. *Topology from the Differentiable Viewpoint*. Charlottesville: University of Virginia Press.

Scarf, H.E. 1967. The approximation of fixed points of a continuous mapping. *SIAM Journal of Applied Mathematics* 15, 1328–43.

Scarf, H.E., with the collaboration of T. Hansen. 1973. *The Computation of Economic Equilibria*. London, New Haven: Yale University Press.

Scarf, H. and Shoven, J.B. (eds) 1984. *Applied General Equilibrium Analysis*. Cambridge: Cambridge University Press.

Shoven, J.B. and Whalley, J. 1972. A general equilibrium calculation of the effects of differential taxation of income from capital in the U.S. *Journal of Public Economy* 1, 281–321.

Shoven, J.B. and Whalley, J. 1984. Applied general-equilibrium models of taxation and international trade. *Journal of Economic Literature* 22, 1007–51.

Smale, S. 1976. A convergent process of price adjustment and global Newton methods. *Journal of Mathematical Economics* 3, 107–20.

Smale, S. 1981. Global analysis and economics. In *Handbook of Mathematical Economics*, ed. K.J. Arrow and M. Intriligator, Amsterdam: North-Holland, Vol. I.

Sperner, E. 1928. Neuer Beweis für die Invarianz der Dimensionszahl und des Gebietes. *Abhandlungen an den mathematischen Seminar der Universität Hamburg* 6, 265–72.

van der Laan, G. and Talman, A.J.J. 1979. A restart algorithm for computing fixed points without an extra dimension. *Mathematical Programming* 17, 74–84.

Whalley, J. 1985. *Trade Liberalization among Major World Trading Areas*. Cambridge, Mass.: MIT Press.

Conjectural Equilibria

F.H. HAHN

In an economy with very many agents the market environment of any one of these is independent of the market actions he decides upon. More generally one can characterize an economy as *perfectly competitive* if the removal of any one agent from the economy would leave the remaining agents just as well off as they were before his removal. (The economy is said to satisfy a 'no surplus' condition; see Makowski, 1980; and Ostroy, 1980.) When an economy is not perfectly competitive, an agent in making a decision must take note of its effect on his market environment, for example, the price at which he can sell. This effect may not be known (or known with certainty) and will therefore be the subject of *conjecture*. A conjecture differs from expectations concerning future market environments which may, say, be generated by some stochastic process. It is concerned with responses to the actions of the agent.

In the first instance then the topic of Conjectural Equilibria is that of an economy which is not perfectly competitive by virtue of satisfying a no surplus condition. But, as we shall see, an economy could fail to satisfy this condition and yet have a perfectly competitive equilibrium.

By an equilibrium in economics we usually mean an economic state which is a rest (critical) point of an (implicit) dynamic system. For instance, it is postulated in the textbooks that when at going prices the amount agents wish to buy does not equal the amount they wish to sell, prices will change. Strictly this should mean that there would, in such a situation, be an incentive for some agent(s) to change prices. This causes difficulties when the economy is perfectly competitive (Arrow, 1959) since it implies that the agent can influence his market environment by his own actions. That is one reason why a fictitious auctioneer has been introduced to account for price changes.

When the economy is not perfectly competitive these difficulties are avoided. A price will be changed if some agent conjectures that such a change would be to his advantage. As a corollary then a conjectural equilibrium must be a state from which it is conjectured by each agent that it would be disadvantageous to depart by actions which are under the individual agent's control. (For a formal definition see below.)

But there are other difficulties. In particular, there is the question of the source of conjectures. If these are taken as given exogenously then there are many states which could be conjectural equilibria for *some* conjectures. It should be noted that a similar objection can be raised in conventional equilibrium analysis. There it is the preferences of agents which are taken as exogenous and there too there are many equilibria which are compatible with some (admissible) preferences. However, while conjectures may turn out to be false and this may occasion a change in conjectures it is less easy to point to equally simple and convincing endogenous mechanisms of preference change. For that reason one may feel that conjectural equilibrium requires that conjectures are in some sense correct ('rational'). For if they are not they will change in the light of experience. This argument is considered below.

The reason why the idea of conjectural equilibria is of interest is that economies which are not intrinsically perfectly competitive (e.g. because of the large number of agents) are of interest and because it allows one to study price formation without an auctioneer.

AN ILLUSTRATION. Consider two agents each of whom can choose an action a_i from a set of action A_i. Let $A = A_1 \times A_2$ with elements $a = (a_1, a_2)$. Then a conjecture c_i is a map from $A \times A_i$ to A_j written as

$$C_i = \theta_i(a, a_i').$$

Its interpretation is this: given the actions of the two agents (a), C_i is the action of j conjectured by i to be result from his choice of a_i'. (In a more general formulation the conjecture can be a probability distribution but that is not considered here.) We require conjectures to be *consistent*:

$$\theta_i(a, a_i) = a_j \tag{1}$$

This says that if agent i continues in his action a_i then he conjectures that j will do likewise. [This use of the word 'consistent' is *not* that of Bresnahan (1981) and others who use it to mean 'correct'.]

Suppose not that there is a function v from A to R^2, written as $v(a) = [v_1(a), v_2(a)]$, which gives the payoffs to the agents as a function of their joint action a. Consider a^* to be one such joint action. One says that a^* is a *conjectural equilibrium* for the two agents if

$$v_i[a_i, \theta_i(a^*, a_i)] \leqslant V_i[a_i^*, \theta_i(a^*)] \qquad \text{all } a_i \in A_i, \quad i = 1, 2 \tag{2}$$

That is, the joint action a^* is a conjectural equilibrium if no agent, given his conjecture, believes that he can improve his position by deviating to a different action.

It is not the case that conjectural equilibrium, as defined, always exists. For instance in the case of a duopoly in a homogeneous product where the action is 'setting the price', v may not be concave and a sensible conjecture may have discontinuities. One thus needs special assumptions to ensure existence or one must face the possibility that agents do not choose actions but probability distributions over actions (mixed strategies); e.g. Kreps and Wilson (1982) in their work on sequential equilibrium employ conjectures which are probability distributions.

Supposing that a conjectural equilibrium exists, one may reasonably argue that until conjectures are less arbitrarily imposed on the theory not much has been gained – almost any pair of actions could be a conjectural equilibrium. A first attempt to remedy this is to ask that conjectures be correct (rational). If that is to succeed in any simple fashion it will be necessary to suppose that each agent has a unique best action under this conjecture. This is very limiting and it means that some of the classical duopoly problems cannot be resolved in this way.

Let the status quo again be a^*. Then if θ_1^* and θ_2^* are correct conjectures it must be that

$$v_2\{\theta_1^*(a^*, a_2), \theta_1^*[(a_1, a_1^*), \theta_2^*(a^*, a_2)]\} > v_1\{a_s', \theta_1^*[(a_1^*, a_2), a_1']\}$$

$$\text{all } a_1' = A_2 \qquad (3)$$

$$v_1\{\theta_2^*(a^*, a_2), \theta_1^*[(a_1^*, a_2), \theta_2^*(a^*, a_2)]\} > v_1\{a_s', \theta_1^*[(a_1^*, a_2), a_1']\}$$

$$\text{all } a_1' = A_1 \qquad (4)$$

A *Rational Conjectural Equilibrium* is then a conjectural equilibrium a^* [with conjectures $\theta_1^*(\cdot)$, $\theta_2^*(\cdot)$ which satisfy (3) and (4)]. It must be re-emphasized that such an equilibrium may not exist for some A and v (see Gale, 1978; Hahn, 1978).

However the idea is simple and where applicable, coherent. It has however been criticized (in a somewhat intemperate and muddled paper) by Makowski (1983). This criticism appears to have had some appeal to some game theorists who like to think of games in extensive form (which they sometimes like to call dynamic). The criticism is this: when agent one deviates from a^* he is interested in the payoffs which he will get given this deviation and agent two's response. This payoff Makowski thinks of as accruing in the 'period' after agent one's deviation. But when agent two responds in that period he is interested in this payoff in the period following this response. So the agents expect 'the game to end' in different periods (Makowski, 1983, p. 8). Moreover, after agent two has responded, agent one, in his turn will again want to respond, i.e. deviate from the deviation he started with. This criticism is then illustrated with an example in which one agent expects the other to return to the status quo *after* he has deviated from it.

All of this however is wrong. Firstly, if one wants to give a time interpretation to conjectures etc. then actions must be thought of as strategies. That is, the deviating agent deviates in one or more elements of his plan over the whole length of the game (perhaps infinite). Under correct conjectures responses and counter responses are taken into account in evaluating the benefits of deviation. Hence, and secondly, a deviating agent is in this situation never surprised by the response of the other, which therefore does not lead him to further revise his deviation. On the definition, agent 1 expects the response to his deviation to be $\theta_1(a^*, a_1)$. Suppose this gives a_2 which is correct. Then that agent knows that the new status quo will be $(a_1, a_2) = a$ and if he has calculated benefits correctly he will not wish to deviate again.

However, there is the following to be said in favour of Makowski's criticism. Deviations in strategies may not be observable by the agent. Therefore in traditional duopoly models with a sequential structure the re-interpretation of actions as strategies may be inappropriate. There is some evidence that in the duopoly literature with conjectures the consequent difficulties have not always been appreciated. It is also the case that too little attention has been paid to the assumption of a unique best response on which the above formulation depends.

An alternative to rational conjectures are *reasonable conjectures* (Hahn, 1978). A conjecture is reasonable if acting on any other conjecture would lower profits given the conjectures of other firms. Suppose that $\bar{\theta}$ is the set of all possible consistent conjectures. For any $\theta_i \in \bar{\theta}$, assume that there is a unique optimizing choice of output by firm i of $y_i(\theta_i)$. Then i's conjecture $\theta_i^0 \in \theta$ is reasonable if given jth conjecture θ_j:

$$v_1[y_i(\theta_i^0), y_j(\theta_j)] \geqslant \hat{v}_i[y_i(\theta_i'), y_j(\theta_j)] \qquad \text{all } \theta_i' \in \theta. \qquad (5)$$

But then a *reasonable conjectural equilibrium* is a pair (θ_1^0, θ_2^0) each in θ such that

$$v_i[y_i(\theta_i^0), y_j(\theta_j^0)] \geqslant \hat{v}[y_i(\theta_i'), y_j(\theta_j^0)], \qquad i, j = 1, 2, \quad \theta_i' \in \bar{\theta} \qquad (6)$$

This is just a Nash-equilibrium where conjectures are interpreted as strategies (Hart, 1982).

While this is still quite demanding it is significantly weaker than (3). If equilibria exist they may be 'bootstrap equilibria', that is they will depend on beliefs about the actions of others, which beliefs may be incorrect. There is certainly no ground for believing that they will be efficient.

One can go one step further in the direction of plausibility by requiring that conjectures be reasonable only for small, or infinitesimal, deviations from the status quo. After all, large experiments are likely to be costlier than small ones. This will allow a larger class of reasonable conjectures and equilibria.

GENERAL CONJECTURAL EQUILIBRIUM. It is fair to say that a present General Equilibrium Theory is in some way complete only for a perfectly competitive economy, that is one where the returns to an individual agent are just equal to the contribution which he makes (Makowski, 1980; Ostroy, 1980). In general (although there are exceptions) such an economy exists when it is large (e.g. it consists of a non-atomic continuum of agents). But there is now another possibility: an economy can be perfectly competitive if agents conjecture that their market actions will have no effect on the prices at which they can trade.

The following assertion will be clear from what has already been discussed. Let us say that an economy is *intrinsically* perfectly competitive if it satisfies the *no-surplus condition*. Then perfectly competitive conjectures are rational if an economy is intrinsically perfectly competitive. But perfectly competitive conjectures can be reasonable even when the economy is not intrinsically perfectly competitive. That is conjectures may be such that if an agent acts on any conjecture other than the perfectly competitive one, his profits will be lower. For instance, this may even be the case for two duopolists with constant marginal costs whose conjectures refer to the price charged by the rival firm. It will also be clear that if we do not require conjectures to be either reasonable or rational then, in general, conjectures can be found to support a competitive equilibrium in an economy which is not intrinsically perfectly competitive.

In a general equilibrium context it is not clear what it is that firms are supposed to conjecture. In some sense the conjecture must refer to the reaction of the whole economy to the action of the conjecturing agent. In other words, it is not obvious how to define a game which adequately represents the economy. But in what sense?

Consider an economy with n produced goods and m non-produced goods. For simplicity suppose that all firms are single product firms and that all firms producing the same good are alike, including their conjectures. There are very many households whose reasonable conjectures are always the competitive one. Households receive the profits of firms. Since the action of any one firm can affect the prices at which households can trade it is not at all clear what it is in the households' interest that the firms should maximize (Gabszewicz and Vial, 1972). If all households are alike it could be their common utility function, but that seems far removed from the world. I shall arbitrarily assume that firms maximize their profits in terms of one of the non-produced goods, say the first. This is arbitrary but it seems to me equally dubious to suppose that firms always choose in the 'best interest of shareholders', especially when that interest is often difficult and sometimes impossible to define.

Let $p \in R^n$, $w \in R_+^{m-1}$ be the price vectors in terms of good m of produced and non-produced goods respectively (so $w_m \equiv 1$). Let $y_j \in Y_j \subset R^{n+m}$ be the production of firm j where $y_{ij} > 0$ is its output of good j, $y_{ii} < 0$ is an input of good i, produced or non-produced. Let $y = \Sigma y_j$, where $y_j \in Y_j$ all j. Let $z \in R_+^m$ be the endowment of non-produced goods and

$$F = \{y \mid y \geqslant (0, -z)\}$$

so that F is the set of feasible net production vectors Y. Let θ_{hj} be the share of household h in firm j.

Given any $y \in F$ we think of each household as endowed with a certain strictly positive stock of non-produced goods and $\theta_{hj} Y_j$ of the production of firm j. To avoid unnecessary complications assume θ_{hj} $(j = 1, \ldots, n)$ to be such that if z_h is the stock of non-produced goods owned by household h:

$$\text{For all } y \in F: z_h + \sum_j \theta_{hj} y_j \geqslant 0 \qquad \text{all } h. \tag{7}$$

Households consume both types of goods. Hence for any $y \in F$ there is now an associated pure exchange economy where each household's endowment is given by (7). Making the usual assumptions there will exist at least one equilibrium $[p(y), w(y)]$. Suppose for the moment that there is only one for each $y \in F$.

Now firm j in this equilibrium observes $[p(y), w(y)]$ and will deviate from y_j (if it deviates at all) if it can thereby increase its conjectured profits. Let

$$\hat{\pi}_j[p(y), w(y), y'_j]$$

be the conjectural profit function of firm j. Then $y^0, p(y^0), w(y^0)$ is a conjectural equilibrium if for all $j = 1, \dots, n$:

$$\hat{\pi}_j[p(y^0), w(y^0), y_j^0] \geqslant \hat{\pi}_j[p(y^0), w(y^0), y'_j] \qquad \text{all } y'_j \in Y. \qquad (8)$$

Such a conjectural equilibrium will exist if all $\hat{\pi}_j(\cdot)$ are quasi-concave, an assumption for which there is scant justification (Hahn, 1978).

If we demand that conjectures be rational then conjectured and actual profit must coincide for all y'_k (the two coincide for $y'_k = y_k^0$ by the requirement that conjectures be consistent). One proceeds as follows. Let $y'_k = y_k^0$. Given the conjectures of the remaining firms find the conjectural equilibrium of the economy $p\{y^*(k), w[y^*(k), y^*(k)]\}$, where $y(k)$ is the vector y with y'_k in the kth place and condition (8) is not imposed for firm k. One then requires that for all $y'_k > 0$.

$$\hat{\pi}_k[p(y^0), w(y^0), y'_k] = \pi_k\{p[y^*(k)], w[y^*(k)], y'_k\}$$

where $\pi_k(\cdot)$ is actual profit. For rational conjectures this should be true for all k.

It will be seen that rational conjectural equilibrium is very demanding. For a certain class of conjectures it will not even exist (Gale, 1978; Hahn, 1978). More importantly, the whole procedure breaks down if given a deviation by k, the conjectural equilibrium is not unique. Lastly, even if by sufficient assumptions one overcomes these difficulties, it is not agreeable to commonsense to suppose that firms can correctly calculate general equilibrium responses to their actions, nor is it obvious that they should always be only concerned with equilibrium states.

Reasonable conjectures do not fare much better, although a notable contribution to their study has recently been made by Hart (1982). Hart notices that conjectures of firms induce a supply correspondence (not generally convex) on their part. Here let us suppose that we can in fact speak of supply functions. These can be thought of as strategies in a manner already discussed. A reasonable conjectural equilibrium then satisfies the condition that, given the supply functions of other firms, no deviation by firm k to another supply response can increase its profits. In (8) one then substitutes on the right-hand side for y'_j, $\eta'_j[p(y^0), w(y^0)]$, an admissible supply function (see Hart, 1982) of j and requires the inequality to hold for all such functions. Of course, one has

$$y_j^0 = \eta_j^0[p(y^0), w(y^0)]$$

for a reasonable conjectural equilibrium.

To show existence of such an equilibrium will require strong assumptions. The technicalities will be found in Hart (1982). However one of the assumptions which he makes is not only technically useful but economically sensible since it leads firms to face a simpler task in forming conjectures. Hart supposes the economy to consist of a number of islands each of which has many consumers and one firm of each type $(j = 1, \ldots, n)$. The islands are small replicas of the whole economy. But households have shares in firms on all islands so that if there are enough islands their share in any firm on their own island is very small. That means that any firm can disregard the effect of a change in its own profits on the demand for the good it produces. To make this work one supposes that produced goods are totally immobile between islands while non-produced goods are totally mobile. By an appropriate assumption on consumers on each island one ensures that they all have the same demand. Lastly, since shares in a firm are held on many different islands the firm, in acting in the shareholder's interest is justified in neglecting the effect of its actions on relative prices on its own island and so is justified in maximizing profits.

From the point of view of conjectural equilibrium the island assumption allows firms (both reasonably and rationally) to ignore effects of their own actions on w – the price vector of non-produced goods. These will be determined by demand and supply over all islands and in this determination any one firm can be regarded as playing a negligible role. This is some gain in realism. But after all allowances have been made it is still true that (a) the assumptions required for the existence of reasonable conjectural equilibrium are uncomfortably strong and (b) even when that is neglected such an equilibrium seems to have small descriptive power.

SIMPLER APPROACHES. Negishi (1960) made the first, justifiably celebrated, attempt to incorporate imperfect competition in general equilibrium analysis. He did this by letting single product firms have consistent inverse demand conjectures (the case he studies most thoroughly makes these linear). Consistency is all he asked for of conjectures but he also needed the uncomfortable postulate that the resulting conjectural profit functions be quasi-concave. Later Hahn (1978), Silvestre (1982) and others added the requirement that besides being consistent, the conjectured demand functions have, if differentiable, the correct slope at equilibrium (i.e. that the conjecture be *infinitesimally* or 'first order' *rational*). It turns out that this extra requirement does not much restrict conjectures, nor thus the set of equilibria which can be generated by some conjectures. The reason roughly is this: in conjectural equilibrium, when conjectured profit functions are twice differentiable, the partial derivative of the conjectured profit function of firm j with respect to its own output must vanish. Suppose the economy to be in such an equilibrium and consider an infinitesimal output deviation by firm k. To find the equilibrium which ensues, differentiate all equilibrium relations, other than that for firm k, with respect to the output of firm k. Amongst these will be the condition that the marginal profit conjectured of every firm (other than k), be zero. Hence differentiation of that condition will yield second order terms. But we can choose these arbitrarily since we are only requiring first order rationality. One can show in fact that these second order terms can be chosen so as to make the first order conjectured change in profit of any firm k correspond to the actual change. (Details in Hahn, 1977.) Hence first order rationality imposes few restrictions.

Both Hahn (1978) and Negishi (1979) have also considered kinked conjectures. The idea is this. If an agent can transact at the going price as much as he desires his conjectures are competitive. If he is quantity constrained (e.g. if a firm cannot sell an amount determined by equality between marginal cost and price) his conjectures are non-competitive. That is he considers that a price change is required to relax the quantity constraint. The fix-price methods of Drèze (1975) and others can be interpreted as an extreme form of such conjectures – for instance to relax a constraint on sales, price, it is conjectured, must be reduced to zero.

To such conjectures there have been two objections. Firstly, they assume that an agent's conjectures are not influenced by constraints on others. For instance, a firm which can hire as much labour as it wants at the going wage while workers cannot sell as much as they like does not conjecture that it could have the same amount of labour at a lower wage. To this one can answer that it is not easy for an agent to observe the quantity constraints on others. For instance, unemployment statistics do not tell us whether workers have chosen not to work or whether they are constrained in their sale of labour. None the less this objection has some force and needs further study with proper attention to the information of agents.

The other objection is that these kinked conjectures are not explained. That is true if explanation turns on what an agent knows or can learn. None the less the hypothesis seems to be to have psychological verisimilitude. If I can always sell my labour at the going wage there is little occasion for the difficult conjecturing of what would happen if I raised my wage. This is not so if I find that I cannot find employment at the going wage.

In any event these simpler approaches allow one to incorporate traditional monopolistic competition in a general equilibrium framework. Of course, some of the assumptions such as concave conjectured profit functions are strong. On the other hand, one can now allow for a certain amount of increasing returns (Silvestre, 1982).

SOME CONCLUSIONS. The conjectural approach has this merit: it takes proper and explicit note of the perceptions by individuals of their market environment. Economic theory perhaps too often neglects the possibility that what is the case may depend on what agents believe to be the case. Historians and others have long since studied the intimate mutual connection between beliefs and events but economists have not made much headway here. The conjectural approach is perhaps a small beginning. For it deals with the theories agents hold and this must plainly enter into our theory of agents.

In particular one should not pay too much attention to the objection that conjectures may not be derivable from some first principles of rationality. It seems to me quite proper to find their description in history. Nor, as has been argued, will an appeal to learning render conjectures in some sense objectively justifiable. This is clear from the discussion of reasonable conjectures and from the costs of experimentation. For hundreds of years witches were burned in the light of a reasonable theory which few would now regard as having proper objective correlatives. There is no reason to suppose that it is possible for businesses or governments now to do better than some of the best minds of the past.

From a more immediately relevant standpoint, conjectural theories are of interest because they attempt a general equilibrium analysis of non-perfect competition. It is good to know that in a proper sense perfectly competitive economies can be viewed as Limiting Cournot Conjectural Equilibrium economies (Novshek and Sonnenschein, 1978). But this knowledge does not contribute to the study of properly imperfectly competitive economies. Again the study of fix-price equilibria has borne some fruits, but not those which were first sought by Triffin (1940) when he proposed a framework for general equilibrium with monopolistic competition. If it is the case that actual economies are not perfectly competitive nor that they behave 'as if' they were, then the task set by Triffin requires serious attention and it is likely that conjectural theories will have a role to play.

Recent developments in game theory (e.g. Kreps and Wilson, 1982) suggest that these two conjectures will have to play a part. Indeed quite generally in that theory, players conjecture that their opponent is 'rational' in an appropriate sense. It is not the case that the conjectural equilibrium approach is an alternative to the game theoretic one.

BIBLIOGRAPHY

Arrow, K.J. 1959. Toward a theory of price adjustment. In M. Abramovitz et al., *The Allocation of Economic Resources*, Stanford: Stanford University Press, 41–51.

Bresnahan, T.F 1981. Duopoly models with consistent conjectures. *American Economic Review* 71(5), 934–45.

Drèze, J. 1975. Existence of equilibrium under price rigidity and quantity rationing. *International Economic Review* 16, 301–20.

Gabszewicz, J.J. and Vial, J.D. 1972. Oligopoly 'à la Cournot' in general equilibrium analysis. *Journal of Economy Theory* 4, 381–400.

Gale, D. 1978. A note on conjectural equilibria. *Review of Economic Studies* 45(1), 33–8.

Hahn, F.H. 1977. Exercise in conjectural equilibria. *Scandinavian Journal of Economics* 79, 210–26.

Hahn, F.H. 1978. On non-Walrasian equilibria. *Review of Economic Studies* 45, 1–17.

Hart, O. 1982. Reasonable conjectures. Suntory Toyota Centre for Economics and Related Disciplines. London School of Economics.

Kreps, D.M. and Wilson, R.B. 1982. Sequential equilibria. *Econometrica* 50, 863–94.

Makowski, L. 1980. A characterization of perfectly competitive economies with production. *Journal of Economic Theory* 22(2), 208–21.

Makowski, L. 1983. 'Rational conjectures' aren't rational and 'reasonable conjectures' aren't reasonable. SSRC Project on Risk, Information and Quantity Signals. Cambridge University Discussion Paper 60.

Negishi, T. 1960. Monopolistic competition and general equilibrium. *Review of Economic Studies* 28, 196–202.

Negishi, T. 1979. *Micro-Economic Foundations of Keynesian Macro-Economics*. Amsterdam: North-Holland.

Novshek, W. and Sonnenschein, H. 1978. Cournot and Walras equilibrium. *Journal of Economic Theory* 19, 223–66.

Ostroy, J. 1980. The no-surplus condition as a characterisation of perfectly competitive equilibrium. *Journal of Economic Theory* 22(2), 183–207.

Silvestre, J. 1977. A model of a general equilibrium with monopolistic behaviour. *Journal of Economic Theory* 16(2), 425–42.

Triffin, R. 1940. *Monopolistic Competition and General Equilibrium Theory*. Cambridge: Mass.: Harvard University Press.

Ulph, D. 1983. Rational conjectures in the theory of oligopoly. *International Journal of Industrial Organization* 1(2), 131–54.

Consumption Sets

PETER NEWMAN

The idea of consumption sets was introduced into general equilibrium theory in July 1954 in Arrow and Debreu (1954, pp. 268–9) and Debreu (1954, p. 588), the name itself appearing only in the latter paper. Later expositions were given by Debreu (1959) and Arrow and Hahn (1971) and a more general discussion by Koopmans (1957, Essay 1). Although there have been several articles concerned with non-convex consumption sets (e.g. Yamazaki, 1978), in more recent years their role in general equilibrium theory has been muted, especially in approaches that use global analysis (see e.g. Mas-Colell, 1985, p. 69). Such sets play no role in partial equilibrium theories of consumer's demand, even in such modern treatments as Deaton and Muellbauer (1980). Since general equilibrium theory prides itself on precision and rigour (e.g. Debreu, 1959, p. x), it is odd that on close examination the meaning of consumption sets becomes unclear. Indeed, three quite different meanings can be distinguished within the various definitions presented in the literature. These are given below (in each case the containing set is the commodity space, usually R^n): M1 The consumption set $C1$ is that subset on which the individual's preferences are defined. M2 The consumption set $C2$ is that subset delimited by a natural bound on the individual's supply of labour services, i.e. 24 hours a day. M3 The consumption set $C3$ is the subset of all those bundles, the consumption of any one of which would permit the individual to survive. Each definition in the literature can (but here will not) be classified according to which of these meanings it includes. In probably the best known of them (Debreu, 1959, ch. 4), the consumption set appears to be the intersection of all three subsets $C1$–$C3$. M1 is plain. After all, preferences have to be defined on *some* proper subset of the commodity space, since the whole space includes bundles with some inadmissibly negative coordinates. M2 is also reasonable, although a full treatment of heterogeneous labour services does raise problems for what is meant by an Arrow–Debreu 'commodity' (see e.g. that of Arrow–Hahn, 1971, pp. 75–6). It is M3 that gives real difficulty, both in itself and in relation to the others.

First, there is little reason to expect either C1 or C3 to be a subset of the other, and so still less to expect M1 and M3 to define the same set. No individual would have any problem in preferring one bundle, the consumption of which would ensure her survival, to a second bundle, the consumption of which would result in her death by starvation. However, she might well prefer the second bundle to a third, whose consumption would cause her to die from thirst (the representation of such preferences by a real-valued utility function might pose problems, but that is another matter). On the other hand, the same individual might not be able to rank in order of preference two bundles each of which contains exotic food and drink, even though fully assured that the consumption of either bundle would allow her to survive.

More importantly, M3 implicitly introduces *consumption* activities, the actual eating and drinking and sheltering that are essential to survival. Such activities constitute what are sometimes called, by analogy with production, the consumption technology. Some partial equilibrium models, such as 'the new home economics' and the theory of characteristics, have treated aspects of such technologies but so far general equilibrium theory has not. In particular, Arrow–Debreu theory has not done so. As a consequence (and unlike some forms of the classical 'corn model') it does not give a coherent account of the birth and death of individual persons, any more than it does of the birth and death of individual firms (*see* GENERAL EQUILIBRIUM). Hence the third meaning M3, which in effect presumes that the model contains such an account when it does not, is hard to interpret. One major difficulty of interpretation arises with the Slater-like condition that each individual's endowment of goods and services, valued at the competitive prices p^*, should be strictly greater than $\inf\{\langle x, p^* \rangle : x \in C\}$, where $\langle .,. \rangle$ denotes inner product and C is 'the' consumption set. This condition is important in proofs of existence of competitive equilibrium, to ensure for example that the budget correspondence is continuous, or that a compensated equilibrium is a competitive equilibrium. It is itself guaranteed by assumptions (discussed by McKenzie, 1981, pp. 821–5) on the relations between 'individual' consumption sets and the aggregate production set.

If C is taken to contain C3 then the assumptions just referred to imply that every consumer survives in every competitive equilibrium, not merely for one period but over the whole (finite) Arrow–Debreu span. This is a breathtaking assertion of fact which recalls irresistibly Hick's wry observation: 'Pure economics has a remarkable way of producing rabbits out of a hat – apparently *a priori* propositions which apparently refer to reality. It is fascinating to try to discover how the rabbits got in' (1939, p. 23).

On the other hand if C is taken to be C1, then the assumptions take on a purely technical (and so less objectionable) aspect, whose role is essentially to ensure that the system stays within the (relative) interior of the sets concerned and so displays appropriate continuity. But then there is no presumption that individual agents survive in a competitive equilibrium, even for one period (cf. Robinson, 1962, p. 3). The multi-period versions of the Arrow–Debreu model are then at risk, since individuals disappear and take their labour service endowments with them. This should not come as a surprise – the problems of time in economics are really too complicated to be overcome simply by adding more dimensions to the one-period model.

Some models that include C3 in C attempt to justify Slater-like conditions directly, on the grounds that 'Not many economies in the present day are so extremely laissez faire as to permit people to starve' (Gale and Mas-Colell, 1975, p. 12). This justification clearly fails as long as the behaviour of the public agency whose actions allegedly prevent such starvation is not modelled *explicitly*, like that of the private agents.

It is usually assumed that consumption sets are bounded below, closed and convex. The first two assumptions are innocuous but the third poses issues of a conceptual kind, which spring from difficulties in interpreting the idea of a convex combination $x^t = tx^1 + (1-t)x^2$ of two bundles x^1 and x^2, where $t \in [0,1]$. Consider the example, sometimes used, in which x^1 is a house in London and x^2 a house in Paris. We cannot take seriously the claim that x^t is a house in the Channel, so t cannot refer to distance. An alternative claim that t refers to the proportion of the period that is spent in London could arise from many different finite partitions of the time interval, not all of which need to be ranked equally by the individual. In effect, convexity of the consumption set comes down to the divisibility of consumer goods, an assumption which in the past has proved not such a bad approximation if one is interested mainly in general equilibrium aspects of market demand, and representative rather than actual consumers. Indivisibilities of producer goods are of course much more serious.

BIBLIOGRAPHY

Arrow, K.J. and Debreu, G. 1954. Existence of an equilibrium for a competitive economy. *Econometrica* 22, 265–90.

Arrow, K.J. and Hahn, F.H. 1971. *General Competitive Analysis.* San Francisco: Holden-Day.

Deaton, A. and Muellbauer, J. 1980. *Economics and Consumer Behaviour.* Cambridge and New York: Cambridge University Press.

Debreu, G. 1954. Valuation equilibrium and Pareto optimum. *Proceedings of the National Academy of Sciences* 40(7), 588–92.

Debreu, G. 1959. *Theory of Value.* Cowles Commission Monograph No. 17. New York: Wiley.

Gale, D. and Mas-Colell, A. 1975. An equilibrium existence theorem for a general model without ordered preferences. *Journal of Mathematical Economics* 2, 9–15.

Hicks, J.R. 1939. *Value and Capital.* Oxford: Clarendon Press; 2nd edn, New York: Oxford University Press, 1946.

Koopmans, T.C. 1957. *Three Essays on the State of Economic Science.* New York: McGraw-Hill.

McKenzie, L.W. 1981. The classical theorem on existence of competitive equilibrium. *Econometrica* 49, 819–41.

Mas-Colell, A. 1985. *The Theory of General Economic Equilibrium. A Differentiable Approach.* Cambridge: Cambridge University Press.

Robinson, J.V. 1962. The basic theory of normal prices. *Quarterly Journal of Economics* 76(1), 1–20.

Yamazaki, A. 1978. An equilibrium existence theorem without convexity assumptions. *Econometrica* 46, 541–55.

Cores

WERNER HILDENBRAND

The *core* of an economy consists of those states of the economy which no group of agents can 'improve upon'. A group of agents can improve upon a state of the economy if, by using the means available to that group, each member can be made better off. Nothing is said in this definition of how a state in the core actually is reached. The actual process of economic transactions is not considered explicitly.

To keep the presentation as simple as possible, we shall consider only the core for exchange economies with an arbitrary number l of commodities, even though the core concept applies to more general situations.

Consider a finite set A of economic agents; each agent a in A is described by his *preference relation* $\precsim_a$ (defined on the positive orthant R^l_+) and his *initial endowments* e_a (a vector in R^l_+). The outcome of any exchange, that is to say, a state (x_a) of the exchange economy $\mathscr{E} = \{\precsim_a, e_a\}_{a \in A}$, is a *redistribution* of the total endowments, i.e.

$$\sum_{a \in A} x_a = \sum_{a \in A} e_a.$$

A *coalition* of agents, say $S \subset A$, can *improve upon* a redistribution (x_a), if that coalition S, by using the endowments available to it, can make each member of that coalition better off, that is to say, there is a redistribution, say $(y_a)_{a \in S}$, such that

$$y_a \succ_a x_a \text{ for every } a \in S \quad \text{and} \quad \sum_{a \in S} y_a = \sum_{a \in S} e_a.$$

The set of redistributions for the exchange economy $\mathscr{E}$ that no coalition can improve upon is called the *core* of the economy $\mathscr{E}$, and is denoted by $C(\mathscr{E})$.

The core is, however, a rather theoretical fundamental equilibrium concept. Indeed, the core provides a theoretical foundation of a more operational equilibrium concept, the *competitive equilibrium* which, in fact, is a very different notion of equilibrium. The allocation process is organized through markets; there is a price for every commodity. All economic agents take the price system as given and make their decisions independently of each other. The equilibrium price system coordinates these independent decisions in such a way that all markets are simultaneously balanced.

More formally, an allocation (x_a^*) for the exchange economy $\mathscr{E} = \{\precsim_a, e_a\}_{a\in A}$ is a *competitive equilibrium* (or a *Walras allocation*) if there exists a price vector $p^* \in R_+^l$ such that for every $a \in A$, $x_a^* \in \phi_a(p^*)$ and

$$\sum_{a\in A} x_a^* = \sum_{a\in A} e_a.$$

Here $\phi_a(p^*)$, or more explicitly, $\phi(p^*, e_a, \precsim_a)$ denotes the demand of agent a with preferences $\precsim_a$ and endowment e_a, i.e. the set of most desired commodity vectors (with respect to $\precsim_a$) in the budget-set $\{x \in R_+^l \mid p^* \cdot x \leqslant p^* \cdot e_a\}$.

The set of all competitive equilibria for the economy $\mathscr{E}$ is denoted by $W(\mathscr{E})$.

The core and the set of competitive equilibria for an economy with two agents and two commodities can be represented geometrically by the well-known Edgeworth–Box (see figure 1). The size of the box is determined by the total endowments $e_1 + e_2$. Every point P in the box represents a redistribution; the first agent receives $x_1 = P$ and the second receives $x_2 = (e_1 + e_2) - P$.

It is easy to show that for every exchange economy $\mathscr{E}$ a competitive equilibrium belongs to the core,

$$W(\mathscr{E}) \subset C(\mathscr{E}).$$

Thus, a state of the economy $\mathscr{E}$ which is decentralized by a price system cannot be improved upon by cooperation. This proposition strengthens a well-known result of Welfare Economics – every competitive equilibrium is Pareto-efficient.

The inclusion $W(\mathscr{E}) \subset C(\mathscr{E})$ is typically strict. Indeed, if the initial allocation of endowments is not Pareto-efficient, which is the typical case, then, if there are any allocations in the core at all, there are core-allocations which are not competitive equilibria.

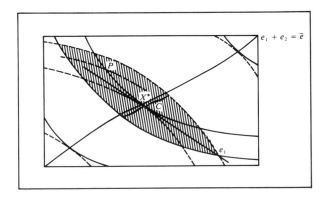

Figure 1

This leads us to the *basic problem* in the theory of the core:

For which kind of economies is the 'difference' between the core and the set of competitive equilibria small? Or in other words, under which circumstances do cooperative barter and competition through decentralized markets lead essentially to the same result?

Naturally, the answer depends on the way one measures the 'difference' between the two equilibrium concepts. However this is done one expects that the economy must have a large number of participants.

In answering the basic question we try to be comprehensible (for example by avoiding the use of measure-theoretic concepts) but not comprehensive. Therefore, if we refer in the remainder of this entry to an economy $\mathscr{E} = \{ \precsim_a, e_a \}_{a \in A}$ we shall always assume that preference relations are continuous, complete, transitive, monotone and strictly convex. The total endowments $\Sigma_{a \in A} e_a$ of an economy are always assumed to be strictly positive. We shall not repeat these assumptions. Furthermore, if we call an economy smooth, then we assume in addition that preferences are smooth (hence representable by sufficiently differentiable utility functions) and individual endowments are strictly positive.

These assumptions simplify the presentation tremendously. For generalizations we refer to the extensive literature.

We remark that under the above assumptions there always exists a competitive equilibrium, and hence, the core is not empty.

LARGE ECONOMIES

The simplest and most stringent measure of difference between the two equilibrium sets, $C(\mathscr{E})$ and $W(\mathscr{E})$, which we shall denote by $\delta(\mathscr{E})$, can be defined as follows.

Let $\delta(\mathscr{E})$ be the smallest number δ with the property: for every allocation $(x_a) \in C(\mathscr{E})$ there exists an allocation $(x_a^*) \in W(\mathscr{E})$ such that

$$|x_a - x_a^*| \leqslant \delta$$

for every agent a in the economy $\mathscr{E}$.

Thus, if $\delta(\mathscr{E})$ is small, then from every agent's view a core allocation is like a competitive equilibrium.

Unfortunately for this measure of difference, it is not true that $\delta(\mathscr{E})$ can be made arbitrarily small provided the number of agents in the economy $\mathscr{E}$ is sufficiently large (even if one restricts the agents' characteristics $(\precsim_a, e_a)$ to an *a priori* given finite set).

Consequently one considers also weaker measures for the 'difference' between the two equilibrium concepts $C(\mathscr{E})$ and $W(\mathscr{E})$. For example, define $\delta_1(\mathscr{E})$ and $\delta_2(\mathscr{E})$, respectively, as the smallest number δ with the property: for every $(x_a) \in C(\mathscr{E})$ there exists a price vector $p \in R_+^i$ such that

(δ_1) $\qquad\qquad |x_a - \phi_a(p)| \leqslant \delta$ $\qquad$ for every agent a in $\mathscr{E}$

113

or

$$(\delta_2) \qquad \frac{1}{\#A}\sum_{a\in A}|x_a - \phi_a(p)| \leqslant \delta.$$

Clearly, the measures δ_1 and δ_2 are weaker than δ since the price vector p is not required to be an equilibrium price vector for the economy $\mathscr{E}$. The number $\delta_1(\mathscr{E})$ (and, *a fortiori*, $\delta_2(\mathscr{E})$) does not measure the distance between the sets $C(\mathscr{E})$ and $W(\mathscr{E})$ but the degree by which an allocation in the core can be decentralized via a price system. Obviously one has $\delta_2(\mathscr{E}) \leqslant \delta_1(\mathscr{E}) \leqslant \delta(\mathscr{E})$.

One can show that $\delta_2(\mathscr{E})$ becomes arbitrarily small for sufficiently large economies. More precisely,

THEOREM 1.   Let T be a finite set of agents' characteristics $(\precsim, e)$ and let b be a strictly positive vector in R^l. Then for every $\varepsilon > 0$ there exists an integer N such that for every economy $\mathscr{E} = \{\precsim_a, e_a\}_{a\in A}$ with $\#A \geqslant N$,

$$\frac{1}{\#A}\sum_{a\in A} e_a \geqslant b$$

and $(\precsim_a, e_a) \in T$ one has

$$\delta_2(\mathscr{E}) \leqslant \varepsilon.$$

(The finite set T in Theorem 1 can be replaced by a compact set with respect to a suitably chosen topology: see Hildenbrand, 1974.) We emphasize that this result does not imply that in large economies core-allocations are near to competitive equilibria. In fact, Theorem 1 does not hold if δ_2 is replaced by the measure of difference δ or even δ_1. Theorem 1 does imply, however, that for sufficiently large economies one can associate to every core-allocation a price vector which 'approximately decentralizes' the core-allocation. Some readers might consider this conclusion as a perfectly satisfactory answer to our basic problem. If one holds this view, then the rest of the paper is a superfluous intellectual pastime. We would like to emphasize, however, that the meaning of 'approximate decentralization' is not very strong. First, the demand $\phi_a(p)$ is not necessarily near to x_a for every agent a in the economy; only the mean deviation

$$\frac{1}{\#A}\sum_{a\in A}|x_a - \phi_a(p)|$$

becomes small. Second, total demand is not equal to total supply; only the mean excess demand

$$\frac{1}{\#A}\sum_{a\in A}[\phi_a(p) - e_a]$$

becomes small.

There are alternative proofs in the literature, e.g. Bewley (1973), Hildenbrand (1974), Anderson (1981) or Hildenbrand (1982). These proofs are based either on a result by Vind (1965) or Anderson (1978).

Sharper conclusions than the one in Theorem 1 will be stated in the following sections. There we consider a sequence $(\mathscr{E}_n)_{n=1,\ldots}$ of economies and then study the asymptotic behaviour of $\delta(\mathscr{E}_n)$.

Before we present these limit theorems we should mention another approach of analysing the inclusion $W(\mathscr{E}) \subset C(\mathscr{E})$. Instead of analysing the asymptotic behaviour of the difference $\delta(\mathscr{E}_n)$ for a sequence of finite economies one can define a large economy where every agent has strictly no influence on collective actions. This leads to a *measure space without atoms* of economic agents (also called a *continuum of agents*). For such economies the two equilibrium concepts coincide. See Aumann (1964).

REPLICA ECONOMIES

Let $\mathscr{E} = \{\precsim_i, e_i\}$ be an exchange economy with m agents. For every integer n we define the n-fold *replica economy* $\mathscr{E}_n$ of $\mathscr{E}$ as an economy with $n \cdot m$ agents; there are exactly n agents with characteristics $(\precsim_i, e_i)$ for every $i = 1, \ldots, m$.

More formally,

$$\mathscr{E}_n = \{\precsim_{(i,j)}, e_{(i,j)}\}_{\substack{1 \leqslant i \leqslant m \\ 1 \leqslant j \leqslant n}}$$

where $\precsim_{(i,j)} = \precsim_i$ and $e_{(i,j)} = e_i$, $1 \leqslant i \leqslant m$ and $1 \leqslant j \leqslant n$. Thus, an agent a in the economy $\mathscr{E}_n$ is denoted by a double index $a = (i,j)$. We shall refer to agent (i,j) sometimes as the jth agent of type i.

Replica economies were first analysed by F. Edgeworth (1881) who proved a limit theorem for such sequences in the case of two commodities and two types of agents. A precise formulation of Edgeworth's analysis and the generalization to an arbitrary finite number of commodities and types of agents is due to Debreu and Scarf (1963).

Here is the basic result for replica economies.

THEOREM 2. For every sequence $(\mathscr{E}_n)$ of replica economies the difference between the core and the set of competitive equilibria tends to zero, i.e.,

$$\lim_{n \to \infty} \delta(\mathscr{E}_n) = 0.$$

Furthermore, if $\mathscr{E}$ is a smooth and regular economy than $\delta(\mathscr{E}_n)$ converges to zero at least as fast as the inverse of the number of participants, i.e., there is a constant K such that

$$\delta(\mathscr{E}_n) \leqslant \frac{K}{n}.$$

The proof of this remarkably neat result is based on the fact that a core–allocation (x_{ij}) assigns to every agent of the same type the same commodity bundle, i.e., $x_{ij} = x_{ik}$. This 'equal treatment' property simplifies the analysis of $\delta(\mathscr{E}_n)$ tremendously. Indeed, an allocation (x_{ij}) in $C(\mathscr{E}_n)$, which can be considered as a vector in $R^{l \cdot m \cdot n}$, is completely described by the commodity bundle of one agent in each type, thus by a vector $(x_{11}, x_{21}, \ldots, x_{m1})$ in $R^{l \cdot m}$, a space whose dimension is independent of n.

Thus, let

$$C_n = \{(x_{11}, x_{21}, \ldots, x_{m1}) \in R^{l \cdot m} | (x_{ij}) \in C(\mathscr{E}_n)\}.$$

One easily shows that $C_{n+1} \subset C_n$. It is not hard to see that Theorem 1 follows if

$$\cap_{n=1}^{\infty} C_n = W(\mathscr{E}_1).$$

But this is the well-known theorem of Debreu and Scarf (1963). The essential arguments in the proof go as follows. Let $(x_1, \ldots, x_m) \in \cap_{n=1}^{\infty} C_n$. One has to show that there is a price vector p^* such that $x \succ_i x_i$ implies $p^* \cdot x > p^* \cdot e_i$. For this it suffices to show that there is a p^* such that

$$p^* \cdot z \geqslant 0 \text{ for every } z \in \cup_{i=1}^{m} (\{x \in R_+^l | x \succ_i x_i\} - e_i) = Z,$$

i.e., there is a hyperplane (whose normal is p^*) which supports the set z. One shows that the assumption $(x_1, \ldots, x_m) \in \cap_{n=1}^{\infty} C_n$ implies that 0 does not belong to the convex hull of z. Minkowski's Separation Theorem for convex sets then implies the existence of the desired vector p^*.

The second part of the conclusion of Theorem 2 is due to Debreu (1975).

TYPE ECONOMIES

The limit theorem on the core for replica economies is not fully satisfactory since replication is a very rigid way of enlarging an economy. The conclusion '$\delta(\mathscr{E}_n) \to 0$' in Theorem 2, to be of general relevance, should be robust to small deviations from the strict replication procedure.

Consider a sequence $(\mathscr{E}_n)$ of economies where the characteristics of every agent belong to a given finite set of types $T = \{(\precsim_1, e_1), \ldots, (\precsim_m, e_m)\}$. We do not consider this as a restrictive assumption (considered as an approximation, one can always group agents' characteristics into a finite set of types). Let the economy $\mathscr{E}_n$ have N_n agents; $N_n(1)$ agents of the first type, $N_n(i)$ agents of type i. Of course the idea is that N_n tends to ∞ with increasing n. Consider the fraction $v_n(i)$ of agents in the economy $\mathscr{E}_n$ which are of type i, i.e.,

$$v_n(i) = \frac{N_n(i)}{N_n}.$$

The sequence $(\mathscr{E}_n)$ is a replica sequence of an economy $\mathscr{E}$ (not necessarily of $\mathscr{E}_1$) if and only if the fractions $v_n(i)$ are all independent of n. It is this rigidity which we want to weaken now.

A sequence $(\mathscr{E}_n)$ of economies with characteristics in a finite set T is called a *sequence of type economies* (over T) if

(i) the number N_n of agents in $\mathscr{E}_n$ tends to infinity and

(ii) $v_n(i) = \dfrac{N_n(i)}{N_n} \xrightarrow[(n \to \infty)]{} v(i) > 0.$

EXAMPLE (random sampling of agents' characteristics):

Let π be a probability distribution over the finite set T. Define the economy $\mathscr{E}_n$ as a random sample of size n from this distribution $\pi(\cdot)$. The law of large numbers then implies property (ii): $v_n(i) \to \pi(i)$.

The step from replica economies to type economies – as small as it might appear to the reader – is conceptually very important. Yet with this 'small' generalization the analysis of the limit behaviour of $\delta(\mathscr{E}_n)$ or $\delta_1(\mathscr{E}_n)$ is made more difficult. Even worse, it is no longer true that for *every* sequence $(\mathscr{E}_n)$ of type economies one obtains $\delta(\mathscr{E}_n) \to 0$ – even if the preferences of all types are assumed to be very nice, say smooth. There are some 'exceptional cases' where the conclusion $\delta(\mathscr{E}_n) \to 0$ does not hold. But these are 'exceptional' cases and the whole difficulty in the remainder of this section is to explain in which precise sense these cases are 'exceptional' and can therefore be ignored. We shall first exhibit the 'cases' where the conclusion fails to hold. Then we shall show that these cases are exceptional.

We denote by $\Pi(\mathscr{E})$ the set of normalized *equilibrium price vectors* for the economy $\mathscr{E} = \{\precsim_a, e_a)\}_{a \in A}$. Thus, for $p^* \in \Pi(\mathscr{E})$ the excess demand is zero, i.e.,

$$\sum_{a \in A} [\phi_a(p^*) - e_a] = 0.$$

To every sequence $(\mathscr{E}_n)$ of type economies we associate a 'limit economy' $\mathscr{E}_\infty$. This economy has an 'indefinitely large' number of agents of every type; the fraction of agents of type i is given by $v(i)$. The mean (per capita) excess demand of that limit economy $\mathscr{E}_\infty$ is defined by

$$z_v(p) = \sum_{i=1}^{m} v(i)[\phi(p, e_i, \precsim_i) - e_i].$$

An equilibrium price vector p^* of the limit economy $\mathscr{E}_\infty$ is defined by $z_v(p^*) = 0$. Let $\Pi(v)$ denote the set of normalized equilibrium price vectors for $\mathscr{E}_\infty$. Obviously for a replica sequence $(\mathscr{E}_n)$ we have $\Pi(\mathscr{E}_n) = \Pi(v)$ for all n. However, for a sequence of type economies the set $\Pi(\mathscr{E}_n)$ of equilibrium prices of the economy $\mathscr{E}_n$ depends on n, and it might happen that the set $\Pi(v)$ is not similar to $\Pi(\mathscr{E}_n)$ even for arbitrarily large n. To fix ideas, it might happen that $\Pi(\mathscr{E}_n) = \{p_n\}$ and $\Pi(v)$ contains not only $p = \lim p_n$ but also another equilibrium price vector. Such a situation has to be excluded.

We call a sequence of type economies *sleek* if $\Pi(\mathscr{E}_n)$ converges (in the Hausdorff-distance) to $\Pi(v)$.

It is known (Hildenbrand, 1974) that the sequence $(\Pi(\mathscr{E}_n))$ converges to $\Pi(v)$ if $\Pi(v)$ is a singleton (i.e., the limit economy has a unique equilibrium) or, in general, if (and only if) for every open set O in R^l with $O \cap \Pi(v) \neq \emptyset$ it follows that $O \cap \Pi(\mathscr{E}_n) \neq \emptyset$ for all n sufficiently large.

We now have exhibited the cases where a limit theorem on the core holds true.

THEOREM 3.   For every sleek sequence $(\mathscr{E}_n)$ of type economies

$$\lim_{n \to \infty} \delta(\mathscr{E}_n) = 0.$$

Unfortunately there seems to be no short and easy proof. The main difficulty arises from the fact that for allocations in the core of a type economy the 'equal treatment' property, which made the replica case so manageable is no longer true. For a proof see Hildenbrand and Kirman (1976) or Hildenbrand (1982) and the references given there. The main step in the proof is based on a result of Bewley (1973).

It remains to show that non-sleek sequences of type economies are 'exceptional cases'.

The strongest form of 'exceptional' is, of course, 'never'. We mentioned already that a sequence $(\mathscr{E}_n)$ is sleek if its limit economy has a unique equilibrium. Unfortunately, however, only under very restrictive assumptions on the set T of agents' characteristics does uniqueness prevail; for example,

(1) if every preference relation leads to a demand function which satisfies gross-substitution (Cobb–Douglas utility functions are typical examples),
(2) if every preference relation is homothetic and the endowment vectors $e_i(i = 1, \ldots, m)$ are collinear.

Since there is no reasonable justification for restricting the set T to such special types of agents we have to formulate a model in which we allow non–sleek sequences to occur provided, of course, this can be shown to be 'exceptional cases'. Let S^{m-1} denote the open simplex in R^m, i.e.

$$S^{m-1} = \left\{ x \in R^m \mid x_i > 0, \sum_{i=1}^{m} x_i = 1 \right\}.$$

The limit distribution $v(i)$ of a sequence of type economies with m types is a point in S^{m-1}.

A cloud subset C in S^{m-1} which has $(m - 1$ dimensional Lebesgue) measure zero is called *negligible*. Thus, if a distribution v is not in C then a sufficiently small change will not lead to C. Furthermore, given any arbitrary small positive number $\mathscr{E}$ one can find a countable collection of balls in S^{m-1} such that their union covers C, and that the sum of the diameters of these balls is smaller than $\mathscr{E}$. Thus, in particular, if $v \in C$ then one can approximate v by points which do not belong to C. Clearly, a negligible set is a small set in S^{m-1}.

THEOREM 4.   Given a finite set T of m smooth types of agents, there exists a negligible subset C in S^{m-1} and a constant K such that for every sequence $(\mathscr{E}_n)$ of type economies over T whose limit distribution v does not belong to C one has $\delta(\mathscr{E}_n) \leqslant K / \# A_n$, thus in particular, $\lim_{n \to \infty} \delta(\mathscr{E}_n) = 0$.

The convergence of $\delta(\mathscr{E}_n)$ follows from Theorem 3 and Theorem 5.4.3 and 5.8.15 in Mas-Colell (1985). For the rate of convergence see Grodal (1975).

BIBLIOGRAPHY

There is an extensive literature on limit theorems on the core which contains important generalizations of the results given here. For a general reference we refer to Hildenbrand (1974) or (1982), Mas-Colell (1985), Anderson (1985) and the references given there.

Anderson, R.M. 1978. An elementary core equivalence theorem. *Econometrica* 46, 1483–7.

Anderson, R.M. 1981. Core theory with strongly convex preferences. *Econometrica* 49, 1457–68.

Aumann, R.J. 1964. Markets with a continuum of traders. *Econometrica* 32, 39–50.

Bewley, T.F. 1973. Edgeworth's conjecture. *Econometrica* 41, 425–54.

Debreu, G. 1975. The rate of convergence of the core of an economy. *Journal of Mathematical Economics* 2, 1–8.

Debreu, G. and Scarf, H. 1963. A limit theorem on the core of an economy. *International Economic Review* 4, 235–46.

Edgeworth, F.Y. 1881. *Mathematical Psychics.* London: Kegan Paul. Reprinted New York: A.M. Kelley, 1967.

Grodal, B. 1975. The rate of convergence of the core for a purely competitive sequence of economies. *Journal of Mathematical Economics* 2, 171–86.

Hildenbrand, W. 1974. *Core and Equilibria of a Large Economy.* Princeton: Princeton University Press.

Hildenbrand, W. 1982. Core of an economy. In *Handbook of Mathematical Economics*, ed. K.J. Arrow and M.D. Intriligator, Vol. II, Amsterdam: North-Holland.

Hildenbrand, W. and Kirman, A.P. 1976. *Introduction to Equilibrium Analysis.* Amsterdam: North-Holland.

Mas-Colell, A. 1985. *The Theory of General Economic Equilibrium, A Differentiable Approach.* Cambridge: Cambridge University Press.

Vind, K. 1965. A theorem on the core of an economy. *Review of Economic Studies* 32, 47–8.

Disequilibrium Analysis

JEAN-PASCAL BENASSY

A convenient way to define 'disequilibrium' is of course as the contrary of 'equilibrium'. Unfortunately this leaves us with no unique definition as the word equilibrium itself has been used in the economic literature with at least two principal meanings. The first one refers to market equilibrium, i.e. the equality of supply and demand on markets. This is the meaning we shall retain in this entry, and therefore the disequilibrium analysis we shall be concerned with here is the study of nonclearing markets, also called non-Walrasian analysis by reference to the most elaborate model of market clearing, the Walrasian model.

The second meaning of equilibrium is somewhat more general. A typical definition is given by Machlup (1958) as '... a constellation of selected interrelated variables, so adjusted to one another that no inherent tendency to change prevails in the model which they constitute'. Dealing with disequilibrium in this second meaning would be a quite formidable (and actually extremely imprecise) task, which is why we want to limit ourselves in this entry to disequilibrium analysis in the first sense.

We should note that the entry RATIONED EQUILIBRIA presents concepts of equilibria in the second, but not in the first sense of the word, i.e. more specifically equilibria without market clearing, or non-Walrasian equilibria.

THE ESSENCE OF THE THEORY. Disequilibrium analysis is best appraised by reference to the standard equilibrium market clearing paradigm, corresponding to the notions of Marshallian or Walrasian equilibrium. There all private agents receive a price signal and assume that they will be able to exchange whatever they want at that price. They express demands and supplies, sometimes called 'notional', which are functions of this price signal. An equilibrium price system is a set of prices for which demand and supply match on all markets. Transactions are equal to the demands and supplies at the equilibrium price system.

Two characteristics deserve to be stressed: all private agents receive price signals and make rational quantity decisions with respect to them. But no agent makes any use of the quantity signals sent to the market. Also no agent actually sets prices, the determination of which is left to the 'invisible hand' or to the implicit Walrasian auctioneer. This logical hole of the theory was pointed out by Arrow (1959) when he noted there was '...a logical gap in the usual formulations of the theory of the perfectly competitive economy, namely, that there is no place for a rational decision with respect to prices as there is with respect to quantities', and more specifically 'each individual participant in the economy is supposed to take prices as given and determine his choices as to purchases and sales accordingly; there is no one left over whose job is to make a decision on price'.

Disequilibrium analysis takes this strong logical objection quite seriously, and its purpose is to build a consistent theory of the functioning of decentralized economies when market clearing is not axiomatically assumed. The consequences of abandoning the market clearing assumption are actually quite far-reaching: (i) The transactions cannot be all equal to demands and supplies expressed on markets. Rationing will be experienced and quantity signals will be formed in addition to price signals (ii) Demand and supply theory must be substantially modified to take into account these quantity signals. One thus obtains a theory of effective demand, as opposed to notional demand which only takes price signals into account (iii) Price theory must also be amended in a way that integrates the possibility of non-clearing markets, the presence of quantity signals, and makes agents themselves responsible for price making, (iv) Finally expectations, which in market clearing models are concerned with price signals only, must now include quantity signals expectation as well.

HISTORY. Though roots may be found earlier, an uncontestable grandfather of disequilibrium analysis in the sense we use here is of course Keynes (1936). He rightfully perceived that one of his main contributions in the *General Theory* was the introduction of quantity adjustments, and more specifically income adjustments, in the economic process, whereas the then dominant 'classical' economists focused on price adjustments only. As Keynes (1937) wrote 'As I have said above, the initial novelty lies in my maintaining that it is not the rate of interest, but the level of incomes which ensures equality between savings and investment'.

Unfortunately for many decades things did not go much further: macro-economists added the level of income in their equations, thereby allowing for unemployment. But concentration on the 'equilibrium' of the goods and money markets, exemplified by the dominant IS–LM model, obscured the 'disequilibrium' nature of the model. As for microeconomics, it was basically unaffected by the Keynesian revolution, and correlatively a growing gap developed between microeconomics and macroeconomics.

A few isolated contributions in the post-war period made some steps toward modern disequilibrium theories. Samuelson (1947), Tobin and Houthakker (1950) studied the theory of demand under conditions of rationing. Bent Hansen (1951) introduced the ideas of active demand, close in spirit to that of effective demand,

121

and of quasi-equilibrium where persistent disequilibrium created steady inflation. Patinkin (1956, ch. 13) considered the situation where the firms might not be able to sell all their 'notional' output. Hahn and Negishi (1962) studied non-tâtonnement processes where trade could take place before a general equilibrium price system was reached. Hicks (1965) discussed the 'fixprice' method as opposed to the flexprice method.

A main impetus came from the stimulating works of Clower (1965) and Leijonhufvud (1968). Both were concerned with the microeconomic foundations of Keynesian theory. Clower showed that the Keynesian consumption function made no sense unless reinterpreted as the response of a rational consumer to a disequilibrium on the labour markets. He introduced the 'dual-decision' hypothesis, a precursor of modern effective demand theory, showing how the consumption function could have two different functional forms, depending on whether the consumer was rationed on the labour market or not. Leijonhufvud (1968) insisted on the importance of short-run quantity adjustments to explain the establishment of an equilibrium with involuntary unemployment.

These contributions were followed by the macroeconomic model of Barro and Grossman (1971, 1976), integrating the 'Clower' consumption function and the 'Patinkin' employment function in the first 'disequilibrium' macroeconomic model.

Then the main development was that of microeconomic concepts of non-Walrasian equilibrium proposed notably by Benassy (1975, 1976, 1977, 1982), Drèze (1975) and Younès (1975). These, which generalize the notion of Walrasian general equilibrium to non-market clearing situations, gave solid microeconomic foundations to the field. The main concepts are reviewed in the entry RATIONED EQUILIBRIA.

From then on, the field has developed quite rapidly, notably in the direction of macroeconomic applications and econometrics, as we shall outline below. We shall now review quickly the main elements of disequilibrium analysis. Longer developments can be found notably in Benassy (1982).

NON-CLEARING MARKETS AND QUANTITY SIGNALS. A most important element of the theory is obviously to show how transactions can occur in a market in disequilibrium, and how quantity signals are generated in the decentralized trading process. To make things clear and intuitive, we shall start with the simple case of two agents, one demander and one supplier in a market which does not necessarily clear. They meet and express, respectively, an effective demand $\tilde{d}$ and supply $\tilde{s}$ (note that we do not use notional demands and supplies which are fully irrelevant in this context). We shall now indicate how transactions and quantity signals are formed in this example. Transactions will be denoted d^* and s^* respectively and they must of course satisfy $d^* = s^*$.

The first principle we shall use is that of voluntary exchange, i.e. that no agent can be forced to trade more than he wants on a market. This condition is quite natural and actually verified on most markets, except maybe for some labour markets which are regulated by more complex contractual arrangements. It is written in this example:

$$d^* \leqslant \tilde{d} \qquad s^* \leqslant \tilde{s}$$

which implies that:

$$d^* = s^* \leqslant \min(\tilde{d}, \tilde{s})$$

Actually in this simple example, there is not reason why these two agents would exchange less than the minimum of demand and supply, as they would be both frustrated in their desires of exchange. This simple 'efficiency' assumption leads us to take the transaction as:

$$d^* = s^* = \min(\tilde{d}, \tilde{s})$$

the well-known 'rule of the minimum'.

Not at the same time as transactions take place, quantity signals are set across the market: faced with the supply $\tilde{s}$, and under voluntary exchange, the demander knows that he will not be able to purchase more than $\tilde{s}$. Symmetrically the supplier knows that he cannot sell more than $\tilde{d}$. Each agent thus receives from the other a quantity signal, respectively denoted as $\bar{d}$ and $\bar{s}$, which tells him the maximum quantity he can respectively buy and sell. In this example:

$$\bar{d} = \tilde{s} \qquad \bar{s} = \tilde{d}$$

and the transactions can thus be expressed as:

$$d^* = \min(\tilde{d}, \bar{d})$$

$$s^* = \min(\tilde{s}, \bar{s})$$

Let us move now now to the general case (which is explored more formally in the entry on RATIONED EQUILIBRIA). Agents, indexed by i, exchange goods indexed by h. On each market h a rationing scheme transforms inconsistent demands and supplies, denoted $\tilde{d}_{ih}$ and $\tilde{s}_{ih}$, into consistent transactions, denoted d_{ih}^* and s_{ih}^*, which balanced identically (i.e. total purchases always equal total sales). At the same time, and continuing to assume voluntary exchange, each agent receives a quantity signal, respectively $\bar{d}_{ih}$ or $\bar{s}_{ih}$ for demanders and suppliers, which tells him the maximum quantity he can buy or sell, and the rationing scheme is equivalently written:

$$d_{ih}^* = \min(\tilde{d}_{ih}, \bar{d}_{ih})$$

$$s_{ih}^* = \min(\tilde{s}_{ih}, \bar{s}_{ih})$$

where $\bar{d}_{ih}$ and $\bar{s}_{ih}$ are functions of the demands and supplies of the other agents on the market. These quantity signals may result from the signals sent to each other by agents in decentralized pairwise meetings (as in the above two agents example) or result from a more centralized process (as in a uniform rationing scheme).

We thus see that on a market we may have unrationed demanders or suppliers, or rationed ones. The rationing scheme is called efficient if there are not both rationed demanders and rationed suppliers in the same market. An efficient rationing scheme implies the well-known 'rule of the minimum', according to which aggregate transactions equal the minimum of supply and demand. Such an assumption, which was very natural for our example with two agents, may not be valid if one considers a macroeconomic market, as not all demanders and suppliers meet pairwise. In particular it is well known that the property of market efficiency may be lost in the process of aggregating submarkets, whereas voluntary exchange remains. Note, however, that the concepts that follow do not require that property of market efficiency.

Not it is clear that the quantity signals received by the agents should have an effect on demand, supply ad price formation. This is what we shall explore now.

EFFECTIVE DEMAND AND SUPPLY. Demands and supplies are signals that agents send to the 'market' (i.e. to the other agents) in order to obtain the best transactions according to their criterion. The traditional 'notional' or Walrasian demands and supplies are constructed under the assumption (which is actually verified ex-post in a Walrasian equilibrium) that each agent can buy and sell as much as he wants on each market. There is thus an equality between the signal the agent sends to the market (demand or supply) and the transaction he will obtained from it.

In disequilibrium analysis there is of course a difference between the signals sent (effective demand and supplies) and their consequences (the transactions actually realized). Effective demands and supplies expressed by an agent in the various markets are the signals which maximize his expected utility of the resulting transactions, knowing that these transactions are related to the demands and supplies by equalities of the type seen above, i.e.:

$$d_{ih}^* = \min(\tilde{d}_{ih}, \bar{d}_{ih})$$
$$s_{ih}^* = \min(\tilde{s}_{ih}, \bar{s}_{ih})$$

The results of such expected utility maximization prgrammes may be quite complex, depending for example on whether quantity constraints are expected deterministically or stochastically, or whether agents act or not as price markers, as we shall see in the next section. In the case of deterministic constraints, there exists a simple and workable definition of effective demand, which generalizes Clower's original 'dual decision' method: effective demand (or supply) on one particular market is the trade which maximizes the agent's criterion subject to the constraints encountered or expected on the other markets. This definition thus naturally integrates the well-known 'spillover effects', which show how disequilibrium in one market affects demands and supplies in the other markets.

We shall immediately give an illustrative example of this definition, due to Patinkin (1956) and Barro and Grossman (1971), that of the employment function of the firm. Consider a firm with a production function $y = F(l)$ exhibiting diminishing returns, and faced with a price p on the output market and a wage w on the labour market. The traditional 'notional' labour demand results from maximization of profit $py - wl$ subject to the production constraint $y = F(l)$, which yields immediately the usual Walrasian labour demand $F'^{-1}(w/p)$. Assume now that the firm faces a constraint $\bar{y}$ on its sales of output (i.e. a total demand $\bar{y}$). According to the above definition the effective demand for labour $\tilde{l}$ is the solution in l of the following programme:

$$\text{Maximize } py - wl \text{ s.t.}$$

$$y = F(l)$$

$$y \leqslant \bar{y}$$

the solution of which is:

$$\tilde{l} = \min\{F'^{-1}(w/p),\ F^{-1}(\bar{y})\}$$

We see that the effective demand for labour may have two forms: the Walrasian demand just seen above if the sales constraint is not binding, or, if this constraint is binding, a more 'Keynesian' form equal to the quantity of labour just necessary to produce the output demand. We see immediately on this example that effective demand may have various functional forms, which intuitively explains why disequilibrium models often have multiple regimes (see for example the three goods–three regimes model in the essay on FIX PRICE MODELS below).

In the case of stochastic demand, the programme yielding the effective demand for labour becomes evidently more complex. One obtains some results quite reminiscent of the inventories literature as developed for example by Arrow, Karlin and Scarf (1958) or Bellman (1957). See Benassy (1982) for the link between these two lines of work.

PRICE MAKING. We shall now address the problem of price making by decentralized agents, and we shall see that there too quantity signals play a prominent role. It is actually quite intuitive that quantity signals must be a fundamental part of the competitive process in a truly decentralized economy. Indeed, it is the inability to sell as much as they want that leads suppliers to propose, or to accept from other agents, a lower price, and conversely it is the inability to buy as much as they want that leads demanders to propose, or accept, a higher price. Various modes of price making integrating these aspects can be envisioned. We shall deal here with a particular organization of the pricing process where agents on one side of the market (usually the suppliers) quote prices and agents on the other side act as price takers. Other modes of pricing (bargaining, contracting) are currently studied, but have not yet been integrated in this line of work. As we shall see this model of price making is quite reminiscent of the imperfect competition line: Chamberlain (1933), Robinson (1933), Triffin (1940), Bushaw and Clower (1957), Arrow (1959), Negishi (1961).

Consider thus, to fix ideas, the case where sellers set the prices (things would be quite symmetrical if demanders were setting the prices), and in order to have only one price per market, let us characterize a market by the nature of the good sold and its seller (we thus consider two goods sold by different sellers as different goods, a fairly usual assumption in microeconomic theory since these goods differ at least by location, quality, etc...). On each 'market' so defined we thus have one seller, the price maker, facing several buyers. As we saw above, for a given price this seller faces a quantity constraint $\bar{s}$, actually equal to the demand of the other agents on that market. But the price level is now a decision variable for the seller, and this quantity constraint (the others' total demand) can be modified by changing the price: for example in general the seller who wants to sell more knows that, other things being equal, he should lower the price. The relation between the maximum quantity he expects to sell and the price set by the price maker is called the expected demand curve. If demand is forecasted deterministically, this expected demand curve will be denoted as:

$$\bar{S}(p, \theta)$$

where θ is a vector of parameters depending on the exact functional form of that curve (for example elasticity and a position factor for isoelastic curves). If demand is forecast stochastically, the expected demand curve will have the form of a probability distribution on $\bar{s}$ (i.e. total demand) conditional on the price.

For a given expected demand curve, the price maker chooses the price which will maximize profits, given the relation between price and maximum sales. For example, continuing to consider a firm with production function $F(l)$, the programme yielding the optimum price is the following in the case of a deterministic expected demand curve:

$$\text{Maximize } py - wl \text{ s.t.}$$

$$y = F(l)$$

$$y \leqslant \bar{S}(p, \theta)$$

$$l \leqslant \bar{l}$$

where $\bar{l}$ is the constraint the firm possibly faces on the labour market, where it is a 'wage taker'. Note that, according to our definition above, the effective demand for labour of this same firm would be given by the above programme, from which the last constraint would be deleted.

Both the price and quantity decisions of price makers depend on the parameters θ. Of course it would require quite heroic assumptions on the computational ability and information available to price setters to assume that they know the 'true' demand function (i.e. the 'true' functional form with the 'true' parameters). But the theory developed here gives a natural way of learning about the demand curve. Indeed, each realization p, $\bar{s}$ in a period is a point on the 'true' demand curve in that period (Bushaw and Clower, 1957). Using the sequence of these observations, plus any extra information available (including for example the price of its competitors), the price maker can use statistical techniques to yield an estimation of the demand curve. Whether this learning would lead to the 'true' demand curve is still an unresolved problem.

EXPECTATIONS. Of course, the modifications we outlined concerning the signal structure affect not only the current period, but the future periods as well, and as compared to traditional 'competitive' analysis, disequilibrium analysis introduces expected quantity signals in addition to expected price signals. Such an introduction allows one for example to rationalize the traditional Keynesian accelerator (Grossman, 1972). The introduction of such quantity expectations into the microeconomic setting was made in Benassy (1975, 1977b, 1982). Macroeconomic applications of the corresponding concepts can be found in Hildenbrand and Hildenbrand (1978), Muellbauer and Portes (1978), Benassy (1982, 1986), Neary and Stiglitz (1983).

SCOPE AND USES OF DISEQUILIBRIUM ANALYSIS. We have briefly outlined the basic elements or building blocks of disequilibrium analysis. We saw that it generalizes the traditional theories of demand, supply and price formation to cases where, in the absence of an auctioneer, markets do not automatically clear. This theory is thus a quite general one, and the scope of its applications very broad. Up to now there have been in the literature three particularly active areas of development: (1) The construction of various concepts of equilibria with rationing, or non-Walrasian equilibria. These concepts, which generalize the traditional notion of Walrasian equilibrium to the cases where not all markets clear, show how mixed price-quantity adjustments can bring about a new type of equilibrium in the short run. (2) The development of numerous macroeconomic applications, which basically use the above concepts in the framework of aggregated macromodels, and derive policy implications, for example to fight involuntary unemployment. (3) Finally new econometric methods have been developed to deal with such models, as traditional methods were more suited to the study of equilibrium markets.

Microeconomic concepts of non-Walrasian equilibria are reviewed in the entry RATIONED EQUILIBRIA. We shall now very briefly outline the macroeconomic and econometric developments.

MACROECONOMIC APPLICATIONS. Many contributions in the field started from a reconsideration of Keynesian models, and it is therefore no surprise that many macroeconomic applications have been made. The early model of Barro and Grossman (1971) has been followed by a huge macroeconomic literature, notably aimed at policy analysis and the study of involuntary unemployment. A very valuable feature of disequilibrium macromodels is that, like the microeconomic models, they endogenously generate multiple regimes in which various policy tools may have quite different impacts. These models are thus a particularly useful tool for synthesizing hitherto disjoint macroeconomic theories. One finds a number of macroeconomic applications in books by Barro and Grossman (1976), Benassy (1982, 1986), Cuddington et al. (1984), Malinvaud (1977), Negishi (1979). We may note that the same methods can also be used to study the problems of centrally planned economies (Portes, 1981).

A few lessons can be drawn from these macrodisequilibrium models. The first

127

is that, even though these models were at the very beginning aimed at bridging the gap with Keynesian analysis, they proved to be of far more general relevance, and able to generate non-Keynesian results as well as the traditional Keynesian results. Secondly, and more generally, whether or not a policy tool is efficient may depend very much on the 'regime' the economy is in. A famous example is the Barro and Grossman fixprice macroeconomic model, with its 'Classical unemployment' and 'Keynesian unemployment' regimes. Finally, it appears that the results of these models are quite sensitive to both the price formation mechanism on each market, as well as on the expectations formation mechanisms on both price and quantities (cf. for example, Benassy (1986), which experiments with various hypotheses).

This quite naturally leads to the need of further theoretical work, and to the necessity of empirically testing these models, an issue to which we now turn.

DISEQUILIBRIUM ECONOMETRICS. In order to estimate microeconomic or macro-economic disequilibrium models a whole new econometric technology has developed in recent years. Let us consider the very simplest case, that of a single market with a rigid price. The most basic system to estimate is then:

$$X^d = a_d Z_d + \varepsilon_d$$

$$X^s = a_s Z_s + \varepsilon_s$$

$$X = \min(X^d, X^s)$$

where X^d is quantity demanded, Z_d is the set of variables affecting demand, a_d is the vector of corresponding parameters and ε_d is a demand disturbance term (and symmetrically on the supply side). The market is assumed for the moment to function efficiently so that transaction X is the minimum of demand and supply X^d and X^s. The problem in estimating such a model, as compared with an equilibrium model, where by assumption

$$X = X^d = X^s$$

is that only X is observed, not X^d or X^s. Techniques for dealing with these problems are reviewed in Quandt (1982). Of course this is the simplest possible model, and numerous extensions are now considered: (1) The prices may be flexible, either within the period of estimation, or between successive periods. The price equation must then be estimated simultaneously with the demand-supply system. (2) Since some applications are made on macroeconomic markets, the 'minimum' condition may not be satisfied, and is replaced by an explicit procedure of aggregation of submarkets. (3) Finally models with several markets in disequilibrium have been estimated, notably at the macroeconomic level.

CONCLUDING REMARKS. The development of disequilibrium analysis has clearly led to an enlargement and synthesis of both traditional microeconomics and macroeconomics.

Usual microeconomic theory in the market clearing tradition has been generalized in a number of directions: the study of the functioning of non-clearing markets and the formation of quantity signals, a theory of demand and supply responding to these quantity signals as well as to price signals, the integration of quantity expectations into microeconomic theory. This line of analysis further includes a theory of price making by agents internal to the system which also bridges the gap with the traditional theories of imperfect competition.

As for the corresponding macroeconomic models, they turn out to be a very useful synthetical tool, as they cover all possible disequilibrium configurations. They are more general than either traditional Keynesian macromodels, which considered only excess supply states, or than 'new classical' macromodels which postulate market clearing at all times. They are of course the natural tool to study problems such as involuntary employment.

Still richer developments lie ahead with further developments in the theories of price and wage formation in markets without an auctioneer. The methodology outlined here will permit us to derive the micro and macro consequences, as well as the consequences in terms of economic policy prescriptions. Much is also to be expected of the development of the associated econometric methods, which should allow us to choose the most relevant hypotheses, and to characterize specific historical episodes.

BIBLIOGRAPHY

Arrow, K.J. 1959. Towards a theory of price adjustment. In *The Allocation of Economic Resources*, ed. M. Abramowitz, Stanford: Stanford University Press.

Arrow, K.J., Karlin, S. and Scarf, H. 1958. *Studies in the Mathematical Theory of Inventory and Production*. Stanford: Stanford University Press.

Barro, R.J., and Grossman, H.I. 1971. A general disequilibrium model of income and employment. *American Economic Review* 61, 82–93.

Barro, R.J., and Grossman, H.I. 1976. *Money, Employment and Inflation*. Cambridge and New York: Cambridge University Press.

Bellman, R. 1957. *Dynamic Programming*. Princeton: Princeton University Press.

Benassy, J.P. 1975. Neo-Keynesian disequilibrium theory in a monetary economy. *Review of Economic Studies* 42, 502–23.

Benassy, J.P. 1976. The disequilibrium approach to monopolistic price setting and general monopolistic equilibrium. *Review of Economic Studies* 43, 69–81.

Benassy, J.P. 1977a. A Neo-Keynesian model of price and quantity determination in disequilibrium. In *Equilibrium and Disequilibrium in Economic Theory*, ed. G. Schwodiauer, Boston: D. Reidel Publishing Company.

Benassy, J.P. 1977b. On quantity signals and the foundations of effective demand theory. *Scandinavian Journal of Economics* 79, 147–68.

Benassy, J.P. 1982. *The Economics of Market Disequilibrium*. New York: Academic Press.

Benassy, J.P. 1986. *Macroeconomics: An Introduction to the Non-Walrasian Approach*. New York: Academic Press.

Bushaw, D.W., and Clower, R. 1957. *Introduction to Mathematical Economics*. Homewood, Ill.: Richard D. Irwin.

Chamberlin, E.H. 1933. *The Theory of Monopolistic Competition*. Cambridge, Mass.: Harvard University Press.

Clower, R.W. 1965. The Keynesian counterrevolution: a theoretical appraisal. In *The Theory of Interest Rates*, ed. F.H. Hahn and F.P.R. Brechling, London: Macmillan; New York: St. Martin's Press.

Cuddington, J.T., Johansson, P.O. and Lofgren, K.G. 1984. *Disequilibrium Macroeconomics in Open Economies*. Oxford: Basil Blackwell.

Drèze, J.H. 1975. Existence of an exchange equilibrium under price rigidities. *International Economic Review* 16, 301–20.

Grossman, H.I. 1972. A choice-theoretic model of an income investment accelerator. *American Economic Review* 62, 630–41.

Hahn, F.H. and Negishi, T. 1962. A theorem on non tatonnement stability. *Econometrica* 30, 463–9.

Hansen, B. 1951. *A Study in the Theory of Inflation*. London: Allen & Unwin; New York: Rinehart.

Hicks, J.R. 1965. *Capital and Growth*. London and New York: Oxford University Press.

Hildenbrand, K. and Hildenbrand, W. 1978. On Keynesian equilibria with unemployment and quantity rationing. *Journal of Economic Theory* 18, 255–77.

Keynes, J.M. 1936. *The General Theory of Money, Interest and Employment*. New York: Harcourt Brace.

Keynes, J.M. 1937. Alternative theories of the rate of interest. *Economic Journal* 47, 241–52.

Leijonhufvud, A. 1968. *On Keynesian Economics and the Economics of Keynes*. Oxford and New York: Oxford University Press.

Machlup, F. 1958. Equilibrium and disequilibrium: misplaced concreteness and disguised politics. *Economic Journal* 68, 1–24.

Malinvaud, E. 1977. *The Theory of Unemployment Reconsidered*. Oxford: Basil Blackwell; New York: Wiley.

Muellbauer, J. and Portes, R. 1978. Macroeconomic models with quantity rationing. *Economic Journal* 88, 788–821.

Neary, J.P. and Stiglitz, J.E. 1983. Towards a reconstruction of Keynesian economics: expectations and constrained equilibria. *Quarterly Journal of Economics* 98, supplement, 199–228.

Negishi, T. 1961. Monopolistic competition and general equilibrium. *Review of Economic Studies* 28, 196–201.

Negishi, T. 1979. *Microeconomic Foundations of Keynesian Macroeconomics*. Amsterdam: North-Holland.

Patinkin, D. 1956. *Money, Interest and Prices*. New York: Row, Peterson & Co.; 2nd edn, New York: Harper & Row, 1965.

Portes, R. 1981. Macroeconomic equilibrium and disequilibrium in centrally planned economies. *Economic Inquiry* 19, 559–78.

Quandt, R.E. 1982. Econometric disequilibrium models. *Econometric Review* 1, 1–63.

Robinson, J. 1933. *The Economics of Imperfect Competition*. London: Macmillan; New York: St. Martin's Press, 1954.

Samuelson, P.A. 1947. *Foundations of Economic Analysis*. Cambridge, Mass.: Harvard University Press.

Tobin, J. and Houthakker, H.S. 1950. The effects of rationing on demand elasticities. *Review of Economic Studies* 18, 140–53.

Triffin, R. 1940. *Monopolistic Competition and General Equilibrium Theory*. Cambridge, Mass.: Harvard University Press.

Younès, Y. 1975. On the role of money in the process of exchange and the existence of a non-Walrasian equilibrium. *Review of Economic Studies* 42, 489–501.

Existence of General Equilibrium

GERARD DEBREU

Léon Walras provided in his *Eléments d'économie politique pure* (1874–7) an answer to an outstanding scientific question raised by several of his predecessors. Notably, Adam Smith had asked in *An Inquiry into the Nature and Causes of the Wealth of Nations* (1776) why a large number of agents motivated by self-interest and making independent decisions do not create social chaos in a private ownership economy. Smith himself had gained a deep insight into the impersonal coordination of those decisions by markets for commodities. Only a mathematical model, however, could take into full account the interdependence of the variables involved. In constructing such a model Walras founded the theory of general economic equilibrium.

Walras and his successors were aware that his theory would be vacuous in the absence of an argument supporting the existence of its central concept. But for more than half a century that argument went no further than counting equations and unknowns and finding them to be equal in number. Yet for a non-linear system this equality does not prove that there is a solution. Nor would it provide a proof even for a linear system, especially when some of the unknowns are not allowed to take arbitrary real values.

A successful attack on the problem of existence of a general equilibrium was made possible by an exceptional conjunction of circumstances in Vienna in the early 1930s. It started from the formulation of the Walrasian model in terms of demand functions which had been given by Gustav Cassel in 1918. As Hans Neisser (1932) noted, certain values of commodity quantities and prices appearing in the solutions of Cassel's system of equations might be negative in such a way as to render those solutions meaningless. Heinrich von Stackelberg (1933) also made a cogent remark. Let x_i be the quantity of the ith final good demanded by consumers, a_{ij} the fixed technical coefficient specifying the input of the jth primary resource required for a unit output of the ith final good, and r_j the available quantity of the jth primary resource. The equality of demand and supply for every resource is expressed by

$$\sum_i a_{ij} x_i = r_j \qquad \text{for all } j.$$

Von Stackelberg observed that if there are fewer final goods than primary resources, the preceding linear system of equations in $(x_1, \ldots, x_m)$ has, in general, no solution. Karl Schlesinger (1933–4) then remarked that equalities should be replaced by inequalities

$$\sum_i a_{ij} x_i \leqq r_j \qquad \text{for all } j,$$

with the condition that a resource for which the strict inequality holds has a zero price. This suggestion, which had already been hinted at by Frederik Zeuthen (1932) in a different context, was essential to the proper formulation of the existence problem.

The problem thus posed received its first solution from Abraham Wald (1933–4), whose work on the existence of a general equilibrium gave rise to three published articles. The first two appeared in *Ergebnisse eines mathematischen Kolloquiums* in 1933–4 and in 1934–5. The third appeared in *Zeitschrift für Nationalökonomie* (1936) and was translated into English in *Econometrica* (1951). In that body of work Wald separately studied a model of production and a model of exchange and proved the existence of an equilibrium for each one.

By the standards prevailing in economic theory at that time, his mathematical arguments were of great complexity, and the major contribution that he had made did not attract the attention of the economics profession. A two-decade pause followed, and when research on the existence problem started again after 1950 it was under the dominant influence of work done, also in the early 1930s, by John von Neumann. His article on the theory of growth, published in *Ergebnisse eines mathematischen Kolloquiums* (1935–6) and translated into English in the *Review of Economic Studies* (1945), contained in particular a lemma of critical importance. That lemma was reformulated in the following far more convenient form, and was also given a significantly simpler proof, by Shizuo Kakutani (1941). Let K be a non-empty, compact, convex set of finite dimension. Associate with every point x in K a non-empty, convex subset $\phi(x)$ of K, and assume that the graph $G = \{(x, y) \in K \times K \mid y \in \phi(x)\}$ of the transformation ϕ is closed. Then ϕ has a fixed point x^*, i.e., a point x^* that belongs to its image $\phi(x^*)$.

Kakutani's theorem was applied by John Nash, in a one-page note of 1950, to establish the existence of an equilibrium for a finite game. It can be used as well (Debreu, 1952) to prove the existence of an equilibrium for a more general system composed of n agents. The ith agent chooses an action a_i in a set A_i of *a priori* possible actions. A state of the social system is therefore described by the list $a = (a_1, \ldots, a_n)$ of the actions chosen by the n agents. The preferences of the ith agent are represented by a real-valued utility function u_i defined for every a in the set of states $A = \times_{i=1}^{n} A_i$. Moreover the ith agent is restricted in the choice of his action in A_i by the actions chosen by the other agents. Formally let N denote the set $\{1, \ldots, n\}$ of all the agents and $N \setminus i$ denote the set of the agents other than the ith. Let also $a_{N \setminus i}$ denote the list of the actions $(a_1, \ldots, a_{i-1}, a_{i+1}, \ldots, a_n)$ chosen by the agents in $N \setminus i$. The ith agent is constrained to choose his own action in a subset $\phi_i(a_{N \setminus i})$ of A_i depending on $a_{N \setminus i}$. In these conditions the ith agent, considering $a_{N \setminus i}$ as given, chooses his action in $\mu_i(a_{N \setminus i})$, the set of the elements of $\phi_i(a_{N \setminus i})$ at which the maximum of the utility function $u_i(\cdot, a_{N \setminus i})$ in $\phi_i(a_{N \setminus i})$ is attained. Consider now the transformation $a \mapsto \mu(a) = \times_{i=1}^{n} \mu_i(a_{N \setminus i})$ associating with any element a of A, the subset $\mu(a)$ of A. A state a^* is an equilibrium if and only if for every $i \in N$, the action a_i^* of the ith agent is best according to his preferences given the actions $a_{N \setminus i}^*$ of the others, that is, if and only if for every $i \in N$, $a_i^* \in \mu_i(a_{N \setminus i}^*)$, that is, if and only if $a^* \in \mu(a^*)$. Thus the concept of an equilibrium for the social system is equivalent to the concept of a fixed point for the transformation $a \mapsto \mu(a)$ of elements of A into subsets of A. Ensuring that the assumptions of Kakutani's theorem are satisfied for the transformation μ yields a proof of existence of an equilibrium for the social system.

In the revival of interest in the problem of existence of a general economic equilibrium after 1950, the first solutions were published in 1954 by Kenneth Arrow and Gerard Debreu, and by Lionel McKenzie. The article by McKenzie emphasized international trade aspects, and the article by Arrow and Debreu dealt with an integrated model of production and consumption. Both rested their proofs on Kakutani's theorem. They were followed over the next three decades by a large number of publications (a bibliography is given in Debreu, 1982) which confirmed the concept of a Kakutani fixed point as the most powerful mathematical tool for proofs of existence of a general equilibrium.

A simple prototype of the various economies that were the subject of those numerous existence results is (following Arrow–Debreu) composed of m consumers and n producers, producing, exchanging and consuming l commodities. The consumption of the ith consumer ($i = 1, \ldots, m$) is a vector x_i in R^l whose positive (or negative) components are his inputs (or outputs) of the l commodities. Similarly the production of the jth producer ($j = 1, \ldots, n$) is a vector y_j in R^l whose negative (or positive) components are his inputs (or outputs) of the l commodities. The ith consumer has three characteristics. (1) His consumption set X_i, a non-empty subset of R^l, is the set of his possible consumptions. (2) A binary relation $\preceq_i$ on X_i defines his preferences, and '$x_i \preceq_i x_i'$' is read as 'x_i' is at least as desired as x_i by the ith consumer'. Formally the preference relation of the ith consumer is the set $\{(x, x') \in X_i \times X_i \mid x \preceq_i x'\}$. (3) A vector e_i in R^l describes his initial endowment of commodities. The jth producer has one characteristic, his production set Y_j, a non-empty subset of R^l defining his possible productions. Finally the number $\theta_{ij} \geq 0$ specifies the fraction of the profit of the jth producer distributed to the ith consumer. These numbers satisfy the equality $\Sigma_{i=1}^{m} \theta_{ij} = 1$ for every j. In summary, the economy $\mathscr{E}$ is characterized by the list of mathematical objects

$$\left[(X_i, \precsim_i, e_i)_{i=1,\ldots,m}, (Y_j)_{j=1,\ldots,n}, (\theta_{ij})_{\substack{i=1,\ldots,m \\ j=1,\ldots,n}} \right].$$

Given a price-vector p in R^l different from 0, the jth producer $(j = 1, \ldots, n)$ chooses a production y_j in Y_j that maximizes his profit, that is, such that the value $p \cdot y_j$ of y_j relative to p satisfies the inequality $p \cdot y_j \geqq p \cdot y$ for every y in Y_j. Thus the ith consumer receives in addition to the value $p \cdot e_i$ of his endowment, $\Sigma_{j=1}^{n} \theta_{ij} p \cdot y_j$ as the sum of his shares of the profits of the n producers. The value $p \cdot x$ of his consumption x is therefore constrained by the budget inequality $p \cdot x \leqq p \cdot e_i + \Sigma_{j=1}^{n} \theta_{ij} p \cdot y_j$. Under the constraint he chooses a consumption x_i in X_i that is best according to his preferences. The list $[p, (x_i)_{i=1,\ldots,m}, (y_j)_{j=1,\ldots,n}]$ of a non-zero price-vector, m consumptions and n productions forms a general equilibrium of the economy $\mathscr{E}$ if for every commodity, the excess of demand over supply vanishes,

$$\sum_{i=1}^{m} x_i - \sum_{j=1}^{n} y_j - \sum_{i=1}^{m} e_i = 0.$$

The existence of a general equilibrium can be proved (following Arrow–Debreu) by casting the economy $\mathscr{E}$ in the form of a social system of the type defined above. For this it suffices to introduce, in addition to the m consumers and to the n producers, a fictitious price-setting agent whose set of actions and whose utility function are now specified. Note first that the definition of a general equilibrium is invariant under multiplication of the price-vector p by a strictly positive real number. In the simple case where all prices are non-negative, one can therefore restrict p to be an element of the simplex $P = \{p \in R^l_+ | \Sigma_{h=1}^{l} p^h = 1\}$, the set of the vectors in R^l whose components are non-negative and add up to one. The set of actions of the price-setter is specified to be P. Given the consumptions $(x_i)_{i=1,\ldots,m}$ chosen by the m consumers, and the productions $(y_j)_{j=1,\ldots,n}$ chosen by the n producers, there results an excess demand

$$z = \sum_{i=1}^{m} x_i - \sum_{j=1}^{n} y_j - \sum_{i=1}^{m} e_i.$$

The utility function of the price-setter is specified to be $p \cdot z$. Maximizing the function $p \mapsto p \cdot z$ over P carries to one extreme the idea that the price-setter should choose high prices for the commodities that are in excess demand, and low prices for the commodities that are in excess supply.

Some of the assumptions on which the theorems of Arrow–Debreu (1954) are based are weak technical conditions: closedness of the consumption-sets, of the production-sets and of the preference relations, existence of a lower bound in every coordinate for each consumption-set, possibility of a null production for each producer. Other assumptions were later shown to be superfluous for economies with a finite set of agents: irreversibility of production (if both y and $-y$ are possible aggregate productions, then $y = 0$), free disposal (any aggregate production $y \leq 0$ is possible), and completeness and transitivity of preferences. Convexity of preferences can be dispensed with, and convexity of consumption-sets can be weakened, in economies with a large number of small consumers. Insatiability of consumers is an acceptable behavioural postulate. There remain, however, two overly strong assumptions. They are the hypothesis that for every i, the endowment e_i yields a possible consumption for the ith consumer (after disposal of a suitable commodity-vector if need be), and the assumption of convexity on the total production-set $Y = \Sigma_{j=1}^n Y_j$ which implies non-increasing returns to scale in the aggregate.

An alternative approach to the problem of existence of a general equilibrium, closer to traditional economic theory, is centred on the concept of excess demand function, or of excess demand correspondence. Given an economy $\mathscr{E}$ defined as before, consider a price-vector p in R_+^l different from 0. The productions $(y_1, \ldots, y_n)$ chosen by the producers, and the consumptions $(x_1, \ldots, x_m)$ chosen by the consumers in reaction to the price-vector p result in an excess demand z in the commodity-space R^l. If z is uniquely determined, the excess demand function f from $R_+^l \setminus 0$ to R^l is thereby defined. If z is not uniquely determined, the set of excess demands in R^l associated with p is denoted by $\phi(p)$, and the excess demand correspondence ϕ is thereby defined on $R_+^l \setminus 0$. Both f and ϕ are homogeneous of degree zero since $f(p)$ and $\phi(p)$ are invariant under multiplication of p by a strictly positive real number. This permits various normalizations of p. For instance, p may be restricted to the simplex P. Moreover, for every $i = 1, \ldots, m$, one has $p \cdot x_i \leq p \cdot e_i + \Sigma_{j=1}^n \theta_{ij} p \cdot y_j$. By summation over i, one obtains

$$p \cdot \sum_{i=1}^m x_i \leq p \cdot \sum_{i=1}^m e_i + p \cdot \sum_{j=1}^n p \cdot y_j,$$

or equivalently $p \cdot z \leq 0$. Therefore for every p in $R_+^l \setminus 0$, one has either $p \cdot f(p) \leq 0$ or $p \cdot \phi(p) \leq 0$. This observation leads to the following proof of existence of a general equilibrium (Gale, 1955; Nikaidô, 1956; Debreu, 1956). Let ϕ be a correspondence transforming points of the simplex P into non-empty convex subsets of R^l. If ϕ is bounded, has a closed graph and satisfies $p \cdot \phi(p) \leq 0$ for every p in P, then, by Kakutani's theorem, there are a point p^* in P and a point z^* in R^l such that $z^* \in \phi(p^*)$ and $z^* \leq 0$. In economic terms, there is a price-vector p^* in P yielding an associated excess demand z^* in $\phi(p^*)$, all of whose components are negative or zero.

If all the consumers in the economy $\mathscr{E}$ are insatiable, every individual budget constraint is binding, and one has for every i, $p \cdot x_i = p \cdot e_i + \Sigma_{j=1}^n \theta_{ij} p \cdot y_j$. By summation over i, $p \cdot z = 0$. Thus in the case where the vector z associated with p is uniquely determined, the excess demand function satisfies

Walras's Law: for every p in $R_+^l \setminus 0$, $p \cdot f(p) = 0$.

In geometric terms, in the commodity-price space R^l the vectors p and $f(p)$ are orthogonal. This prompts one to normalize the price-vector p so that it belongs to the positive part of the unit sphere $\bar{S} = \{p \in R_+^l \mid \|p\| = 1\}$, for then $f(p)$ can be represented as a vector tangent to $\bar{S}$ at p. The excess demand function is now seen as a vector field on $\bar{S}$. This in turn suggests another proof of existence of a general equilibrium (Dierker, 1974) for the particular case of an exchange economy $\mathscr{E}$ whose consumers have continuous demand functions, monotone preferences and strictly positive endowments of all commodities. In that case for every $i = 1, \ldots, m$, the consumption-set X_i of the ith consumer is R^l_+, and $x < x'$ implies $x \prec_i x'$ (if x' is at least equal to x in every component and $x' \neq x$, then x' is preferred to x). Since the demand of a consumer with monotone preferences is not defined when some prices vanish, one must restrict the price-vector p to be strictly positive in every component, that is, to belong to $S = \{p \in \text{Interior } R^l_+ \mid \|p\| = 1\}$. Moreover let p_q be a sequence of price vectors in S converging to p_0 in the boundary $\bar{S} \setminus S$ of S. Thus for every q, the vector p_q is strictly positive in each component, while, in the limit, p_0 has some zero components. Then the associated sequence of excess demands $f(p_q)$ is unbounded. As a consequence, the vector field f points inward towards S near the boundary of S. In these conditions Brouwer's fixed point theorem yields the existence of an equilibrium price-vector p^* in S for which excess demand vanishes, $f(p^*) = 0$.

The preceding solutions of the problem of existence of a general equilibrium all rest directly on fixed point theorems. Three different lines of approach are provided by (1) combinatorial algorithms for the computation of approximate general equilibria, (2) differential processes converging to general equilibria, (3) the theory of the fixed point index of a mapping.

(1) The past two decades have witnessed the development of algorithms of a combinatorial nature for the computation of an approximate general equilibrium (*see* COMPUTATION OF GENERAL EQUILIBRIA above). Given any number $\varepsilon > 0$, a constructive procedure thereby yields a price-vector p such that the norm $|f(p)|$ of the associated excess demand is smaller than ε. A compactness argument then gives a sequence of price-vectors p_q in S converging to p_0 for which $|f(p_1)|$ tends to 0. In the limit, $f(p_0) = 0$.

(2) Global Analysis was introduced into economic theory at the beginning of the 1970s to study the set of general equilibria of an economy and the manner in which it depends on the economy. In that framework Stephen Smale proposed in (1976) a differential process which starts from a point in the boundary of the set of normalized price-vectors, and which converges to the set of equilibria provided that the initial point does not lie in a negligible exception set (*see* GLOBAL ANALYSIS). Another constructive procedure thus gives, from a differentiable viewpoint, conditions under which the set of general equilibria is not empty.

(3) In the same differentiable framework Egbert Dierker (1972) used the theory of the fixed point index of a mapping to prove that a regular economy (as defined by him in REGULAR ECONOMIES below) whose excess demand points inward near the boundary of S has an odd (hence non-zero) number of general equilibria. The significance of this theorem rests on the fact that under its assumptions almost every economy is regular.

The previous existence results have been extended in many directions. The study of the core of an economy led to the consideration of a set of agents, all of whom are negligible relative to their totality. This concept was formalized first as an atomless measure space of agents, and later by means of non-standard analysis. In both cases the existence of a general equilibrium had to be proved for economies with infinitely many agents.

In order to specify a commodity one lists its physical characteristics, the date, the location, and the event at which it is available. As soon as one of those four variables can take infinitely many values, the analysis of general equilibrium must be set in the framework of infinite-dimensional commodity spaces. Several existence results were obtained in that context.

In yet another direction, external effects called for extensions. When the characteristics of each agent (e.g. his preferences, his production set, ...) depend on the actions chosen by the other agents, formulating the economy as a social system of the type described earlier immediately yields an existence theorem. Still other extensions have covered economies with public goods, with indivisible commodities, and with non-convex production sets.

BIBLIOGRAPHY

Arrow, K.J. and Debreu, G. 1954. Existence of an equilibrium for a competitive economy. *Econometrica* 22, 265–90.

Arrow, K.J. and Intriligator, M.D. (eds) 1981–6. *Handbook of Mathematical Economics*, Vols I–III, Amsterdam: North-Holland.

Cassel, K.G. 1918. *Theoretische Sozialökonomie.* Leipzig: C.F. Winter Trans. as *The Theory of Social Economy*, New York: Harcourt, 1932.

Debreu, G. 1952. A social equilibrium existence theorem. *Proceedings of the National Academy of Sciences* 38, 886–93.

Debreu, G. 1956. Market equilibrium. *Proceedings of the National Academy of Sciences* 42, 876–8.

Debreu, G. 1982. Existence of competitive equilibrium. Ch. 15 in Arrow and Intriligator (1981–6).

Dierker, E. 1972. Two remarks on the number of equilibria of an economy. *Econometrica* 40, 951–3.

Dierker, E. 1974. *Topological Methods in Walrasian Economics.* Berlin, New York: Springer-Verlag.

Gale, D. 1955. The law of supply and demand, *Mathematica Scandinavica* 3, 155–69.

Kakutani, S. 1941. A generalization of Brouwer's fixed point theorem. *Duke Mathematical Journal* 8, 457–9.

McKenzie, L.W. 1954. On equilibrium in Graham's model of world trade and other competitive systems. *Econometrica* 22, 147–61.

Nash, J.F. 1950. Equilibrium points in N-person games. *Proceedings of the National Academy of Sciences of the USA* 36, 48–9.

Neisser, H. 1932. Lohnhöhe und Beschäftigungsgrad im Marktgleichgewicht. *Weltwirtschaftliches Archiv* 36, 415–55.

Neumann, J. von 1935–36. Über ein ökonomisches Gleichungssystem und eine Verallgemeinerung des Brouwerschen Fixpunktsatzes. *Ergebnisse eines mathematischen Kolloquiums* 8, 73–83. Trans. by G. Morgenstern as 'A model of general economic equilibrium', *Review of Economic Studies* 13(1), 1945, 1–9.

Nikaidô, H. 1956. On the classical multilateral exchange problem. *Metroeconomica* 8, 135–45.

Schlesinger, K. 1933–4. Über die Produktionsgleichungen der ökonomischen Wertlehre. *Ergebnisse eines mathematischen Kolloquiums* 6, 10–20.

Smale, S. 1976. A convergent process of price adjustment and global Newton methods. *Journal of Mathematical Economics* 3, 107–20.

Smith, A. 1776. *An Inquiry into the Nature and Causes of the Wealth of Nations.* 2 vols, ed. R.H. Campbell, A.S. Skinner and W.B. Todd, Oxford: Clarendon Press, 1976.

von Stackelberg, H. 1933. Zwei kritische Bemerkungen zur Preistheorie Gustav Cassels. *Zeitschrift für Nationalökonomie* 4, 456–72.

Wald, A. 1933–4. Über die eindeutige positive Lösbarkeit der neuen Produktionsgleichungen. *Ergebnisse eines mathematischen Kolloquiums* 6, 12–20.

Wald, A. 1934–5. Über die Produktionsgleichungen der ökonomischen Wertlehre. *Ergebnisse eines mathematischen Kolloquiums* 7, 1–6.

Wald, A. 1936. Über einige Gleichungssystem der mathematischen Ökonomie. *Zeitschrift für Nationalökonomie* 7, 637–70. Trans. by Otto Eckstein as 'On some systems of equations of mathematical economics', *Econometrica* 19(4), October 1951, 368–403.

Walras, L. 1874–7. *Éléments d'économie politique pure.* Lausanne: L. Corbaz. Trans. by William Jaffé as *Elements of Pure Economics*, Homewood, Ill.: Richard D. Irwin, 1954.

Zeuthen, F. 1932. Das Prinzip der Knappheit, technische Kombination und ökonomische Qualität. *Zeitschrift für Nationalökonomie* 4, 1–24.

Fixed Point Theorems

HUKUKANE NIKAIDO

An economic system, which consists of a number of relationships among the relevant factors, is modelled as a system of equations or inequalities of certain unknowns, whose solution represents a specific state in which the system settles. This is typically exemplified by the Walrasian competitive economy (Walras, 1874), consisting of the interaction of manifold behaviours of many individual agents with different motivations, whose specific state is a competitive equilibrium in which certain prices of goods solve the system of equations representing the simultaneous clearing of all the markets of goods so as to make those individual behaviours mutually consistent.

An economic theory is the formulation of an economic system and the elucidation of its structural and performance characteristics. It is then a primary premise of the theory, on which all its developments are built, that its modelled system be consistent in the sense that the corresponding system of equations or inequalities has a solution. Without this consistency the theory is void. For the Walrasian competitive economy the existence of a competitive equilibrium is the premise.

Conventionally, economists satisfied themselves about the existence of a solution of the relevant system of equations on the ground that there are as many equations as unknowns, a rule of thumb, which, though it is a criterion for the consistency of a system of equations in general, is neither necessary nor sufficient for the existence of a solution of a given specific system of equations.

It was generally realized in the 1950s that to deal properly with the existence of solutions of systems of equations it is necessary to rely on more sophisticated mathematical methods, among others concepts and theorems in topology, which was dawning around the beginning of the 20th century and has by now grown to a highly advanced field in contemporary mathematics. Fixed point theorems are the most notable ones among them.

Stated in the most indefinite form, a fixed point theorem is a proposition which asserts that a mapping f that transforms each point x of a set X to a point $f(x)$

139

within X has a fixed point x^* that is transformed to itself, so that $f(x^*) = x^*$. An arbitrary mapping need not have a fixed point, and the truth of a fixed point theorem hinges on the behavioural properties of the mapping and the structural properties of the set on which the mapping is defined.

A fixed point theorem, the first of such theorems in topology, was formulated and proved by Brouwer (1910), a great master in mathematics. It asserts the existence of a fixed point in the case where X is the set of all those points in the n-dimensional Euclidean space whose coordinates are non-negative and add up to unity, called a *simplex*, and where the mapping f transforms points within X in a continuous way.

This theorem has been used in existence problems arising in many fields, mainly in physical sciences. In economics it was used for the first time by von Neumann (1937) to prove the existence of a balanced growth path and an associated set of equilibrium prices in his multisectoral model of an expanding economy. Later in the 1950s it was applied in its original or extended versions to prove the existence of a competitive equilibrium in the Walrasian economy almost simultaneously by several authors (Arrow and Debreu, 1954; McKenzie, 1954; Gale, 1955 and Nikaido, 1956).

Brouwer's theorem still holds good in cases where the set X is not the simplex but a set topologically equivalent to the simplex, which is by definition the image of the simplex under a one-to-one continuous mapping. Bounded, closed, convex sets in the Euclidean space are sets of the simplest structure among the sets topologically equivalent to the simplex. The boundedness of a set means that the distance between any two points within it can not be indefinitely large, but has a uniform bound. The closedness of a set means that there is no point outside it which can be approached as closely as one likes from its inside. The convexity of a set means that any two points x, y can be joined by a segment within it that is represented by $tx + (1 - t)y$, $(1 \geqslant t \geqslant 0)$. These three properties are often possessed by sets of relevant variables that arise in economic models.

The procedure by which von Neumann reduced the solution of the existence problem for his model of an expanding economy to Bouwer's fixed point theorem was very involved, but suggested a generalization of the concept of a fixed point on which to formulate an extension of the theorem, that fits economic models better in dealing with the existence problems arising in them. This extension was carried out by Kakutani (1941).

Kakutani's fixed point theorem pertains to a multi-valued mapping, a generalized version of the ordinary single-valued mapping. In the generalization a mapping f associates with each point x of a set X a set $f(x)$. Such a mapping is called a *point-to-set* mapping, a *set-valued* mapping or a *correspondence*. For a set-valued mapping f a fixed point x^* is a point which is included in its image, $x^* \in f(x^*)$. Regarding the way a set-valued mapping transforms points to sets there is a concept of continuity which is a counterpart of that for ordinary single-valued mappings. f is said to be *upper semi-continuous*, or *upper hemi-continuous*, if at each point x the image sets $f(y)$ of its nearby points y are very close to $f(x)$; formally, if for any neighbourhood U of $f(x)$ at each point x there is a neighbourhood V of x such that the image $f(y)$ of any point y belonging to V is included in U.

Kakutani's fixed point theorem states that if a set-valued mapping f transforms each point x of a bounded closed convex set X in the Euclidean space to a non-empty closed convex subset of X in an upper semi-continuous way, then there is a fixed point $x^* \in f(x^*)$.

Fixed point theorems in the Brouwer–Kakutani line are very powerful in solving existence problems arising in a number of important economic models. The following are typical examples of their use in the solution of such problems.

(a) Existence of an equilibrium point in a many-person noncooperative game (Nash, 1950). Let $K_i(x_1, x_2, \ldots, x_n)$ be the payoff function of the ith player, continuous with respect to the n-tuple of the players' strategies x_i, each of which is chosen from among the strategy set X_i, closed, bounded and convex for $i = 1, 2, \ldots, n$, where n is the number of players. An equilibrium point, which is such a special n-tuple of strategies $(x_1^*, x_2^*, \ldots, x_n^*)$ that x maximizes the ith player's payoff given that the other players' strategies are x_j^* ($j \neq 1$), is obtained as a fixed point of a mapping. The relevant set-valued mapping f is that which transforms each n-tuple of strategies $(x_1, x_2, \ldots, x_n)$ to the cartesian product of M_i ($i = 1, 2, \ldots, n$), where M_i is the set of the ith player's strategies that maximize his payoff given that the other players' strategies are x_j ($j \neq i$), and is assumed to be convex. f transforms each point $(x_1, x_2, \ldots, x_n)$ to the closed convex set $M_1 \times M_2 \times \ldots \times M_n$ within the cartesian product $X_1 \times X_2 \times \ldots \times X_n$, a bounded closed convex set in the Euclidean space in an upper semi-continuous way, and has a fixed point by virtue of Kakutani's fixed point theorem.

(b) Existence of a competitive equilibrium in the Walrasian competitive economy. The Walrasian competitive economy is modelled as a national economy-wide system consisting of profit-maximizing producers and utility-maximizing households in the most articulate fashion by Arrow and Debreu (1954) and Debreu (1959). A competitive equilibrium is a specific state of the system where at some prices of goods these manifold individual price-taking maximization behaviours are mutually consistent. It can be characterized as simultaneous market clearing for all goods in terms of excess demand functions of the prices that are derived from the individual maximization behaviours, and its possibility is ensured by Kakutani's fixed point theorem (Gale, 1955; Nikaido, 1956; Debreu, 1959).

Simultaneous market clearing, which is referred to as Walras's theorem can be stated as follows: Let an excess demand function ϕ associated with each n-tuple of prices $p_1, p_2, \ldots, p_n$ non-negative and adding up to unity a non-empty bounded, closed and convex subset $\phi(p_1, p_2, \ldots, p_n)$ of an n-dimensional Euclidean space, consisting of points with coordinates that represent excess demands for goods, in an upper semi-continuous way; and let Walras's Law,

$$\sum_{i=1}^{n} p_i e_i = 0$$

be satisfies for any excess demand vector $(e_1, e_2, \ldots, e_n)$ included in $\phi(p_1, p_2, \ldots, p_n)$.

Then there are specific prices $(p_1^*, p_2^*, \ldots, p_n^*)$ at which the corresponding set $\phi(p_1^*, p_2^*, \ldots, p_n^*)$ includes a special excess demand vector $(e_1^*, e_2^*, \ldots, e_n^*)$ with nonpositive excess demands $e_i^* \leqslant 0$ for all goods $i = 1, 2, \ldots, n$, and $e_i^* = 0$ for goods whose prices p_i^* are positive.

The excess demand function ϕ turns out to be bounded in the sense that there is a bounded closed convex set E large enough to include $\phi(p_1, p_2, \ldots, p_n)$ for all points $p = (p_1, p_2, \ldots, p_n)$ in the simplex. Thus the competitive equilibrium is obtained by Kakutani's fixed point theorem as a fixed point of the mapping f which transforms each pair (p, d) of a point p in the simplex and an excess demand vector $d = (d_1, d_2, \ldots, d_n)$ in E to the set of all pairs (q, e), e chosen from among $\phi(p_1, p_2, \ldots, p_n)$ and $q = (q_1, q_2, \ldots, q_n)$ with the coordinates

$$q_i = [p_i + \max(d_i, 0)] \bigg/ \left[1 + \sum_{j=1}^{n} \max(d_j, 0) \right], \qquad (i = 1, 2, \ldots, n).$$

The mapping f transforms points to closed convex sets in an upper semi-continuous way within the cartesian product X of the simplex and E, a bounded closed convex set, so that Kakutani's fixed point theorem applies to f on X. At a fixed point (p^*, e^*) hold.

$$e^* \in \phi(p_1^*, p_2^*, \ldots, p_n^*)$$

$$p_i^* = [p_i^* + \max(e_i^*, 0)] \bigg/ \left[1 + \sum_{j=1}^{n} \max(e_j^*, 0) \right]$$

so that

$$\sum_{i=1}^{n} p_i^* e_i^* = 0$$

$$p_i^* \sum_{j=1}^{n} \max(e_j^*, 0) = \max(e_i^*, 0), \qquad (i = 1, 2, \ldots, n),$$

which rules out the possibility that some e_i^* are positive, and implies $e_i^* = 0$ for i such as $p_i^* > 0$.

As a mathematical result Brouwer's fixed point theorem is deeply rooted in the profound topological nature of Euclidean space, which necessitates the complexity of its methods of proof. The most straightforward proof, which is due to Knaser, Kuratowski and Mazurkiewicz (1929), is based on a combinatorial theorem known as Sperner's lemma (Sperner, 1928) on subdivisions of the simplex to small simplices. Kakutani's fixed point theorem is proved by applying Brouwer's theorem to single-valued mappings approximating the given set-valued mapping.

In the late 1960s computational algorithms were developed by Scarf (1973) to approximate as closely as one likes the fixed points in the theorems in the Brouwer–Kakutani line, based on his new combinatorial theorem, similar to but distinct from Sperner's lemma, on fine grids of small simplices lying in the simplex. They serve as efficient procedures to locate fixed points explicitly, and also effect an alternative proof of Brouwer's theorem.

142

The Kakutani fixed point theorem has by now been further extended to cases where the set X, on which the relevant mapping f works, is of a more complex structure. The result due to Eilenberg and Montgomery (1946), which is representative of these extensions, asserts the existence of a fixed point in the case where a mapping f transforms points to *acyclic* subsets in an upper semi-continuous way within a set X which is a *compact, acyclic, absolute neighbourhood retract,* Compactness is a property of a set that is a counterpart in general spaces to boundedness and closedness combined together in Euclidean space, meaning that any nonvoid subset has at least an accumulation point within the set. The acyclicity of a set means that the set has the same homology groups as does a set consisting of a single point, and weakens *contractibility* in the sense that the set is continuously deformable to a single point within it, a very much generalized concept of convexity. Absolute neighbourhood retracts form so broad a category of sets that they include compact acyclic sets in infinite-dimensional linear spaces. The infinite-dimensional direct counterpart results of the Kakutani fixed point theorem by Fan (1952) and Glicksberg (1952) prove special cases of the Eilenberg–Montgomery theorem in direct elementary ways. These remarkable relaxations of assumptions of the Kakutani theorem broaden its applicability to economic models in which the sets of relevant variables are of more complex structures.

BIBLIOGRAPHY

Arrow, K.J. and Debreu, G. 1954. Existence of an equilibrium for a competitive economy. *Econometrica* 22, July, 265–90.

Brouwer, L.E.J. 1910. Über ein eindeutige, stetige Transformationen von Flächen in sich. *Mathematische Annalen* 69, 176–80.

Debreu, G. 1959. *Theory of Value: an Axiomatic Analysis of Economic Equilibrium,* Cowles Foundation Monograph No. 17, New York: John Wiley & Sons.

Eilenberg, S. and Montgomery, D. 1946. Fixed point theorems for multi-valued transformations. *American Journal of Mathematics* 68, 214–22.

Fan, K. 1952. Fixed point and minimax theorems in locally convex topological linear spaces. *Proceedings of the National Academy of Sciences of the USA* 38, 121–6.

Gale, D. 1955. The law of supply and demand. *Mathematica Scandinavica* 3, 155–69.

Glicksberg, I.L. 1952. A further generalization of the Kakutani fixed point theorem with application to Nash equilibrium points. *Proceedings of the American Mathematical Society* 3, 170–74.

Kakutani, S. 1941. A generalization of Brouwer's fixed point theorem. *Duke Mathematical Journal* 8(3), 457–9.

Knaster, B., Kuratowski, C. and Mazurkiewicz, S. 1929. Ein Beweis des Fixpunksatzes für n-dimensionale Simplexe. *Fundamenta Mathematica* 14, 132–7.

McKenzie, L.W. 1954. On equilibrium in Graham's model of world trade and other competitive systems. *Econometrica* 22, April, 147–61.

Nash, J.F. 1950. Equilibrium points in n-person games. *Proceedings of the National Academy of Sciences of the USA* 36, 48–9.

Neumann, J. von, 1937. Über ein ökonomisches Gleichungssystem und eine Verallgemeinerung des Brouwerschen Fixpunktsatzes, *Ergebnisse eines mathematischen Kolloquiums* 8.

Translated as 'A model of general economic equilibrium', *Review of Economic Studies* 13(33), 1945–6, 1–9.

Nikaido, H. 1956. On the classical multilateral exchange problem. *Metroeconomica* 8, August, 135–45; A supplementary note, 9, December 1957, 209–10.

Scarf, H. (with T. Hansen.) 1973. *The Computation of Economic Equilibria.* Cowles Foundation Monograph 24, New Haven and London: Yale University Press.

Sperner, E. 1928. Neuer Beweis für die Invarianz der Dimesionszahl und des Gebietes. Abhandlungen an den mathematischen, Seminar der Universität, Hamburg 6, 265–72.

Walras, L. 1874–7. *Eléments d'économie politique pure.* Lausanne: Corbaz. Trans. by W. Jaffé as *Elements of Pure Economics*, London: Allen & Unwin, 1954; New York: Orion, 1954.

Fixprice Models

JOAQUIM SILVESTRE

Modern fixprice theory (Benassy, 1975, 1976, 1982; Drèze, 1975; Younès, 1975) studies trade and production at non-Walrasian prices in general environments with possibly many agents and goods. The name and the basic logic originate in Hicks (1965) where a multiperiod economy is contemplated. Hicks defines two analytical methods: the Flexprice Method, which assumes that prices adjust within each period so that current transactions equal both demand and supply (such very short-run equilibration being, in his words, 'hard to swallow') and the Fixprice Method, where prices are given at the beginning of each period and transactions may differ from supply or demand. Both the Flexprice and the Fixprice methods are 'pure' or extreme ones. Hicks's own preference is 'for something which lies between', knowing that 'anything that does so must partake to some extent the difficulties of the two'. The general models discussed here follow Hicks's Fixprice Method. They are rather abstract, and they may alternatively be applied to the short period of *Capital and Growth* or to an atemporal economy.

In the Flexprice Method transactions take place at prices for which excess demand is zero. It may be interpreted that prices adjust very rapidly in response to excess demand and that no transactions occur before equilibrium is reached. A rigorous formulation of this idea is the Walras–Samuelson tâtonnement process. Consider an exchange economy with two commodities and two agents, agent i being initially endowed with ω_{ij} units of commodity $j (i, j = 1, 2)$. Let the aggregate Walrasian excess demand functions be $z^1(p_1, p_2|\omega)$. (Here the vector $\omega = (\omega_{ij})$ is fixed.) As long as $z^i(p_1, p_2|\omega) \neq 0$ or $z^2(p_1, p_2|\omega) \neq 0$ no transactions occur and prices adjust according to the differential equation:

$$(\mathrm{d}p_i/\mathrm{d}t) = z^i(p_1(t), p_2(t)|\omega), \qquad i = 1, 2.$$

The Walrasian excess demands provide the 'market signals' for the adjustment of prices.

The Walrasian excess demand functions express the plans of price taking agents, i.e., plans made under the conjecture that any quantities can be bought and sold at the going prices. If transactions at non-Walrasian prices occur then such a conjecture will be falsified, since some agents will be unable to realize their plans (see Arrow, 1959). This led Patinkin (1956) to postulate that disequilibrium transactions in a market create spillover effects on others, so that, e.g., 'the pressure of excess demand in the one market affects the price movements in all other markets' (p. 157). One could, for instance, write:

$$(dp_i/dt) = f_i(z^1(p_1(t), p_2(t)|\omega), z^2(p_1(t), p_2(t)|\omega)), \qquad i = 1, 2,$$

where f_1 is some function. Patinkin's formulation was imprecise (Negishi, 1965; Clower, 1965), but his search for the 'relevant market signals' motivates Clower's (1965) 'dual decision hypothesis' as a microeconomic foundation of Keynesian macroeconomics. This idea also developed by Leijonhufvud (1968) and generalized by Barro–Grossman (1971, 1976), is central to Benassy's fixprice model.

It was discovered in the late 1950s that the Walras–Samuelson tâtonnement process fails to converge unless some restrictive assumptions are imposed. This difficulty, now well understood but somehow surprising at the time, led to the formulation of the non-tâtonnement adjustment process. Here two simultaneous movements occur: the distribution of the endowments changes according to some rule for trading at non-Walrasian prices, and prices adjust in response to Walrasian excess demands at the current endowments, e.g. for some rule g_{ij},

$$(d\omega_{ij}/dt) = g_{ij}(p_1(t), p_2(t), \omega(t)),$$

$$(dp_i/dt) = z^i(p_1(t), p_2(t)|\omega(t)), \qquad i, j = 1, 2.$$

This process is hard to interpret except possibly as depicting the sequential exchange of durable goods (the mineral bourse mentioned in Smale, 1976). Moreover, it ignores the irrelevance of the Walrasian signals when transactions occur at non-Walrasian prices. But some conditions on disequilibrium trading (formally, on the functions g_{ij}, see Hahn–Negishi, 1962 and Uzawa, 1962) originally meant to guarantee the convergence of the non-tâtonnement process inspired basic features of the modern fixprice models (see Younès, 1975).

A third theoretical development of the early Sixties, namely the monopolistic general equilibrium analysis pioneered by Negishi (1960–61), led to extensions of the Fixprice model where agents on one side of the market may face nonhorizontal demand (oligopoly) or supply (oligopsony) curves and have price setting power. Such market power may be based on structural conditions on the economy as in Benassy (1976, 1977, 1982), Hart (1982), Silvestre (1987) (see also DISEQUILIBRIUM ANALYSIS and RATIONED EQUILIBRIA): prices and quantities are determined simultaneously and, usually, oligopoly (or oligopsony) is formally parallel to excess supply (or excess demand). Alternatively, an inequality between supply and demand gives temporary market power to agents on the short side who may then face nonhorizontal demand or supply curves for large enough quantities (see Arrow, 1959; Negishi, 1974, 1979; Hahn, 1978; John, 1985).

CONCEPTS

Modern fixprice analysis postulates explicit trading institutions called markets: in each market a commodity is exchanged against a common medium of exchange (money). Thus, there are $n + 1$ goods (from 0 to n) in the case of n markets, the zeroth good being money. This sharply contrasts with the institutional imprecision of the models alluded to in the previous section. The analysis addresses two questions: (1) Given a price vector p (normalized with respect to money), what allocations are compatible with it? (2) Given a p and an allocation compatible with it, which is the type of disequilibrium in each market? (Question 2 is a prerequisite to the study of the 'market signals' for price adjustment.) The answers are derived from three basic principles which reflect the operation of the market institution: (i) voluntary trading; (ii) absence of market frictions, and (iii) effective demand. The latter requires the explicit recognition of the interaction among markets. The first two impose conditions on trade in a market, namely that, at the going price: (i) no trader may gain by trading less; (ii) no pair formed by a buyer and a seller may gain by trading more.

The fixprice model provides a general framework (that includes perfect competition as a special case) for price-guided allocation mechanisms (see Silvestre, 1986). It has several applications (i) *short-run analysis* that assumes, as in *Capital and Growth*, that it takes time for prices and quantities to adjust (perfect competition corresponding to very fast adjustment); (ii) *monopolistic competition* (including perfect competition as the special case where market power is nil: see previous section); (iii) *price (wage or rent) controls*; this in particular motivates Drèze's formulation; (iv) *price (or wage) negotiation* (representatives of buyers and sellers negotiate prices that are taken as given by individual traders: see Silvestre, 1987). Fixprice analysis can be viewed as abstracting from specific behaviour features (say, particular oligopoly models, adjustment paths, Government policies or negotiation procedures) and focusing instead on basic market principles common to alternative specifications.

The definitions of fixprice equilibrium due to Benassy, Drèze and Younès vary in form and motivation, but turn out to be equivalent under some assumptions (see Silvestre, 1982, 1983). Rather than reproducing them in all generality, we exemplify the common concepts in two simple but important cases.

Case 1: Differentiable exchange economics. Let there be $n + 1$ goods, indexed, $0, 1, \ldots, n$ (i.e. n markets). There are m traders: trader i is endowed with an $(n + 1)$ dimensional vector of initial endowments ω_i and a differentiable utility function $u_i: R^{n+1} \to R$. A net trade allocation is an m-tuple of n-dimensional net trade vectors $(z_i) = (z_{i1}, \ldots, z_{in})$, one for each trader, satisfying: $\Sigma_i z_i = 0$. It is understood that, for $j = 1, \ldots, n$, if $z_{ij} > 0$ (or < 0) then trader i is buying (or selling) in market j. The (normalized) price vector $p = (p_1, \ldots, p_n)$ is given. The vector $\hat{x}_i(p; z_i) = (\omega_{i0} - p \cdot z_i, \omega_{i1} + z_{i1}, \ldots, \omega_{in} + z_{in})$ is then the consumption vector associated with $(p; z_i)$. We only consider situations where the vectors p and $\hat{x}_i(p; z_i)$ are strictly positive. Define i's marginal utility of trading in market j at the going price as: $u_{ij}(p; z_i) = \partial u_i / \partial x_{ij} - p_j \cdot \partial u_i / \partial x_{i0}$, with derivatives evaluated at $\hat{x}(p; z_i)$.

147

Definition: A net trade allocation (z_i^*) is a *Fixprice Equilibrium for p* if, writing $\mu_{ij}^* \mu_{ij}(p; z_i)$, (a) *Voluntariness*: For $i = 1, \ldots, m$, $z_{ij}^* \cdot \mu_{ij}^* \geqslant 0$; (b) *Absence of market frictions*: For $j = 1, \ldots, n$ and for any pair of consumers i, h, $\mu_{ij}^* \cdot \mu_{hj}^* \geqslant 0$.

Figure 1 illustrates the case of $n = 1$ and $m = 2$ in an Edgeworth box: point A represents the (unique) fixprice equilibrium at the price vector p: there trader 1 is a buyer $(z_{11} > 0)$. The straight line through points ω and A depicts the budget constraints. Allocations in the segment $[\omega, A]$ would violate condition (b). Those in the segment $[A, B]$ (in particular the Pareto efficient point D) would violate condition (a) for trader 1.

The graphically more complex case of $n = m = 2$ is illustrated in Figures 2a–d. Figure 2(a) depicts trader 1's budget set in R_3^+. Rather than drawing a three-dimensional Edgeworth box, we graph first separately (Fig. 2(b–c)) and then together (Fig. 2(d)) the two-dimensional budget triangles of the traders. Figure 2(a–b) also depicts the intersections of some indifference surfaces of trader 1 with his budget set, Q_1 being his most preferred point in the budget set. At point A he is selling in both markets (i.e. $z_{11} < 0$, $z_{12} < 0$: he gets money in exchange), $\mu_{12} < 0$ (he would like to sell more in market 2) and $\mu_{11} = 0$. Figure 2(c) corresponds to trader 2: at point A he is buying in both markets (i.e. $z_{20} > 0$, $z_{21} > 0$, $z_{22} > 0$), and $\mu_{21} > 0$, $\mu_{22} = 0$. Figure 2(d) superimpose the two graphs (with the axes corresponding to trader 2 reversed and with the initial endowment points coinciding at ω). Points A in Figures 2(b–c) have been chosen so that they also coincide in Figure 2(d), i.e., $z_{2j} + z_{2j} = 0$, $j = 1, 2$. These trades constitute a Fixprice Equilibrium.

Case 2: The Three Good Model. This by now popular model originated in Barro–Grossman (1971, 1976) and was further elaborated by Benassy (1977,

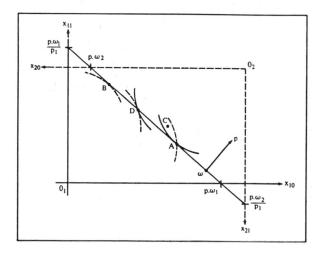

Figure 1

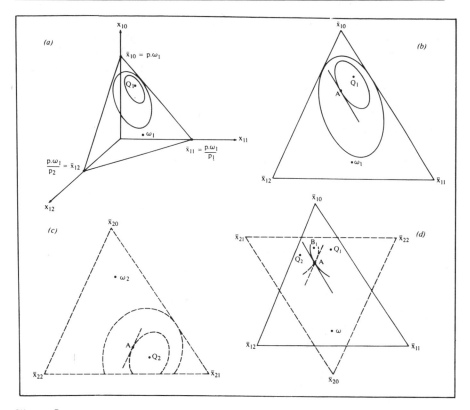

Figure 2

1982, 1986) and Malinvaud (1977) among others. Our presentation follows Silvestre (1986).

Let there be three goods, money, denoted by M, initially available in M_0 units, labour, denoted by L, initially available in L_0 units, and output, denoted by Y, which is initially non-available but is produced by labour according to the production function $Y = f(L)$. There are two markets, the labour market, with (nominal) wage w, and the output market, with price p. There is one firm and one consumer (the homogeneity of U makes this assumption inessential) who owns M_0 and L_0, receives all profits and is endowed with a utility function $U(Y, M)$. Note that the labour supply is fixed at L_0.

Define the marginal rate of substitution as $V'(Y) = (\partial U / \partial Y)/(\partial U / \partial M)$, with derivatives evaluated at (Y, M_0). Define the marginal cost curve as $C'_w = w(f^{-1})'(Y)$, and the full employment output as $Y_0 = f(L_0)$. Then:

Definition: The level of output Y is a *Fixprice Equilibrium output for the price–wage pair* (p, w) if:

$$Y = \min \{(V')^{-1}(p), (C'_w)^{-1}(p), Y_0\}.$$

149

This equality embodies in a compact way several conditions that can be interpreted as follows. First, $Y \leqslant Y_0$, i.e., output cannot exceed the full employment level. Second, $Y \leqslant (V')^{-1}(p)$, or alternatively $p \leqslant V'(Y)$: this means that the consumer cannot gain by buying less output at the going price: it is a condition of 'voluntary trading' for the consumer. Third, $Y \leqslant (C'_w)^{-1}(p)$, or, alternatively, $p \geqslant C'_w(Y)$, i.e. the price cannot be lower than the marginal cost: it is a condition of 'voluntary trading' for the firm (profits cannot increase by selling less at the going price). Finally, at least one of these weak inequalities must be an equality: this is the condition of frictionless markets,.

Figure 3 partitions the (p, w) plane according to which one of the three possible equalities determines output (solid lines). In region E (full employment), $Y = Y_0$. In region K (Keynesian unemployment) $p = V'(Y)$, and in region C (for Classical Unemployment of Full Capacity) $p = C'_w(Y)$. In the boundaries between regions the two relevant equalities hold. At the Walrasian point W all three equalities hold. There is full employment in Region E and unemployment outside it. The dashed lines are isoemployment loci, with the arrows indicating the directions of increasing employment.

Within the short-run interpretation (see Silvestre, 1986, for alternative ones) the labour market is in excess supply (or, excess demand) in the interior of Regions K and C (or Region E), and the output market is in excess supply (or demand) in the interior of region K (or regions C and E). At the Walrasian point W both markets are balanced. In the Keynesian region the condition for determination of output $p = V'(Y)$ can be rewritten in terms of the consumption function as in the textbook Keynesian multiplier model. The homogeneity of U implies that demand for output, as a function of p and wealth I, can be written as $h(p)I$, where the function $h(p)$ satisfies: (i) $ph(p) < 1$ and (ii) the marginal

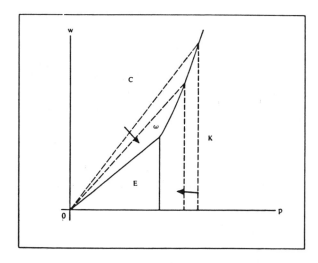

Figure 3

equality $(\partial U/\partial Y)/(\partial U/\partial M) = p$ whenever the consumption vector is a multiple of $(h(p), 1 - ph(p))$. By setting $I = M_0 + pY$ we obtain the effective demand for output (see the entry DISEQUILIBRIUM ANALYSIS) $C(Y) = h(p)(M_0 + pY)$: this is the traditional consumption function, with marginal propensity to consume equal to $ph(p) < 1$. The satisfaction of effective demand requires $Y = C(Y)$, i.e., $Y/M_0 = h(p)/[1 - ph(p)]$, which by the above marginal equality implies that $p = V'(Y)$.

The distinction of the two types of excess supply of labour has important implications for economic policy and for comparative statics. In Region C output is determined by the condition 'price = marginal cost'. Hence, lowering wages (nominal or real) will increase employment, but an increase in demand will have no effect on employment. In Region K, a decrease in the nominal wage has no effect on employment: only lowering the price or otherwise stimulating demand will work. This analysis also offers insights on the effects of different kinds of shocks (see Malinvaud, 1977; Silvestre, 1986): a business cycle driven by demand shocks will fluctuate between Keynesian unemployment and full employment, whereas productivity shocks will yield fluctuations between the Keynesian and the Classical types of unemployment.

INEFFICIENCIES

The budget equality and the market institution impose constraints on trades. Thus, the resulting allocation may very well be Pareto dominated by other allocations that do not satisfy these constraints. The study of such inefficiencies is important for the normative analysis of the situations covered by fixprice theory (short-run market disequilibria, price controls, monopolistic competition).

Inefficiency relative to the set of physically attainable allocations. Consider Figure 1. Note that the allocation given by A is not Pareto efficient: both traders would be better off at C, but C cannot be reached without violating some budget constraint.

A similar phenomenon may occur if there are two traders in one side of the market. Modify the example of Figure 1 by duplicating Trader 2: i.e., Traders 1 and 2 are unchanged, but now there is a Trader 3 with the same preferences and endowments as Trader 2. Let $z_{21} = (-1/4)z_{11}$, and $z_{31} = (-3/4)z_{11}$. Then there are mutually beneficial reallocations between traders 2 and 3, but they violate the budget constraint.

One can say that this type of inefficiency is caused by 'wrong prices'. Note, however, that trade at non-Walrasian prices does not *per se* imply inefficiency. Point D in Figure 1, for instance, is Pareto efficient, and all budget constraints are satisfied there. (A general treatment of allocations of this type is given by Balasko, 1979, and Keiding, 1981). But there is forced trading at point D. It is the combination of non-Walrasian prices and the market institution (reflected by the voluntariness condition) that implies inefficiency. This point is made rigorous in Silvestre (1985).

151

Inefficiencies relative to allocation satisfying the budget constraints. When there is only one market (see Figure 1) because of the absence of frictions no allocation that satisfies the budget constraint is Pareto superior to a Fixprice Equilibrium, i.e., a Fixprice Equilibrium is efficient relative to allocations that satisfy the budget constraints. This ceases to be true with several markets: for instance, point *B* in Figure 2(d) Pareto dominates point *A* and satisfies all budget constraints. (Note that point *B* violates voluntariness.) Such inefficiencies have been studied in Benassy (1975, 1977, 1982) and Younès (1975). A particularly striking case occurs in Keynesian allocations of the Three Good Model: the markets for labour and output are in excess supply, and a direct barter of labour against output would benefit both the firm and the worker (and improve welfare). This phenomenon was viewed by Clower (1965) and Leijonhufvud (1968) as a failure of coordination among markets. It is often alleviated in modern economies by Keynesian policies rather than by the direct exchange of labour against output.

Again, the inefficiencies relative to allocations satisfying the budget constraints are based on the institutional arrangements for trade: the exchange of money against a good in each market. They could conceivably disappear under alternative trading institutions. For instance, Drèze–Müller (1980) presents a scheme where traders must satisfy, in addition to the usual budget constraint, a balance condition on 'coupons' associated with trading on each (nonmoney) commodity. The equilibria of this scheme are always efficient relative to trades that do not violate the budget constraints. (Thus, point *A* in Figure 2(d) is not an equilibrium of this kind.) Their model captures institutions that may appear under persistent excess demand, as in wartime or in planned economies.

BIBLIOGRAPHY

Arrow, K.J. 1959. Towards a theory of price adjustment. In *The Allocation of Economic Resources*, ed. M. Abramovitz, Stanford: Stanford University Press.

Balasko, Y. 1979. Budget constrained Pareto-efficient allocations. *Journal of Economic Theory* 21, 359–79.

Barro, R.J. and Grossman, H.I. 1971. A general equilibrium model of income and employment. *American Economic Review* 61, 82–93.

Barro, R.J. and Grossman, H.I. 1976. *Money, Employment and Inflation.* Cambridge and New York: Cambridge University Press.

Benassy, J.P. 1975. Neo-Keynesian disequilibrium theory in a monetary economy. *Review of Economic Studies* 42, 503–23.

Benassy, J.P. 1976. The disequilibrium approach to monopolistic price setting and general monopolistic equilibrium. *Review of Economic Studies* 43(1), 69–81.

Benassy, J.P. 1977. A Neo-Keynesian model of price and quantity determination in disequilibrium. In *Equilibrium and Disequilibrium in Economic Theory*, ed. G. Schwödiauer, Boston: Reidel.

Benassy, J.P. 1982. *The Economics of Market Disequilibrium.* New York: Academic Press.

Benassy, J.P. 1986. *Macroeconomics: An Introduction to the Non-Walrasian Approach.* New York: Academic Press.

Clower, R.W. 1965. The Keynesian counter-revolution: a theoretical appraisal. In *The Theory of Interest Rates*, ed. F.H. Hahn and F.P.R. Brechling, London: Macmillan; New York: St. Martin's Press.

Drèze, J. 1965. Existence of an exchange equilibrium under price rigidities. *International Economic Review* 16, 301–20.

Drèze, J. and Müller, H. 1980. Optimality properties of rationing schemes. *Journal of Economic Theory* 23, 131–49.

Hahn, F.H. 1978. On non-Walrasian equilibria. *Review of Economic Studies* 45(1), 1–17.

Hahn, F.H. and Negishi, T. 1962. A theorem on non-tâtonnement stability. *Econometrica* 30, 463–9.

Hahn, F.H. and Brechling, F.P.R. (eds) 1965. *The Theory of Interest Rates*, London: Macmillan; New York: St. Martin's Press.

Hart, O. 1982. A model of general equilibrium with Keynesian features. *Quarterly Journal of Economics* 97, 109–38.

Hicks, J.R. 1965. *Capital and Growth*. Oxford and New York: Oxford University Press.

John, R. 1985. A remark on conjectural equilibria. *Scandinavian Journal of Economies* 87(1), 137–41.

Keiding, H. 1981. Existence of budget constrained Pareto-efficient allocations. *Journal of Economic Theory* 24, 393–7.

Leijonhufvud, A. 1968. *On Keynesian Economics and the Economics of Keynes*. Oxford and New York: Oxford University Press.

Malinvaud, E. 1977. *The Theory of Unemployment Reconsidered*. Oxford: Basil Blackwell; New York: Wiley.

Negishi, T. 1960. Monopolistic competition and general equilibrium. *Review of Economic Studies* 28, 196–201.

Negishi, T. 1965. Market clearing processes in a monetary economy. In *The Theory of Interest Rates*, ed. F.H. Hahn and F.P.R. Brechling, London: Macmillan; New York: St. Martin's Press.

Negishi, T. 1974. Involuntary unemployment and market imperfection. *Economic Studies Quarterly* 25(1), 32–46.

Negishi, T. 1979. *Microeconomic Foundations of Keynesian Macroeconomics*. Amsterdam: North-Holland.

Patinkin, D. 1956. *Money, Interest and Prices*, Evanston, Ill: Row Peterson.

Silvestre, J. 1982. Fixprice analysis in exchange economies. *Journal of Economic Theory* 26, 28–58.

Silvestre, J. 1983. Fixprice analysis in productive economies. *Journal of Economic Theory* 30, 401–9.

Silvestre, J. 1985. Voluntary and efficient allocations are Walrasian. *Econometrica* 53, 807–16.

Silvestre, J. 1986. The elements of fixprice microeconomies. In *Microeconomic Theory*, ed. L. Samuelson, Boston: Kluwer Nijhoff.

Smale, S. 1976. A convergent process of price adjustment and global Newton methods. *Journal of Mathematical Economics* 3, 107–20.

Uzawa, H. 1962. On the stability of Edgeworth's barter process. *International Economic Review* 3(2), May, 218–32.

Younès, Y. 1975. On the role of money in the process of exchange and the existence of a non-Walrasian equilibrium. *Review of Economic Studies* 42, 489–501.

Free Disposal

TED BERGSTROM

'I should like to buy an egg, please' she said timidly. 'How do you sell them?'
'Fivepence farthing for one – twopence for two,' the Sheep replied.
'Then two are cheaper than one?' Alice said, taking out her purse.
'Only you must eat both if you buy two,' said the Sheep.
'Then I'll have one please', said Alice, as she put the money down on the counter. For she thought to herself, 'They mightn't be at all nice, you know.'

Lewis Carroll, *Through the Looking-Glass*

If I dislike a commodity, you may have to pay to get me to accept it. But so long as some otherwise non-sated consumer finds this commodity to be desirable, or at least harmless, it could not have a negative price in competitive equilibrium. Likewise, if some firm can dispose of arbitrary amounts of a commodity without using any other inputs or producing any other (possibly noxious) outputs, its price in competitive equilibrium cannot be negative. Therefore competitive equilibrium analysis can be confined to the case of non-negative prices if every commodity is either harmless to someone or freely disposable.

If a commodity is not freely disposable and is a 'bad' in the sense that everyone prefers less of it to more, it is possible to redefine the 'commodity' as the absence of the bad. The commodity so defined can then be treated as a good with a positive price. More generally, it might be possible to choose some alternative coordinate system in which to measure commodity bundles so that in the new coordinate system either there is free disposability or more is preferred to less. But if people are willing to pay a positive sum for a small amount of a commodity and less for a large amount, then the question of whether that commodity will have a positive or negative price in competitive equilibrium cannot be decided in advance. The sign of the equilibrium price will in general depend on supplies of this and other goods and on the detailed configuration of preferences in the economy.

154

Sometimes a noxious by-product of production or consumption can be transformed into a useful output if sufficient other resources are used. Then the equilibria price for the by-product may be either positive or negative, depending on the prices of the other inputs and of the output into which it is transformed. This is particularly evident when commodities are distinguished by location. Garbage located in the centre of a city is undesirable to everyone. To bury or incinerate it is costly and generates no valuable outputs. Therefore, if garbage is disposed of in this way, its equilibrium price must be negative. But the garbage could be transported to the country, boiled and fed to pigs. Depending on the costs of this process and the price of pork, it may turn out that converting garbage to pig feed is profitable even when garbage at the city centre has a zero or positive price. Both the ultimate disposition of garbage and the sign of its price have to be determined endogenously in the competitive process.

Early proofs of the existence of competitive equilibrium (Arrow and Debreu, 1954; Gale, 1955; Debreu, 1959) assumed that all commodities are freely disposable or, equivalently, defined equilibrium so as to allow the possibility that in equilibrium some goods might be in excess supply but have zero price. Debreu (1956) shows how the assumptions of free disposal and monotonicity can be greatly relaxed. McKenzie (1959) and Debreu (1962) present general theorems on the existence of equilibrium in which free disposal is not assumed. Rader (1972), Hart and Kuhn (1975), Bergstrom (1976) and Shafer (1976) suggest further generalizations and simplifications in dealing with negative prices in equilibrium.

The formal treatment of negative prices in existence proofs presents an interesting mathematical problem. Most of the standard existence proofs apply the Kakutani fixed-point theorem to a correspondence that maps the set of possible equilibrium prices into itself in such a way that a fixed point for the mapping is a competitive equilibrium price vector. The Kakutani theorem applies to an upper hemicontinuous mapping from a closed bounded convex set to its compact, convex subsets. If the only prices to be considered are non-negative, then the domain for this correspondence can be chosen to be the unit simplex. If all price vectors, positive and negative must be considered, then an obvious candidate for the domain of this mapping would be the unit sphere. $\{p \in R^n | p \cdot p = 1\}$. But this is not a convex set. The closed unit ball $\{p \in R^n | p \cdot p \leqslant 1\}$ is a convex set, but it contains the vector zero, at which point the excess demand mapping is not upper hemicontinuous.

Debreu (1956) solved this problem neatly in a brief, elegant paper that has received less attention than it deserves. The existence proofs that assume free disposability of all goods had shown that there exists a non-negative price vector at which the excess demand vector is either zero or belongs to the negative orthant. Debreu generalized this result to show that if there is free disposability on any convex cone which is not a linear subspace, then a price vector can be found at which excess demand is either zero or belongs to the cone of free disposability. Furthermore, this price vector gives a non-positive value to every activity in the cone of free disposability. In particular, consider the case where one good is assumed to be freely disposable. Then, from Debreu's theorem, it follows that there exists some price vector at which excess demand for all goods other than the freely disposable good is zero, and at which there is either zero or negative excess demand for the freely disposable good. From Walras's Law and the fact that excess demand for all other goods is zero, it follows that the price of the freely disposable good can be positive only if excess demand is zero. Therefore this price vector is a competitive equilibrium. Thus Debreu weakened the free disposability assumption from 'all goods are freely disposable' to 'at least one good is freely disposable'.

We can take Debreu's argument one step further and eliminate the assumption of even one freely disposable good. Nowhere in Debreu's proof is it necessary to assume that the freely disposable good is desirable to anyone. This suggests that the existence of a freely disposable good is not likely to be essential for the existence of equilibrium. For suppose that there is an economy with no freely disposable goods. A fictional good could be introduced which is freely disposable but totally useless and totally harmless to everyone. For the augmented economy found by adding this fictional good to the original economy, by Debreu's theorem there would exist a competitive equilibrium. In this new economy it turns out that the equilibrium price of the useless, freely disposable good must be zero and the vector of equilibrium prices for the other goods can serve as a competitive equilibrium price vector for the original economy.

The approach taken by Bergstrom (1976) is equivalent to introducing a useless and harmless fictional good into Debreu's model. Taking the formal steps of this argument directly without intermediary fictions leads to an upper hemicontinuous mapping from the unit ball into itself for which there is a fixed point on the boundary of the unit ball. This fixed point turns out to be a competitive equilibrium price vector. An interesting alternative approach was taken by Rader (1972) and by Hart and Kuhn (1975). Instead of the Kakutani theorem, they use a theorem about fixed and antipodal points of a continuous mapping from the unit sphere into itself, and are thereby able to deal with all prices on the unit sphere as potential equilibrium prices.

The first and second welfare theorems and the theorems about the equivalence between the core and the set of competitive equilibria apply straightforwardly when there is not free disposal. For example, in order to prove the Pareto optimality of competitive equilibrium in an exchange economy, we simply argue along the usual lines that if any allocation is Pareto superior to a competitive equilibrium, then at the original competitive prices, the aggregate value of consumption in the proposed Pareto superior allocation must exceed the aggregate value of initial endowments. But if the proposed allocation is feasible, then the aggregate consumption vector in the proposed allocation must equal the aggregate initial endowment vector. It follows, whether prices are positive, negative or zero that if the two vectors are equal they must have the same value at the competitive price vector. Therefore there cannot be a feasible allocation which is Pareto superior to a competitive equilibrium. Similar arguments apply to the core theorem. The only matter in which a bit of care must be taken is in defining the activities available to a potential blocking coalition so as to exclude the possibility of dumping undesirable commodities. This simply amounts to the assumption that a blocking coalition must exactly equalize its total consumption of all goods to its total endowment.

BIBLIOGRAPHY

Arrow, K.J. and Debreu, G. 1954. Existence of an equilibrium for a competitive economy. *Econometrica* 22, July, 265–90.

Bergstrom, T. 1976. How to discard free disposability – at no cost. *Journal of Mathematical Economics* 3(2), 131–4.

Debreu, G. 1956. Market equilibrium. *Proceedings of the National Academy of Sciences of the USA* 42, 876–8.

Debreu, G. 1959. *The Theory of Value.* New York: Wiley.

Debreu, G. 1962. New concepts and techniques for equilibrium analysis. *International Economic Review* 3, 257–73.

Gale, D. 1955. The law of supply and demand. *Mathematica Scandinavica* 3, 155–69.

Hart, O. and Kuhn, H. 1975. A proof of the existence of equilibrium without the free disposal assumption. *Journal of Mathematical Economics* 2(3), 335–43.

McKenzie, L. 1959. On the existence of general equilibrium for a competitive market. *Econometrica* 27(1), 54–71.

Rader, T. 1972. *Theory of General Economic Equilibrium.* New York: Academic Press.

Shafer, W. 1976. Equilibrium in economies without ordered preferences or free disposal. *Journal of Mathematical Economics* 3(2), 135–7.

Free Goods

IAN STEEDMAN

Free goods are 'goods', whether consumer goods or productive inputs, which are useful but not scarce; they are in sufficiently abundant supply that all agents can have as much of them as they wish at zero social opportunity costs (cf. ch. 11, §3, of Carl Menger's *Principles of Econonomics*, 1871). Goods which have a positive social opportunity cost but a zero price – for example, because there are no property rights in them, or because they are fully subsidized – are *not* free goods. Any 'gift of nature', whether it be a good such as air, or a primary input such as labour or land (in the narrow sense), might be a free good under certain circumstances. But a produced commodity can be a free good, other than in the market period, only if it is a joint product. As is at once obvious from the example of air, the free nature of a good is not an intrinsic property; thus air above the earth's surface is, in most circumstances, a free good but air under water or in deep mines is not. More abstractly, then, a free good is a good for which supply is not less than demand at a zero price (in the sense of social opportunity cost). But since both supply of and demand for any good depend on the prices of all goods, it is clear that whether a particular good is or is not a free good is a general equilibrium, not a partial equilibrium, issue.

Consider first a Walrasian analysis of general equilibrium. Under the standard assumptions of such an analysis, Walras's Law (or identity) holds, so that $pS \equiv 0$, where p is a row vector of prices and S a column vector of excess supplies. (This is an *identity*, holding at all prices, not only at equilibrium prices.) Now, by definition, in a Walrasian analysis any equilibrium excess supply vector satisfies $S^* \geqslant 0$. Hence if it is ensured that any equilibrium price vector satisfies $p^* \geqslant 0$, it follows – from $pS \equiv 0$ and $S^* \geqslant 0$ – that if $S_j^* > 0$ then $p_j^* = 0$. That is, the Rule of Free Goods holds in such a Walrasian equilibrium, applying to all 'goods', whether produced or non-produced. Two points are to be noted. The less important one is that while $S_j^* > 0$ implies $p_j^* = 0$, $p_j^* = 0$ does not imply $S_j^* > 0$, since $p_j^* = 0 = S_j^*$ is possible. The more important point is that the Rule of Free Goods is not implied by $pS \equiv 0$ and $S^* \geqslant 0$ alone; they must be supported by the condition $p^* \geqslant 0$. This last condition if often underpinned by an assumption of the possibility of *free disposal* (see below). Such an assumption rules out the possibility that any $p_j^* < 0$, for there would be an unlimited demand for a good for which one 'paid' a negative price – that is *received* a positive price – and which one could dispose of at zero cost.

It was noted above that the Rule of Free Goods is applied in Walrasian flex-price analyses to both products and primary inputs. With respect to the latter, it is instructive to consider the linear programming formulation which is sometimes given for the 'supply' side of a general equilibrium existence proof for an economy with linear technical conditions. In the primal problem one is asked to maximize the value of net output, at parametrically given product prices, subject to not using more than the exogenously fixed supply of any primary input. The complementary slackness conditions, corresponding to these last constraints, give immediate expression to the Rule of Free Goods, as applied to the primary inputs. And the non-negativity constraints in the dual problem stipulate, of course, that the solution factor prices cannot be negative. Thus every solution factor price will be non-negative and will be zero if the relevant factor is less than fully utilized.

It is essential to note that not all types of economic analysis impose the Rule of Free Goods with respect to all primary inputs. In the von Neumann model, for example, that rule is certainly imposed with respect to all the produced commodities, but it is not applied to labour, which receives an exogenously given real wage bundle which is independent of the degree of utilization of labour. At most, one could say that a 'Rule of Zero 'Excess Wages' is applied because labour is less than fully employed. Similarly, in Keynes's analysis the presence of involuntarily unemployed labour does not drive the wage to a zero but only to an exogenously given minimum (a market level reservation price). Clearly, then, the three assertions $pS \equiv 0$, $S^* \geqslant 0$ and $p^* \geqslant 0$ are not all accepted within Keynes's analysis. But since $S^* \geqslant 0$ and $p^* \geqslant 0$ *are* accepted, it can only be Walras's Law which is being rejected – and this is indeed the case, for in Keynes's analysis we have only the condition that, the elements of S being defined in terms of *desired* supplies and demands, $pS \geqslant 0$. The weaker relation is, of course, perfectly consistent with $S_j^* \geqslant 0$ and $p_j^* \geqslant 0$ (see Morishima, 1976, pp. 203–11).

It was noted above that the 'free-disposal' assumption has the convenient consequence that no equilibrium price can be negative; this means that the search for Walrasian equilibrium price vectors can be confined to the unit simplex. Although this restriction on prices is *not* a necessary ingredient of all general equilibrium existence proofs, the free-disposal assumption is sufficiently widely adopted (it is sometimes even described as obviously reasonable) to merit a close examination of its justification. Consider first the proposal that the commodity to be disposed of in a disposal process is the *only* input to the latter. This means that the only form of 'disposal activity' allowed is that of simply *leaving* the commodity to be disposed of *where* it is and leaving it *as* it is. If it moves or changes its form, that must be the result solely of non-human and non-produced agencies. (Note that one cannot defend the disposal activity assumption by saying that it applies only to the 'last stage' of a real-world-like disposal process, which first uses labour, lorries, etc. to take waste chemicals, for example, to a particular place. This is because the assumption is supposed to apply to *all* commodities, including, for example, the chemical waste *situated at the point of its production*.)

This leads us naturally to a consideration of the second – and even more objectionable – aspect of the disposal activity assumption, the proposal that the activity has *no* outputs. Taken literally, this proposal simply contradicts one of *the* most fundamental laws constituting our conception of the physical universe – the law of conservation of mass-energy. If one takes the conservation law for granted, for the purposes of economic theory, then *either* the zero-output assumption is incomprehensible *or* it means that all the outputs from the disposal process lie outside the commodity set which is taken as the basis for the economic analysis. A defence of the latter interpretation would have to involve both an account of the principles according to which that set is defined on a non-arbitrary basis and an explanation of why the outputs of disposal processes can be supposed – non-arbitrarily – to lie outside that set.

It might be said that the disposal-activity assumption simply provides one interpretation of the basic axiom of free disposal ($x \in X$ and $x' \leqslant x$ implies $x' \in X$, where X is the production set) and that the latter may be acceptable even while the former is not. How then might the axiom be understood in the absence of disposal processes? Suppose that together with all the other inputs and outputs (which will be held constant), a certain input of fertilizer and a certain output of maize define an activity belonging to the production set. It is then proposed that, *ceteris paribus*, the same fertilizer input and a smaller maize output also define a feasible activity. We cannot suppose that some of the fertilizer is simply not used, for then an output (that of fertilizer) would have been increased. Thus all the fertilizer must be used. If it is used in the same way as 'before' then a smaller maize output, *ceteris paribus*, involves different laws of nature. If it is used but used differently from 'before', then some other input has changed, contrary to hypothesis. Hence the presence of a disposal activity is, after all, required.

In the above example, the 'other input' which has changed when fertilizer is used differently is some human agency. For to say that fertilizer is used differently is precisely to say that *someone* has acted differently. Suppose then that we now change the example, replacing the given fertilizer input by a given quantity of a specified type of labour input and including fertilizer amongst the (given) 'other' inputs and outputs. In the absence of disposal processes, does the fact that a certain labour input and a certain maize output define an activity in the production set, mean that the *same* labour input and a *smaller* maize output (perhaps even a *negative* one) also define such an activity? If free disposal is ruled out, the laws of nature are constant and labour is precisely defined, the answer would again seem to be No. Thus, again, the free-disposal axiom does indeed rest on the presence of disposal activities. Objections to the disposal-activity assumption are thus also objections to the axiom of free disposal itself.

It has already been noted that general equilibrium existence proofs can dispense with the free-disposal axiom and that Keynes's theory does not apply the Rule of Free Goods to labour. More generally, the rule of free goods should not simply be assumed to apply to non-produced inputs, for it must always be considered whether their owners place a positive reservation price on them. With respect to produced commodities, free disposal should not be assumed (for the reasons given above), as it commonly is in linear programming models, in studies of balanced growth within closed production models with convex cone production sets, and in proofs of turnpike theorems. In each case, on dispensing with the free-disposal axiom, one must decide how to represent preferences over 'bads'. These apparently abstract issues are, of course, of immediate relevance in the discussion of such policy issues as pollution control, environmental protection and waste disposal. (If there were no joint production, or if free disposal were possible, there could be no problems of pollution control and waste disposal.) When there are disposal activities which involve a negligible private cost but a significant social cost, policy will involve bringing the positive costs of disposal to bear on the individual agents concerned. This may induce them, in turn, to discover or invent new uses for the previously undesired 'commodities'; the costly nature of disposal has spurred changes in technical knowledge.

BIBLIOGRAPHY

Morishima, M. 1976. *The Economic Theory of Modern Society*. Cambridge and New York: Cambridge University Press.

Global Analysis in Economic Theory

STEVE SMALE

The goal here is to illustrate 'global analysis in economics' by putting the main results of classical equilibrium theory into a global calculus context. The advantages of this approach are fourfold:

(1) The proofs of existence of equilibrium are simpler. Kakutani's fixed point theorem is not used, the main tool being the calculus of several variables.
(2) Comparative statics is integrated into the model in a natural way, the first derivatives playing a fundamental role.
(3) The calculus approach is closer to the older traditions of the subject.
(4) In so far as possible the proofs of equilibrium are constructive. These proofs may be implemented by a speedy algorithm, which is Newton's method modified to give global convergence. On the other hand, the existence proofs are sufficiently powerful to yield the generality of the Arrow–Debreu theory.

Only two references are given at the end of this entry, each containing an extensive bibliography with historical notes. The two references themselves give detailed, expanded accounts of the subject of global analysis in economic theory.

Let us proceed to an account of this model. The basic equation of equilibrium theory is 'supply equals demand', or in symbols, $S(p) = D(p)$. Since we are in a situation of several markets, there are several variables in this equation. Equilibrium prices are obtained by setting the excess demand $z = D - S$ equal to zero and solving. Consider this function z on a more abstract level.

Suppose that given an economy of l markets, or of l commodities with corresponding prices written as $p_1, \ldots, p_l$, the excess demand for the ith commodity is a real valued function $z_i = z_i(p_1, \ldots, p_l)$ $p_j \geqslant 0$ and we form the vector $z = (z_1, \ldots, z_l)$. Thus the excess demand can be interpreted as a map, which we take to be sufficiently differentiable, from $\mathbb{R}_+^l$ to $\mathbb{R}^l$, where $\mathbb{R}^l$ is Cartesian l-space and $\mathbb{R}_+^l = \{p \in \mathbb{R}^l / p_i \geqslant 0\}$. An economic equilibrium is a set of prices $p = (p_1, \ldots, p_i)$ for which excess demand is zero, that is, $z(p) = 0$.

Economic theory imposes some conditions on the function z which go as follows.

First and foremost is Walras's Law, which is expressed simply by $p \cdot z(p) = 0$ (inner product). Written out, this is

$$\sum_{i=1}^{l} p_i \cdot z_i(p_1, \ldots, p_l) = 0$$

and states that the value of the excess demand is zero. This is a budget constraint which asserts that the excess demand is consistent with the total assets of the economy. It can be proved from a reasonable microeconomic foundation, as can be seen below.

Second is the homogeneity condition $z(\lambda p) = z(p)$ for all $\lambda > 0$. Changing all prices by the same factor does not affect excess demand. This condition reflects the fact that the economy is self-contained; prices are not based on anything lying outside the model.

The final condition is the boundary condition that $z_i(p) \geq 0$ if $p_i = 0$. This may be interpreted as: if the ith good is free, then there will be a non-negative excess demand for it.

The following result and its generalizations and ramifications lie at the heart of economic theory.

Existence Theorem. Suppose that an excess demand z satisfies Walras's Law, homogeneity, and the boundary condition. Then there is a price equilibrium.

We will give the proof under the additional mild non-degeneracy condition that the derivative of z is non-singular somewhere on the boundary of $\mathbb{R}_+^l$. This proof is based on Sard's theorem and the inverse function theorem, two basic theorems of global analysis.

Consider a differentiable map f from a set U contained in $\mathbb{R}^k$ to $\mathbb{R}^n$. A vector $y \in \mathbb{R}^n$ is said to be a *regular* value if at each point $x \in U$ with $f(x) = y$, the derivative $Df(x): \mathbb{R}^k \to \mathbb{R}^n$ is surjective. A subset of $\mathbb{R}^n$ is of *full measure* if its complement has measure zero.

Sard's Theorem. If a map $f: U \to \mathbb{R}^n$ is of sufficient differentiability class $(C^r, r > k - n, 0)$ then the set of regular values of f has full measure.

A subset V of $\mathbb{R}^n$ is called a k-dimensional *submanifold* if for each point, there is a neighbourhood U in V and a change of coordinates of $\mathbb{R}^n$ which throws U into a coordinate subspace of dimension k.

Inverse Function Theorem. If $y \in \mathbb{R}^n$ is a regular value of a smooth map $f: U \to \mathbb{R}^n$, $U \subset \mathbb{R}^k$, then either $f^{-1}(y)$ is empty or it is a submanifold of dimension $k - n$.

Let us sketch out the proof of the Existence Theorem. Define the space of normalized prices by

$$\Delta_1 = \left\{ p \in \mathbb{R}_+^l \middle/ \sum p_i = 1 \right\}$$

A space auxiliary to the commodity space is defined by

$$\Delta_0 = \left\{ z \in \mathbb{R}^l \middle/ \sum z_i = 0 \right\}.$$

For the excess demand map z: $\mathbb{R}^l_+ - 0 \to \mathbb{R}^l$, define an associated map ϕ: $\Delta_1 \to \Delta_0$ by $\phi(p) = Z(p) - \Sigma z^i(p)p$. Note that $\phi(p)$ is well-defined (i.e. $\phi(p) \in \Delta_0$) and also smooth. Note moreover that if $\phi(p) = 0$, then $z(p) = 0$, and that p is a price equilibrium. This follows from Walras's Law as follows. If $\phi(p) = 0$, then $z(p) = \Sigma z^i(p)p$ and so $p \cdot z(p) = \Sigma z^i(p)p \cdot p = 0$. Therefore $\Sigma z^i(p) = 0$, since $p \cdot p \neq 0$. By the previous equation $z(p)$ must be zero.

The boundary condition on z implies that ϕ satisfies a similar boundary condition. That is, if $p_i = 0$ then $\phi_i(p) = z_i(p) \geqslant 0$.

It is now sufficient to show that $\phi(p) = 0$ for some $p \in \Delta_1$. The argument for this proceeds by defining yet another map $\hat{\phi}$ by

$$\hat{\phi}(p) = \frac{\phi(p)}{\| \phi(p) \|}$$

where $E = \phi^{-1}(0)$ and S^{l-2} is the set of unit vectors in Δ_0.

By definition the set E is the set of price equilibria, which is to be shown not empty.

Let p_0 be a price vector on the boundary of Δ_1 where the derivative $D\phi(p_0)$ is non-degenerate (our special hypothesis implies the existence of this p_0). One applies Sard's theorem to obtain a regular value y of $\hat{\phi}$ in S^{l-2} near $\hat{\phi}(p_0)$, where $\hat{\phi}^{-1}(y)$ is non-empty.

From the inverse function theorem it follows that $\hat{\phi}^{-1}(y)$ is a smooth curve in Δ_1 (a 1-dimensional submanifold). From the boundary condition and a short argument which we omit, it follows that this curve cannot leave Δ_1.

Since the curve $\hat{\phi}^{-1}(y)$ is a closed set in $\Delta_1 - E$ and has no end points (the inverse function theorem implies that) it must tend to E. In particular, E is not empty and therefore the existence theorem is proved.

The above proof is 'geometrically' constructive in that a curve $\gamma = \hat{\phi}^{-1}(y)$ is constructed which leads to a price equilibrium. This picture can be made analytic by showing that γ is a solution of the ordinary differential equation 'Global Newton', $d\phi/dt = \lambda D\phi(p)^{-1}\phi(p)$, where λ is $+1$ or -1 determined by the sign of the determinant of $D\phi(p)$. As a consequence the Euler method of approximating the solution of an ordinary differential equation can be used to obtain a discrete algorithm for locating a price equilibrium. By an appropriate choice of steps, ± 1, this discrete algorithm near that equilibrium is Newton's Method; thus the appellation 'Global Newton' for the differential equation.

One would like to understand the process of convergence to equilibrium in terms of decentralized mechanics of price adjustment. Unfortunately the situation in this respect is unclear.

Next we give a brief picture of how global analysis relates to a pure exchange economy. This will allow a microeconomic derivation of the excess demand function discussed above, so that the existence theorem just proved will imply an existence theorem for a price equilibrium of a pure exchange economy. Continuing in this framework one can prove Debreu's theorem on generic finiteness of price equilibria, by putting the structure of a differentiable manifold on the big set of price equilibria. The equilibrium manifold is a natural setting for comparative statics.

A trader's preferences will be supposed to be represented by a smooth utility function $u: P \to \mathbb{R}$, where $p = \{x \in \mathbb{R}^l, x_i > 0\}$ is commodity space. The indifference surfaces are those $u^{-1}(c) \subset P$. We make strong versions of classical hypotheses on this function.

Monotonicity. The gradient, grad $u(x)$, has positive coordinates.

Convexity. The second derivative $D^2 u(x)$ is negative difinite on the tangent space at x of the corresponding indifference surface.

Boundary condition. The indifference surfaces are closed sets in $\mathbb{R}^l$ (not just P).

From the utility function, one defines for the individual trader a demand function. $f: \mathbb{R}^l_+ \times \mathbb{R}_+ \to P$ of prices $p \in \mathbb{R}^l_+$ and wealth $w > 0$. For this, consider the budget set $B_{p,w} = \{x \in P | p \cdot x = w\}$. Then $f(p,w)$ is the maximum of f on $B_{p,w}$.

One can prove:

Proposition. The demand function f satisfies

   (a) grad $u(f(p,w)) = \lambda p,$ for some $\lambda > 0$
   (b) $p \cdot f(p,w) = w$
   (c) $f(\lambda p, \lambda w) = f(p,w)$ any $\lambda > 0$
   (d) f is smooth.

A pure exchange economy will be a set of m traders, each with preferences as discussed above, associated to utility functions $u_i, i = 1, \ldots, m$ defined on the same commodity space P. Also associated to the ith trader is an endowment vector $e_i \in P$. At prices p, this trader's wealth is the value of his endowment $p \cdot e_i = w_i$. A *state* is an allocation $(x_1, \ldots, x_m)$, $x_i \in P$ and a price system $p \in \mathbb{R}_+$.

Feasibility is the condition:

$$(F) \qquad\qquad \sum x_i = \sum e_i$$

A kind of satisfaction condition of a state is

(S) For each i, x_i maximizes u_i on the budget set

$$B = \{y \in P | p \cdot y = p \cdot e_i\}$$

An economic equilibrium of a pure exchange economy $(e_1, \ldots, e_m, u_1, \ldots, u_m)$ is a state $[(x_1, \ldots, x_m), p]$ satisfying (F) and (S).

Theorem. There exists a price equilibrium of every pure exchange economy.

The proof goes by applying the previous existence theorem above. Define the excess demand $Z = D - S$ as follows:

$$S(p) = \sum e_i, \qquad D(p) = \sum f_i(p, p \cdot e_i),$$

where f_i is the above defined demand of the ith trader. One then shows Walras's Law:

$$p \cdot Z(p) = p \cdot D(p) - p \cdot S(p) = \sum p \cdot f_i(p, p \cdot e_i) - p \cdot \sum e_i = 0$$

using (b) of the proposition above.

Use (c) of the proposition to confirm the homogeneity of z. The use of the boundary condition is more technical. But under the rather strong hypotheses, this gives a fairly complete existence proof for a price equilibrium of a pure exchange economy.

This existence proof extends to prove the Arrow–Debreu theorem in the generality of the latter's *Theory of Value*.

BIBLIOGRAPHY

Mas-Colell, A. 1985. *The Theory of General Economic Equilibrium, a Differentiable Approach.* Cambridge: Cambridge University Press.

Smale, S. 1981. Global analysis and economics. In *Handbook of Mathematical Economics*, Volume 1, ed. K. J. Arrow and M. D. Intriligator. Amsterdam: North-Holland.

Intertemporal Equilibrium and Efficiency

E. MALINVAUD

People, corporations and governments take decisions for the future. What kind of consistency exists between these decisions? What role does the price system play in this respect? Is the resulting evolution efficient? How can economic organization be improved in order to permit a more satisfactory growth?

Confronted with such huge questions, economists have often answered quickly. Even when attention is limited to formal theory, which this article exclusively considers, many statements can be found which, taken as valid for a time, were later disproved. They had been obtained on special models and too easily given a broad validity. Indeed, the preliminary step should have been to find a general formal representation of economic activity through time, but this step was not given sufficient attention until the late 19th century (Böhm-Bawerk, 1888; Fisher, 1907). The central model with reference to which the whole theory can be built and developed clearly emerged only in the 1950s.

A survey on the subject must then start from first principles and note which major features of reality are still today neglected in main-stream theory. The significance of the most far-reaching results and the importance of some big question marks will then have to be assessed.

INTERTEMPORAL DECISIONS. Households save for future consumption, employees work overtime so as to have enough to enjoy their vacation, students strive to get a diploma so as to hold good jobs later, parents want to leave bequests to their children. Firms produce to inventories in the expectation of future sales, recruit and train staff that will later improve their competitiveness, install equipment to be used for many years, build new factories.

The main theories dealing with intertemporal economic problems see such decisions as part of plans that the relevant agents make for all their future activities. Any household for instance is assumed not only to decide its present

167

supply of labour and demand for goods, but also simultaneously to choose its plan for labour to be later supplied and the goods to be later consumed, and this up to the end of its existence.

The notion of this plan can in principle be made richer by taking *uncertainties* into account; the future decisions are then conditional on events to be later observed, but they are already specified for all conceivable combinations of events. In principle again the structure of the plan must then depend on the structure of the *information* that the agent will receive. In the main intertemporal theories these complications coming from uncertainties and information are, however, neglected, so that the concept of a plan does not appear to be unduly abstract. When the relevance of these theories is assessed, one has to wonder about the consequences of the simplification, as will be seen in the sequel.

Analysis of intertemporal behaviour can adopt the familiar approach: the constraints to which the plan is subject and the objectives that it strives to achieve must be identified; then the optimization problem is solved. The purest of all theories simply transpose the classical analysis of consumer and producer behaviour (Debreu, 1959). They assume the existence of a full system of discounted prices, with one such price for each commodity at each present or future date, a price at which agents will be able to buy or sell as much of this commodity as they may wish. They then directly reinterpret as follows the constraints and objectives that static atemporal theories made familiar.

As between the many plans that he can think of, a consumer is assumed to have a system of preferences that is often conveniently represented by a utility function, whose argument is a consumption vector with as many components as there are commodites and dates. A budget constraint requires that the discounted value of the consumption vector does not exceed a given amount, the consumer's initial wealth. The chosen plan maximizes the utility function subject to the budget constraint. It then follows that the consumption of the various commodities (and the supply of labour) depend on what are the discounted prices and the initial wealth. The present saving of the consumer may be said to be equal to the interest income earned on his initial wealth *minus* the value of his present consumption (labour income appears negatively in this value). It is immaterial in this theory to know how saving is invested. Hence, the consumption plan and the resulting saving plan are seen as involving the whole future *life cycle* of the consumer (Modigliani and Brumberg, 1954).

The plan of a producer is subject only to the constraints that technology imposes. The producer acts as a price taker. His objective is to maximize the discounted value of the plan. It follows that demand for inputs and supply of outputs are functions of the discounted prices. The balance between the value of present outputs and present inputs gives the financial surplus if positive or requirement if negative; this is subject to no direct constraint.

Such a theory of consumer and product behaviour does not claim to apply to all problems concerning this behaviour. Clearly, analysis of the firm in particular must usually go far beyond the stylized description given above, even simply when investment behaviour is being studied (Nickell, 1978). But the theory is supposed to be appropriate for fitting into the discussion of the broad questions raised by intertemporal equilibrium and efficiency.

Even when it is so circumscribed, the intent cannot be considered as fully achieved. Significant limitations must be kept in mind, since they may forbid application of the theory to some of the problems raised by equilibrium and efficiency over time; indeed, some of these limitations have been the motivation for theoretical developments that will not be discussed at length here, but must be mentioned.

Full knowledge of the system of discounted prices for purchases of sales at all relevant future dates is of course an abstraction. Forward prices exist for only a few basic commodities and a limited horizon. Whereas the interest rates at which one can borrow or lend for more or less long durations are fairly well defined, with non-negligible transaction costs and fiscal interference, however, prices that will apply to future transactions have to be forecast by the agents. The uncertainties that their forecast necessarily contains are neglected. Among the many consequences of this major simplification, one particularly notes that it rules out fundamental problems concerning the characterization of decision criteria of business firms (Drèze, 1982).

Constraints on individual choices are also reduced to a minimum. No consideration is given to quantitative constraints, such as those following from mass unemployment on individuals looking for jobs or from business depression on firms looking for customers. When such constraints are binding, not only must the plans meet them, but also spill-over effects from one period to others occur, according to laws that follow from the theory of individual behaviour under rationing (Samuelson, 1947). In particular, consumers willing but unable to borrow are constrained by their current resources, a phenomenon that gives some justification to the Keynesian consumption function relating current consumption to current income.

Neglect of financial constraints may be considered as following from other theoretical simplifications, lack of uncertainty and full knowledge of discounted prices, which rule out insolvency; but it is often particularly restrictive. The role of financial constraints on investment behaviour indeed play a major part in the development of trade cycle theories (Haberler, 1937).

Another notable feature of the theory is the simplicity of the trading relations that it assumes. Consumers and producers buy from 'the market' or sell to 'the market'. A worker need not establish ties with a particular employer, nor a manufacturing firm to a particular supplier of raw material. Actually, intertemporal decisions are often subject to quite significiant irreversibilities. Long-term commitments are frequent for easily understandable reasons, some of which having to do with the specificities that characterize many production processes (for instance, most equipment, once bought, cannot be resold). Long-term contracts are also predominant on the labour market, even though many of their clauses often remain implicit. This feature motivates significant research nowadays, under the heading of 'implicit contracts' (Rosen, 1985).

Limited as it is, the classical theory of individual intertemporal decisions is, however, indispensable as a starting point, from which the study of the many complexities of real life can proceed. It has moreover brought to light some quite relevant results, such as the fact that, contrary to common belief, the saving of a household need not be an increasing function of interest rates or that individual choice is bound to exhibit some degree of impatience (Koopmans, 1960).

AN INTERTEMPORAL ECONOMY. The theory of general intertemporal equilibrium can also transpose the more familiar static theory. But clearly when so doing it does not go very far; new complications, specific to intertemporal problems, must be faced.

The simple transposition of the general competitive equilibrium assumes the existence of a terminal date, 'the horizon', a given set of consumers and producers whose activities end at this date, if not before. They all decide their plans at the initial date, on the basis of a full system of discounted prices, and acting as price takers. Perfect competition is assumed to imply that discounted prices are such that all markets clear; more precisely for a given date and a given commodity, aggregate supply and demand are defined by addition of corresponding individual supplies and demands contained in individual plans, which may then be considered as fully announced; at equilibrium the aggregate supply is precisely equal to aggregate demand, and this applies for any date and commodity. Hence, all individual plans are, from the initial date, mutually consistent for all future dates.

The usefulness of such an abstract equilibrium concept cannot be judged independently of its application, in particular for the discussion of properties linking discounted prices to the agents' individual characteristics. Before facing this discussion, it is enlightening to consider how the model can be revised; this was done in three ways.

First, the hypothesis of a full system of markets, one for each date and commodity, has been relaxed and the notion of a *temporary equilibrium* made explicit (Hicks, 1930; Arrow and Hahn, 1971; Grandmont, 1977). Markets then exist only for the exchange of commodities at the (initial) present date, as well as for the loans of one numeraire commodity from the present to the next future date. Thus, present prices and the interest rate of the first period are assumed to be determined by the law of supply and demand, individual plans being made mutually consistent for the initial data. But in deciding their plans, individual agents have to form anticipations about future prices. Nothing guarantees that these anticipations are correct, so that individual plans will be revised with the passage of time, as actual prices are found to differ from what was expected.

Formal properties of this more realistic model will not be discussed here. Cases can be defined in which anticipations are later realized. It is then possible, but not always necessary when the future is unbounded, that the sequence of temporary equilibria coincides with the equilibrium defined from the hypothesis of a full system of markets. Thus, two sources of difficulty can arise: false anticipations and on the other hand instability following from the myopic functioning of the market system (Hahn, 1968).

Second, coming back to the case of a full system of markets, one has relaxed the assumption of a finite horizon with a fixed set of agents. The problem of knowing which firms exist has not been considered as specific to the intertemporal models, and has not been discussed thus far in the framework of these models, given that infinitely lived firms have been assumed. But since the initial proposals of Allais (1947) and Samuelson (1958), consumers are more and more assumed to belong to overlapping generations, each generation living only for a finite time. Such a representation of the consumption sector is clearly more appropriate for long-term analysis than the assumption of a given set of consumers living for ever, but it raises new difficulties (Balasko–Shell, 1980–81).

Third, since long-term phenomena are often involved, it has been found natural and convenient to concentrate attention on specifications in which the exogenous conditions of economic activity, such as technology, tastes, size of the population, natural resources, remain the same through time or change in a simple way; for instance, population increasing at a constant rate while technology exhibits constant returns to scale and natural resources are unbounded. Within such specifications one has dealt with the particular case of a stationary equilibrium, or else with equilibria in which production and consumption all increase at the same constant rate, that is, the case of 'proportional growth'. The analytical usefulness of this assumption of stationarity was at the centre of an important debate on the building of the theory of capital during the 1930s (Knight, 1935; Hayek, 1936). It follows from the simple form that has the price system of a stationary equilibrium: all discounted prices can be computed from the prices of the present commodities using a single interest rate that applies to all future periods of unit duration. 'The interest rate' is then unambiguously defined (Malinvaud, 1953).

ANY GENERAL LAW? A clear formalization of intertemporal equilibrium not only serves to aid progress in the fundamental conceptualization of economic activity (hence indirectly in the rigour of the discussions concerning many particular questions) but should also lead to comparative statics properties, which, dealing with intertemporal equilibria, have also been called 'comparative dynamics properties'. Particular importance has been given to the question of knowing how the interest rate changes from one stationary equilibrium to another when some specific change is being brought to its exogenous determinants.

The study of the question concentrated on a number of conjectures, which turned out to be about as many disappointments for those who had expected to find rigorous proofs of their general validity. It is now realized that the rate of interest is related in a very complex way to the many exogenous determinants of equilibrium and that changes of relative prices, which are associated with changes of interest, may be responsible for paradoxical effects. A brief survey of this theoretical search, that extended over many years, nevertheless reveals some basic issues.

Does a high preference of individuals for present consumption necessarily imply a high interest rate? The property was often asserted. When first publishing his *Theory of Interest* in 1907, Irving Fisher called it an impatience theory. Only later when he revised the book for the 1930 edition did he add the subtitle 'as determined by impatience to spend income and opportunity to invest it', which recognizes the role of the productivity of investment (Samuelson, 1967). Quite significant cases have indeed been found in the overlapping generation model for which changes of impatience leave the interest rate unchanged (Samuelson, 1958).

Does a decrease of the rate of interest mean a lengthening of the production process? The positive answer was taken for granted, at least as long as technology was given, by many economists and was at the head of the 'Austrian Theory' as developed mainly by Böhm-Bawerk (1888) and Hayek (1941). Actually, description of the production process was usually organized in such a way as to focus on the conjectured property, this being true also with such non-Austrian authors as Wicksell (1901). Final output, available for consumption at some date, was seen as resulting from a number of well identified primary inputs made at previous dates and having 'matured' since then. The notion of an average period of production looked natural; an inverse relationship between this period and the rate of interest was expected. However, it turned out that, even restricting attention to the case of one primary input and one final output, one could not prove the relationship unless a special definition was given to the production period and a special phrasing to the property (Hicks, 1939, 1973). Generalization to many primary inputs, many final outputs and many interdependent production processes raises the fundamental difficulty resulting from induced variations in relative prices; it is quite unlikely that a generalized property could be proved (Sargan, 1955).

A somewhat similar property was expected with another formalization that seems to be much more appropriate for describing technology in modern industry. The property concerns the choice of techniques and the notion that different techniques should be selected at various stages of development, as relative scarcity of the two main factors, labour and capital, changes and the interest rate moves accordingly. Its formal specification actually requires a particular model. The production possibility set is seen as resulting from a combination of a number of elementary processes, each one operating at constant returns to scale, with fixed input–output coefficients, and requiring a time just equal to one period. Specifying further this model and applying it to an economy with one primary factor (labour), n produced goods and no joint production (the 'Samuelson–Leontief technology'), one defines a technique as a selection of n processes, one for the production of each good.

In this model, given any value of the interest rate, one can determine one technique that is fully appropriate for production, no matter what is the consumption basket. It then seemed natural to conjecture that techniques thus appearing as efficient at different interest rates were ordered from the less capitalistic (high interest) to the most capitalistic ones (low interest). However, this conjecture is not generally valid, even in this special model: as the interest rate progressively declines, one may have to switch at some point away from some technique but have to switch back to it at a later point: this is the case of 'reswitching of techniques' (Morishima, 1966).

Is the interest rate systematically smaller when, with a given technology, one shifts from a stationary equilibrium to another one using the same labour input but more productive capital? Again, this looked like a natural property to be stated. Since in a perfect equilibrium with no uncertainty the net rate of profit must be equal to the interest rate, the property was associated with the notion that capital accumulation must depress profit rates.

The property holds in a purely aggregated model with just one produced commodity, used both for consumption and as productive capital (Solow, 1956). The significance of this model for a more general situation was at the heart of hot debates in the late 1950s and early 1960s, the main opponents being located in the two academic cities named Cambridge (Robinson, 1956; Lutz and Hague, 1961). A side issue was whether one could give unambiguous definitions to such aggregate notions as the volume of productive capital and the marginal productivity of capital. Eventually, both counterexamples and formal analysis of the problem showed that the property was not generally valid (Burmeister and Turnovsky, 1972).

The significance of these various negative theoretical results should of course not be overstated. While reflecting the basic complexity of the relationship between the full system of discounted prices and its determinants, the results do not prove that 'pathological cases' are often empirically relevant.

INTERTEMPORAL EFFICIENCY. In the same way as the classical theory of individual behaviour, the theory of the optimum allocation of resources can be transposed to the intertemporal framework. Pareto efficiency of a 'programme' made of a set of individual plans, also called 'Pareto optimality', is generalized in an obvious way that need not be spelled out. The two classical duality theorems directly apply as long as the horizon is bounded: the programme resulting from a competitive equilibrium of the type described above is Pareto efficient if no external effect occurs; conversely, under a convexity or atomicity assumption, to any Pareto efficient programme can be associated a set of discounted prices supporting this programme. Properties of this system of prices are similar to those of the competitive price system.

Interesting new applications of these properties may give insights on the evolution of prices through time. In particular it is easily found that, if extraction costs are negligible, the discounted efficiency price of an exploited exhaustible resource is the same for all future dates, which means that the undiscounted price increases at a rate equal to the interest rate of the numeraire (Hotelling, 1931). When forming decisions on the use of exhaustible resources, one should give as much weight to the distant future as to the present; discounting gives no comfort for such decisions.

Theoretical difficulties, however, occur when the more realistic case of an unbounded horizon is being considered. The most relevant of these difficulties concerns the Pareto efficiency of competitive equilibria; efficiency is still proved to hold if the discounted value of the productive capital that exists at date t decreases to zero when one lets t increase to infinity (Malinvaud, 1953); but examples of competitive equilibria that do not fulfil this condition and are not Pareto efficient can be found. Such examples may be characterized as cases of overcapitalization, an excessive capital stock being indefinitely maintained without this ever benefiting consumption.

When attention is limited to stationary equilibria, a negative interest rate reveals lack of efficiency, whereas a positive one implies efficiency (if no external effect exists). Similarly, the interest rate of the price system supporting an efficient proportional growth programme cannot be smaller than the rate of growth (Starrett, 1970). The borderline case of an interest rate equal to the growth rate corresponds to what was called 'the golden rule'. More precisely, a new notion of optimality has been defined as follows for proportional growth programmes: an optimal programme is feasible and no other feasible programme leads to larger consumptions (i.e. a larger consumption of some commodity at some date and no smaller consumption of any commodity at any date). This definition neglects the conditions at the initial date since an 'optimal' programme can require a large input of capital at this date, larger than is required by other Pareto efficient proportional growth programmes. It was proved that a price system exists that supports such an optimal programme and contains an interest rate equal to the rate of growth (Desrousseaux, 1961; Phelps, 1961). This is another case in which discounting does not make the distant future negligible.

When it is considered in the preceding terms, the theory of intertemporal efficiency has a somewhat unrealistic aspect; or rather it seems to be quite partial in its treatment of the various questions that intertemporal efficiency raises both for planning and for the study of actual economic evolution. Indeed, the restrictions mentioned in the first section of this article are often serious.

For the theory of planning, even restricted to the medium and long terms, for which intertemporal choices are particularly important, problems concerning the gathering and exchange of information should not be neglected. If a system of discounted prices is to be used for supporting consistency of individual decisions with national objectives, its determination must be given very serious consideration. Moreover, planning often aims at correcting handicaps, distortions or market failures preventing economic development. Its long-term achievement then depends on how well it deals with problems that are not considered here but have motivated an important literature, dealing in particular with the determination of the best shadow discount rate to be used in project evaluation (Dasgupta et al., 1972).

Similarly, for assessing the performance of actual economic systems, one has still to face many questions that again often relate to problems of information. Three of them seem to deserve particular attention. First, the vision of agents exchanging in markets abstracts too much from the complexities of actual contractual arrangements, some of which deal precisely with intertemporal choices; one does not yet clearly see how these complexities react on the behaviour of the full economy, nor even how theory could approach the issue.

Second, the notion of an intertemporal competitive equilibrium should be replaced by that of a sequence of competitive temporary equilibria. It is then known that, even if anticipations are self-fulfilling along this sequence, intertemporal efficiency is not guaranteed; more precisely, the short-sightedness of equilibria seems to increase the likelihood of an overcapitalization of the type exhibited by the theory of the golden rule. This may occur because of too high saving propensities, because of risk aversion or because of oligopolistic market structures (Malinvaud, 1981). But the question of knowing whether and when this likelihood will materialize remains obscure.

Third, the dual assumption of permanent market clearing and permanently equilibrating prices rules out of consideration many issues, such as those arising from variations in the degree of unemployment or in the stimulus given by profitability. A rather common view among supporters of the market system sees these variations as negligible from a long-term perspective, economic evolution being supposed simply to oscillate around the long-term path determined by equilibrium analysis. But critics of the market system and some other economists have the opposite view: economic disequilibria would provide the main clue for an understanding of the comparative growth of nations (Schumpeter, 1934; Beckerman, 1966). Theory remains conspicuously weak with respect to solving this major debate.

BIBLIOGRAPHY

Allais, M. 1947. *Economie et intérêt*. Paris: Imprimerie Nationale.

Arrow, K. and Hahn, F. 1971. *General Competitive Analysis*. San Francisco: Holden-Day.

Balasko, Y. and Shell, K. 1980–81. The overlapping generations model. *Journal of Economic Theory*. I. The case of pure exchange without money, December 1980, 23(3), 281–306; II. The case of pure exchange with money, February 1981, 24(1), 112–42.

Beckerman, W. 1966. The determinants of economic growth. In *Economic Growth in Britain*, ed. P.D. Henderson, London: Weidenfeld & Nicolson.

Böhm-Bawerk, E. von. 1889. *Positive Theories des Kapitales*. Trans. as Vol. II of *Capital and Interest*, South Holland, Ill.: Libertarian Press, 1959.

Burmeister, E. and Turnovsky, S.J. 1972. Capital deepening response in an economy with heterogeneous capital goods. *American Economic Review* 62(5), December, 842–53.

Dasgupta, P., Marglin, S. and Sen, A. 1972. *Guidelines for Project Evaluation*. New York: UNIDO, United Nations.

Debreu, G. 1959. *Theory of Value: An Axiomatic Analysis for Economic Equilibrium*. New York: Wiley.

Desrousseaux, J. 1961. Expansion stable et taux d'intérêt optimal. *Annales des Mines*, November, Paris.

Drèze, J. 1982. Decision criteria for business firms. In *Current Developments in the Interface: Economics, Econometrics, Mathematics*, ed. M. Hazewinkel and A. Rinney Khan, Dordrecht: D. Reidel.

Fisher, I. 1907. *The Rate of Interest*. New York: Macmillan, 2nd edn, 1930.

Grandmont, J.-M. 1977. Temporary general equilibrium theory. *Econometrica* 45(3), April, 535–72.

Haberler, G. 1937. *Prosperity and Depression*. Geneva: League of Nations. 3rd enlarged edn, 1943; Lake Success, New York: United Nations, 1946.

Hahn, F. 1968. On warranted growth paths. *Review of Economic Studies* 35, 175–84.

Hayek, F.A. von. 1936. The mythology of capital. *Quarterly Journal of Economics* 50, February, 199–228.

Hayek, F.A. von. 1941. *The Pure Theory of Capital*. London: Routledge & Kegan Paul; Chicago: University of Chicago.

Hicks, J. 1939. *Value and Capital*. Oxford: Clarendon; 2nd edn, New York: Oxford University Press, 1946.

Hicks, J. 1973. *Capital and Time*. Oxford: Clarendon.

Hotelling, H. 1931. The economics of exhaustible resources. *Journal of Political Economy* 39, 137–75.

Knight, F. 1935. The theory of investment once more: Mr. Boulding and the Austrians. *Quarterly Journal of Economics* 50, November, 36–67.

Koopmans, T.C. 1960. Stationary ordinal utility and impatience. *Econometrica* 28, April, 287–309.

Lutz, F. and Hague, D. (eds) 1961. *The Theory of Capital*. London: Macmillan.

Malinvaud, E. 1953. Capital accumulation and efficient allocation of resources. *Econometrica* 21, April, 233–68.

Malinvaud, E. 1962. Efficient capital accumulation: a corrigendum. *Econometrica* 30, July, 570–73.

Malinvaud, E. 1981. *Théorie macroéconomique*, Vol. 1. Paris: Dunod.

Modigliani, F. and Brumberg, R. 1954. Utility analysis and the consumption function: an interpretation of cross-section data. In *Post-Keynesian Economics*, ed. K. Kurihara, New Brunswick, NJ: Rutgers University Press; London: George Allen & Unwin, 1955.

Morishima, M. 1966. Refutation of the nonswitching theorem. *Quarterly Journal of Economics* 80, November, 520–25.

Nickell, S. 1978. *The Investment Decisions of Firms*. Cambridge: Cambridge University Press; Cambridge, Mass.: Harvard University Press.

Phelps, E. 1961. The golden rule of capital accumulation. *American Economic Review* 51(4), September, 638–42.

Robinson, J. 1956. *The Accumulation of Capital*. London: Macmillan; Homewood, Ill.: R.D. Irwin.

Rosen, S. 1985. Implicit contracts. *Journal of Economic Literature* 23(3), September, 1144–75.

Samuelson, P. 1947. *Foundations of Economic Analysis*. Cambridge, Mass.: Harvard University Press.

Samuelson, P. 1958. An exact consumption-loan model of interest with or without the social contrivance of money. *Journal of Political Economy* 66, December, 467–82.

Samuelson, P. 1967. Irving Fisher and the theory of capital. In *Ten Economic Studies in the Tradition of Irving Fisher*, ed. W.J. Fellner et al., New York: John Wiley & Sons.

Sargan, J.D. 1955. The period of production. *Econometrica* 23, April, 151–65.

Schumpeter, J. 1934. *The Theory of Economic Development*. Cambridge, Mass.: Harvard University Press.

Solow, R. 1956. A contribution to the theory of economic growth. *Quarterly Journal of Economics* 70, February, 65–94.

Starrett, D. 1970. The efficiency of competitive programmes. *Econometrica* 38(5), September, 704–11.

Wicksell, K. 1901. *Vorlesungen über Nationalökonomie*. Trans. as *Lectures on Political Economy*, London: Routledge and Kegan Paul, 1934, Vol. I; New York: A.M. Kelley.

Large Economies

JOHN ROBERTS

Economists have often claimed that our theories were never intended to describe individual behaviour in all its idiosyncracies. Instead, in this view, economic theory is supposed to explain only general patterns across large populations. The prime example is the theory of competitive markets, which is designed to deal with situations in which the influence of any individual agent on price formation is 'negligible'.

As in so many aspects of economics, Cournot (1838) was the first to make the role of large numbers explicit in his analysis. Cournot provided a theory of price and output which, as the number of competing suppliers increases without bound, asymptotically yields the competitive solution of price equals marginal and average cost. However, for any given finite number of competitors, an imperfectly competitive outcome results.

It took over a century for Cournot's insights on the role of large numbers to be fully appreciated. Edgeworth (1881) argued the convergence of his contract curve as the economy grew, and increasing numbers of authors assumed that the number of agents was 'sufficiently large' that each one's influence on quantity choices was negligible, but it was not until the contributions of Shubik (1959) and Debreu and Scarf (1963) to the study of the asymptotic properties of the core that the number of agents took a central role in economic analysis.

The crucial step in this line of analysis was taken by Aumann (1964). Arguing that, in terms of standard models of behaviour, an individual agent's actions could be considered to be negligible only if the individual were himself arbitrarily small relative to the collectivity, Aumann modelled the set of agents as being (indexed by) an atomless measure space. In this context, an individual agent corresponds to a set of measure zero, while aggregate quantities are represented as integrals (average, per capita amounts). Then changing the actions of a single individual (or any finite number) actually has no influence on aggregates.

The non-atomic measure space formulation brings three mathematical properties that have proven important. The first is that it provides a consistent modelling of the notion of individual negligibility: only in such a context is an individual truly able to exert no influence on prices. Thus, this model correctly represents the primary reason for appealing to 'large numbers': in it, competitive price-taking behaviour is rational. Moreover, this individual negligibility, when combined with an assumption that individual characteristics are sufficiently 'diffuse', means that discontinuities in individual demand disappear under aggregation (Sondermann, 1975).

The second property is that a (non-negligible) subset of agents drawn from an economy with a non-atomic continuum of agents is essentially sure to be a representative sample of the whole population. This property has proven crucial in the literature relating the core and competitive equilibrium. (See Hildenbrand (1974) for a broad-ranging treatment of these issues.) It is also used in showing equivalence of core and value allocations (Aumann, 1975).

The other important property of the non-atomic continuum model is the convexifying effect. Even though individual entities (demand correspondences, upper-contour sets, production sets) may not be convex, Richter's theorem implies that the aggregates of these are convex sets when the set of agents is a non-atomic continuum. This property yields existence of competitive equilibrium in large economies even when the individual entities are ill behaved and no 'diffuseness' is assumed.

In the non-atomic continuum modelling, the individual agent formally disappears. Instead, one has coalitions (measurable sets of agents), and an individual is formally indistinguishable from any set of measure zero. The irrelevance of individuals is made very clear in the model of Vind (1964), where only coalitions are defined and individual agents play no part. Debreu (1967) showed the equivalence of Vind's and Aumann's approaches. A further extension of this line is to consider economies in terms only of the distributions of individual characteristics and allocation in terms of distributions of commodities. The strengths of this approach are shown in Hildenbrand (1974).

This disappearance of the individual is intuitively bothersome: economists are used to thinking about individual agents being negligible, but not about individuals having no existence whatsoever. Brown and Robinson (1972) provided an escape from this dilemma by their modelling of a large set of agents via nonstandard analysis. This approach gives formal meaning to such notions as an infinitesimal that had been swept out of mathematics and replaced by 'epsilon-delta' arguments. In interpreting nonstandard models, one distinguishes between how things appear from 'inside the model' and what they look like from 'outside'. From outside, these models may have an infinity of (individually negligible, infinitesimal) agents, yet from inside each agent is a well-defined, identifiable entity. Using this mathematical modelling eases the interpretation of large economies and also allows formalization of some very intuitive arguments that otherwise could not be made. Unfortunately, the difficulties of mastering the mathematics of nonstandard analysis has limited the number of economists using this approach.

While these formal models capture the essential intuition about the nature of economic behaviour of large economies, results obtained in this context should be of interest only to the extent that these models provide a good approximation to large but finite economies. This point was first emphasized by Kannai (1970), and its elaboration was the central issue confronting mathematical general equilibrium theory through the 1960s and early 1970s. The issue is one of continuity: in what sense are infinite economy models the limits of finite economies as the economy grows, and do the various constructs of interest (competitive or Lindhal allocations, cores, value allocations, etc.) of the finite economies approach those of the limit, infinite economies? These questions are extremely subtle. A good introduction to them is Hildenbrand (1974).

The study of the limiting, asymptotic properties of various economic concepts represents an alternative, more direct (but often less tractable) approach to large economy questions than does working with infinite economies. This line begins with Cournot's (1838) treatment of the convergence of oligopoly to perfect competition, the general equilibruim development of which has been a major focus of recent activity (see Mas-Colell, 1982 and the references there). The work growing out of Edgeworth (1881) and Debreu and Scarf (1963) on the core-competitive equilibrium equivalence noted above also follows this line.

Once such convergence is established, the crucial question becomes that of the rate of convergence because asymptotic results are of limited interest if convergence is too slow. This question was first addressed for the core by Debreu (1975), who showed convergence at a rate of at least one over the number of agents.

A more direct approach to this issue of how large a market must be for its outcomes to be approximately competitive is to employ a model in which price formation is explicitly modelled. (Note that this is not a property of the Cournot or Arrow–Debreu analyses.) In a partial equilibrium context the Bertrand (1883) model of price-setting homogeneous oligopoly indicates that 'two is large', in that duopoly can yield price equal to marginal cost. Recent striking results in the same line for the double auction are due to Gresik and Satterthwaite (1985), who show that even with individual reservation prices being private information, equilibrium under this institution can yield essentially competitive, welfare-maximizing volumes of trade with as few as six sellers and buyers.

This work is very heartening, for it tends to justify the profession's traditional reliance on competitive models which make formal sense only with an infinite set of agents. Another basis for optimism on this count comes from experimental work which shows strong tendencies for essentially competitive outcomes to be attained with quite small numbers. The further study of such institutions is clearly indicated.

BIBLIOGRAPHY

Aumann, R.J. 1964. Markets with a continuum of traders. *Econometrica* 32, 39–50.
Aumann, R.J. 1975. Values of markets with a continuum of traders. *Econometrica* 43, 611–46.
Bertrand, J. 1883. Théorie mathématique de la richesse sociale. *Journal des Savants* 48, 499–508.

Brown, D.J. and Robinson, A. 1972. A limit theorem on the cores of large standard exchange economies. *Proceedings of the National Academy of Sciences of the USA* 69, 1258–60.

Cournot, A. 1838. *Recherches sur les principes mathématiques de la théorie des richesses.* Paris: Hachette. Trans. as *Researches into the Mathematical Princples of the Theory of Wealth*, New York: Kelley, 1960.

Debreu, G. 1967. Preference functions on measure spaces of economic agents. *Econometrica* 35, 111–22.

Debreu, G. 1975. The rate of convergence of the core of an economy. *Journal of Mathematical Economics* 2, 1–8.

Debreu, G. and Scarf, H. 1963. A limit theorem on the core of an economy. *International Economic Review* 4, 235–46.

Edgeworth, F.Y. 1881. *Mathematical Psychics.* London: Kegan Paul. Reprinted New York: A.M. Kelley, 1960.

Gresik, T. and Satterthwaite, M. 1984. The rate at which a simple market becomes efficient as the number of traders increases: an asymptotic result for optimal trading mechanisms. Discussion Paper 641, Center for Mathematical Studies in Economics and Management Science, Northwestern University.

Hildenbrand, W. 1974. *Core and Equilibria of a Large Economy.* Princeton: Princeton University Press.

Kannai, Y. 1970. Continuity properties of the core of a market. *Econometrica* 38, 791–815.

Mas-Colell, A. (ed.) 1982. *Non-cooperative Approaches to the Theory of Perfect Competition.* New York: Academic Press.

Shubik, M. 1959. *Strategy and Market Structure; Competition, Oligopoly, and the Theory of Games.* New York: Wiley.

Sondermann, D. 1975. Smoothing demand by aggregation. *Journal of Mathematical Economics* 2, 201–24.

Vind, K. 1964. Edgeworth-allocations in an exchange economy with many traders. *International Economic Review* 5, 165–77.

Lindahl Equilibrium

JOHN ROBERTS

Lindahl equilibrium attempts to solve the problem of determining the levels of public goods to be provided and their financing by adapting the price system in a way that maintains its central feature of an efficient allocation being the outcome of voluntary market activities within the context of private property rights. Instead of some political choice mechanism and coercive taxation, under the Lindahl approach each individual faces personalized prices at which he or she may buy total amounts of the public goods. In equilibrium, these prices are such that everyone demands the same levels of the public goods and thus agrees on the amounts of public goods that should be provided. Since each individual buys and consumes the total production of public goods, the price to producers is the sum of the prices paid by individuals, and equilibrium involves the supply at these prices equalling the common demand. Thus, Lindahl equilibrium brings unanimity about the level of public goods provision, with costs being shared in proportion to (marginal) benefits.

The basic idea of a market solution to the problem of providing public goods is due to Erik Lindahl (1919). In its modern formulation, Lindahl equilibrium has come to play a benchmark role in the study of economies with public goods, externalities, and government expenditure which parallels that played by Walrasian competitive equilibrium in the analysis of questions where these factors are absent. For example, tax incidence can be measured relative to the Lindahl equilibrium. On the other hand, the Lindahl concept does not share the competitive equilibrium's centrality of position as a predictor of the actual outcomes of economic activity.

This latter point involves some irony, because Lindahl's original exposition of the idea treats it as having both normative and descriptive/predictive value.

Lindahl considered a legislature in which two parties represent the two homogeneous classes that constitute the electorate. (He also indicates how to extend the analysis to more classes and their representatives.) The issue is how much government activity should be carried out and how the costs of this activity should be shared between the two groups.

Lindahl identified two functions, say $f_A(s)$ and $f_B(s)$, which give, respectively, the expenditure on public activity that group A would want if it had to pay a fraction s of the corresponding costs and the level that B would want if it had to pay the complementary fraction $1 - s$. The value $x = f_A(s)$ is just the solution to the problem of maximizing the utility of after-tax income and public expenditure for group A, given that it will pay $100s\%$ of the costs, while f_B solves the corresponding problem for B. Ignoring income effects, Lindahl obtained $s = v'_A(f_A(s))$, where v_A is A's utility for public expenditure, and, correspondingly, $1 - s - v'_B(f_B(s))$. Note that f_A is decreasing and f_B is increasing. Thus, assuming $f_A(0) > f_B(0)$ or $f_A(1) < f_B(1)$, so that a group bearing all the costs wants less expenditure than does the group paying nothing, there is a unique value s^* strictly between zero and one at which the two groups agree on the desired level of expenditure, i.e., $x^* = f_A(s^*) = f_B(s^*)$.

Much of Lindahl's analysis is in terms of bargaining between the two groups over x and s under the assumption that, at any partition of the costs, the smaller of the two proposed quantities will be implemented. (This reflects the connection to voluntary exchange, where no one is forced to transact.) He recognized that such bargaining would not automatically lead to s^*, x^*. However, he claimed that if both groups were equally adept at defending their interests, this outcome would result.

Foley (1970) provided the basic general equilibrium treatment of Lindahl's idea in the context of an Arrow–Debreu private ownership economy with both private and pure public goods (no rivalry in consumption and no possibility of exclusion) where there are zero endowments of public goods, these goods are never used as inputs, and production takes place under constant returns to scale. (See Milleron (1972), Roberts (1973), and Kaneko (1977) for extensions and Roberts (1974) for a survey.)

Foley's model focuses on prices for the public goods rather than cost shares. Individual demand functions for public goods, as depending on the prices of both private and public goods, are defined (exactly as for private goods) as the choices of quantities to consume that maximize utility subject to the budget constraint defined by the prices and the agent's endowment. Thus, the quantity demanded of any public good at a particular price vector differs with individual preferences and endowments. However, the nature of pure public goods requires that all agents' consumption of any of these goods be equal. Thus, if prices are to lead different individuals all to demand the same quantities of public goods, it is clear that the prices charged to consumers must be personalized, differing across individuals to reflect differences in preferences and incomes. The price received by a producer of public goods is then the sum of the price paid by individuals, because each unit of each public good is allocated to and paid for by every individual. Meanwhile, private goods markets involve standard competitive pricing. With this, Lindahl equilibrium is a vector p of private goods prices, a vector q_i of public goods prices for each consumer i, an allocation of private goods x_i to each i and a vector of public goods y such that: (x_i, y) is the most preferred consumption bundle for consumer i from those affordable at prices (p, q_i), given

i's wealth as determined by p and i's initial endowment of private goods ω_i; and also such that the net input–output vector $(\Sigma_i x_i - \omega_i, y)$ is profit-maximizing at the producer prices $(p, \Sigma_i q_i)$. Note that both consumers and producers are following standard, competitive, price-taking behaviour just as in the Walrasian equilibrium.

Further appreciation of the connection between Lindahl and Walrasian equilibria can be gained using Arrow's insight (1970) that externalities (and the public goods problem in particular) can be viewed as a phenomenon of missing markets. Given a public goods economy with I consumers, M private goods and N public goods such as studied by Foley, consider an associated economy with I consumers, $(M + K)$ private goods, and no public goods, where $K = IN$. In this economy, each public good n in the original economy is replaced by a collection of I private goods, each of which is of interest to and consumable by only one consumer and which together are joint products in production. A net input–output vector in this economy of the form

$$(z, \tilde{y}), \qquad z \in R^M,$$

$$\tilde{y} = (y^1, \dots, y^{IN}) = (y_1, y_2, \dots, y_N, y_1, y_2, \dots, y_N, \dots, y_1, y_2, \dots, y_N) \in R_+^{IN}$$

is producible if and only if $(z, y_1, \dots, y_N)$ is in the production set of the original public goods economy. A Walras equilibrium in this economy is a price vector $(p, q^1, \dots, q^{IN}) \in R_+^{MK}$ and consumption vectors $(x_i, y_i^1, \dots, y_i^{IN}) \in R^{M+K}$, $i = 1, \dots, I$, where $(x_i, y_i^1, \dots, y_i^{IN})$ is the most preferred bundle for i from among those costing no more than $p\omega_i$ and where $(\Sigma_i x_i - w_i, \Sigma_i y_i^1, \dots, \Sigma_i y_i^{IN})$ is profit maximizing at prices $(p, q^1, \dots, q^{IN})$. Clearly, these conditions imply $y_i^{jn} = 0$ for $i \neq j$, so that no consumer receives positive amounts of another's personalized goods, and $y_i^{in} = y_j^{jn}$ for all i, j, and n, so that each individual consumes the same quantities of these personalized goods. Thus, Walras equilibria of the artificial economy exactly correspond to the Linahl equilibria of the original economy, with a parallel correspondence between the feasible allocations in the two economies and between the Pareto optima.

This construction, which was used by Foley to prove existence of Lindahl equilibrium, illuminates the claim that the Lindahl equilibrium involves voluntary exchange in the context of maintaining private property rights. It also makes clear that Lindahl equilibria are Pareto optimal and that any optimum can be supported as an equilibrium with a reallocation of resources. (In fact, Silvestre (1984) has characterized Lindahl allocations in terms of optimality plus a condition that no agent wants to reduce his or her contribution to paying for public goods if the level of provision would be proportionately reduced.) The Lindahl equilibrium's role as a benchmark is largely attributable to its having these properties, plus the fact that the Lindahl equilibrium allocations belong to the core if blocking is defined by a group being able to produce a more preferred consumption bundle for each of its members, even if non-members contribute nothing to public goods production (Foley, 1970). However, this construction also suggests some of the problems with the Lindahl equilibrium which prevent it from having great appeal as a positive prediction.

In particular, the usual complaint against a price-based solution to the public goods problem is that there would be no reason for an individual to take the Lindahl prices as given: misrepresentation of preferences should be profitable. Of course, as long as there are only a finite number of participants in a market, the behaviour of each typically has some influence on price formation, and so the assumption of price-taking in Walrasian, private goods equilibrium is questionable too.

Progress on this incentives question requires being more specific about the mechanism used to determine the allocation as a function of the initially dispersed information about the economic environment. In this context, Hurwicz (1972) formalized the idea that there must be incentive problems even with only private goods by showing that if a mechanism always yields Pareto optima and if participation is voluntary, so that its outcomes must be unanimously preferred to the no-trade point, then it cannot be a dominant strategy always to report one's preferences (demand) correctly. The exactly parallel result for public goods was achieved by Ledyard and Roberts (see Roberts, 1976). Thus neither Walrasian nor Lindahl equilibria can be the outcome of a mechanism which is incentive compatible in this dominant-strategy sense.

Of course, the standard case in which the Walrasian equilibrium seems appealing is a 'large numbers' one where each individual's influence is small. This intuition has been formalized in a number of ways: revealing one's true demand for private goods generically is asymptotically a dominant strategy as the number of participants in the economy becomes large; only competitive allocations are in the core of large economies; Nash equilibria of various models in which individuals recognize their influence on prices converge to the competitive solution as the economy grows. However, with public goods the situation is much different: increasing the size of the economy makes price-taking less attractive. This too has been shown in various ways. Roberts (1976) showed that increasing numbers can worsen the incentives for correct revelation of preferences for public goods and that as the numbers grow, the departure of the outcome from efficiency can also increase. Muench (1972) showed that the core and Lindahl equilibria do not coincide in large economies, and Champsaur, Roberts and Rosenthal (1975) demonstrated that the core of a public goods economy may actually expand when the number of consumers increases. In terms of the artificial economy, the essential intuition is that the market for each of the personalized goods is monopsonized, and the joint-product interaction constrains the bargaining power of the producer which otherwise might permit an efficient outcome to the bilateral monopoly situation. Thus, it seems that in the large numbers situations that have been the traditional concern of economics, the price-taking assumption renders the Lindahl solution of little predictive or descriptive value.

These essentially negative results are in some contrast with the results on incentives for correct revelation in iterative planning procedures for determining public goods. This literature was begun by Malinvaud (1971a, 1971b) and Drèze and de la Vallée Poussin (1971) and is surveyed in Roberts (1986).

In this context, the notion of incentive compatible behaviour is Nash equilibrium: each agent selects his/her responses to the central planning authority's proposals so as to maximize his/her payoff, given the strategies being used by the other agents to determine their responses. Such behaviour typically involves misrepresentation of preferences. However, various authors (Roberts (1979), Champsaur and Laroque (1982), and Truchon (1984) for example), have shown that this misrepresentation need not prevent convergence to a Pareto optimum and, in particular, to the Lindahl allocation.

However, as argued in Roberts (1986), these results are of limited interest because they rely on the implausible assumption that each agent is perfectly informed about the other's preferences. (A similar criticism can be laid against the static mechanisms for obtaining Walrasian or Lindahl allocations as Nash equilibria (Hurwicz, 1979).) Moreover, once the (self-selection or truthful reporting) constraints associated with preferences being private information are recognized, it is not clear that any mechanism can achieve Lindahl allocations (see Laffont and Maskin, 1979; d'Aspremont and Gerard–Varet, 1979). This gives a further reason for doubting the empirical relevance of Lindahl equilibrium.

BIBLIOGRAPHY

Arrow, K.J. 1970. The organization of economic activity: issues pertinent to the choice of market versus non-market allocation. In *Public Expenditures and Policy Analysis*, ed. R.H. Haveman and J. Margolis, Chicago: Markham.

Champsaur, P. and Laroque, G. 1982. Strategic behaviour in decentralized planning procedures. *Econometrica* 50, 325–44.

Champsaur, P., Roberts, J. and Rosenthal, R. 1975. Cores in economies with public goods. *International Economic Review* 16, 751–64.

d'Aspremont, C. and Gerard-Varet, L.A. 1979. On Bayesian incentive compatible mechanisms. In *Aggregation and Revelation of Preferences*, ed. J. Laffont, Amsterdam: North-Holland, 269–88.

Drèze, J. and de la Vallée Poussin, D. 1971. A tâtonnement process for public goods. *Review of Economic Studies* 38, 133–50.

Foley, D. 1970. Lindahl's solution and the core of an economy with public goods. *Econometrica* 38, 66–72.

Hurwicz, L. 1972. On informationally decentralized systems. In *Decision and Organization: A Volume in Honor of Jacob Marschak*, ed. C.B. McGuire and R. Radner, Amsterdam: North-Holland, 297–336.

Hurwicz, L. 1979. Outcome functions yielding Walrasian and Lindahl allocations at Nash equilibrium points. *Review of Economic Studies* 46, 217–27.

Kaneko, M. 1977. The ratio equilibrium and a voting game in a public goods economy. *Journal of Economic Theory* 16, 123–36.

Laffont, J. and Maskin, E. 1979. A differential approach to expected utility maximizing mechanisms. In *Aggregation and Revelation of Preferences*, ed. J. Laffont, Amsterdam: North-Holland.

Lindahl, E. 1919. *Die Gerechtigkeit der Besteuerung*. Lund: Gleerup. Part I, ch. 4, 'Positive Lösung', trans. by E. Henderson and reprinted as 'Just taxation – a positive solution', in *Classics in the Theory of Public Finance*, ed. R.A. Musgrave and A.T. Peacock, London: Macmillan, 1958.

Malinvaud, E. 1971a. A planning approach to the public goods problem. *Swedish Journal of Economics* 11, 96–112.

Malinvaud, E. 1971b. Procedures for the determination of a program of collective consumption. *European Economic Review* 2, 187–217.

Milleron, J. 1972. Theory of value with public goods: a survey article. *Journal of Economic Theory* 5, 419–77.

Muench, T. 1972. The core and the Lindahl equilibrium of an economy with a public goods: an example. *Journal of Economic Theory* 4, 241–55.

Roberts, J. 1973. Existence of Lindahl equilibrium with a measure space of consumers. *Journal of Economic Theory* 6, 355–81.

Roberts, J. 1974. The Lindahl solution for economies with public goods. *Journal of Public Economics* 3, 23–42.

Roberts, J. 1976. The incentives for correct revelation of preferences and the number of consumers. *Journal of Public Economics* 6, 359–74.

Roberts, J. 1979. Incentives in planning procedures for the provision of public goods. *Review of Economic Studies* 46, 283–92.

Roberts, J. 1986. Incentives, information and iterative planning. In *Information, Incentives, and Economic Mechanisms*, ed. T. Groves, R. Radner and S. Reiter, Minneapolis: University of Minnesota Press.

Silvestre, J. 1984. Voluntariness and efficiency in the provision of public goods. *Journal of Public Economics* 24, 249–56.

Truchon, M. 1984. Nonmyopic strategic behaviour in the MDP planning procedure. *Econometrica* 52, 1179–89.

Money and General Equilibrium Theory

JOSEPH M. OSTROY

Taking general equilibrium theory to be the model introduced by its founder, the topic of money and general equilibrium theory is as old as the subject itself. In the Preface to the fourth edition of the *Elements*, Walras wrote: 'Chiefly, however, it was my theory of money that underwent the most important chnges as a result of my research on the subject from 1876 to 1899.'

We are still working on Walras's model, but while the non-monetary aspects of the model have been the subject of steady improvement marked by comparatively harmonious logical development, research on the monetary side has been greeted with doubts and misgivings. Why? There is an outward-looking reason: the subject of money in general equilibrium is thought to be related to the problems of macroeconomics, subjects of great consequence and contentiousness. There is also an inward-looking reason: it is not clear if what we know as Walrasian general equilibrium is compatible with a model in which money as a medium of exchange plays an essential role.

This essay will take the inward-looking perspective on money and general equilibrium theory. No claim is, or need be, made that only after the inward-looking issues of logical consistency have been settled will the problems of money and macroeconmics be resolved. The only claim we make is the rather obvious one that monetary exchange is an example *par excellence* of a universal economic phenomenon, and if there is one branch of the discipline that is suited to its study, it is certainly general equilibrium theory. We shall argue that the incorporation of monetary exchange tests the limits of general equilibrium theory, exposing its implicitly centralized conception of trade and calling for more decentralized models of exchange.

1. THE WALRAS–HICKS–PATINKIN TRADITION: INTEGRATING MONETARY INTO VALUE THEORY. Walras presents his framework first by addressing the problem of

equilibrium in exchange and then introducing production and capital accumulation as extensions of the basic model of exchange. With this structure in place, Walras brings in money by introducing the equation of the offer and demand for money so as to conform with the rest of his system. This is accomplished by making a distinction between the stock of money, an object without any utility of its own, and the 'services of availability' of the stock, which does enter into the household utility functions and firm production functions.

Similarly, Hicks's (1935) suggestion for simplifying the theory of money is to make it conform to the (non-monetary) theory of value. Since 'marginal utility analysis is nothing other than a general theory of choice' and people do choose the amounts of money they hold, monetary theory can be embedded into value theory.

Patinkin's work (1965) represents the culmination of this tradition. Here Walras's 'service of availability' of money is somewhat fancifully recast as avoidance of 'embarassment from default'. Important to the money and general equilibrium agenda for Patinkin is the proper formulation of the real-balance effect so that nominal and real magnitudes are jointly determined as well as more precise statements of propositions on the short-run and long-run neutrality of money.

The presumption in this integration of money into value theory is that monetary theory is the weak partner and that by the exercise of reshaping it to fit the more rigorous choice-theoretic principles of value theory, including capital theory, monetary theory will be strengthened. There can be no doubt as to the influence of this regimen. Numerous contributions have demonstrated that the mechanism of exchange in a money economy, whatever it may be, can be usefully approximated by the mechanism of choice for a money commodity. Writers such as Friedman (1956) and Tobin (1961) each subscribe to the incorporation of money into the framework of value theory as the basis for their outward-looking approach to monetary theory.

When subjected to the scrutiny of the inward-looking approach to money and general equilibrium, this goal of integration does not appear to be very satisfying. By introducing money after he had completed his theory of exchange, Walras clearly made monetary phenomena on optional add-on rather than an integral component of the mechanism of exchange. Further, it was an add-on that would have to be valued for its own sake rather than as a component enhancing the performance of the rest of the system.

A succinct illustration of the inability of the model to leave room for monetary exchange is Walras's Theorem of Equivalent Distributions. Let p, x_i, and w_i stand for prices, individual i's final allocation and i's initial distribution of commodities, respectively, all elements of a given vector space. If $[p,(x_i)]$ is an equilibrium final allocation for individuals having certain tastes and initial distributions of commodities (w_i), then $[p,(x_i)]$ is also an equilibrium final allocation for individuals having the same tastes and any other initial distributions (w_i') such that $\Sigma w_i' = \Sigma w_i'$ and $pw_i' = pw_i$, for all i. Thus the no-trade distribution $(w_i' = x_i)$ is in the same equivalence class with an initial distribution in which the pattern of net trades among individuals and commodities is much less trivial. Trade or no trade, it is all the same to this model of exchange.

2. TRANSACTIONS COSTS. The inward-looking approach to money and general equilibrium asserts that Walras's class of equivalent redistributions is much too coarse, certainly too coarse to provide a role for the exchange facilitating properties of money. One way to refine these equivalence classes is to revise the conventional budget-constraint, $p(x_i - w_i) = 0$, by postulating that the value of all commodities purchased, $p(\max[x_i - w_i, 0])$, cannot exceed the value of the beginning of the period holdings of, say commodity 1, $p_1 w_i^1$. This is the so-called 'cash-in-advance' constraint of Clower (1967). The presumed real-world inferiority of barter exchange – purchasing commodities directly with other commodities – compared to money becomes a given. Of course, the added monetary constraint begs the question as to why it is necessary, particularly since as an added constraint it cuts down on the opportunities available under Walrasian barter. What is needed is a more comprehensive approach from which we may derive as a conclusion something resembling the cash-in-advance constraint as a solution to the problem of economizing on transaction costs.

Monetary exchange does not follow automatically once the costs of transacting are introduced. The costs of trading A for B directly must be greater than the indirect trade of A for money and then money for B. Oft-repeated lists of the properties of money (portability, durability, divisibility, etc.) call attention to attributes of an object with lower costs of exchange, but these lists merely describe the desirable features of a common medium of exchange that has already been adopted rather than provide an explanation of why the adoption should take place.

Just as in the single-period version of an exchange economy (characterized by the Theorem of Equivalent Distributions) where there is no role for money, the same conclusion holds for a multi-period extension with future markets. After indexing commodities by date and contingencies the model is indistinguishable from the one-period version. The key is that the individual faces a single budget-constraint for trades over the entire time horizon. Now modify this intertemporal model by making transactions costly, particularly that futures transactions are more costly than spot transactions. Thus, we leave behind models where the Theorem of Equivalent Redistributions holds, but we do not necessarily enter the world of monetary exchange. In fact, if we again permit individuals to face a single budget-constraint, a pattern of exchange that could be identified as monetary would require that one commodity is singled out to have much lower costs of transacting whenever it is used to buy or sell any other commodity. The question then would be 'Why?' and the answer 'That this is simply a feature of the transactions technology' would not be very satisfactory.

Suppose, however, we use the time index to create breaks in the budget-constraint. Each individual faces a sequence of budget-constraints in each of which his/her trades must balance. This will typically lead to a Walrasian equilibrium allocation that is Pareto-inferior. (Note that the definition of

Pareto-inferiority takes transactions costs for granted, i.e., feasible reallocations must respect the given transactions technology and distribution of initial endowments.) Now introduce an additional object of exchange, money, the terminal holding of which must coincide with its initial holding for each individual. Then it is possible to have budget-balance in each period in all commodities including money without having period-by-period balance in non-money commodities. The end result is to return to the single budget-constraint for the non-money commodities over the whole trading horizon. Hahn (1973) and Starrett (1973) show that an equilibrium allocations under such an arrangement would be Pareto-optimal.

The moral we draw from this story is that there are two types of transactions costs, technological and strategic. The technological ones have a transportation cost character – the unavoidable costs of sending commodity A from person i at time t to person j at time s. They may set the stage, but they are not sufficient to rationalize monetary exchange. The strategic costs are reflected by the demand that budget-balance be imposed at each period. Presumably, if individuals were not required to balance their budgets at each period there would be no monitoring and enforcement mechanism to get them to balance their budget over time, and they would cheat. It is the implicit costs of monitoring and enforcing budget-balance – the strategic costs – that yield a rationale for monetary exchange.

3. MONEY AND THE OVERLAPPING GENERATIONS MODELS OF GENERAL EQUILIBRIUM. It is useful to think of general equilibrium models as coming in two versions, the predominant one due to Walras and another, called the overlapping generations model, due to Samuelson (1958). Both share what seem to be the main features of market clearance conditions obtained from price-taking maximizers, but in one important conclusion they diverge. With inessential qualifications, a Walrasian equilibrium is always Pareto-optimal while the corresponding price-taking, market-clearing equilibrium in an overlapping generations model readily admits the possibility of Pareto inefficiency. The presence of this Pareto-gap holds out the promise that it might be filled by the introduction of a tradeable asset which, although intrinsically worthless, would allow individuals of adjacent generations to reach a Pareto-optimal allocation. And this promise can be fulfilled.

There is a certain similarity between the rationale for money in the transactions costs and overlapping generations models. In each case an intertemporal equilibrium without money may be inefficient, while the introduction of an intrinsically worthless object of exchange can remove the inefficiency. Ignoring the subtle mathematical complexities of the overlapping generations model's double infinity of individuals and commodities, the hypothesis that time and future generations are unending can be accepted as a fact-of-life. Thus, without having to appeal to transactions costs, it has been boldly argued by Wallace (1980) and Cass and Shell (1980) that the overlapping generations framework is the natural vehicle for describing money in general equilibrium theory.

Taking an outward-looking view of the problem, there is much to recommend the overlapping generations models. They lead to definite, policy-relevant macroeconomic conclusions, whereas the transactions cost approach has, at this stage at least, little to say about policy. However, taking an inward-looking view, the overlapping generations model appears less satisfying. Certainly it provides a role for money as a transfer mechanism between generations but there is no role for money as a medium of exchange. There are many circumstances in which full Pareto-efficiency can be achieved in a non-monetary equilibrium and the conditions under which efficiency does or does not require a positively valued money follows a logic of its own independent of the exchange enhancing properties commonly associated with money.

4. MONEY AND DECENTRALIZED EXCHANGE. In comparison to the aggregative style of macroeconomics, general equilibrium theory is held out as the micro-economically detailed description of an economy which highlights the decentralized character of the price system. In the Walras–Hicks–Patinkin tradition, general equilibrium theory provides the standard of rigour and detail to which monetary theory should aspire. However, when one adopts an inward-looking view of the problem of money and general equilibrium, it becomes apparent that these aspirations are set too low. The (implicit) description of market exchange in general equilibrium theory exhibits a substantial amount of as-if centralization, certainly too much to permit a role for money. Alternatively put, the Walrasian model of exchange is not much concerned with how commodities are exchanged.

Suppose the mythical auctioneer has just completed the task of finding equilibrium prices. It now remains for trades to be executed. Consider, first, a centralized story in which individuals come to the auctioneer to make their exchanges. Assuming that the auctioneer has no inventories of commodities and that not everyone can converge on the auctioneer at once, a record-keeping problem emerges. All individuals will leave their excess supplies with the auctioneer but at least the first few will not be able to pick up all their excess demands. They will have to return at a later date. Thus, actual purchase and sale will be separated in time. It would, therefore, be advisable for the auctioneer to keep a record of each individual's transactions. This can be simply and conveniently accomplished by issuing an IOU recording the value of supplies given up minus purchases received, all computed at equilibrium prices. In this way the auctioneer does not have to rely on his memory to discourage those who would cheat by saying that they had given more or taken less than they actually had in their previous trips to the auctioneer.

The strategic issues are similar to those described in the transactions cost models, above, except that here the record-keeping problem occurs whenever there is trade and not simply when there is intertemporal trade in the general equilibrium sense. Physical limitations on the executions of trades make it either inefficient or impossible to balance purchase sale transactions at every trading opportunity. But this creates the problem of how to enforce the overall budget-constraint when efficient execution of trades requires that an individual's trading position be out of balance along the way.

191

The auctioneer story is rather centralized. We may also consider a more decentralized trading arrangement in which individuals exchange sequentially in pairs. Ostroy (1973) and Ostroy and Starr (1974) investigate the trade-offs among time, information required beyond knowledge of equilibrium prices, inventories of commodities on hand, and centralized enforcement of budget constraints to execute trades. Also using a model of sequential pairwise exchange, Jones (1976) has addressed a theme which goes to the heart of the decentralization issue. The issue, raised by Menger (1871), is whether money is necessarily a creature of the state or whether a monetary trading pattern could arise endogenously through individuals being led by their self-interest to single out some commodity as a common medium of exchange.

There is hardly a more universal economic phenomenon than monetary trade. Thus, it would seem an explanation of money would be at the core of a theory of exchange. That it is not is neither a cause of anguish nor for complacency. The received theory arose to explain the prices of commodities. While obviously well-suited to its purpose, it is simply too centralized to cope with the economic issues underlying monetary exchange. But current research indicates that economic theory is moving along several fronts towards a more decentralized level of abstraction. Complementary developments in theories of search, of contracting and of incentive compatibility are all examples of what is sometimes called a 'micro-micro' attempt to go beyond the levels of aggregation that constitute the more traditional modes of analysis in general equilibrium theory. Perhaps in several decades we shall look back on traditional general equilibrium theory and say that in its microeconomic detail it stands in relation to the new theory as classical Ricardian analysis stands in relation to it. At that point, we can expect monetary exchange to be a routine application of general equilibrium theory.

BIBLIOGRAPHY

Cass, D. and Shell, K. 1980. In defense of a basic approach. In *Models of Monetary Economics*, ed. J.H. Kareken and N. Wallace, Minneapolis: Federal Reserve Bank of Minneapolis.

Clower, R.W. 1967. A reconsideration of the microfoundations of monetary theory. *Western Economic Journal* 6, December, 1–8.

Friedman, M. 1956. The quantity theory of money – a restatement. In *Studies in the Quantity Theory of Money*, ed. M. Friedman, Chicago: University of Chicago Press.

Hahn, F.H. 1973. On transactions costs, inessential sequence economics and money. *Review of Economic Studies* 40(4), October, 449–61.

Hicks, J.R. 1935. A suggestion for simplifying the theory of money. *Economica* 2, February, 1–19.

Jones, R.A. 1976. The origin and development of media of exchange. *Journal of Political Economy* 84(4), August, Part I, 757–75.

Menger, C. 1871. *Principles of Economics*. Trans. J. Dingwell and B. Hoselitz, New York: New York University Press.

Ostroy, J.M. 1973. The informational efficiency of monetary exchange. *American Economic Review* 63(4), September, 597–610.

Ostroy, J.M. and Starr, R. 1974. Money and the decentralization of exchange. *Econometrica* 42(6), November, 1093–1113.

Patinkin, D. 1965. *Money, Interest and Prices*. 2nd edn, New York: Harper & Row.

Samuelson, P.A. 1958. An exact consumption-loan model of interest with or without the social contrivance of money. *Journal of Political Economy* 66, December, 467–82.

Starrett, D. 1973. Inefficiency and the demand for 'money' in a sequence economy. *Review of Economic Studies* 40, October, 437–48.

Tobin, J. 1961. Money, capital and other stores of value. *American Economic Review Papers and Proceedings* 51, May, 26–37.

Wallace, N. 1980. The overlapping generations model of fiat money. In *Models of Monetary Economics*, ed. J.H. Kareken and N. Wallace, Minneapolis: Federal Reserve Bank of Minneapolis.

Walras, L. 1874–7. *Elements of Pure Economics*. Trans. W. Jaffé, Homewood, Ill.: Richard D. Irwin, 1954.

Monopolistic Competition and General Equilibrium

TAKASHI NEGISHI

Traditional general equilibrium theory, as exemplified in Walras (1874–7) and Hicks (1939), was concerned only with perfect competition, though it was preceded by Cournot's theory of oligopoly (1838), where perfect competition is only a limiting case of oligopoly. Walras (1874–7, p. 431) admitted that perfect competition is not the only possible system of economic organization and that we must consider the effects of other systems, such as those of monopolies, in order to make a choice between perfect competition and the other systems, as well as to satisfy our scientific curiosity. His theory of monopoly, however, remains a partial equilibrium analysis and no general equilibrium model is developed for an economy which contains monopolies. Hicks was more explicit in excluding monopolies from general equilibrium theory. He insisted that 'a universal adoption of the assumption of monopoly, must have very destructive consequences for economic theory' (1939, p. 83). The effect of an increase in demand on price is indeterminate, if the expansion of the firm is stopped not by rising costs, as in the case of competition, but by the limitation of the market, as in the case of monopoly.

But it is exactly on this problem of the rising costs versus the limitation of demand that Sraffa (1926) based his arguments against the empirical relevance of perfect competition. He argued that the chief obstacle to increasing production 'does not lie in the cost of production but in the difficulty of selling the larger quantity of goods without reducing the price' (p. 543). Although the theory for firms facing downwardly sloping demand curves suggested by Sraffa was first developed by Chamberlin (1933) and Robinson (1933) within the framework of Marshallian partial equilibrium theory, Triffin (1940, p. 89) emphasized that 'the new wine of monopolistic competition should not be poured into the old goatskins of particular equilibrium methodology'. For Triffin, the main contribution of monopolistic competition theory lay in its focus on the interdependence of firms.

194

Since partial or particular equilibrium theory deals only with relations between firms in an industry (or a group), the general theory of economic interdependence has to be constructed so as to encompass interrelations among all firms in an economy. Modern theories of monopolistic competition and general equilibrium such as Negishi (1961), Kuenne (1967), Arrow and Hahn (1971), Gabszewicz and Vial (1972), Fitzroy (1974), Marschak and Selten (1974) should be seen in this historical perspective.

Let us start with the simple model of monopolistic competition and general equilibrium considered by Negishi (1961). Suppose an economy is composed of perfectly competitive customers, perfectly competitive firms and monopolistically competitive firms. As usual, a perfectly competitive firm is assumed to maximize its profit by choosing a combination of input (vector) and output (vector) from a technologically given convex set of feasible combinations of input and output when prices are given. Similarly, a perfectly competitive consumer is assumed to maximize his utility subject to budget constraint, when prices and the distribution of profit from all firms are given.

A monopolistically competitive firm is assumed to perceive a *subjective* inverse demand curve when a currently observed combination of price and quantity is given. A subjective demand curve is different from an objective or true demand curve, which is a locus of actually realized or observable combinations of price and quantity. Suppose customers actually demand x^* of its product at the price of p^*. Then the firm perceives a possible relation between the demand x and the price p such that

$$p = D(x, p^*, x^*), \qquad \partial p/\partial x < 0. \tag{1}$$

To make the perceived demand curve rational in the weakest sense, the condition that

$$p^* = D(x^*, p^*, x^*) \tag{2}$$

must be imposed, so that the perceived demand curve passes the observed point (p^*, x^*). In other words, it intersects the objective demand curve at the given observed point. If (1) is simplified so that p is linear with respect to x; that is,

$$p = a(p^*, x^*) - b(p^*, x^*)x \tag{3}$$

where a and b are positive, the profit of the firm is a concave quadratic function of inputs and outputs. The firm is assumed to maximize its profit by choosing a combination of outputs and inputs when the currently observed combination of quantity demanded and price is given in markets where the firm is a price-maker, and prices are given in all the other markets.

Finally, all the markets must be cleared. In products markets the quantity demanded by consumers and by all the firms as input has to be equal to the quantity of output of all the supplying firms. In markets of factors of production, the quantity demanded by all the firms as input has to be equated to the quantity supplied by consumers. Price is raised (lowered) if quantity demanded exceeds (falls short of) quantity supplied, which we will call here the law of supply and demand.

Suppose we are given a set of values for all the prices, the inputs and outputs of all the firms, and quantities demanded and supplied for all the consumers. Then through the behaviour of markets, consumers and firms, there will be generated a new set of values of these prices and quantities corresponding to the given original set. Firms choose new combinations of inputs and outputs so as to maximize profits in view of given prices and quantities, while consumers choose new quantities demanded and supplied so as to maximize utilities, since the profits distributed are calculated from given prices and quantities. A new vector of prices is generated in markets through the law of demand and supply. Generally, the new vector of prices and quantities is different from the original. Under standard technical assumptions, however, we can show by the use of Kakutani's fixed-point theorem that there exists a vector completely identical to itself.

It is easily seen that such an unchanging vector of prices and quantities represents a general equilibrium of an economy which contains monopolistic competition. Since prices are unchanging, all the markets are cleared with quantities demanded and supplied, chosen by utility and profit maximization. Since price and quantity are unchanged, we see from (2) that perceived profit of a monopolistically competitive firm is maximized at the observed, realized price and quantity demanded; that is, the firm perceives demand for its product correctly. In other words, the existence of a general equilibrium is proved for an economy with monopolistic competition.

Certainly the model described above has many unsatisfactory aspects, and many criticisms, modifications and generalizations have been suggested, some of which are reviewed below.

The increasing returns to scale is presumably one reason for the existence of monopoly and monopolistic competition. Therefore, Arrow and Hahn (1971, pp. 151–67), Fitzroy (1974), Silvestre (1977, 1978) and others have emphasized the importance of the case where the feasible set of combinations of input and output is not convex for monopolistically competitive firms, and have developed interesting models to deal with this problem. For example, the model considered by Arrow and Hahn is very general with respect to the behaviour of monopolistically competitive firms, since each firm's reaction function is simply assumed to be continuous with respect to relevant variables, and the maximization of profit is not explicitly considered.

This is not unrelated to the objection against profit maximization raised by Gabszewicz and Vial (1972) for the case of monopolistically competitive firms. The owners of a firm may be interested not in profit itself but rather in what the profit can buy. The owners of price-making firms may, then, prefer a lower profit but favourable prices for consumption goods, to higher profit and unfavourable prices. To some extent, however, this difficulty has been solved by Hart (1982, 1984).

Nikaido (1975, pp. 7–10) was very critical of the use of the perceived or subjective demand curve (1) on the grounds: (a) that in monopolistically competitive markets disequilibrium does not consist in excess demand or supply (Lange, 1944, p. 35), and (b) that monopolistically competitive firms must perceive demand correctly not only at equilibrium (which is guaranteed by condition (2)) but also at disequilibria. Confining himself to the use of the Leontief model of production and additive logarithmic utility functions, however, Nikaido also found difficulties in the construction of the objective demand curve, which may not be downward sloping (1975, pp. 53–6).

Hart's (1984) criticism on the use of the subjective demand curve (1) and (2) is that the class of possible equilibria is very large so that the model gives us very little predictive power. In this respect, his consideration of the case of the reasonable conjecture (Hahn, 1978) is very interesting, since it reduces the class of possible equilibria by imposing restrictions more stringent than (2).

Unlike the case of the subjective or perceived demand curve (1), the objective demand curve is derived explicitly from the behaviour of consumers; that is, utility maximization. Models with monopolistically competitive firms facing such objective demand curves were developed first by Gabszewicz and Vial (1972) and Fitzroy (1974) on the basis of the *Cournot–Nash equilibrium* concept. They were followed by Marschak and Selten (1974), Laffont and Laroque (1976), Silvestre (1978) and others, who contributed to an interesting development of concepts of equilibrium.

In the model with the subjective demand curve, the restriction (3) is imposed in order that the profit function of a monopolistically competitive firm be concave with respect to the level of output, so that the level of output becomes a continuous function of the given values of prices and quantities. Similarly, in models with objective demand curves corresponding conditions must be imposed to make the profit function concave and the reaction function continuous, for otherwise it is difficult to prove the existence of a general equilibrium. However, Roberts and Sonnenschein (1977) have produced a number of non-pathological examples where these conditions are not satisfied, and have argued for the non-desirability of imposing any such conditions that are not derived from hypotheses on the fundamental data of preferences, endowments and technology. Therefore, it cannot be said that the problem of the existence of a general equilibrium is solved satisfactorily for an economy with monopolistically competitive firms facing objective demand curves.

Perhaps Kuenne's criticism (1967) deserves a separate mention. He argued against Triffin's interpretation (1940) of the relation between Walras–Pareto general equilibrium theory and Chamberlin's theory of monopolistic competition, and criticized the model of Negishi (1961) on the ground that it does not cope with the problem of product differentiation, interproduct competition being eliminated in both its rivalrous and non-rivalrous aspects. He developed a general equilibrium model to study interrelated product markets, by adopting the assumption of non-rivalrous inter-firm competition and by employing the concept of industry and group in the sense of Chamberlin.

Recently an interesting model was constructed by Dixit and Stiglitz (1977) to study the problem of product differentiation in the spirit of Chamberlin. Following Krugman (1979), we may sketch a simplified version of their model as follows. Let us consider an economy with only one scarce factor of production, labour.

The number of products differentiated is a variable which is denoted by n. The utility function of the representative consumer, into which all products enter symmetrically, is

$$U = \sum v(c_i), \qquad v' > 0, \, v'' < 0, \qquad (4)$$

where c_i is the consumption of the ith product. All products are assumed to be produced with the same cost function. The labour used in producing each product is a linear function of output:

$$y_i = a + bx_i \qquad (5)$$

where y_i is labour used in production of the ith product, x_i is the output of the ith product, and a and b are positive constants. Since all the products are symmetric, it follows that $x_i = x$, $y_i = y$, $c_i = c$, for all i. If c is known from the condition that the maximized profit is zero, the number of products differentiated is obtained from (5) as

$$n = L/(a + bx) \qquad (6)$$

since $x = Lc$ and $ny = L$, where L is the given labour force.

We cannot discuss here in detail all the critical arguments and suggestions for new concepts cited above, nor can our survey be exhaustive of the rapidly growing literature; fortunately some of it is nicely surveyed in Hart (1984).

We have seen that there is little agreement achieved among scholars on how monopolistic competition should be modelled in general equilibrium theory. Many scholars are critical of the model that uses the subjective demand curve perceived with weak consistency conditions and try to develop models using the objective demand curve derived explicitly from the utility maximization of consumers. In other words, they insist that monopolistically competitive firms should be modelled as rational agents fully informed of market conditions summarized in objective demand curves. We do not deny, of course, the importance of the problem of whether the behaviour of such fully informed rational firms is mutually consistent in the sense that there exists an equilibrium in the model using an objective demand curve. Unfortunately, it is difficult to solve this problem in view of Nikaido (1975) and Roberts and Sonnenschein (1977).

In the case of a perfectly competitive economy, however, it is only recently that existence problems were solved for a model in which agents are fully informed of market conditions. But long before that, there were already important and useful applications of general equilibrium theory to many problems, where the existence of an equilibrium was assumed as a part of hypotheses (Hicks, 1983, p. 374). Similarly, there have already been several interesting applications of the theory of general equilibrium with monopolistic competition, even though no particular model has won general acceptance. Since there is no reason why different models should not be used for different applications, however, we can use a model with the subjective demand curve or a model with very strong assumptions, provided that it yields an interesting result in a particular field.

The theory of international trade is set apart from other parts of economics by its concern with general equilibrium. Since scale economies play a crucial role in explaining the postwar growth in trade among the industrial countries (Kaldor, 1966; Balassa, 1967), general equilibrium theory with monopolistic competition should be applied in order to deal with those problems of increasing returns that cannot be dealt with by the theory of the perfect competition. A representative contribution in this area is Krugman (1979), who showed that trade is a way of extending the market and allowing exploitation of scale economies, and need not be a result only of international differences in technology or factor endowments. This is a revival of Adam Smith's argument that the division of labour is limited by the extent of the market (1776, p. 31). Though he used a Dixit–Stiglitz model, Krugman also surveyed related contributions based on other models of monopolistic competition.

Recent literature on Keynesian economics considers Keynesian equilibria by assuming that prices and wages are fixed, and effective demands and supplies equilibrated through the adjustment of quantities. One problem here is why prices and wages are fixed in the face of the existence of involuntary unemployment and excess capacities or inventories. Since the theory of perfect competition cannot solve this problem, it is natural to consider applications of the theory of monopolistic competition. An interesting example of the rapidly growing literature on this topic is Hart (1982), which also contains references to other contributions.

Having assumed that firms know the objective demand curves facing them, Hart (1982) had to admit a serious nonexistence problem pointed out by Roberts and Sonnenschein (1977). However, it is particularly in Keynesian economics that we should use subjective demand curves. Unlike the case of Walrasian homogeneous markets, where agents are fully informed of market conditions, markets in Keynesian economics should be Marshallian heterogeneous markets, where agents are not fully informed of conditions necessary to know the objective demand curves. In such a market, even competitive firms cannot perceive the demand curves to be infinitely elastic if demand falls short of supply. This is the reason why prices are fixed in the face of excess supplies, and demand and supply are equilibrated through the adjustment of the supply.

There is a strong reason why the perceived demand curve has a kink at the currently realized point, due to asymmetric behaviour of consumers in a world of imperfect information. Competitive firms cannot exceed the current price ruling in the market, since a higher price would induce customers to search for low-price suppliers. The perceived demand curve is infinitely elastic to the left of the currently realized point. A lower price, on the other hand, may not be fully advertised to customers who are currently buying from firms that are not lowering their prices. The perceived curve is, therefore, rather inelastic to the right of the realized point. The existence of this kink makes profit function of the firm concave with respect to the level of the output, which is convenient for proving the existence of an equilibrium (Negishi, 1979).

BIBLIOGRAPHY

Arrow, K.J., and Hahn, F. 1971. *General Competitive Analysis.* San Francisco: Holden-Day.

Balassa, B. 1967. *Trade Liberalization among Industrial Countries.* New York: McGraw-Hill.

Chamberlin, E.H. 1933. *The Theory of Monopolistic Competition.* Cambridge, Mass.: Harvard University Press.

Cournot, A.A. 1838. *Recherches sur les principes mathématiques de la théorie des richesses.* Trans. N.T. Bacon. New York: Macmillan, 1897.

Dixit, A. and Stiglitz, J. 1977. Monopolistic competition and optimum product diversity. *American Economic Review* 67(3), June, 297–308.

Fitzroy, F. 1974. Monopolistic equilibrium, non-convexity and inverse demand. *Journal of Economic Theory* 7(1), January, 1–16.

Gabszewicz, J.J. and Vial, J. 1972. Oligopoly 'à la Cournot' in a general equilibrium analysis. *Journal of Economic Theory* 4(3), June, 381–400.

Hahn, F.H. 1978. On non-Walrasian equilibria. *Review of Economic Studies* 45(1), February, 1–17.

Hart, O.D. 1982. A model of imperfect competition with Keynesian features. *Quarterly Journal of Economics* 97(1), February, 109–38.

Hart, O.D. 1984. Imperfect competition in general equilibrium: an overview of recent work. In *Frontiers of Economics*, ed. K.J. Arrow and S. Honkapohja, Oxford: Blackwell.

Hicks, J.R. 1939. *Value and Capital.* 2nd edn, Oxford: Oxford University Press, 1946; 2nd edn, New York: Oxford University Press, 1946.

Hicks, J.R. 1983. *Classics and Moderns. Collected Essays on Economic Theory*, Vol. III. Oxford: Blackwell; Cambridge, Mass.: Harvard University Press.

Kaldor, N. 1966. *Causes of the Slow Rate of Economic Growth in the United Kingdom.* Cambridge: Cambridge University Press.

Krugman, P.R. 1979. Increasing returns, monopolistic competition, and international trade. *Journal of International Economics* 9(4), November, 469–79.

Kuenne, R.E. 1967. Quality space, interproduct competition, and general equilibrium theory. In *Monopolistic Competition Theory: Studies in Impact*, ed. R.E. Kuenne, New York: J. Wiley.

Laffont, J.J. and Laroque, G. 1976. Existence d'un équilibre général de concurrence imparfaite: une introduction. *Econometrica* 44(2), March, 283–94.

Lange, O. 1944. *Price Flexibility and Employment.* Cowles Commission Monograph No. 8, Bloomington: Principia Press.

Marschak, T. and Selten, R. 1974. *General Equilibrium with Price-Making Firms.* Lecture Notes in Economics and Mathematical Systems No. 91, Berlin: Springer.

Negishi, T. 1961. Monopolistic competition and general equilbrium. *Review of Economic Studies* 28, June, 196–201.

Negishi, T. 1979. *Microeconomic Foundations of Keynesian Macroeconomics.* Amsterdam: North-Holland.

Nikaido, H. 1975. *Monopolistic Competition and Effective Demand.* Princeton: Princeton University Press.

Roberts, J. and Sonnenschein, H. 1977. On the foundations of the theory of monopolistic competition. *Econometrica* 45(19), January, 101–13.

Robinson, J. 1933. *The Economics of Imperfect Competition.* London: Macmillan; New York: St. Martin's Press, 1954.

Silvestre, J. 1977. General monopolistic equilibrium under non-convexities. *International Economic Review* 18(2), June, 425–34.

Silvestre, J. 1978. Increasing returns in general non-competitive analysis. *Econometrica* 46(2), March, 397–402.

Smith, A. 1776. *An Inquiry into the Nature and Causes of the Wealth of Nations.* Ed. R.H. Campbell, A.S. Skinner and W.B. Todd, Oxford: Oxford University Press, 1976.

Sraffa, P. 1926. The laws of returns under competitive conditions. *Economic Journal* 36, December, 535–50.

Triffin, R. 1940. *Monopolistic Competition and General Equilibrium Theory.* Cambridge, Mass.: Harvard University Press.

Walras, L. 1874–7. *Éléments d'économie politique pure ou théorie de la richesse sociale.* Definitive edn, Lausanne: Corbaz. Trans. W. Jaffé, Homewood, Ill.: Richard D. Irwin, 1954.

Numéraire

MICHAEL ALLINGHAM

In general equilibrium theory the price of one good in terms of another is interpreted as the amount of the second which can be exchanged for a given amount of the first. There is thus no essential role for a standard of value, or *numéraire*, though it is frequently helpful to introduce this. Such a *numéraire* is a commodity in terms of which, by convention, other commodities are valued.

The concept seems to have been introduced by Steuart (1767), albeit with some confusion between the properties of 'money' and 'units of account'. Walras (1874–7) clarified the concept, and showed how prices expressed in terms of one *numéraire* could be translated into prices in terms of another, without any introduction of 'money'. In the present discussion we commence with a justification of the use of *numéraire*. We then discuss the choice of a *numéraire* and some problems which may arise through the use of this.

We may represent an economy with n commodities by the excess demand function $f: S \to R^n$, where $S = R^n_+ - 0$. The interpretation is that $f(p)$ is the vector of aggregate excess demands (positive) or excess supplies (negative) expressed at the price system p. A basic property of f is that it is homogeneous of degree zero, that is $f(tp) = f(p)$ for all positive t.

It is this property which justifies the use of a *numéraire*. We can, for example, take commodity n to be *numéraire*, that is, ensure that $p_n = 1$, by setting the scalar t appropriately. Thus the price system q can be replaced by the *numéraire* price system p with $p_n = 1$ by multiplying q by $t = 1/q_n$; nothing real changes, since $f(p) = f(q)$. However, this is only possible if we can ensure that q_n is positive; since q is restricted only to S this may prove difficult.

The problem of the price of a chosen *numéraire* possibly being zero may be avoided by using a composite *numéraire*, that is a basket of goods. The scalar t may then be set as $u \cdot q$, where u is the unit vector in R^n: this has the effect of restricting p to the unit simplex in R^n. Alternatively, a non-linear normalization may be used, for example setting $t = q \cdot q$: this has the effect of restricting p to the surface of a sphere in R^n_+.

However, in reality prices are usually quoted in terms of some single unit of account, or *numéraire*, and it may be useful for the model of the economy to recognize this. Provided that all commodities are desirable, in the sense that $f_i(p)$ is infinite is $p_i = 0$, there is no possibility of any price being zero in equilibrium, that is some p where $f(p) = 0$. But there may be a problem of p_i being zero on some adjustment path of prices. Whether this is indeed a problem will depend on both the nature of f and on the adjustment process governing this path. For example, if the adjustment process is given by $\dot{p} = h(f(p))$, where h is a continuous sign-preserving function (and a dot indicates differentiation with respect to time) and if f has the above desirability property, then there is no problem. Alternatively, if the adjustment process is $\dot{p}_i = 0$ if $p_i \leqslant 0$ and $f_i(p) < 0$, while $\dot{p}_i = h_i(f_i(p))$ otherwise, then again there is no problem, provided of course that initial prices are positive (Arrow and Hahn, 1971). However, if these properties do not apply, and particularly if the adjustment process is discrete, there may be a problem.

Provided we can use a simple *numéraire* it is clear that if equilibrium is unique in terms of one *numéraire* then it will be unique in terms of another. However, the choice of *numéraire* may be relevant to considerations of stability: that is, for some given adjustment process involving a *numéraire* the economy may be stable for some *numéraire* but not for some other. Some sufficient conditions for stability, such as the condition that f have the revealed preference property, are clearly independent of any choice of a *numéraire*, while others are not (Hahn, 1982). For example, the diagonal dominance condition that all commodities are normal and that there are some units in which commodities can be measured such that each of their excess demands is more sensitive to a change in its own price than it is to change in all other non-*numéraire* prices combined, is clearly dependent on the choice of *numéraire*; indeed, because of homogeneity it makes no sense to attempt to extend it to include the *numéraire*. An economy may have this property, which is sufficient for stability, for one *numéraire* but not for some other. Since this condition is not necessary for stability it does not follow that the economy will be unstable with the second *numéraire*, but neither can stability be guaranteed.

The reason why uniqueness, for example, does not depend on the choice of *numéraire* while stability may, is that stability depends on the adjustment process. Strictly speaking, a change of *numéraire* is simply a change of adjustment process: it is quite natural that the economy may be stable under one adjustment process but not under another.

The question of a *numéraire* has a practical as well as a theoretical importance. In many cases 'money' is the natural *numéraire* – though the introduction of money in an essential sense, as opposed to simply as a unit of account, introduces its own problems (Clower, 1967).

BIBLIOGRAPHY
Arrow, K.J. and Hahn, F. 1971. *General Competitive Analysis.* San Francisco: Holden Day.
Clower, R.W. 1967. A reconsideration of the microfoundation of monetary theory. *Western Economic Journal* 6, December, 1–8.

Hahn, F. 1982. Stability. In *Handbook of Mathematical Economics*, Vol. 2, ed. K.J. Arrow and M.D. Intriligator, Amsterdam: North-Holland.

Steuart, Sir J. 1767. *Principles* (Book 1). London.

Walras, L. 1874–7. *Eléments d'économie politique pure*. Definitive edn, Lausanne: Corbaz, 1926. Trans. by W. Jaffé as *Elements of Pure Economics*, London: George Allen & Unwin, 1954; New York: Orion, 1954.

Overlapping Generations Model of General Equilibrium

JOHN GEANAKOPLOS

The consumption loan model that Paul Samuelson introduced in 1958 to analyse the rate of interest, with or without the social contrivance of money, has developed into what is without doubt the most important and influential paradigm in neoclassical general equilibrium theory outside of the Arrow–Debreu economy. A vast literature in public finance and macroeconomics is based on the model, including studies of the national debt, social security, the incidence of taxation and bequests on the accumulation of capital, the Phillips curve, the business cycle, and the foundations of monetary theory. In the following pages I give a hint of these myriad applications only in so far as they illuminate the general theory. My main concern is with the relationship between the Samuelson model and the Arrow–Debreu model.

Samuelson's innovation was in postulating a demographic structure in which generations overlap, indefinitely into the future; up until then it had been customary to regard all agents as contemporaneous. In the simplest possible example, in which each generation lives for two periods, endowed with a perishable commodity when young and nothing when old, Samuelson noticed a great surprise. Although each agent could be made better off if he gave half his youthful brithright to his predecessor, receiving in turn half from his successor, in the marketplace there would be no trade at all. A father can benefit from his son's resources, but has nothing to offer in return.

This failure of the market stirred a long and confused controversy. Samuelson himself attributed the suboptimality to a lack of double coincidence of wants. He suggested the social contrivance of money as a solution. Abba Lerner suggested changing the definition of optimality. Others, following Samuelson's hints about the financial intermediation role of money, sought to explain the consumption loan model by the incompleteness of markets. It has only gradually become clear that the 'Samuelson suboptimality paradox' has nothing to do with the absence of markets or financial intermediation. Exactly the same equilibrium allocation would be reached if all the agents, dead and unborn, met (in spirit) before the beginning of time and traded all consumption goods, dated from all time periods, simultaneously under the usual conditions of perfect intermediation.

Over the years Samuelson's consumption loan example, infused with Arrow–Debreu methods, has been developed into a full blown general equilibrium model with many agents, multiple kinds of commodities and production. It is equally faithful to the neoclassical methodological assumptions of agent optimization, market clearing, and rational expectations as the Arrow–Debreu model. This more comprehensive version of Samuelson's original idea is known as the overlapping generations (OLG) model of general equilibrium.

Despite the methodological similarities between the OLG model and the Arrow–Debreu model, there is a profound difference in their equilibria. The OLG equilibria may be Pareto suboptimal. Money may have positive value. There are robust OLG economies with a continuum of equilibria. Indeed, the more commodities per period, the higher the dimension of multiplicity may be. Finally, the core of an OLG economy may be empty. None of this could happen in any Arrow–Debreu economy.

The puzzle is why? One looks in vain for an externality, or one of the other conventional pathologies of an Arrow–Debreu economy. It is evident that the simple fact that generations overlap cannot be an explanation, since by judicious choice of utility functions one can build that into an Arrow–Debreu model. It cannot be simply that the time horizon is infinite, as we shall see, since there are classes of infinite horizon economies whose equilibria behave very much like Arrow–Debreu equilibria. It is the combination, that generations overlap indefinitely, which is somehow crucial. In sections 4 and 5 I explain how.

Note that in the Arrow–Debreu economy the number of commodities, and hence of time periods, is finite. One is tempted to think that if the end of the world is put far enough off into the future, that could hardly matter to behaviour today. But recalling the extreme rationality hypotheses of the Arrow–Debreu model, it should not be surprising that such a cataclysmic event, no matter how long delayed, could exercise a strong influence on behaviour. Indeed the OLG model proves that it does. One can think of other examples. Social security, based on the pay-as-you-go principle in the United States in which the young make payments directly to the old, depends crucially on people thinking that there might always be a future generation; otherwise the young will not contribute. Another similar example comes from game theory, in which cooperation depends on an infinite horizon. On the whole, it seems at least as realistic to suppose that everyone believes the world is immortal as to suppose that everyone believes in a definite date by which it will end. (In fact, it is enough that people believe, for every T, that there is positive probability the world lasts past T.)

In sections 1 and 3 I describe a simple one commodity example illustrating the four differences mentioned above between OLG and Arrow–Debreu equilibria. These are known to hold equally for economies with many commodities, as pointed out in sections 4 and 5. Section 2 discusses the possibility of equilibrium cycles in a one commodity, stationary, OLG economy.

Section 6 takes up the question of comparative statics. If there is a multiplicity of equilibria, what sense can be made of comparative statics? Section 6 summarizes the work showing that for perfectly anticipated changes, there is only one equilibrium in the multiplicity that is 'near' an original 'regular' equilibrium. For unanticipated changes, there may be a multidimensional multiplicity. But it is parameterizable. Hence by always fixing the same variables, a unique prediction can be made for changes in the equilibrium in response to perturbations. In section 7 we see how this could be used to understand some of the New Classical–Keynesian disputes about macroeconomic policy. Different theories hold different variables fixed in making predictions. Section 8 considers a neoclassical–classical controversy and section 9 summarizes some work on sunspots in the OLG model. Uncertainty in dynamic models seems likely to be very important in the future. An understanding of the one commodity model is sufficient to read all sections except 4 and 5.

The explanation of the puzzles of OLG equilibria given in section 4 is lack of market clearing 'at infinity'. By appealing to nonstandard analysis, the mathematics of infinite and infinitesimal numbers, it can be shown that there is a 'finite-like' Arrow–Debreu economy whose 'classical equilibria', those price sequences which need not clear the markets in the last period, are isomorphic to the OLG equilibria. Lack of market clearing is also used to explain the suboptimality and the positive valuation of money.

Recall the classical economists' conception of the economic process as a never ending cycle of reproduction. The state of physical commodities is always renewed. Samuelson attempted to give a completely neoclassical explanation of the rate of interest in just such a setting. It now appears that the market forces of supply and demand are not sufficient to determine the rate of interest in the OLG model. In other infinite horizon models they do. The difference, we speculate in section 5, comes from the fact that in the OLG model, no matter how large t is, there is always someone who values consumption more at date t than at date 1. In those infinite horizon models where equilibrium behaviour is like that in Arrow–Debreu, the economy is uniformly impatient.

1. INDETERMINACY AND SUBOPTIMALITY IN A SIMPLE OLG MODEL. In this section we analyse the equilibrium set of a one commodity per period, overlapping generations (OLG) economy. Although the definition of equilibrium seems firmly in the Walrasian tradition of agent optimization and market clearing, we discover three surprises. There are robust examples of OLG economies that possess an uncountable multiplicity of equilibria, that are not in the core, or even Pareto optimal. The lack of optimality (in a slightly different model, as we shall see) was pointed out by Samuelson in his seminal (1958) paper. The indeterminacy of equilibrium in the one commodity case is usually associated first with Gale (1973). In later sections we shall show that these puzzles are robust to an extension

of the model to multiple commodities and agents per period, and to a nonstationary environment. We shall add still another puzzle in section 3, the positive valuation of money, which is also due to Samuelson.

A large part of this section is devoted to developing the notation and price normalization that we shall use throughout. In any Walrasian model the problem of price normalization (the 'numeraire problem') arises. Here the most convenient solution in the long run is not at first glance the most transparent.

Consider an overlapping generation (OLG) economy $E = E_{-\infty,\infty}$ in which discrete time periods t extend indefinitely into the past and into the future, $t \in \mathcal{Z}$. Corresponding to each time period there is a single, perishable consumption good x_t. Suppose furthermore that at each date t one agent is 'born' and lives for two periods, with utility

$$u^t(\ldots, x_t, x_{t+1}, \ldots) = a^t \log x_t + (1 - a^t) \log x_{t+1}$$

defined over all vectors

$$x = (\ldots, x_{-1}, x_0, x_1, \ldots) \in L = R_+^{\mathcal{Z}}.$$

Thus we identify the set of agents A with the time periods $\mathcal{Z}$. Let each agent $t \in A$ have endowment

$$e^t = (\ldots, 0, e_t^t, e_{t+1}^t, 0, \ldots) \in L$$

which is positive only during the two periods of his life. Note that

$$\sum_{t \in A} e_s^t = e_s^{s-1} + e_s^s \qquad \text{for all} \quad s \in \mathcal{Z}.$$

An equilibrium is defined as a price vector

$$p = (\ldots, p_{-1}, p_0, \ldots) \in L_{++}$$

and allocation

$$\bar{x} = [x^t = (\ldots, x_t^t, x_{t+1}^t, \ldots); t \in A]$$

satisfying $\bar{x}$ is feasible, i.e.

$$\sum_{t \in A} x_s^t = \sum_{t \in A} e_s^t, \qquad \text{for all} \quad s \in \mathcal{Z} \tag{1.1}$$

and

$$\sum_{s \in Z} p_s e_s^t < \infty \qquad \text{for all} \quad t \in A \tag{1.2}$$

and

$$x^t \in \operatorname*{Arg\,Max}_{X \in L} \left\{ u^t(x) \mid \sum_{s \in \mathcal{Z}} p_s x_s \leqslant \sum_{s \in \mathcal{Z}} p_s e_s^t \right\} \tag{1.3}$$

The above definition of equilibrium is precisely in the Walrasian tradition, except that it allows for both an infinite number of traders and commodities. All prices are finite, and consumers treat them as parametric in calculating their budgets. The fact that the definition leads to robust examples with a continuum of Pareto-suboptimal equilibria calls for an explanation. We shall give two of them, one at the end of this section, and one in section 4. Note that condition (1.2) becomes necessary only when we consider models in which agents can live for an infinite number of time periods.

As usual, the set of equilibrium price sequences displays a trivial dimension of multiplicity (indeterminacy), since if p is an equilibrium, so is kp for all scalars $k > 0$. We can remove this ambiguity by choosing a price normalization $q_t = p_{t+1}/p_t$, for all $t \in \mathcal{Z}$. The sequence $q = (\ldots, q_{-1}, q_0, \ldots)$ and allocations $(x^t; t \in \mathcal{Z})$ form an equilibrium if (1) above holds together with

$$x^t \in \operatorname*{Arg\,Max}_{x \in L} \{u^t(x) | x_t + q_t x_{t+1} \leqslant e_t^t + q_t e_{t+1}^t\}. \tag{1.4}$$

Notice that we have taken advantage of the finite lifetime of the agents to combine (1.2) and (1.3) into a single condition (1.4). We could have normalized prices by choosing a numeraire commodity, and setting its price equal to one, say $p_0 = 1$. The normalization we have chosen instead has three advantages as compared with this more obvious system. First, the q system is time invariant. It does not single out a special period in which a price must be 1; if we relabelled calendar time, then the corresponding relabelling of the q_t would preserve the equilibrium. In the numeraire normalization, after the calendar shift, prices would have to be renormalized to maintain $p_0 = 1$. Second, on account of the monotonicity of preferences, we know that if the preferences and endowments are uniformly bounded

$$0 < a \leqslant a^t \leqslant \bar{a} < 1, \quad 0 < \underline{e} \leqslant e_t^t, \quad e_{t+1}^t \leqslant \bar{e} \leqslant 1 \qquad \text{for all} \quad t \in A,$$

then we can specify uniform *a priori* bounds $\underline{k}$ and $\bar{k}$ such that any equilibrium price vector q must satisfy $\underline{k} \leqslant q_t \leqslant \bar{k}$ for all $t \in \mathcal{Z}$. Thirdly, it is sometimes convenient to note that each generation's excess demand depends on its own price. We define

$$[Z_t^t(q_t), Z_{t+1}^t(q_t)] = (x_t^t - e_t^t, x_{t+1}^t - e_{t+1}^t)$$

for x^t satisfying (1.4), as the excess demand of generation t, when young and when old. We can accordingly rewrite equilibrium condition (1.1) as

$$Z_t^{t-1}(q_{t-1}) + Z_t^t(q_t) = 0 \qquad \text{for all} \quad t \in \mathcal{Z}. \tag{1.5}$$

Let us now investigate the equilibria of the above economy when preferences and endowments are perfectly stationary. To be concrete, let

$$a^t = a \qquad \text{for all} \qquad t \in A,$$

and let

$$e_t^t = e, \qquad \text{and} \qquad e_{t+1}^t = 1 - e, \qquad \text{for all} \quad t \in A,$$

where $e > a \geqslant \frac{1}{2}$. Agents are born with a larger endowment when young than when old, but the aggregate endowment of the economy is constant at 1 in every time period. Furthermore, each agent regards consumption when young as at least as important as consumption when old ($a \geqslant \frac{1}{2}$), but on account of the skewed endowment, the marginal utility of consumption at the endowment allocation when young is lower than when old:

$$\frac{a}{e} < \frac{1-a}{1-e}.$$

If we choose

$$q_t = \bar{q} = \frac{1-a}{1-e}\frac{e}{a} > 1$$

for all $t \in \mathscr{T}$, then we see clearly that at these prices each agent will just consume his endowment; $q = (\dots, \bar{q}, \bar{q}, \bar{q}, \dots)$ is an equilibrium price vector, with $x^t = e^t$ for all $t \in A$. Note that if we had used the price normalization $p_0 = 1$, the equilibrium prices would be described by

$$(\dots, p_0, p_1, p_2, \dots) = (\dots, 1, \bar{q}, \bar{q}^2, \dots)$$

where $p_t \to \infty$ as $t \to \infty$.

But there are other equilibria as well. Take $q = (\dots, 1, 1, 1, \dots)$, and

$$(x_t^t, x_{t+1}^t) = (a, 1-a) \qquad \text{for all} \quad t \in A.$$

This 'golden rule' Pareto equilibrium dominates the autarkic equilibrium previously calculated, thereby raising the most important puzzle of overlapping generations economies: why is it that equilibria can fail to be Pareto optimal? We shall discuss this question at length, in section 4. For now, let us observe one more curious fact. We can define the *core* of our economy in a manner exactly analogous to the finite commodity and consumer case. We say that a feasible allocation $x = (x^t; t \in A)$ is in the core of the economy E if there is no subset of traders $A' \subset A$, and an allocation $y = (y^t; t \in A')$ for A' such that

$$\sum_{t \in A'} y^t = \sum_{t \in A'} e^t,$$

and

$$u^t(y) > u^t(x^t) \qquad \text{for all} \quad t \in A'.$$

A simple argument can be given to show that the core of this economy is empty. For example, the golden rule equilibrium allocation is Pareto optimal, but not in the core. Since $a < e$, every agent is consuming less when young than his initial endowment. Thus for any $t_0 \in A$, the coalition $A' = \{t \in A \mid t \geqslant t_0\}$ consisting of all agents born at time t_0 or later can block the golden rule allocation.

Let us continue to investigate the set of equilibria of our simple, stationary economy. One can show that for any $\bar{q}_0$, with $1 < \bar{q}_0 < \bar{q}$, there is an equilibrium price sequence

$$q = (\ldots, q_{-1}, q_0, q_1, \ldots)$$

with $q_0 = \bar{q}_0$. In other words, there is a whole continuum of equilibria, containing a nontrivial interval of values. Incidentally, it can also be shown that for all such equilibria q, $q_t \to \bar{q}$ as $t \to \infty$, and $q_t \to 1$ as $t \to -\infty$. Moreover, these equilibria, together with the two steady state equilibria, constitute the entire equilibrium set.

This raises the second great puzzle of overlapping generations economies. There can be a nondegenerate continuum infinity of equilibria, while in finite commodity and agent economies there are typically only a finite number. Thus if we considered the finite truncated economy $E_{-T,T}$ consisting of those agents born between $-T$ and T, and no others, then it can easily be seen that there is only a unique equilibrium $(q_{-T}, \ldots, q_T) = (\bar{q}, \ldots, \bar{q})$, no matter how large T is taken. On the other hand, in the overlapping generations economy, there are a continuum of equilibria. Moreover, the differences in these equilibria are not to be seen only at the tails. In the OLG economy, as $\bar{q}_0$ varies from 1 to $\bar{q}$, the consumption of the young agent at time zero varies from a to e, and his utility from $a \log e = (1 - a) \log(1 - e)$ (which for e near 1 is close to $-\infty$), all the way to $a \log a + (1 - a) \log(1 - a)$. By pushing the 'end of the world' further into the future, one does not approximate the world which does not end. We shall take up this theme again in section 4.

It is very important to understand that the multiplicity of equilibria is not due to the stationarity of the economy. If we choose a^t near a and (e_t^t, e_{t+1}^t) near $(e, 1 - e)$, we would find the same multiplicity. One might hold the opinion that in a steady state economy, one should only pay attention to steady state equilibria, i.e. only to the autarkic and golden rule equilibria. In nonsteady state economies, there are not steady state equilibria to stand out among the continuum. One must face up to the multiplicity.

Let us reconsider how one might demonstrate the multiplicity of equilibria, even in a nonstationary economy. This will lead to a first economic explanation of indeterminacy similar to the one originally proposed by Samuelson. Suppose that in our nonstationary example we find one equilibrium $\hat{q} = (\ldots, \hat{q}_{-1}, \hat{q}_0, \hat{q}_1, \ldots)$ satisfying:

$$Z_t^{t-1}(\hat{q}_{t-1}) + Z_t^t(\hat{q}_t) = 0 \qquad \text{for all} \quad t \in \mathscr{Z}. \tag{1.6}$$

Let us look for 'nearby' equilibria.

We shall say that generation t is expectations sensitive at q_t if both $[\partial Z_t^t(\hat{q}_t)/\partial q_t] \neq 0$ and $[\partial Z_{t+1}^t(\hat{q}_t)/\partial q_t] \neq 0$. If the first inequality holds, then the young's behaviour at time t can be influenced by what they expect to happen at time $t + 1$. Similarly, if the second inequality holds, then the behaviour of the old agent at time $t + 1$ depends on the price he faced when he was young, at time t. Recalling the logarithmic preferences of our example, it is easy to calculate that the derivatives of excess demands, for any $q_t > 0$, satisfy

$$\frac{\partial Z_t^t(q_t)}{\partial q_t} = a^t e_{t+1}^t \neq 0$$

and

$$\frac{\partial Z_{t+1}^t(q_t)}{\partial q_t} = \frac{-(1-a^t)e_t^t}{q_t^2} \neq 0.$$

Hence by applying the implicit function theorem to (1) we know that there is a nontrivial interval I_{t-1}^F containing $\hat{q}_{t-1}$ and a function F_t with domain I_{t-1}^F such that $F_t(\hat{q}_{t-1}) = \hat{q}_t$, and more generally,

$$Z_t^{t-1}(q_{t-1}) + Z_t^t[F_t(q_{t-1})] = 0, \qquad \text{for all} \quad q_{t-1} \in I_{t-1}^F.$$

Similarly there is a nontrivial interval I_t^B containing $\hat{q}_t$, and a function B_t with domain I_t^B such that $B_t(\hat{q}_t) = \hat{q}_{t-1}$, and more generally, $Z_t^{t-1}[B_t(q_t)] + Z_t^t(q_t) = 0$, for all $q_t \in I_t^B$. Of course, if $F_t(q_{t-1}) = q_t \in I_t^B$, then $B_t(q_t) = q_{t-1}$.

These forward and backward functions F_t and B_t, respectively, hold the key to one understanding of indeterminacy. Choose any relative price $q_0 \in I_0^F \cap I_0^B$ between periods 0 and 1. The behaviour of the generation born at 0 is determined, including its behaviour when old at period 1. If $q_0 \neq \hat{q}_0$, and generation 1 continues to expect relative prices $\hat{q}_1$ between 1 and 2, then the period 1 market will not clear. However, it will clear if relative prices q_1 adjust so that $q_1 = F_1(q_0)$. Of course, changing relative prices between period 1 and 2 from $\hat{q}_1$ to q_1 will upset market clearing at time 2, if generation 2 continues to expect $\hat{q}_2$. But if expectations change to $q_2 = F_2(q_1)$, then again the market at time 2 will clear. In general, once we have chosen $q_t \in I_t^F$, we can take $q_{t+1} = F_{t+1}(q_t)$ to clear the $(t+1)$ market. Similarly, we can work backwards. The change in q_0 will cause the period 0 market not to clear, unless the previous relative prices between period -1 and 0 were changed from $\hat{q}_{-1}$ to $q_{-1} = B_0(q_0)$. More generally, if we have already chosen $q_t \in I_t^B$, we can set $q_{t-1} = B_t(q_t)$ and still clear the period t market.

Thus we see that it is possible that an arbitrary choice of $q_0 \in I_0^F \cap I_0^B$ could lead to an equilibrium price sequence q. What happens at time 0 is undetermined because it depends on expectations concerning period 1, and also the past. But what can rationally be expected to happen at time 1 depends on what in turn is expected to happen at time 2 etc.

There is one essential element missing in the above story. Even if $q_t \in I_t^F$, there is no guarantee that $q_{t+1} = F_{t+1}(q_t)$ is an element of I_{t+1}^F. Similarly, $q_t \in I_t^B$ does not necessarily imply that $q_{t-1} = B_t(q_t) \in I_{t-1}^B$. In our steady state example, this can easily be remedied. Since all generations are alike,

$$F_t = F_1, \ B_t = B_0, \ I_t^F = I_0^F \qquad \text{and} \qquad I_t^B = I_0^B \qquad \text{for all} \quad t \in \mathcal{Z}$$

One can show that the interval $(1, \bar{q}) \subset I_0^F \cap I_0^B$, and that if $q_0 \in (1, \bar{q})$, then $F_1(q_0) \in (1, \bar{q})$, and $B_0(q_0) \in (1, \bar{q})$. This establishes the indeterminacy we claimed.

In the general case, when there are several commodities and agents per period, and when the economy is nonstationary, a more elaborate argument is needed. Indeed, one wonders, given one equilibrium $\hat{q}$ for such an economy, whether after a small perturbation to the agents there is any equilibrium at all of the perturbed economy near $\hat{q}$. We shall take this up in section 6.

2. ENDOGENOUS CYCLES. Let us consider another remarkable and suggestive property that one commodity, stationary OLG economies can exhibit. We shall call the equilibrium $q = (\ldots, q_{-1}, q_0, q_1, \ldots)$ periodic of period n if $q_0, q_1, \ldots, q_{n-1}$ are all distinct, and if for all integers i and j, $q_i = q_{i+jn}$. The possibility that a perfectly stationary economy can exhibit cyclical ups and downs, even without any exogenous shocks or uncertainty, is reminiscent of 1930s–1950s business cycle theories. In fact, it is possible to construct a robust one commodity per period economy which has equilibrium cycles of every order n! Let us see how.

As before, let each generation t consist of one agent, with endowment $e^t = (\ldots, 0, e, 1 - e, 0, \ldots)$ positive only in period t and $t + 1$, and utility $u^t(x) = u_1(x_t) + u_2(x_{t+1})$. Again, suppose that $\bar{q} = u_2'(1 - e)/u_1'(e) > 1$. It is an immediate consequence of the separability of u^t, that for

$$q_t \leqslant \bar{q}, \qquad \frac{\partial Z_{t+1}^t(q_t)}{\partial q_t} < 0.$$

From monotonicity, we know that $Z_{t+1}^t(q_t) \to \infty$ as $q_t \to 0$. Hence it follows that for any $0 < q_0 < \bar{q}$, there is a unique $q_{-1} = B_0(q_0)$ with

$$Z_0^{-1}[B_0(q_0)] + Z_0^0(q_0) = 0.$$

From the fact that $Z_0^0(q_0) \geqslant -e$, for all q_0 it also follows that there is some $\underline{q} \leqslant 1$ such that if $q_0 \in [\underline{q}, \bar{q}]$, then $B_0(q_0) \in [\underline{q}, \bar{q}]$.

Now consider the following theorem due to the Russian mathematician Sarkovsky.

Sarkovsky's theorem: Let B: $[\underline{q}, \bar{q}] \to [\underline{q}, \bar{q}]$ be a continuous function from a nontrivial closed interval into itself. Suppose that there exist a 3-cycle for B, i.e. distinct points q_0, q_1, q_2, in $[\underline{q}, \bar{q}]$ with $q_1 = B(q_0), q_2 = B(q_1), q_0 = B(q_2)$. Then there are cycles for B of every order n.

Grandmont (1985), following related work of Benhabib–Day and Benhabib–Nishimura, gave a robust example of a one commodity, stationary economy (u_1, u_2, e) giving rise to a 3-cycle for the function B_0. Of course a cycle for B_0 is also a cyclical equilibrium for the economy, hence there are robust examples of economies with cycles of all orders.

Theorem (Grandmont): There exist robust examples of stationary, one-commodity OLG economies with cyclical equilibria of every order n.

This result is extremely suggestive. Note first, however, that all of the cyclical equilibria, except for the autarkic one-cycle $(\ldots, \bar{q}, \bar{q}, \bar{q}, \ldots)$ can be shown to be Pareto optimal (see section 4). The theory of macroeconomic business cycles is concerned with the welfare losses from cyclical fluctuations. (On the other hand, the fact that cyclical behaviour is not incompatible with optimality is perhaps an important observation for macroeconomics.) More significantly, it must be pointed out that Sarkovsky's theorem is a bit of a mathematical curiosity. No comparable general theorem is known for maps of the square, or any higher dimensional cube, into itself. The best that could be hoped for in general are robust examples of two cycles. And of course nonstationary economies, even with one commodity, will typically not have any periodic cycles. By contrast, the multiplicity and suboptimality of nonperiodic equilibria that we saw in section 1 are robust properties that are maintained in OLG economies with multiple commodities and heterogeneity across time. The main contribution of the endogenous business cycle literature is that it establishes the extremely important, suggestive principle, that very simple dynamic models can have very complicated ('chaotic') dynamic equilibrium behaviour.

In the next section we turn to another phenomenon that can generally occur in overlapping generations economies, but never in finite horizon models.

3. MONEY. Money very often has value in an overlapping generations model, but it never does in a finite horizon Arrow–Debreu model. The reason for its absence in the latter model is familiar: in the last period its marginal utility to every consumer is zero, hence so is its price. In the second to last period nobody will pay to end up holding any money, because in the last period it will be worthless. By induction it will have no value even in the first period. Evidently this logic fails in the infinite horizon setting, since there is no last period. On the other hand, there are infinite horizon models where again money can have no value. The difference between the OLG model and these other infinite horizon models will be discussed in section 5.

Strictly speaking, the overlapping generations model we have discussed so far has been modelled along the lines of Arrow–Debreu: each agent faces only one budget constraint and equilibrium is defined as if all markets met simultaneously at the beginning of time ($-\infty$). In such a model money has no function. However, we can define another model, similar to that first considered by Samuelson, in which agents face a sequence of budget constraints and markets meet sequentially, where money does have a store of value role. Surprisingly, this model turns out to have formally the same properties as the OLG model we have so far considered. To distinguish the two models we shall refer to this latter monetary model as the Samuelson model.

Suppose that we imagine a one-good per period economy in which the markets meet sequentially, according to their dates, and not simultaneously at the beginning of time. In such a setting it is easy to see that there could be no trade, since, as Samuelson put it, there is no double coincidence of wants. The old and the young at any date t both have the same kind of commodity, so they have no mutually advantageous deal to strike. But as Samuelson pointed out, introducing a durable good called money, which affects no agent's utility, might allow for much beneficial trade. The old at date t could sell their money to the young for commodities, who in turn could sell their money when old to the next period's young. In this manner new and more efficient equilibria might be created. The 'social contrivance of money' is thus connected to both the indeterminacy of equilibrium and the Pareto suboptimality of equilibrium, at least near autarkic equilibria. The puzzle, we have said, is how to explain the positive price of money when it has no marginal utility.

A closer examination of the equilibrium conditions of Samuelson's monetary equilibrium reveals that although it appears much more complicated, it reduces to the OLG model we have defined above, but with one difference, that the budget constraint of the generation endowed with money is increased by the value of the money. The introduction of the asset money thus 'completes the markets', in the sense of Arrow (1953), by which we mean that the equilibrium of the sequential economy can be understood as if it were an economy in which money did not appear and all the markets cleared at the beginning of time (except, as we said, that the income of several agents is increased beyond the value of their endowments). The puzzle of how money can have positive value in the Samuelson model can thus be reinterpreted in the OLG model as follows. How is it possible that we can increase the purchasing power of one agent beyond the value of his endowment, without decreasing the purchasing power of any other agent below his, and yet continue to clear all the markets? Before giving a more formal treatment of the foregoing, let me re-emphasize an important point. It has often been said that the Samuelson consumption loan model can be understood from the point of view of incomplete markets. Adding money to the model does indeed complete the markets, in the precise sense of Arrow–Debreu, but the result is the OLG model in which the puzzles remain.

Consider now a truncated example $E_{0,\infty}$ in which time begins at date $t = 0$, but continues to infinity. Once again there is a new agent 'born' at each date $t \geq 0$, whose utility depends only on two goods dated during his lifetime, and whose endowment is positive only in those same commodities. At each date $t \geq 1$ there will be two agents alive, a young one and an old one. At date 0 there is only one agent. To this truncation of our earlier model we now add one extra commodity, which we call money. Money is a perfectly durable commodity that affects no agent's utility. Agents are endowed with money (M_t^t, M_{t+1}^t), in addition to their commodity endowments.

A price system is defined as a sequence

$$(\pi; p) = (\pi_0, \pi_1, \pi_2, \ldots; p_0, p_1, p_2, \ldots)$$

of money prices π_t and commodity prices p_t for each $t = 0$. The budget set for any agent t is defined by

$$\{(m_t, m_{t+1}, x_t, x_{t+1}) \geq 0 \,|\, \pi_t m_t + p_t x_t \leq \pi_t M_t^t + p_t e_t^t$$

and

$$\pi_{t+1} m_{t+1} + p_{t+1} x_{t+1} \leq \pi_{t+1} M_{t+1}^t + p_{t+1} e_{t+1}^t + \pi_{t+1} m_t\}.$$

The budget constraint expresses the principle that in the Samuelson model agents cannot borrow at all, and cannot save, i.e. purchase more when old than the value of their old endowment, except by holding over money m_t from when they were young. Let $m_t^t(\pi, p)$ and $m_{t+1}^t(\pi, p)$ be the utility maximizing choices of money holdings by generation t when young and when old. As before the excess commodity demand is defined by $Z_t^t(\pi, p)$ and $Z_{t+1}^t(\pi, p)$.

To keep things simple, we suppose that agent 0 is endowed with $M_0^0 = M$ units of money when he is young, but all other endowments M_s^t are zero. Since money is perfectly durable, total money supply in every period is equal to M. Equilibrium is defined by a price sequence (π, p) such that $m_0^0(\pi, p) = M$ and $Z_0^0(\pi, p) = 0$, and for all

$$t \geq 1, \ m_t^{t-1}(\pi, p) + m_t^t(\pi, p) = M \qquad \text{and} \qquad Z_t^{t-1}(\pi, p) + Z_t^t(\pi, p) = 0.$$

At first glance this seems a much more complicated system than before.

But elementary arguments show that in equilibrium either $\pi_t = 0$ for all t, and there is no intergenerational trade of commodities, or $\pi_t > 0$ for all t. In the latter case $m_{t+1}^t(\pi, p) = 0$ for all t, hence money market clearing is reduced to

$$m_t^t(\pi, p) = M \qquad \text{for all} \quad t \geq 0.$$

And for the period by period Walras's Law, if the goods market clears at date t, so must the money market. So we never have to mention money market clearing. Moreover, by taking $q_t = (\pi_t p_{t+1})/(\pi_{t+1} p_t)$ we can write the commodity excess demands for agents $t \geq 1$ just as in section 1, by

$$[Z_t^t(q_t), Z_{t+1}^t(q_t)]$$

and they are the same as

$$[Z_t^t(\pi, p), Z_{t+1}^t(\pi, p)].$$

The only agent who behaves differently is agent 0, whose budget set must now be written

$$D^0(\mu, q_0) = \{x \mid x_0 + q_0 x_1 \leq e_0^0 + q_0 e_1^0 + \mu M\},$$

where

$$\mu = \frac{\pi_0}{p_0}.$$

We can then write agent 0's excess demand for goods as

$$[Z_0^0(\mu, q_0), Z_1^0(\mu, q_0)].$$

A monetary equilibrium in the OLG economy E_0, is any (μ, q), $\mu \geq 0$, satisfying

$$Z_0^0(\mu, q_0) = 0, \qquad Z_1^0(\mu, q_0) + Z_1^1(q_1) = 0,$$

and

$$Z_t^{t+1}(q_{t-1}) + Z_t^t(q_t) = 0 \qquad \text{for all} \quad t \in Z.$$

4. UNDERSTANDING OLG ECONOMIES AS LACK OF MARKET CLEARING AT INFINITY. In this section we point out that the suboptimality of competitive equilibria, the indeterminacy of nonstationary equilibria, the non-existence of the core, and the positive valuation of money can all occur robustly in possibly nonstationary OLG economies with multiple consumers and $L > 1$ commodities per period. We also note the important principle that the potential dimension of indeterminacy

is related to L. In the two-way infinity model, it is $2L - 1$. In the one-way infinity model without money it is $L - 1$; in the one-way infinity model with money the potential dimension of indeterminacy is L.

None of these properties can occur (robustly) in a finite consumer, finite horizon, Arrow–Debreu model. In what follows we shall suggest that a proper understanding of these phenomena lies in the fact that the OLG model is isomorphic, in a precise sense, to a '*-finite' model in which not all the markets are required to clear.

One of the first explanations offered to account for the differences between the Arrow–Debreu model and the Samuelson model with money centred on the finite lifetimes of the agents and the multiple budget constraints each faced. These impediments to intergenerational trade (e.g. the fact that an agent who is 'old' at time t logically cannot trade with an agent who will not be 'born' until time $t + s$) were held responsible. Indeed in a finite horizon model under uncertainty (with incomplete asset markets), if agents are confronted with a series of budget constraints, it is possible to generate robustly many dimensions of Pareto-suboptimal equilibria. But there is no uncertainty in the Samuelson model. And as we saw in the last section, without uncertainty, the presence of a single asset like money is enough to connect all the markets. Formally, as we saw, the model is identical to what we called the OLG model in which we could imagine all trade taking place simultaneously at the beginning of time, with each agent facing a single budget constraint involving all the commodities. What prevents trade between the old and the unborn is not any defect in the market, but a lack of compatible desires and resources.

Another common explanation for the surprising properties of the OLG model centres on the 'paradoxes' of infinity. In finite models, one proves the generic local uniqueness of equilibrium by counting the number of unknown prices, less one for homogeneity, and the number of market clearing conditions, less one for Walras's Law, and notes that they are equal. In the OLG model there are an infinity of prices and markets, and who is to say that one infinity is greater than another? We already saw that the backward induction argument against money fails in an infinite horizon setting, where there is no last period. Finally, it was pointed out that in many of the OLG equilibria (with unnormalized prices p) the value $\Sigma_t p_t(e_t^{t-1} + e_t^t) = \Sigma_t p \cdot e^t$ of the social endowment is infinite. No consumer is able to afford any fraction of the social endowment, no matter how small. This suggested to some a radically different kind of budget constraint from that in the Arrow–Debreu model. Surely it is right that infinity is at the heart of the problem. But this explanation does not go far enough. In the model considered by Bewley (1972) there are an infinite number of time periods (but a finite number of consumers). In that model all equilibria are Pareto optimal, and money never has value, even though there is no last time period. And by considering a sophisticated extension of the real numbers to infinite and infinitesimal magnitudes, it is possible for consumers to imagine purchasing a positive fraction (albeit infinitesimal) of the social endowment. The problem of infinity shows that there may be a difference between the Arrow–Debreu model and the OLG model.

In itself, however, it does not predict the qualitative features (like the potential dimension of indeterminacy) that characterize OLG equilibria.

Consider now a general OLG model with many consumers and commodities per period. We index utilities $u^{t,h}$ by the time of birth t, and the household $h \in H$, a finite set. Household (t, h) owns initial resources $e_t^{t,h}$ when young, an L-dimensional vector, and resources $e_{t+1}^{t,h}$ when old, also an L-dimensional vector, and nothing else. As before utility $u^{t,h}$ depends only on commodities dated either at time t or $t + 1$. Given prices

$$q_t = (q_{ta}, q_{tb}) \in R_{++}^{2L}, \qquad \sum_{i=1}^{2L} q_{ti} = 1.$$

consisting of all the $2L$ prices at date t and $t + 1$, each household in generation t has enough information to calculate the relevant part of its budget set. Hence we can write household excess demand $[Z_t^{t,h}(q_t), Z_{t+1}^{t,h}(q_t)]$ and the aggregate excess demand of generation t as $[Z_t^t(q_t), Z_{t+1}^t(q_t)]$, where

$$Z_{t+s}^t(q_t) = \sum_{h \in H} Z_{t+s}^{t,h}(q_t), \qquad s = 0, 1.$$

Suppose that time goes from $-\infty$ to ∞. We can write the market clearing condition for equilibrium exactly as we did in the one commodity, one consumer case, as

(A) $$Z_t^{t-1}(q_{t-1}) + Z_t^t(q_t) = 0 \qquad t \in \mathbb{Z}.$$

Of course we need to put restrictions on the q_t to ensure their compatibility, since q_{tb} and $q_{t+1,a}$ refer to the same period $t + 1$ prices. But this is easily done.

Similarly we can define the one way infinity economy $E_{0,\infty}$, in which time begins in period 0. We retain the same market clearing conditions for $t \geq 1$, changing only the $t = 0$ condition.

$$(A_+) Z_0^0(q_0) = 0 \qquad \text{and} \qquad Z_t^{t-1}(q_{t-1}) + Z_t^t(q_t) = 0, \qquad t \geq 1$$

Finally, let us define equilibrium in a one-way infinity model with money, E_0^M, when agents $(0, h)$ are endowed with money M^h, in addition to their commodities, by (μ, q), $\mu \geq 0$, satisfying

$$(A_+^M) \sum_{h \in H} Z_0^{0h}(q_0, \mu M^h) = 0 \qquad \text{and} \qquad \sum_{h \in H} Z_1^0(q_0, \mu M^h) + Z_1^1(q_1) = 0,$$

and

$$Z_t^{t-1}(q_{t-1}) + Z_t^t(q_t) = 0, \qquad \text{for} \quad t \geq 2.$$

With these preliminary definitions out of the way, we are ready to proceed with 'lack of market clearing at infinity'. For concreteness we shall concentrate first on $E_{0,\infty}$. Consider the truncated economy $E_{0,T}$ consisting of all the agents born between periods 0 and T. Market clearing in $E_{0,T}$ is identical to that in $E_{0,\infty}$ for $t = 0$ to $t = T$. But at $t = T + 1$, we require $Z_{T+1}^T(q_t) = 0$ in $E_{0,T}$. We have already seen in section 1 what a great deal of difference this can make: the economies $E_{0,T}$ and $E_{0,\infty}$ may be very different, for all finite T. The interesting point is that by appealing to nonstandard analysis, which makes rigorous the mathematics of infinite and infinitesimal numbers, one can easily show that the behaviour of $E_{0,T}$, for T an infinite number is very similar to the behaviour of $E_{0,T}$ for T finite. Thus the properties of the economy $E_{0,\infty}$ do not stem from infinity alone. We shall need to modify $E_{0,T}$ before it corresponds to $E_{0,\infty}$. Nevertheless, the economies $E_{0,T}$ to provide some information about $E_{0,\infty}$.

Theorem: (Cass–Balasko–Shell and Wilson): Under mild conditions, at least one equilibrium for $E_{0,\infty}$ always exists.

To see why this is so, note that $E_{0,T}$ is well-defined for any finite T. From nonstandard analysis we know that the sequence $E_{0,T}$, for $T \in \mathscr{F}$ and the original economy $E_{0,\infty}$, has a unique extension to the infinite integers. Now fix T at an infinite integer. We know that $E_{0,T}$ has at least one equilibrium, since $E_{0,s}$ does for all finite s. But if T is infinite, $E_{0,T}$ includes all the finite markets $t = 1, 2, \ldots$, so all those must clear at an equilibrium q^* of $E_{0,T}$. Taking the standard parts of the prices q_t^* for the finite t (and ignoring the infinite t) gives an equilibrium q for $E_{0,\infty}$.

To properly appreciate the force of this proof, we shall consider it again, when it might fail, in section 5, where we deal with infinite lived consumers.

In terms of the existence of equilibrium $E_{0,\infty}$ (and similarly $E_{0,\infty}^M$ and E) behaves no differently from an Arrow–Debreu economy. But the indeterminacy is a different story.

Definition: A classical equilibrium for the economy $E_{0,T}$ is a price sequence $q^* = (q_0, q_1, \ldots, q_T)$ that clears the markets for $0 \leqq t \leqq T$, but at $t = T + 1$, market clearing is replaced by

$$Z_{T+1}^T(q_T) \leqq \sum_{h \in H} e_{T+1}^{T+1,h}.$$

Thus in a classical equilibrium there is lack of market clearing at the last period. The aggregate excess demand in that period, however, must be less than the endowment the young of period $T + 1$ would have had, were they part of the economy. Economies in which market clearing is not required in every market are well understood in economic theory. Note that in a classical equilibrium the agents born at time T are not rationed at $T + 1$; their full Walrasian (notional) demands are met, out of the dispossessed endowment of the young. But we do not worry about how this gift from the $T + 1$ young is obtained. The significance of our classical equilibrium for the OLG models can be summarized:

Theorem (Geanakoplos–Brown): Fix T at an infinite integer. The equilibria q for $E_{0,\infty}$ correspond exactly to the standard parts of classical equilibria q^* of $E_{0,T}$.

The Walrasian equilibria of the economy $E_{0,\infty}$, which apparently is built on the usual foundations of agent optimization and market clearing, correspond to the 'classical equilibria' of another finite-like economy $E_{0,T}$ in which the markets at $T + 1$ ('at infinity') need not clear. The existence of equilibrium in $E_{0,\infty}$ is not a problem, because market clearing is a special case of possible non-market clearing, and $E_{0,T}$, being finite-like, always has market clearing equilibria. Thus even though the number of prices and the number of markets in $E_{0,\infty}$ are both infinite, we see that it is possible to say which is bigger, and by how much. From Walras's Law we know that if all the markets but one clear, that must clear as well. Hence having L markets that do not clear provides for $L-1$ potential dimensions of indeterminacy.

Corollary (Geanakoplos–Brown): For a generic economy $E_{0,\infty}$, there are at most $L-1$ dimensions of indeterminacy in the equilibrium set.

It is by no means true that there must be $L-1$ dimensions of indeterminacy in a generic economy. If we consider a classical equilibrium q^* for $E_{0,T}$, then generically we will be able to fix arbitrarily $L-1$ prices anywhere near their q^* values, and then choose the rest of the prices to clear all the markets up through time T. But which $L-1$ prices there are depends on which square submatrix N (of derivatives of excess demands with respect to prices) is invertible. For example, call the economy $E_{0,\infty}$ intertemporally separable if each generation t consists of a single agent whose utility for consumption at date t is separable from his utility for consumption at date $t+1$. Then the $L-1$ free parameters must all be chosen at date $T+1$ (as part of $q_{T,b}$), i.e. way off at infinity.

Corollary (Geanakoplos–Brown–Polemarchakis): Intertemporally separable economies $E_{0,\infty}$ generically have locally unique (in the product topology) equilibria.

Even when the $L-1$ degrees of freedom may be chosen at time $t=0$, there still may be no indeterminacy, if the matrix N has an inverse (in the nonstandard sense) with infinite norm. But when the free $L-1$ parameters may be chosen at $t=0$ and also the matrix N has an inverse with finite norm, then all nearby economies must also display $L-1$ dimensions of indeterminacy.

Theorem (Kehoe–Levine and Geanakoplos–Brown). In the $E_{0,\infty}$ OLG model there are robust examples of economies with $L-1$ dimensions of indeterminacy. In the monetary economy, $E_{0,\infty}^M$, there are robust examples of economies with L dimensions of indeterminacy.

In the monetary case, one can image L parallel and independent one good monetary economies of the kind studied in section 1. This is a knife-edge example of an L-commodity OLG monetary economy with L dimensions of indeterminacy, parametrized at $t=0$. A rather simple modification of this example yields another in which the N matrix has an inverse with a finite norm. This latter example is therefore robust, which implies that there are other nearby economies with L dimensions of indeterminacy in which no utilities are separable between commodities. A similar approach works in $E_{0,\infty}$, but with a dimension less. Let us now turn our attention to the question of Pareto optimality.

Definition: An allocation $\bar{x} = (x^{t,h}; 0 \le t \le T)$ is classically feasible for the economy $E_{0,T}$ if $\Sigma_{(t,h) \in A} x_s^{t,h} \le \Sigma_{(t,h) \in A} e_s^{t,h}$, for $0 \le s \le T + 1$. The classically feasible allocation $\bar{x}$ for $E_{0,T}$ is a classic Pareto optimum if there is no other classically feasible allocation $\bar{y}$ for $E_{0,T}$ with $u^t(y^{t,h}) > u^t(x^{t,h})$ for all $(t,h) \in A$ with $0 \le t \le T$, with at least one inequality representing a noninfinitesimal difference.

Theorem (Geanakoplos–Brown): The Pareto-optimal allocations $\bar{x}$ for the OLG economy $E_{0,\infty}$ are precisely the standard parts of classical Pareto-optimal allocations $\bar{x}^*$ for $E_{0,T}$, if T is fixed at an infinite integer.

The upshot of this theorem is that the effective social endowment includes the commodities e_{T+1}^{T+1} of the generation born at time $s = T + 1$, even though they are not part of the economy $E_{0,T}$. Since the socially available resources exceed the aggregate of private endowments, it is no longer a surprise that a Walrasian equilibrium, in which the value of aggregate spending every period must equal the value of aggregate private endowments, is not Pareto optimal.

On the other hand, this does not mean that all equilibrium are Pareto suboptimal. If the equilibrium prices $p_t \to 0$ as $t \to \infty$ (equivalently, if p_{T+1} is infinitesimal) then the value of the extra social endowment is infinitesimal, and there are no possible noninfinitesimal improvements. Let $(p, \bar{x})$ be an equilibrium for the OLG economy $E_{0,\infty}$. Consider the concave-convex programming problem of maximizing the utility of agent $(0, \bar{h})$, holding all other utilities of agents (t, h) with $0 \le t \le T$ at the levels $u^{t,h}(x^t)$ they get with $\bar{x}$, over all possible classically feasible allocations in $E_{0,T}$ that do not use more resources, even at time $T + 1$, than $\bar{x}$. Clearly $\bar{x}$ itself is a solution to this problem. But now let us imagine raising the constraints at time $T + 1$ from

$$\sum_{h \in H} x_{T+1}^{T,h} \qquad \text{to} \qquad \sum_{h \in H} (e_{T+1}^{Th} + e_{T+1}^{T+1,h}).$$

What is the rate of change of the utility $u^{0,\bar{h}}$? For the first infinitesimal additions to period $T + 1$ resources, the rate of change of $u^{0,\bar{h}}$ is on the order of p_{T+1}. But as the increases get larger, this rate of change could drop quickly, as higher derivatives come into play (assuming that agents have strictly concave utilities). One can easily calculate that the second derivative $\partial^2 u^{0,\bar{h}} / \partial e_{T+1}^2$, and all higher derivatives, depend on $\Sigma_{t=0}^T |1/p_t|$. Arguing this way, or even more directly, one can show:

Theorem (Cass, 1972; Benveniste–Gale, 1975; Balasko–Shell, 1980; Okuno–Zilcha, 1981): If agents have uniformly strictly concave utilities, then the equilibrium $(p, \bar{x})$ for an OLG economy $E_{0,\infty}$ is Pareto optimal if and only if $\Sigma_{t=0}^{\infty} |1/p_t| = \infty$.

Note that in this theorem it is the unnormalized prices that play the crucial role. It follows immediately from this theorem that the golden rule equilibrium $q = (\dots, 1, 1, 1, \dots)$ for the simple one good, stationary economy of section 1 is Pareto optimal, since the corresponding unnormalized price sequence is also $(\dots, 1, 1, 1, \dots)$. In fact, a moment's reflection shows that any periodic, nonautarkic equilibrium must also be periodic in the unnormalized prices p. Hence, as we have said, the cyclical equilibria of section 2 are all Pareto optimal.

Having explained the indeterminacy and Pareto suboptimality of equilibria for $E_{0,\infty}$ in terms of lack of market clearing at infinity, let us reexamine the monetary equilibria of OLG economies $E_{0,\infty}^M$, where $M = (M^h; h \in H)$ is the stock of aggregate money holdings by the agents $(0, h)$ at time 0.

Definition: Let $z \in R^L$ be a vector of commodities for time $T + 1$. Suppose that $-\Sigma_{h \in H} e_{T+1}^{T,h} \leqq \Sigma_{h \in H} M^h z \leqq \Sigma_{h \in H} e_{T+1}^{T+1,h}$. Let the augmented economy $E_{0,T}^M(z)$ be identical to the economy $E_{0,T}$, except that the endowment of each agent $(0, h)$ is augmented by $M^h \cdot z$ units of commodities at time $T + 1$.

Theorem (Geanakoplos–Brown): The equilibria q of the monetary economy E_0^M are precisely obtained by taking standard parts of full market clearing equilibria q^* of the augmented economies $E_{0,T}^M(z)$ for which $q_{T,b}^* z \geqq 0$, if T is fixed at an infinite integer.

The above theorem gives another view of why there are potentially L dimensions of monetary equilibria. It also explains how money can have positive value: it corresponds to the holding of extra physical commodities. In fact, this explains how the 'social contrivance of money' can lead to Pareto-improving equilibria, even in OLG economies where there is already perfect financial intermediation. The holding of money can effectively bring more commodities into the aggregate private endowment. The manifestation of the 'real money balances' is the physical commodity bundle z at date $T + 1$. Money plays more than just an intermediation role.

Before concluding this section let us consider a simple generalization. Suppose that agents live for three periods. What plays the analogous role to $E_{0,T}$? The answer is that prices need to be specified through time $T + 2$, but markets are only required to clear through time T. There are therefore $2L - 1$ potential dimensions of indeterminacy, even in the one-sided economy. In general, we must specify the price vector up until some time s, and then require market clearing only in those commodities whose excess demands are fully determined by those prices.

This reasoning has an important generalization to production. Suppose that capital invested at time t can combine with labour at time $t + 1$ to produce output at time $t + 1$, and suppose that all agents live two periods. Is there any difference between the case where labour is inelastically supplied, and the case where leisure enters the utility? In both cases the number of commodities is the same, but in the latter case the potential dimension of indeterminacy is one higher, since the supply of labour at any time might depend on further prices.

5. IMPATIENCE AND UNIFORM IMPATIENCE. We have already suggested that it is useful in understanding the OLG model to consider variations, for example in which consumers live forever. By doing so we shall also gain an important perspective on what view of consumers is needed to restore the usual properties

of neoclassical equilibrium to an infinite horizon setting, a subject to which we return in section 8.

Let us now allow for consumers $t \in A$ who have endowments e^t that may be positive in all time periods, and also for arbitrary utilities u^t defined on uniformly bounded vectors $x \in L$. For ease of notation we assume one consumer per period. A minimal assumption we need about utilities u^t is continuity on finite segments i.e. fixing x_s for all $s > n, u^t(x)$ should be continuous in $(x_1, \ldots, x_n)$. We also assume $\Sigma_{t \in A} e^t$ is uniformly bounded. In short, consumers may live forever. We shall find that in order to have Walrasian equilibria, the consumers must be impatient. In order for the equilibria to resemble Arrow–Debreu equilibria, the consumers need to be uniformly impatient.

Suppose we try to form the truncated economy $E_{0,T}$ as before, say for T finite. Since utility potentially depends on every commodity, we could not define excess demands in $E_{0,T}$ unless we knew all the prices. To make it into a finite economy, let us call $E'_{0,T}$ the version of $E_{0,T}$ in which every agent $0 \leq t \leq T$ is obliged to consume his initial endowment during periods $t > T$. Clearly $E'_{0,T}$ has an equilibrium. For this to give information about the original economy $E_{0,\infty}$, we need that consumers do not care very much about what happens to them after T, as T gets very far away. This is the notion of impatience.

For any vector x, let $_n\hat{x}$ be the vector which is zero for $t > n$, and equal to x up until n. Thus $_n\hat{x}$ is the initial n-segment of x. To say that agent $t \in A$ is impatient means that for any two uniformly bounded consumption streams x and y, if $u^t(x) > u^t(y)$, then for all big enough n, $u^t(_n\hat{x}) > u^t(y)$. Let us suppose that all consumers are impatient.

Note that the OLG agents are all impatient, since none of them cares about consumption after he dies.

The truncation argument, applied at an infinite T, still does not guarantee the existence of an equilibrium. For once we take standard parts, ignoring the infinitely dated commodities, it may turn out that the income from the sale of an agent's endowed commodities at infinite t, which he used to finance his purchase of commodities at finite t, is lost to the agent. It must also be guaranteed that the equilibria of $E_{0,T}$ give infinitesimal total value to the infinitely dated commodities. Wilson (1981) has given an example of an economy, composed entirely of impatient agents, that does not have an equilibrium precisely for this reason.

On the other hand, if there are only finitely many agents, even if they are infinitely lived, then we have:

Theorem (Bewley, 1972): Let the economy E be composed of finitely many, impatient consumers. Then there exists an equilibrium, and all equilibria are Pareto optimal.

Thus in the Bewley model there is no end to time, and no diminution in the physical size (endowment) of the economy over time. Yet unlike OLG models, equilibria are always Pareto optimal. What is the essential difference between the models?

Notice that in both the OLG model and Bewley's model, all consumers are impatient. The crucial difference is that in the OLG model, the *economy* is not impatient; for any date $t = n$, there is somebody who cares more about consumption at date n than at date $t = 0$. In order to discuss the notion of uniform impatience, let us introduce one more notation. Let 1 be the bundle of goods which consists of one unit of every commodity, at all dates. If a consumer has monotonic preferences, then there is some k such that strictly more of all goods up until date k makes him better off. Thus we can re-express impatience for agent t by saying that for all uniformly bounded x, and all $\varepsilon > 0$, there exists n such that

$$u^t(\varepsilon \cdot_k \hat{1} +_n \hat{x}) > u^t(x).$$

Definition: The agents $t \in A$ are said to be uniformly impatient if there is a fixed finite integer k with the following property. Let $(x^t; t \in A)$ be an allocation such that

$$x = \sum_{t \in A} x^t$$

is uniformly bounded. Let $\varepsilon > 0$ be fixed. Then there are $\varepsilon^t > 0$ and n satisfying

$$\sum_{t \in A} \varepsilon^t = \varepsilon$$

and

$$u^t(\varepsilon^t \cdot_k \hat{1} +_n \hat{x}^t) > u^t(x^t) \qquad \text{for all} \quad t \in A.$$

Of course any finite set of impatient consumers is uniformly impatient.

Theorem (Geanakoplos–Brown, 1982, 1985, 1986): Let the economy E be composed of agents $t \in A$ that are uniformly impatient. Then an equilibrium exists, all equilibria are Pareto optimal and in the core, the core equivalence holds for replications of the economy, and money never has positive value.

This theorem establishes a criterion for an economy, composed possibly of infinitely many goods and consumers, to behave like an Arrow–Debreu economy. The story would be complete if one could show, analogously to section 4, that there is an economy $E_{0,T}$ for some infinite T whose equilibria (as opposed to classical equilibria) corresponded, by taking standard parts, precisely to the equilibria of E. One could then derive information about the number of equilibria in E. Unfortunately this remains an open question.

Consider, however, the special case when there are finitely many agents, $h = 1, \ldots, H$, with separable, discounted utilities of the form $u^h(x) = \sum_{t=0}^{\infty} \delta_h^t v^h(x_t)$, with $\delta_h < 1$. This is clearly an economy with uniformly impatient consumers. And here there is a result:

Theorem (Kehoe–Levine, 1985): In finite agent, separable, discounted utility economies, there are generically a finite number of equilibria.

It is extremely interesting to investigate the change in behaviour of an economy that evolves from individually impatient to uniformly impatient. Muller and

Woodford (1983) consider an example with one infinitely lived agent, and infinitely many, overlapping, finite-lived agents. Wilson (1981) guarantees the existence of at least one equilibrium. They show that when the single agent's proportion of the aggregate endowment is low enough, there are a continuum of equilibria, but if it is high enough, there is no local indeterminacy.

6. COMPARATIVE STATICS FOR OLG ECONOMIES. A celebrated theorem of Debreu asserts that almost any Arrow–Debreu economy is regular, in the sense that it has a finite number of equilibria, each of which is locally unique. Small changes to the underlying structure of the economy (tastes, endowments, etc.) produce small, unique changes in each of the equilibria.

We have already seen that there are robust OLG economies with a continuum of equilibria. If attention is focused on one of them, how can one predict to which of the continuum of new equilibria the economy will move if there is a small change in the underlying structure of the economy, perhaps caused by deliberate government intervention? In what sense is any one of the new equilibria near the original one? In short, is comparative statics possible?

It is helpful at this point to recall that the OLG model is, in spirit, meant to represent a dynamic economy. Trade may occur as if all the markets cleared simultaneously at the beginning of time, but the economy is equally well described as if trade took place sequentially, under perfect foresight or rational expectations. Indeed this is surely what Samuelson envisaged when he introduced money as an asset into his model. Accordingly, when a change occurs in the underlying structure of the economy, we can interpret it as if it came announced at the beginning of time, or as if it appeared at the date in which it actually affects the economy.

We distinguish two kinds of changes to the underlying structure of an economy $\bar{E}_{-\infty,\infty}$ starting from an equilibrium $\bar{q}$. Perfectly anticipated changes, after which we would look for a new equilibrium that cleared all the markets from the beginning of time, represent one polar case, directly analogous to the comparative statics experiments of the Arrow–Debreu economy. At the other extreme we consider perfectly *un*anticipated changes, say at date $t = 1$. Beginning at the original economy and equilibrium $\bar{q} = (\ldots, \bar{q}_{-1}, \bar{q}_0, \bar{q}_1, \ldots)$, we would look, after the change from $\bar{E}_{-\infty,\infty}$ to $E_{-\infty,\infty}$, at time $t = 1$ (say to the endowment or preferences of the generation born at time 1), for a price sequence $q = (\ldots, q_{-1}, q_0, q_1, \ldots)$ in which $q_t = \bar{q}_t$ for $t \leq 0$, and $Z_t^{t-1}(q_{t-1}) + Z_t^t(q_t) = 0$ for $t \geq 2$. But at date $t = 1$ we would require q_1 to satisfy $Z_1^0(q_{1a}|\bar{q}_0) + Z_1^1(q_1) = 0$, where $Z_1^0(q_{1a}|\bar{q}_0)$ represents the excess demand of the old at time 1, given that when they were young they purchased commodities on the strength of the conviction that they could surely anticipate prices $\bar{q}_{0,b}$ when they got old, only to discover prices q_{1a} instead.

To study these two kinds of comparative statics, we must describe what we mean by saying that two price sequences are nearby. Our definition is based on the view that a change at time $t = 1$ ought to have a progressively smaller impact the further away in time from $t = 1$ we move. We say that q is near $\bar{q}$ if the difference $|q_t - \bar{q}_t|$ declines geometrically to zero, both as $t \to \infty$ and as $t \to -\infty$.

We have already noted in section 1 that the multiplicity of OLG equilibria is due to the fact that at any time t the aggregate behaviour of the young generation is influenced by their expectations of future prices, which (under the rational expectations hypothesis) depend on the next generation's expectations etc. Accordingly we restrict our attention to generations whose aggregate behaviour Z^t satisfies the expectations sensitivity hypothesis:

$$\text{rank} \frac{\partial Z_t^t(p_t, p_{t+1})}{\partial p_{t+1}} = \text{rank} \frac{\partial Z_{t+1}^t(p_t, p_{t+1})}{\partial p_t} = L.$$

For economies composed of such generations we can apply the implicit function theorem, exactly as in section 1, around any equilibrium q to deduce the existence of the forward and backward functions F_t and B_t. We write their derivatives at $\bar{q}$ as D_t and D_t^{-1}, respectively.

For finite Arrow–Debreu economies, Debreu gave a definition of regular equilibrium based on the derivative of excess demand at the equilibrium. He showed that comparative statics is sensible at a regular equilibrium, and then he showed that a 'generic' economy has regular equilibria. We follow the same programme.

We say that the equilibrium $\bar{q}$ for the expectations sensitive OLG economy $\bar{E}$ is Lyapunov regular if the long-run geometric mean of the products $D_t^* D_t D_{t-1}^* D_{t-1} \dots D_1^* D_1$ and $D_{-t}^{-1} * D_{-t}^{-1} \dots D_{-1}^{-1} * D_{-1}^{-1}$ converge and if to these products we can associate at most $2L - 1$ numbers, called Lyapunov exponents. The equilibrium is also nondegenerate if in addition none of these Lyapunov exponents is equal to one.

Theorem (Geanakoplos–Brown, 1985): Let $\bar{E} = \bar{E}_{-\infty,\infty}$ be an expectations-sensitive economy with a regular, nondegenerate equilibrium $\bar{q}$. Then for all sufficiently small perturbations E of $\bar{E}$ (including $\bar{E}$ itself), E has a unique equilibrium q near $\bar{q}$.

Thus the comparative statics of perfectly anticipated changes in the structure of $\bar{E}$, around regular, nondegenerate equilibria, is directly analogous to the Arrow–Debreu model. Note incidentally that one implication of the above theorem is that neutral policy changes, i.e. those for which $\bar{q}$ itself remains an equilibrium cannot have any effect if they are perfectly anticipated. (A structural change is always taken to mean with respect to real magnitudes, e.g. if the government buys a certain number of capital goods.) The situation is quite different for unanticipated changes.

Theorem (Geanakoplos–Brown, 1985): Let $\bar{E}$ be an expectations-sensitive economy with a regular equilibrium $\bar{q}$. Then for all sufficiently small perfectly unanticipated perturbations E of $\bar{E}$ (including $\bar{E}$ itself), the set of unanticipated equilibria q of E near $\bar{q}$ is either empty, or a manifold of dimension r,

$0 \leq r \leq L(L-1)$ if there is no money in the economy), independent of the perturbation.

The above theorem allows for the possibility that an unanticipated change may force the economy onto a path that diverges from the original equilibrium; the disturbance could be propagated and magnified through time. And if there are nearby equilibria, then there may be many of them. (Indeed that is basically what was shown in section 4.) In particular, an unanticipated neutral policy change could be compatible with a continuum of different equilibrium continuations. The content of the theorem is that if there is a multiplicity of equilibrium continuations, it is parametrizable. In other words, the same r variables can be held fixed, and for any sufficiently small perturbation, there is exactly one nearby equilibrium which also leaves these r variables fixed. We shall discuss the significance of this in the next section.

This last theorem was proved first, in the special case of steady-state economies, by Kehoe–Levine, in the same excellent paper to which we have referred already several times. The theorem quoted here, together with the previous theorem on the comparative statics of perfectly anticipated policy changes, refers to economies in which the generations may be heterogeneous across time.

Let us suppose that A is a compact collection of generational characteristics, all of which obey the expectations-sensitive hypothesis. Let us suppose that each generation's characteristics are drawn at random from A, according to some Borel probability measure. If the choices are made independently across time, then the product measure describes the selection of economies. Almost any such collection will have a complex demographic structure, changing over time. The equilibrium set is then endogenously determined, and will be correspondingly complicated. It can be shown, however, that

Theorem (Geanakoplos–Brown, 1985): If the economy E is randomly selected, as described above, then with probability one, E has at least one Lyapunov regular equilibrium.

Note that the regularity theory for infinite economies stops short of Arrow–Debreu regularity. In the finite economies, with probability one all the equilibria are regular.

7. KEYNESIAN MACROECONOMICS. Keynesian macroeconomics is based in part on the fundamental idea that changes in expectations, or animal spirits, can affect equilibrium economic activity, including the level of output and employment. It assets, moreover, that publicly announced government policy also has predictable and significant consequences for economic activity, and that therefore the government should intervene actively in the marketplace if investor optimism is not sufficient to maintain full employment.

The Keynesian view of the indeterminacy of equilibrium and the efficacy of public policy has met a long and steady resistance, culminating in the sharpest attack of all, from the so-called new classicals, who have argued that the time-honoured microeconomic methodological premises of agent optimization and market clearing, considered together with rational expectations, are logically inconsistent with animal spirits and the non-neutrality of public monetary and bond financed fiscal policy.

The foundation of the new classical paradigm is the Walrasian equilibrium model of Arrow–Debreu, in which it is typically possible to prove that all equilibria are Pareto optimal and that the equilibrium set is finite; at least locally, the hypothesis of market clearing fixes the expectations of rational investors. In that model, however, economic activity has a definite beginning and end. Our point of view is that for some purposes economic activity is better described as a process without end. In a world without a definite end, there is the possibility that what happens today is underdetermined, because it depends on what people tomorrow expect to happen the day after tomorrow, etc.

Consider the simple one good per period overlapping generations economy with money E_0^M, which we discussed in section 1. Generation 0 is endowed with money when young, and equilibrium can be described either with the unnormalized prices $p = (\bar{p}_0, \bar{p}_1, \ldots)$, or with the normalized prices $(\bar{\gamma}, \bar{q}) = (\bar{\gamma}, \bar{q}_0, \bar{q}_1, \ldots)$ where $\bar{q}_t = \bar{p}_{t+1}/\bar{p}_t$, and $\bar{\gamma} = M/\bar{p}_0$. It is helpful to reinterpret the model as a simple production economy. Imagine that the endowment e_t^t in the first period of life is actually labour, which can be transformed into output, y_t, according to the production function, $y_t = e_t$. We would then think of any purchases of goods by the old generation as demand for real output to be produced by the young. The young in turn now derive utility from leisure in their youth and consumption in their old age. Notice that the quantity equation $\bar{p}_t y_t = M$, holds for this economy. (Velocity equals one.)

The indeterminacy of rational expectations equilibrium has the direct implication that optimistic expectations *by themselves* can cause the economy's output to expand or contract. In short the economy has an inherent volatility. The Keynesian story of animal spirits causing economic growth or decline can be told without invoking irrationality or non-market-clearing.

In fact, the indeterminacy of equilibrium expectations is especially striking when seen as a response to public (but unanticipated) policy changes. Suppose the economy is in a long-term rational expectations equilibrium $\bar{p}$, when at time 1 the government undertakes some expenditures, financed either by lump sum taxation on the young or by printing money. How should rational agents respond? The environment has been changed, and there is no reason for them to anticipate that $(\bar{p}_2, \bar{p}_3, \ldots)$ will still occur in the future. Indeed, in models with more than one commodity (such as we will shortly consider) there may be no equilibrium $(p_1, p_2, p_3, \ldots)$ in the new environment with $p_2 = \bar{p}_2$, $p_3 = \bar{p}_3$, etc. There is an ambiguity in what can be rationally anticipated.

We argue that it is possible to explain the differences between Keynesian and monetarist policy predictions by the assumptions each makes about expectational responses to policy, and not by the one's supposed adherence to optimization, market clearing, and rational expectations, and the other's supposed denial of all three.

Consider now the government policy of printing a small amount of money,

ΔM, to be spent on its own consumption of real output – or equivalently to be given to generation $t = 0$ (when old) to spend on its consumption. Imagine that agents are convinced that this policy is not inflationary, i.e. that $\bar{p}_1$ will remain the equilibrium price level during the initial period of the new equilibrium. This will give generation $t = 0$ consumption level $(M + \Delta M)/\bar{p}_1$. As long as ΔM is sufficiently small and the initial equilibrium was one of the Pareto-suboptimal equilibria described in section 1, there is indeed a new equilibrium price path p beginning with $p_1 = \bar{p}_1$. Output has risen by $\Delta M/\bar{p}_1$, and in fact this policy is Pareto improving. On the other hand, imagine that agents are convinced that the path of real interest rates

$$(q_1^{-1} - 1, q_2^{-1} - 1, \ldots) = \left(\frac{p_1}{p_2} - 1, \frac{p_2}{p_3} - 1, \ldots\right)$$

will remain unchanged. In this economy, price expectations are a function of p_1. Recalling the initial period market-clearing equation, it is clear that prices rise proportionally to the growth in the money stock. The result is 'forced savings'; output is unchanged and generation $t = 1$ must pay for the government's consumption. If the government's consumption gives no agent utility, the policy is Pareto worsening.

This model is only a crude approximation of the differences between Keynesian and monetarist assumptions about expectations and policy. It is quite possible to argue, for example, that holding $q_1 = \bar{p}_2/\bar{p}_1$ (the inflation rate) fixed is the natural *Keynesian* assumption to make. This ambiguity is unavoidable when there is only one asset into which the young can place their savings. We are thereby prevented from distinguishing between the inflation rate and the interest rate. Our model must be enriched before we can perform satisfactory policy analysis. Nevertheless the model conveys the general principle that expected price paths are not locally unique. There is consequently no natural assumption to make about how expectations are affected by policy. A sensible analysis is therefore impossible without externally given hypotheses about expectations. These can be Keynesian, monetarist, or perhaps some combination of the two.

Geanakoplos–Polemarchakis (1986) builds just such a richer model of macroeconomic equilibrium by adding commodities, including a capital good, and a neoclassical production function. With elastically supplied labour, there are two dimensions of indeterminacy. It is therefore possible to fix both the nominal wage, and the firm's expectations ('animal spirits'), and still solve for equilibrium as a function of policy perturbations to the economy. These institutional rigidities are more convincingly Keynesian, and they lead to Keynesian policy predictions. Moreover, taking advantage of the simplicity of the two-period lived agents, the analysis can be conducted entirely through the standard Keynesian (Hicksian) IS–LM diagram.

Keynesians themselves often postulate that the labour market does not clear. In Keynesian models that has at least a threefold significance, which it is perhaps important to sort out. Since labour is usually taken to be inelastically supplied, it makes it possible to conceive of (Keynesian) equilibria with different levels of output and employment. It makes the system of demand and supply under-determined, so that endogenous variables like animal spirits (i.e. expectations) which are normally fixed by the equilibrium conditions can be volatile. It creates unemployment that is involuntary. By replacing lack of labour market clearing at time 1 with elastic labour supply and lack of market clearing 'at infinity' one no longer needs to rely on what has seemed to many an *ad hoc* assumption in order to get at least the first two *desiderata* of Keynesian analysis.

8. NEOCLASSICAL EQUILIBRIUM VS CLASSICAL EQUILIBRIUM. The Arrow–Debreu model of general equilibrium, based on agent optimization, rational expectations, and market clearing, is universally regarded as the central paradigm of the neoclassical approach to economic theory. In the Arrow–Debreu model, consumers and producers, acting on the basis of individual self-interest, combine, through the aggregate market forces of demand and supply, to determine (at least locally) the equilibrium distribution of income, relative prices, and the rate of growth of capital stocks (when there are durable goods). The resulting allocations are always Pareto optimal.

Classical economists at one time or another have rejected all of the methodological principles of the Arrow–Debreu model. They replace individual interest with class interest, ignore (marginal) utility, especially for waiting, doubt the existence of marginal product, and question whether the labour market clears. But by far the most important difference between the two schools of thought is the classical emphasis on the long-run reproduction of the means of production, in a never-ending cycle.

Thus the celebrated classical economist Sraffa writes in Appendix D to his book:

> It is of course in Quesnay's *Tableau Economique* that is found the original picture of the system of production and consumption as a circular process, and it stands in striking contrast to the view presented by modern theory, of a one-way avenue that leads from 'Factors of Production' to 'Consumption Goods'.

The title of his book, *Production of Commodities by Means of Commodities*, itself suggests a world that has no definite beginning, and what is circular can have no end.

In the Arrow–Debreu model time has a definite end. As we have seen, that has strong implications. With universal agreement about when the world will end, there can be no reproduction of the capital stock. In equilibrium it will be run down to zero. Money, for example, can never have positive value. Rational expectations will fix, at each moment, and for each kind of investment, the expected rate of profit.

In the classical system, by contrast, the market does not determine the distribution of income. Sraffa writes

> The rate of profits, as a ratio, has a significance which is independent of any prices, and can well be 'given' before the prices are fixed. It is accordingly

susceptible of being determined from outside the system of production, in particular by the money rates of interest. In the following sections the rate of profits will therefore be treated as the independent variable (Sraffa (1960, p. 33)).

Other classical writers concentrate instead on the real wage as determined outside the market forces of supply and demand, for example by the level of subsistence, or the struggle between capital and labour. Indeterminacy of equilibrium seems at least as central to classical economists as it is to Keynesians.

Like Keynesians, classicals often achieve indeterminacy in their formal models by allowing certain markets not to clear in the Walrasian sense. (Again like Keynesians, the labour market is usually among them.) Thus we have called the equilibrium in section 4 in which some of the markets were allowed not to clear a 'classical equilibrium'.

What the OLG model shows is that by incorporating the classical view of the world without definite beginning or end, it is possible to maintain all the neoclassical methodological premises and yet still leave room for the indeterminacy which is the hallmark of both classical and Keynesian economics. In particular this can be achieved while maintaining labour market clearing. The explanation for this surprising conclusion is that the OLG model is isomorphic to a finite-like model in which indeed not all the markets need to clear. But far from being the labour markets, under pressure to move toward equilibrium from the unemployed clamouring for jobs, these markets are off 'at infinity', under no pressure toward equilibrating.

We have speculated that once one has agreed to the postulate that the resources of the economy are potentially as great at any future date as they are today, then uniform impatience of consumers is the decisive factor, according to Walrasian principles, which may influence whether the market forces of supply and demand determine a locally unique, Pareto-optimal equilibrium, or leave room for extra-market forces to choose among a continuum of inefficient equilibria. In these terms, the Arrow–Debreu model supposes a short-run impatient economy, and OLG a long-run patient economy.

9. SUNSPOTS. So far we have not allowed uncertainty into the OLG model. As a result we found no difference in interpreting trade sequentially, with each agent facing two budget constraints, or 'as if' the markets all cleared simultaneously at the beginning of time, with each agent facing one budget constraint. Once uncertainty is introduced these interpretations become radically different. In either case, however, there is a vast increase in the number of commodities, and hence in the potential for indeterminacy.

If we do not permit agents to make trades conditional on moves of nature that occur before they are born, then agents will have different access to asset markets. Even in finite horizon economies, differing access to asset markets has been shown by Cass and Shell to lead to 'sunspot effects'.

A 'sunspot' is a visible move of nature which has no real effect on consumers, either on account of preferences, or endowments, or through production. In the

Arrow–Debreu model it also could have no effect on equilibrium trade; this is no longer true when access to asset markets differs.

The sunspot effect is intensified when combined with the indeterminacy that can already arise in an OLG economy. Consider the simple one good, steady state OLG economy of sections 1 and 2. Suppose that there is an equilibrium two cycle $q = (\ldots, q_{-1}, q_0, q_1, \ldots)$ with $q_{2t} = q^s$ and $q_{2,+1} = q^s$ and $q_{2,+1} = q^R$, for all $t \in \mathscr{Z}$. Now suppose that the sun is known to shine on even periods, and hide behind rain on odd periods. The above equilibrium is perfectly correlated with the sun, even though no agent's preferences or endowments are. As usual, the same prices for $t \geq 0$ support an equilibrium, given the right amount of money, in $E_{0,\infty}^M$.

More generally, suppose that the probability of rain or shine, given the previous period's weather, is given by the Markov matrix $\pi = (\pi_{SS}, \pi_{SR}, \pi_{RS}, \pi_{RR})$. A steady state equilibrium for $E_{0,\infty}^M$, given π, is an assignment of a money price for the commodity, depending only on that period's weather, such that if all agents maximize their expected utility with respect to π, then in each period the commodity market and money market clears. Azariadis (1981) essentially showed that if there is a 2-cycle of the certainty economy, then there is a continuum of steady state sunspot equilibria.

The sunspot equilibria, unlike the cyclical equilibria of section 2, are Pareto suboptimal whenever the matrix π is nondegenerate.

The combination of the dynamic effects of the infinite horizon OLG model with the burgeoning theory of incomplete markets under real uncertainty, is already on the agenda for next generation's research.

BIBLIOGRAPHY

Arrow, K.J. 1953. The role of securities in the optimal allocation of risk-bearing. Reprinted in K.J. Arrow, *Essays in the Theory of Risk Bearing*, Chicago: Markam, 1971.

Azariadis, C. 1981. Self-fulfilling prophecies. *Journal of Economic Theory* 25(3), 380–96.

Balasko, Y., Cass, D. and Shell, K. 1980. Existence of competitive equilibrium in a general overlapping-generations model. *Journal of Economic Theory* 23(3), 307–22.

Benveniste, L. and Gale, D. 1975. An extension of Cass' characterization of infinite efficient production programs. *Journal of Economic Theory* 10, 229–38.

Bewley, T. 1972. Existence of equilibria in economies with infinitely many commodities. *Journal of Economic Theory* 4, 514–40.

Cass, D. 1972. On capital overaccumulation in the aggregative, nonclassical model of economic growth. *Journal of Economic Theory* 4(2), 200–23.

Cass, D. and Yaari, M.E. 1966. A re-examination of the pure consumption loan model. *Journal of Political Economy* 74(2), 200–23.

Debreu, G. 1970. Economies with a finite set of equilibria. *Econometrica* 38, 387–92.

Diamond, P.A. 1965. National debt in a neo-classical growth model. *American Economic Review* 55(5), 1126–50.

Gale, D. 1973. Pure exchange equilibrium of dynamic economic models. *Journal of Economic Theory* 6(1), 12–36.

Geanakoplos, J. 1978, 1980. Sraffa's *Production of Commodities by Means of Commodities*: indeterminacy and suboptimality in neoclassical economics. RIAS Working Paper

(1978), also ch. 3 of Four essays on the model of Arrow–Debreu. Ph.D. dissertation, Harvard University (1980).

Geanakoplos, J. and Brown, D. 1982. Understanding overlapping generations economies as lack of market clearing at infinity. Yale mimeo, revised 1985, 1986.

Geanakoplos, J. and Polemarchakis, H.M. 1984. Intertemporally separable overlapping generations economies. *Journal of Economic Theory* 34, 207–215.

Geanakoplos, J. and Polemarchakis, H.M. 1985. Walrasian indeterminacy and Keynesian macroeconomics. Forthcoming in *Review of Economic Studies*.

Geanakoplos, J. and Brown, D. 1985. Comparative statics and local indeterminacy in OLG economies: an application of the multiplicative ergodic theorem. Cowles Foundation Discussion Paper No. 773.

Grandmont, J.M. 1985. Endogenous, competitive business cycles. *Econometrica* 53(5), 995–1046.

Kehoe, T.J. and Levine, D.K. 1984. Regularity in overlapping generations exchange economies. *Journal of Mathematical Economics* 13, 69–93.

Kehoe, T.J. and Levine, D.K. 1985. Comparative statics and perfect foresight in infinite horizon models. *Econometrica* 53, 433–53.

Kehoe, T.J., Levine, D.K. and Romer, P.M. 1986. Smooth valuation functions and determinacy in economies with infinitely lived consumers. Unpublished manuscript.

Keynes, J.M. 1936. *The General Theory of Employment, Interest and Money.* London: Macmillan; New York: Harcourt, Bracc.

Lucas, R.E. 1972. Expectations and the neutrality of money. *Journal of Economic Theory* 4(2), 102–121.

Muller, W.J. and Woodford, M. 1983. Stationary overlapping generations economies with production and infinite lived consumers: II. Determinacy of equilibrium. Discussion Paper 326, Department of Economics, M.I.T.

Samuelson, P.A. 1958. An exact consumption loan model of interest, with or without the social contrivance of money. *Journal of Political Economy* 66(5), 467–82.

Sraffa, P. 1960. *Production of Commodities by Means of Commodities.* Cambridge: Cambridge University Press.

Wilson, C. 1981. Equilibrium in dynamic models with an infinity of agents. *Journal of Economic Theory* 24(1), 95–111.

Own Rates of Interest

JOHN EATWELL

The concept of the own-rate of interest on a commodity was introduced (though not named) by Piero Sraffa in his review (1932) of Friedrich von Hayek's book *Prices and Production* (1931), and was later taken up, and labelled, by Maynard Keynes in his analysis of the role of money in the theory of employment (1936, ch. 17). Sraffa introduced the concept by means of the example of a cotton spinner who borrows money to purchase a quantity of raw cotton today (at the spot price) which he simultaneously sells forward (Sraffa, 1932, p. 50). The spinner is actually borrowing cotton for the period of the transaction, say, one year. The own-rate of interest on cotton is then the spot price of a bale of cotton divided by the future price of a bale discounted at the going money rate of interest; less one. So if the price of 100 bales of cotton for delivery today is $20, and the price to be paid for delivery of 100 bales in one year's time is $21.40, whilst the money rate of interest is 5%, then the own-rate of interest on cotton is

$$\frac{20}{21.40/1.05} - 1 = c. - 2\% \text{ (See Keynes, 1930, p. 223)}.$$

Sraffa's interpretation of the role of the money rate of interest in the calculation was *not* that it was simply the rate of interest on a numeraire. 'Money' in his discussion, is the actual financial medium. So the money rate represents the normal rate of interest (which is assumed equal to rate of profit) in the economy as a whole. The difference between the money rate and own-rate of interest on a commodity therefore indicates that the *spot market* for that commodity is not in normal long-run equilibrium.

In equilibrium the spot and forward price coincide, for cotton as for any other commodity; and all the 'natural' or commodity rates are equal to one another, and to the money rate. But if, for any reason, the supply and the demand for a commodity are not in equilibrium (*i.e.* its market price exceeds or falls short of its cost of production), its spot and forward prices diverge, and the 'natural'

234

rate of interest on that commodity diverges from the 'natural' rates on other commodities. Suppose there is a change in the distribution of demand between various commodities; immediately some will rise in price, and others will fall; the market will expect that after a certain time, the supply of the former will increase, and the supply of the latter fall, and accordingly the forward price, for the date on which equilibrium is expected to be restored, will be below the spot price in the case of the former and above it in the case of the latter; to the effecting of the [restoration of equilibrium] as is the divergence of prices from the costs of production; it is, in fact, another aspect of the same thing (1932, p. 50).

In terms of the example, the equilibrium price is $21.40 and the equilibrium rate of interest is 5%. However, the current price of 100 bales of cotton is $20, which invested at the going rate of interest, would be worth only $21 at the end of a year, and this would buy c.98 bales of cotton at the equilibrium price then ruling. Thus the own-rate of interest on cotton is c. -2%. The concept of the own-rate of interest on a commodity interpreted in this way, can only be defined with respect to normal prices and to the normal interest rate, represented by the money rate of interest. For example, if the money rate of interest in the above instance were 10% the own-rate of interest on cotton would be c. 3%; if 0%, then c. -7%.

Keynes used Sraffa's ideas in his analysis of the determination of the level of investment. His theory of the rate of interest was derived from an analysis of the demand for the stock of monetary assets – that demand being the sum of transactions, precautionary, and speculative demands – with only the latter being regarded as a function of the rate of interest.

The elasticity of the liquidity preference schedule with respect to the rate of interest was based on two rates of interest, the rate which actually holds, and the rate which is expected to hold in the future (the long-run rate). The ambiguity introduced into Keynes's analysis by the construction of the liquidity preference schedule on the basis of the short-run and the long-run rate of interest was not totally clear in the *General Theory*, other than in Keynes's ambivalence over whether the rate of interest was a 'psychological' or a 'conventional' variable (see Keynes, 1936, pp. 200–202). The reference to 'convention' established the idea that 'institutional' or 'historical' factors might be the underlying determinants of the long-run rate of interest; he is content to point to forces other than supply and demand and leave the issue there.

The ambiguity in Keynes's theory is exposed in his theory of investment. There, he associates the equalization of rates of return on different categories of assets with the determination of the volume of investment. The idea that rates of return are equalised is characteristic of long-run analyses. Yet Keynes is suggesting that this equality is attained with respect to a rate of interest which is determined as a short-run phenomenon. This ambiguity is unresolved in the *General Theory*. Subsequent discussion by Kaldor (1960) although the issue was clearly identified, left the problem unresolved.

The definition and interpretation of the own-rate of interest in modern general equilibrium theory (see Debreu, 1959) are quite different from those advanced by Sraffa – although there is a formal similarity in the method of calculation. The set of equilibrium prices refer to commodities located at different points in time and yet include no interest charge. The prices are discounted prices *which would be paid today* for commodities to be traded at a future date. The rate of interest at which the prices are discounted is not specified.

The own-rate of interest on a commodity in one production period, say time t to time $t + 1$, is defined as the ratio of the appropriate discounted prices, less one: i.e. the own-rate of interest on commodity q over the time period t is

$$p_{qt} = \frac{p_{qt}}{p_{qt+1}} - 1$$

where p_{qt}, p_{qt+1} are the discounted prices in period 1 of the commodity q available at the beginning (resp. the end) of period t, the prices being determined in the manner shown. The calculation just shown contains no reference to a normal rate of interest. The own-rate of return is defined independently of any normal or money rate. By analogy with the case of a-capitalistic production, the ratio of the discounted prices p_{qt}, p_{qt+1} is equal to the marginal rate of substitution in consumption between q_t and q_{t+1}, and to the marginal rate of transformation in production.

So although commodities q_t and q_{t+1}, are defined as *different* commodities for the purpose of price determination, they are regarded as the *same* commodity for the purpose of the definition of the own-rate of interest, the difference in the prices being due to their temporal location.

Although there is some technical similarity in the calculation of the own-rate of interest on a commodity by both Sraffa and Debreu, the definition advanced by Sraffa is quite different from that adopted by Debreu. This difference stems from their different conceptions of prices and their formation. In Sraffa's formulation the own-rate of interest is a reflection of the divergence of the market price from normal equilibrium price (and the normal rate of interest). In Debreu's definition this latter distinction has no meaning. The discounted prices used in his calculation are equilibrium prices, but there is no normal rate of interest of normal long-run prices in the Marshallian sense of those terms. Thus differences in the own-rate of interest as between commodities arise not out of market price 'deviations', but out of his definition of a 'commodity'.

It should also be noted that markets of the type referred to by Debreu, on which payment is made today for commodities to be traded in the future, do not exist. On such futures markets as there are the prices set are those which will be paid at the time the trade is actually made (Debreu, 1959, p. 33). Such prices could not be the basis for the calculation of the own-rate of interest on a commodity in the manner of Debreu.

BIBLIOGRAPHY
Debreu, G. 1959. *Theory of Value*. New Haven: Yale University Press.

Hayek, F.A. von. 1931. *Prices and Production.* London: Routledge & Kegan Paul; 2nd edn, New York: A.M. Kelley, 1967.

Kaldor, N. 1960. Keynes' theory of the own-rates of interest. In N. Kaldor, *Essays on Economic Stability and Growth.* London: Duckworth.

Keynes, J.M. 1936. *The General Theory of Employment, Interest and Money.* London: Macmillan; New York: Harcourt, Brace.

Sraffa, P. 1932. Dr Hayek on money and capital. *Economic Journal* 42, March, 42–53.

Perfect Competition

M. ALI KHAN

An allocation of resources generated under *perfect competition* is an allocation of resources generated by the pursuit of individual self-interest and one which is insensitive to the actions of any single agent. Self-interest is formalized as the maximization of profits by producers and the maximization of utility by consumers, both sets of actions being taken at a price system which cannot be manipulated by any single agent, producer or consumer. An essential ingredient then in the concept of perfect competition in the idea of *economic negligibility* which, in a set-up of equally powerful economic agents, is captured by the related notion of *numerical negligibility* and by considering an economy with *many* agents. Perfect competition is thus an idealized construct akin (say) to the mechanical idealization of a frictionless system or to the geometric idealization of a straight line.

A formalization of perfect competition hinges on how the intuitive notions of 'negligibility' and 'many' agents are made precise. In this entry we shall discuss four alternative formalizations of these notions. Since the essence of these ideas can be fully communicated in the context of an economy without producers, that is, an *exchange economy*, we shall confine ourselves to this case and develop some notation and terminology regarding it.

An *exchange economy* consists of a commodity space L, a set of traders, T, a space of characteristics $\mathscr{P}$ and a mapping $\mathscr{E}$ from T into $\mathscr{P}$ with the value of $\mathscr{E}$ at a particular t in T being given by the triple $(X(t), \succsim_t, e(t))$. The space of characteristics is thus a product space constituted by consumption sets $X(t) \subset L$, by binary relations $\succsim_t$ over $X(t) \times X(t)$ and by initial endowments $e(t) \in X(t)$. The relation $\succsim_t$ formalizes preferences and is read 'preferred or indifferent to'.

An *allocation* $x: T \to L$ is an assignment of commodity bundles such that $x(t) \in X(t)$ for all t in T and such that the summation, suitably formalized, of $(x(t) - e(t))$ over T is zero. A *price system* is a non-zero, continuous linear function on the commodity space L. Note that we have already presumed that L has enough structure on it that summation and the specifications of continuity and

238

linearity make sense. A *competitive equilibrium* is a pair (p, x) where p is a price system and x an allocation such that for all t in T, $x(t)$ is a maximal element for $\succsim_t$ in the budget set $\{y \in X(t): \langle y, p \rangle \leqslant e(t), p \rangle\}$. Here $\langle y, p \rangle$ denotes the valuation of the commodity bundle y by the function p and, in case L is the Euclidean space R^n, it can be written as the scalar product

$$(p \cdot y) = \sum_{n=1}^{n} p_i y_i.$$

For any competitive equilibrium $(p, x), x$ will be referred to as a *competitive allocation*.

We shall illustrate four formalizations of perfect competition. Our illustrations will be based on Farrell's (1959) conjecture on the existence of competitive equilibria without any convexity assumptions; and through Edgeworth's (1881) conjecture on the identity of core and competitive allocations. Both conjectures were made for economies satisfying conditions of perfect competition, i.e. for economies with 'many' economically negligible agents. Note that x is said to be an allocation in the *core* if there does not exist any other allocation y and a coalition S, suitably formalized, such that $y(t) \succsim_t x(t)$ and not $x(t) \succsim_t y(t)$ for all t in S and the summation of $(y(t) - e(t))$ over S is zero. If one views competitive allocations as making precise the idea of individual rationality, one can view core allocations as making precise the idea of group rationality.

The first formalization of perfect competition that we discuss is due to Aumann (1964) and contemporaneously to Vind (1964). Aumann considered the set of traders to be an *atomless measure space* (T, Σ, λ), the commodity space to be R^n, the summation in the definitions of allocations and the core to be the Lebesgue integral, the set of admissible coalitions to be the σ-algebra Σ and $\mathscr{E}$ to be a measurable map. For details of these basic concepts of measure theory, the reader is referred, for example, to Hildenbrand (1974).

Aumann's formalization of the set of agents as an atomless measure space is a precise formulation of the intuitive idea of an economy with 'many' agents, i.e., a 'large' economy, in which every agent is numerically and economically negligible. The seminal nature of this conception was quickly realized. In 1964, Aumann showed that the set of competitive allocations of such an economy coincides with its set of core allocations and in 1966, followed this up by showing that neither set is empty. What is of special significance is that neither result depends on any 'convexity' hypothesis on preferences. The importance of the Lyapunov theorem on the range of an atomless vector measure in the derivation of these results, is, by now, well understood; see Hildenbrand (1974) for details. We shall not touch upon the various elaborations and refinements of Aumann's results that continue up to the present nor on alternative formulations of an atomless measure-theoretic economy by Vind and Richter (1971). The latter omission is justified, at least in the context of R^n, in view of Debreu's (1967) work and in view of Armstrong–Richter (1984).

Another formulation of perfect competition is due to Brown–Robinson (1975) and utilizes methods of *nonstandard analysis*, a specialization in mathematical logic due to A. Robinson (1960). Brown–Robinson (1975) considered the set of traders T to be an *internal star finite set*, the commodity space to be $*R^n$, the summation in the definitions of allocations and core to be summation over internal sets, the set of admissible coalitions to be the set of all internal subsets of T and $\mathscr{E}$ to be an internal map. For details of these concepts, the reader is referred, for example, to Hurd–Loeb (1985).

Since internal, star finite sets may have cardinality of the order of the continuum, the Brown–Robinson formalization of perfect competition is another way of making precise the concepts of many agents and of their negligibility. Moreover, since the nonstandard universe has in it finitely large and infinitesimally small numbers which can be manipulated just as ordinary real numbers, one can speak of an individual trader's actions have a positive, but infinitesimal effect on the price system. On replacing equality by equality modulo infinitesimals in the definitions of allocation and the core, Brown–Robinson (1975), and without their ad-hoc standardly bounded assumption on allocations, Brown–Khan (1980) showed the equivalence of core and competitive allocations of a nonstandard economy. Brown (1976) followed this up by showing the existence of competitive equilibria in such an economy. Both results dispensed with the convexity assumption on preferences and used in an essential way Loeb's (1973) combinatorial analogue of Lyapunov's theorem. These basic contributions led to several results being established for nonstandard economics; see Rashid (forthcoming) for details. However, one is missing the point if one sees the motivation of this research as simply an attempt to prove for nonstandard economies what had already been proved for measure-theoretic economies; its importance has to be gauged in the context of a third formalization of perfect competition.

The third formalization of perfect competition is motivated, in part, by the observation that there do not exist economies with uncountably many agents and, in part, by a methodological curiosity as to whether the results established for nonstandard and measure-theoretic economies are artifacts of the way 'negligibility' and 'large' economies were modelled. This led to an investigation of the question as to whether the equivalence and existence results are approximately valid for a 'large but finite' economy. Taking the lead from the replicated sequences of Debreu–Scarf (1963), the idea is to consider a sequence $\mathscr{G} = \{\mathscr{E}_k\}_{k=1}^{\infty}$ of finite economies where $\mathscr{E}_k$ is an economy with k agents, i.e., T_k is a set of cardinality k. For each $\mathscr{E}_k$, we can define competitive equilibrium and core in the conventional way without encountering any difficulty in the formalization of summation of a coalition. The commodity space is taken to be R^n. It is clear that as k becomes large, the number of agents in the economy $\mathscr{E}_k$ get increasingly numerically negligible. If we now add to this the assumption that the initial endowments are uniformly bounded, i.e., there exists a positive number M such that $0\|e(t)\| \leqslant M$ for all $t \in T_k$, for all $\mathscr{E}_k \in \mathscr{G}$, we also ensure that each agent is getting economically negligible.

One can now ask the following question. For any positive number ε, however small, does there exist an integer k such that all economies in $\mathscr{G}$ with the number of agents larger than k have approximate competitive equilibria and are such that their cores can be sustained as approximate competitive equilibria, with ε indicating, in either instance, the degree of approximation? This question was answered in the affirmative under varying degrees of generality and the answers constituted *asymptotic* equivalence and existence theorems.

Asymptotic equivalence theorems under convexity of preferences and compactness of the space of characteristics were first proved by Bewley (1973) and Grodal–Hildenbrand (reported in Hildenbrand, 1974, section 3.2) and without such assumptions, and even without continuity of preferences, by Khan (1974a); also see Hildenbrand (1974, section 3.3) and Nishino (1971).. Asymptotic existence theorems were first proved by Hildenbrand–Schmeidler–Zamir (1974) and by Khan (1975). We shall not touch upon subsequent refinements and extensions of these results except to refer to Anderson (1985) and in the case of the equivalence theorem and to Khan–Rashid (1982) in the case of the existence theorem.

These asymptotic results have been proved using rather disparate techniques. The first approach is to conceive of an economy as a measure on the space of characteristics and utilize Skorokhod's theorem and the theory of weak convergence measures. This is the approach of Hildenbrand (1970) and is dependent on a topology (typically metrizable) on the space of characteristics $\mathscr{P}$. Such topologies were formulated by Debreu (1969), Kannai (1970) and Hildenbrand (1970). The second approach is based on the observation that 'any sentence which is true in the standard universe is true for internal entities in the nonstandard universe'. Brown–Robinson (1974) were the first to use this observation to 'flip over', as it were, an equivalence theorem for a nonstandard exchange economy to an asymptotic result. Thus, the fact that asymptotic results could be derived without any topology on the space of preference relations is no accident but rather a direct consequence of the difference in the two approaches. Indeed, there are circumstances, as in Khan (1974b) or in Khan–Rashid (1982), where it is far from clear how one would proceed with the weak convergence approach. It is curious and somewhat unfortunate for the subject that in the several available surveys of this research, the asymptotic theorems have never been compared and it is only the recent work of Anderson (1986) that does this for the equivalence theorem.

We now turn to a fourth formalization of perfect competition. Our third formalization relates to a sequence of economies and a natural question arises as to whether given an arbitrary economy rather than an arbitrary degree of approximation, one can find the error, depending on the parameters of the economy, with which the equivalence and existence theorems hold. If this error is shown to depend only on the size of the agents' endowments and the number of commodities but not on the number of agents, we obtain results that yield as corollaries asymptotic theorems. Such a formulation of perfect competition is due to Starr (1969) and Arrow–Hahn (1971) and is an abstract formalization of perfect competition in that 'negligibility' and 'largeness' are seen in the way the error depends on the number of agents.

As the nonstandard approach to asymptotic results succeeded in dispensing with compactness assumptions on the space of characteristics, Anderson observed that the argument in Khan–Rashid (1978) could be carried out entirely in standard terms, that is without any reference to nonstandard analysis. This led to an elementary equivalence theorem; Anderson (1978), a result which can be cited as definitive. The same observation applied to Khan–Rashid (1982) led to an elementary existence theorem; Anderson–Kahn–Rashid (1982). This has been strengthened by Geller (1986) and extended to production by Vohra (forthcoming). These results, which, in hindsight, can be seen as sharpened versions of those of Arrow–Hahn–Starr, rely on the Shapley–Folkman theorem (Arrow–Hahn, 1971, p. 392). It is important to be clear, however, that the elegance and simplicity of these results lies in the weak competitive equilibrium notions on which they are based.

We have illustrated four different formalizations of perfect competition in terms of the so-called core equivalence and existence theorems. Alternatively, we could have illustrated them by the value equivalence theorem or by the equivalence of competitive and Nash equilibria or in yet other ways. But the illustration is not the point; what is to be emphasized is that we now have four robust and logically related methods of studying perfect competition.

BIBLIOGRAPHY

Anderson, R.M. 1978. An elementary core equivalence theorem. *Econometrica* 46, 1483–7.

Anderson, R.M. 1985. Strong core theorems with nonconvex preferences. *Econometrica* 53, 1283–94.

Anderson, R.M. 1986. Notions of core convergence. In *Contributions to Mathematical Economics in Honour of Gerard Debreu*, ed. W. Hildenbrand and A. Mas-Colell, Amsterdam: North-Holland.

Anderson, R.M., Khan, M. Ali and Rashid, S. 1982. Approximate equilibria with bounds independent of preferences. *Review of Economic Studies* 49, 473–5.

Armstrong, T. and Richter, M.K. 1984. The core – Walras equivalence. *Journal of Economic Theory* 33, 110–51.

Arrow, K.J. and Hahn, F.H. 1971. *General Competitive Analysis*. San Francisco: Holden-Day.

Aumann, R.J. 1964. Markets with a continuum of traders. *Econometrica* 32, 39–50.

Aumann, R.J. 1966. Existence of competitive equilibria in markets with a continuum of traders. *Econometrica* 34, 1–17.

Bewley, T.F. 1973. Edgeworth's conjecture. *Econometrica* 41, 425–54.

Brown, D.J. 1976. Existence of competitive equilibrium in a non-standard exchange economy. *Econometrica* 44, 537–47.

Brown, D.J. and Khan, M. Ali. 1980. An extension of the Brown–Robinson equivalence theorem. *Applied Mathematics and Computation* 6, 167–75.

Brown, D.J. and Robinson, A. 1974. The cores of large standard economies. *Journal of Economic Theory* 9, 245–54.

Brown, D.J. and Robinson, A. 1975. Nonstandard exchange economies. *Econometrica* 43, 41–55.

Debreu, G. 1967. Preference functions on measure spaces of economic agents. *Econometrica* 35, 111–22.

Debreu, G. 1969. Neighboring economic agents. In *La Décision*, Paris: CNRS.

Debreu, G. and Scarf, H. 1963. A limit theorem on the core of an economy. *International Economic Review* 4, 235–46.

Edgeworth, F.Y. 1881. *Mathematical Physics*. London: Kegan Paul. Reprinted New York: Augustus M. Kelley, 1967.

Farrell, M.J. 1959. The convexity assumption in the theory of competitive markets. *Journal of Political Economy* 67, 377–91.

Geller, W. 1986. An improved bound for approximate equilibria. *Review of Economic Studies* 53, 307–8.

Hildenbrand, W. 1970. On economies with many agents. *Journal of Economic Theory* 2, 161–88.

Hildenbrand, W. 1974. *Core and Equilibria of a Large Economy*. Princeton: Princeton University Press.

Hildenbrand, W., Schmieidler, D. and Zamir, S. 1974. Existence of approximate equilibria and cores. *Econometrica* 41, 1159–66.

Hurd, A.E. and Loeb, P.A. 1985. *An Introduction to Nonstandard Analysis*. New York: Academic Press.

Kannai, Y. 1970. Continuity properties of the core of a market. *Econometrica* 38, 791–815. A correction in *Econometrica* 40, 1972, 955–8.

Khan, M. Ali. 1974a. Some equivalence theorem. *Review of Economic Studies* 41, 549–65.

Khan, M. Ali. 1974b. Some remarks on the core of a 'large' economy. *Econometrica* 42, 633–42.

Khan, M. Ali. 1975. Some approximate equilibria. *Journal of Mathematical Economics* 2, 63–86.

Khan, M. Ali and Rashid, S. 1978. A limit theorem for an approximate core of a large but finite economy. *Economic Letters* 1, 297–302. Abridged version of 'Limit theorems on cores with costs of coalition formation', Johns Hopkins Working Paper No. 24, 1976.

Khan, M. Ali and Rashid, S. 1982. Approximate equilibria in markets with indivisible commodities. *Journal of Economic Theory* 28, 82–101.

Loeb, P.A. 1973. A combinatorial analog of Lyapunov's theorem for infinitesimally generated atomic vector measures. *Proceedings of the American Mathematical Society* 39, 585–6.

Nishino, H. 1971. On the occurrence and existence of competitive equilibria. *Keio Economic Studies* 8, 33–47.

Rashid, S. 1987. *Economies with Many Agents: a Nonstandard Approach*. Baltimore: Johns Hopkins Press.

Richter, M.K. 1971. Coalitions, cores and competition. *Journal of Economic Theory* 3, 323–34.

Robinson, A. 1966. *Nonstandard Analysis*. Amsterdam: North-Holland Publishing Co. Revised edn, 1974.

Starr, R.M. 1969. Quasi-equilibria in markets with non-convex preferences. *Econometrica* 37, 25–38.

Vind, K. 1964. Edgeworth-allocations in an exchange economy with many traders. *International Economic Review* 5, 165–77.

Vohra, R. 1987. Local public goods as indivisible commodities. *Regional Science and Urban Economics*.

Production as Indirect Exchange

TROUT RADER

Relative to classical doctrines, neoclassical economics was distinguished early on by the addition of utility to the arsenal of theoretical tools, especially with respect to mathematical methods (e.g. Jevons (1871); Marshall (1890) and Walras (1874–7) as a supplement to such as Adam Smith (1776), Ricardo (1817) and Cournot (1838). In his *Éléments*, Walras conjectured that groping or *tâtonnement* led to general equilibrium where supply equalled demand for each, even in a many-commodity, many-dimensional world. Also utility was shown to be equivalent to abstract properties of preferences on bundles of consumer goods (Hicks and Allen, 1934). For example, not only was choice by rational agents expostulated but, consistent with modern psychoanalysis or its milder variants, many non-rationalities were permitted Sonnenschein, 1972 and Shafer, 1974). Thereby application of economics was greatly expanded to cover non-transitive preferences.) However, the story did not end there.

INDUCED PREFERENCES ON TRADE. With my thesis on Edgeworth's *Mathematical Psychics* (1881) I began a long study of the foundations of trade. Along these lines the tool from economic theory of interest is that which, on the basis of the underlying preferences and production technology, imputes consumer well-being to trades with properties in common usage by theorists (Rader, 1963, 1964). The basic problem then is to evaluate feasible *trade* vectors, $T = \{t: t \in W + Y\}$, where Y is the *general* production possibility set (positive coordinates for outputs, negative for inputs) and W the initial endowments. The induced preference ordering is $s \succ_i t$, i.e. agent i prefers proposed exchange s to trade t, if given s, the optimal attainable final consumption is preferred to all attainable consumptions given t. In turn for this to be sensible we should know that the

244

optimum exists for all s (and t as well), which is known if the relevant set of trades is compact and either:

(1) $\succ_i$ is transitive and irreflexive and the complement of $P_i(s) = \{t : t \succ_i s\}$ is open or, unexpectedly,

(2) Y is convex, compact, $\succ_i$ is irreflexive and complete (i.e. total) and $P_i(x)$ is convex, $P_i(s)$ is open as is its complement (Sonnenschein, 1972).

Condition (1) follows for a consumer who evaluates final consumption by an upper semi-continuous, quasi-concave utility function. For instance, not only condition (1) but a relevant part of (2) is implied by the strong property of a concave utility function. However (2) applies much more widely, even to whole economies with social preferences where the properties except for transitivity are sometimes canonical (as will be seen), or perhaps more bizarrely even to political preferences based on such as majority rule which is well known to be intransitive (cf. Kramer, 1972). By this construction there is a transparent derivation of induced preferences, with or without transitivity depending on which case (1) or (2) applies (Rader, 1978a). In effect, *for every economy with exchange, there are preferences on trades whereupon given convexity and such, we can theorize for the whole as though there were only pure exchange.* The construction is such that basic ordering, continuity, and convexity properties can be derived and results known for exchange economies go over even if production is applied. Consequently many results of welfare economies of pure exchange are imputed to production – exchange economies by the foregoing *Principle of Equivalence,* e.g. implied is the old Fundamental Theorem of Welfare Economics that shows the equivalence of equilibrium with Pareto optimality (Gale and Mas-Colell, 1977) or the newer results, Edgeworth's conjecture stated in his *Mathematical Psychics* to the effect that equilibrium is exactly that state for a large economy which does no worse for a subgroup than the group's best in autarky (Scarf, 1962; Aumann, 1964; Debreu and Scarf, 1973). As such the Equivalence is a unification of otherwise apparently disparate materials.

APPLICATION TO HEDONIC THEORY. This and the next three sections present applications. First, induced preferences can be applied in a Lancaster (1966) set-up where goods are demanded not for their own sake but for their underlying characteristics. Then preferences on goods are not inherent but in turn, induced. Therefore there is the sequence,

production + initial wealth → characteristics → consumption,

and preferences are (potentially) defined in reverse at each stage. Furthermore at each stage, properties are inherited from those preceding. Mathematically, except for elementary and straightforward (if at times unexpected) syllogisms, the main relevant tools are those of the theory of linear topological spaces and more commonly finite dimensional vector spaces. This involves among other things the generalized matrix inverse used in statistics (Graybill, 1969), and the formal equality of algebraic internality and topological interiority (Kelley and Namioka, 1963).

PAIRWISE OPTIMALITY. In the case of bilateral trade, the achievement of optimality among pairs, *pairwise optimality*, often implies Pareto or consumer efficiency. By our analysis, this will apply to consumer-producers as well as those with fixed endowments. The basic requirement is interconnectedness of potential trade gains and quasi-concavity of induced utility, or more generally convexity of induced preferences (see Rader, 1968; also Polterovich, 1970; and Goldman and Starr, 1982, or such as ensured by the existence of a 'money good' always of use to all consumers (cf. Feldman, 1973)). (A unified treatment using Helley's theorem for sets was offered by Madden in 1975.) In cases of non-convexity there will still be mutual tangency of indifference hypersurfaces. By smoothness of underlying preferences, the induced preferences are smooth and by definition, there the tangent hyperplane is uniquely determined, a property inherited from the earlier stages (Rader, 1976). The normal to this hyperplane defines prices and for optimality they must be equal for different consumers (since otherwise there would be exploited gains to supplementary trade). However, there is nothing to ensure that the consequent value of final consumption does or even can equal the value of initial wealth. Hence optimal trades may entail Pareto superior gifts, a subject of current research interest especially with regard to inter-country transfers, such as reparations or foreign aid (J.M. Keynes, 1919; Leontief, 1938; Samuelson, 1952, 1954).

WORLD TRADE AND TRANSFERS. A direct application is to countries in international commerce, following Meade (1955) or Chipman (1979), each with community preferences of his own. Under a regime of free trade not only are prices equalized of final goods between countries but often so are per-unit factor costs, even for those that are immobile, so called factor price equalization (Rader, 1977, 1978b; (I now prefer the phase factor cost equalization). Therefore results for distribution of factor shares are implied as well.

The theory described above is at a relatively general level. However, there are cases of special interest. For example, if all consumers have gross substitutable demand so that an increase in one price always increases excess demand for the other goods then, even though not social utility maximizing, the economy's excess demand locally satisfies the weak law of revealed preference,

$$\delta P \Delta e < 0,$$

where e = excess demand and p = generalized price (the vector p includes not only prices of manufactured goods but also unit costs of productive factors.)

Suppose e is chosen at p, $\bar{e}$, at $\bar{p}$. Then the weak axiom of revealed preference (WA) is that e affordable at $\bar{p}$ implies $\bar{e}$ is too expensive at p ($p\bar{e} > 0 = pe$).

Specifically, suppose the economy is partitioned into two sectors, one for consumers with gross substitutable demand and the other consisting of profit maximizing firms, then *near any equilibrium* (WA) *holds*, as stated in Rader (1972). Furthermore in this instance (WA) is easily verified for all other p near equilibrium. Also the weak law (WA) follows if consumer-traders of a given taste class are distributed with respect to expenditures over a line interval beginning at zero *expense* and ending at zero *frequency*, the frequency always non-increasing (Hildenbrand, 1983). In still another case, the economy behaves as if it were one transitive consumer. It is required that all traders are homothetic and that expenditures are in constant proportions, one to the other, and the strong law (SA) is said to hold (Chipman, 1972).

In these various instances, the whole economy acts like a single representative consumer with various rationality properties. The Marshallian idealization where marginal utility of income or money is assumed constant so that the whole acts like a single consumer is more than metaphor that permits aggregation of consumer demand. The 'offer' curve is indeed the result of social optimization and also choice is still the intersection of the community feasibility set with a social indifference hypersurface. It is only that disjoint surfaces may intersect, reflecting the absence of transitivity.

TRANSACTION COSTS. One particular technology which was mentioned in Debreu (1959, ch. 7) has, evidently independently, received much attention and continues to have prospects, namely that of the technology of transferring a good from one location to another or more generally, transaction costs (cf. Coase, 1960). Since the conditions sufficient for induced preferences to be upper-semi continuous are very weak, the set of Pareto optima is very likely non-empty. However, if the technical possibilities do not form a convex set, whence induced preferences on trades may not be convex even when those for direct consumption are, then the welfare equivalence between optimality and equilibrium may not be, whence non-competition may be appropriate.

BIBLIOGRAPHY

Aumann, R.J. 1964. Markets with a continuum of traders. *Econometrica* 32, 39–50.

Aumann, R.J. 1966. Existence of competitive equilibria in markets with a continuum of traders. *Econometrica* 34, 1–17.

Birkhoff, G. and Rota, G.C. 1962. *Ordinary Differential Equations.* Boston: Ginn & Co.

Chipman, J. 1974. Homothetic preferences and aggregation. *Journal of Economic Theory* 8(1), May, 26–38.

Chipman, J. 1979. The theory and application of trade utility functions. In *General Equilibrium, Growth, and Trade*, ed. J.R. Green and J.A. Scheinkman, New York: Academic Press.

Coase, R.H. 1960. The problem of social cost. *Journal of Law and Economics* 3, October, 1–44.

Coddington, E.A. and Levinson, N. 1955. *Theory of Ordinary Differential Equations.* New York: McGraw-Hill.

Cournot, A. 1838. *Recherches sur les principes mathématiques de la théorie des richesses.* Trans., New York: Macmillan, 1983.

Debreu, G. 1959. *Theory of Value.* New York: Wiley.

Debreu, G. and Scarf, H. 1963. A limit theorem on the core of an economy. *International Economic Review* 4, 236–46.

Edgeworth, F.Y. 1881. *Mathematical Psychics.* London: Kegan Paul. Reprinted New York: Augustus M. Kelley, 1967.

Feldman, A.M. 1973. Bilateral trading processes, pairwise optimality and Pareto optimality. *Review of Economic Studies* 40, October, 463–79.

Gale, D. and Mas-Colell, A. 1975. An equilibrium existence theorem for a general model without ordered preferences. *Journal of Mathematical Economics* 2, 9–15.

Gale, D. and Mas-Colell, A. 1976–7. On the role of complete, transitive preferences in equilibrium theory. In *Equilibrium and Disequilibrium in Economics*, ed. G. Schwodiauer, Dordrecht: Reidel.

Gantmacher, F.R. 1959. *The Theory of Matrices*. Vol. 1, New York: Chelsea.

Girsanov, I.V. 1972. *Lectures on Mathematical Extremum Problems*. New York: Springer.

Goldman, S. and Starr, R. 1982. Pairwise, t-wise, and Pareto optimalities. *Econometrica* 50, 593–606.

Graybill, F. 1969. *Introduction to Matrices*. Belmont: Wadsworth.

Hicks, J.R. and Allen, R.G.D. 1934. A reconsideration of the theory of value. *Economica*, NS 1, 52–76.

Hildenbrand, W. 1983. On the law of demand. *Econometrica* 51, 997–1019.

Jevons, W.S. 1871. *The Theory of Political Economy*. London: Macmillan; 5th edn, New York: Kelley and Millman, 1957.

Kelley, J. and Namioka, I. 1963. *Linear Topological Spaces*. New York: Van Nostrand.

Keynes, J.M. 1919. *The Economic Consequences of the Peace*. London: Macmillan; New York: Harper & Row, 1971.

Kihlstrom, R., Mas-Colell, A. and Sonnenschein, H. 1976. The demand theory of the weak axiom of revealed preference. *Econometrica* 44, 971–8.

Kramer, G.H. 1972. Sophisticated voting over multi-dimensional choice spaces. *Journal of Mathematical Sociology* 2, 165–80.

Lancaster, K. 1966. A new approach to consumer theory. *Journal of Political Economy* 74, 132–57.

Leontief, W. 1936. Note on the pure theory of transfer. In *Explorations in Economics*, New York: McGraw-Hill.

Leontief, W. 1941. *The Structure of American Economy, 1919–1939*. London and New York: Oxford University Press, 1951.

Madden, P. 1975. Efficient sequences of non-monetary exchange. *Review of Economic Studies* 44, 581–96.

Marshall, A. 1890. *Principles of Economics*. London: Macmillan; New York: Macmillan, 1948.

Mas-Colell, A. 1974. An equilibrium existence theorem without complete or transitive preferences. *Journal of Mathematical Economics* 1, 237–46.

McKenzie, L. 1960. Matrices with dominant diagonals and economic theory. In *Mathematical Methods in the Social Sciences*, ed. K. Arrow, S. Karlin and P. Suppes, Stanford: Stanford University Press.

Meade, J.E. 1955. *Trade and Welfare*. London and New York: Oxford University Press.

Polterovich, M. 1970. A model of resource distribution. *Matekon* 7(3), Spring, 245–62.

Rader, T. 1963. Edgeworth exchange and general economic equilibrium. Unpublished dissertation, Yale University. Synopsis in *Yale Economic Essays* 4, 1964, 133–80.

Rader, T. 1968. Pairwise optimality and non-competitive behavior. In *Papers in Quantitative Economics*, Vol. I, ed. J. Quirk and A.M. Zarley, Lawrence, Kansas: University of Kansas Press.

Rader, T. 1970. Resource allocation with increasing returns to scale. *American Economic Review* 60, 814–25.

Rader, T. 1972. General equilibrium theory with complementary factors. *Journal of Economic Theory* 4, 372–80.

Rader, T. 1976. Pairwise optimality, multilateral optimality and efficiency, with and without externalities. In *Theory and Measurement of Economic Externalities*, ed. S.Y. Lin, New York: Academic Press.

Rader, T. 1977–8. Many good multiplier analysis: classical, neoclassical and Keynesian. In *Equilibrium and Disequilibrium in Economics*, ed. G. Schwodiauer, Dordrecht: Reidel Press.

Rader, T. 1978a. Induced preferences on trades when preferences may be intransitive and incomplete. *Econometrica* 46, 137–46.

Rader, T. 1978b. On factor price equalization. *Journal of Mathematical Economics* 5, 71–82.

Rader, T. 1979. Factor price equalization with more industries than factors. In *General Equilibrium Growth and Trade*, ed. J. Green and Scheinkman, New York: Academic Press.

Ricardo, D. 1817. *The Principles of Political Economy and Taxation.* London: Murray.

Samuelson, P.A. 1952–4. The transfer problem and transport costs. I: The terms of trade when impediments are absent; II: Analysis of effects of trade impediments. *Economic Journal* 57, 278–304; 59, 264–90.

Scarf, H. 1962. An analysis of markets with a large number of participants. In *Recent Advances in Game Theory*, ed. H. Scarf, Princeton: Princeton University Press.

Shafer, W. 1974. The nontransitive consumer. *Econometrica* 42(5), 913–19.

Smith, A. 1776. *An Inquiry into the Nature and Causes of the Wealth of Nations.* London: W. Strahan & T. Cadell; New York: Modern Library, 1937.

Sonnenschein, H. 1971. Demand theory without transitive preferences. In *Preferences, Utility and Demand*, ed. J. Chipman, M. Hurwicz, M. Richter and H. Sonnenschein, New York: Harcourt, Brace.

Walras, L. 1874–7. *Eléments d'économie politique pure.* Lausanne: L. Corbaz. Definitive edn 1926, trans. W. Jaffé as *Elements of Pure Economics*, New York: Orion, 1954.

Rationed Equilibria

JEAN-PASCAL BENASSY

DEFINITION AND SCOPE. Equilibria with rationing, also called non-Walrasian equilibria, are a wide class of equilibrium concepts which generalize the traditional notion of Walrasian equilibrium by allowing markets not to clear (in the traditional sense) and therefore quantity rationing to be experienced. Their scope is best described by examining first Walrasian equilibrium as a reference.

In a Walrasian equilibrium by definition all markets clear, that is, demand equals supply for each good. This consistency of the actions of all agents is achieved by price movements solely. No rationing is experienced as each agent is able to exchange as much as he wants at the Walrasian equilibrium price system. As noted by Arrow (1959), there is a 'missing element' in the concept, in that, whereas quantity actions by the agents result from rational behaviour, market clearing is assumed axiomatically. Non-Walrasian theory thus simply abandons this last assumption, allowing prices to be determined by other mechanisms than market clearing. An almost immediate corollary is that in order to obtain equilibrium concepts, quantity signals and quantity adjustments will have to be introduced together with price adjustments. To summarize briefly, the Walrasian equilibrium concept is generalized in the following directions:

(1) More general price mechanisms are considered, ranging from full rigidity to full flexibility, with intermediate forms of imperfect competition. Moreover each market may have its own price determination scheme.

(2) Quantity signals are introduced in addition to price signals. They intervene in both demand-supply and price making behaviour.

(3) Equilibrium in the short run is achieved by quantity adjustments as well as by price adjustments.

(4) Expectations about the future concern not only price signals, but quantity signals as well.

HISTORY. Equilibria with rationing have a double ancestry: Keynes (1936) because he developed (at the macroeconomic level) a concept of equilibrium where adjustment was made by quantities (the level of income) as well as by prices, and Walras (1874) because he developed a model of general equilibrium with interdependent markets. The Walrasian model has been beautifully developed into a highly elaborate and rigorous concept, notably in Hicks (1939), Arrow and Debreu (1954), Debreu (1959), Arrow and Hahn (1971).

The gap between these two lines of thought was unfortunately total until the stimulating contributions of Clower (1965) and Leijonhufvud (1968), who reinterpreted Keynesian analysis in terms of labour market rationing and quantity adjustments. These insights were included in the first fixprice macroeconomic model by Barro and Grossman (1971, 1976).

Rigorous microeconomic concepts of equilibrium with quantity rationing were then developed: Drèze (1975) built an equilibrium concept with prices variable between preset limits; Benassy (1975a, 1977b, 1982) constructed an alternative concept of fixprice equilibrium, and introduced expectations into that framework. A third concept of fixprice equilibrium was built by Younès (1975). Benassy (1976, 1977a, 1982) also developed a non-Walrasian equilibrium concept with price markets which bridged the gap with another important line of work, that dealing with general equilibrium under imperfect competition, notably associated with the name of Negishi (1961).

Still other concepts of equilibria with rationing were proposed by Glustoff (1968), Hahn (1978), Böhm and Levine (1979), Heller and Starr (1979).

We shall now describe the main concepts of the theory. In order to set the stage and introduce notation, let us first describe the economy considered and the corresponding Walrasian equilibrium concept.

THE ECONOMY AND WALRASIAN EQUILIBRIUM. We shall describe the various concepts in the framework of an exchange economy. One good, which we shall call money, serves as numeraire, medium of exchange and reserve of value (non-monetary exchange has been considered in Benassy, 1975b). There are l markets where nonmonetary goods, indexed by $h = 1, \ldots, l$, are exchanged against money at the price p_h. Call p the l-dimensional vector of these prices. Agents are indexed by $i = 1, \ldots, n$. Agent i has an initial endowment of good $h\omega_{ih}$, and of money $\bar{m}_i$. Call d_{ih} his purchase of good h, s_{ih} his sale of good h. Define $z_{ih} = d_{ih} - s_{ih}$ his net purchase of good h and z_i the vector of these net purchases. His final holdings of non-monetary goods and money are respectively

$$x_i = \omega_i + z_i. \qquad m_i = \bar{m}_i - p z_i$$

and we shall assume that the agent has a utility function $U_i(x_i, m_i) = U_i(\omega_i + z_i, m_i)$ which we shall assume throughout strictly quasi-concave in its arguments.

Having described the economy, let us now turn to the notion of Walrasian equilibrium. As indicated above, each agent is assumed to be able to exchange as much as he wants on each market. He thus transmits demands and supplies which maximize his utility subject to the budget constraint, i.e. the Walrasian net demand function is the solution in z_i of the following programme:

$$\text{Maximize } U_i(\omega_i + z_i, m_i) \quad \text{s.t.}$$

$$pz_i + m_i = \bar{m}_i.$$

This yields a vector of Walrasian net demands $z_i(p)$. A Walrasian equilibrium price vector p^* is defined by the condition that all markets clear, i.e.:

$$\sum_{i=1}^{n} z_i(p^*) = 0.$$

Transactions realized by agent i are simply equal to $z_i(p^*)$.

EQUILIBRIUM WITH BOUNDED PRICES. This concept, due to Drèze (1975), develops a notion of equilibrium valid when prices are subject to inequality constraints. We shall describe here, for simplicity of exposition, the case where absolute prices are subject to limits of the form:

$$\bar{p}_h \leqslant p_h \leqslant \bar{\bar{p}}_h.$$

Price limits linked to a price index were considered as well in Drèze (1975) (see also Van der Laan, 1980; Dehez and Drèze, 1984).

The basic idea behind this concept of equilibrium is that rationing becomes operative when prices hit one of the limits. The rationing considered will take the form of an upper bound on trades. (We shall see in the next section a possible justification for this type of rationing.) More specifically, as in Drèze (1975), consider a uniform rationing on each market, and call $\bar{d}_h$ the upper bound on purchases on market h, $\bar{s}_h$ the upper bound on sales. Net purchases of agent i on market h, z_{ih}, are thus limited to the interval:

$$-\bar{s}_h \leqslant z_{ih} \leqslant \bar{d}_h.$$

An equilibrium with price rigidities 'à la Drèze' can be now defined as a set of prices p_h^*, transactions z_{ih}^* and quantity constraints $\bar{d}_h$ and $\bar{s}_h$ such that:

(i) $\bar{p}_h \leqslant p_h^* \leqslant \bar{\bar{p}}_h \qquad \forall h$

(ii) $\sum_{i=1}^{n} z_{ih}^* = 0 \qquad \forall h$

(iii) The vector z_i^* is solution in z_i of

Maximize $U_i(\omega_i + z_i, m_i)$, s.t.

$$\begin{cases} pz_i + m_i = \bar{m}_i \\ -\bar{s}_{ih} \leqslant z_{ih} \leqslant \bar{d}_{ih} \qquad \forall h \end{cases}$$

(iv) $\forall h \quad z_{ih}^* = \bar{d}_h$ for some i implies $z_{jh}^* > -\bar{s}_h \qquad \forall j$

$\qquad z_{ih}^* = -\bar{s}_h$ for some i implies $z_{jh}^* < \bar{d}_h \qquad \forall j$

(v) $\forall h$ $p_h < \bar{p}_h$ implies $z_{ih}^* < \bar{d}_h$ $\forall i$

$\quad\quad p_h > \bar{p}_h$ implies $z_{ih}^* > -\bar{s}_h$ $\forall i$.

Condition (i) simply reminds us that prices are bounded upward and downward. Condition (ii) says that transactions should be consistent on every market. Condition (iii) says that transactions must be individually rational, i.e. they must maximize utility subject to the budget constraint and quantity constraints on all markets. Condition (iv) says that rationing may affect either supply or demand, but not both simultaneously. This condition is usually presented as a condition of market by market efficiency. Note also that money is never rationed. This condition is aimed at suppressing trivial equilibria where all agents would be constrained to trade nothing. Condition (v) says that upward (downward) price rigidity must be binding if there is quantity rationing of demand (supply). It thus expresses in an intuitive way that quantity rationing is a substitute for price variations.

We should note at this stage that this concept contains as particular cases both a fixprice equilibrium concept (when both price limits are equal) and Walrasian equilibrium (when the lower bound is zero and the upper bound infinite).

Existence of such an equilibrium with uniform bounds on net trades was proved in Drèze (1975). The concept is easily extended to some non-uniform bounds (Grandmont and Laroque, 1976, Greenberg and Müller, 1979), but in this last case it is not specified in the concept how shortages are allocated among rationed demanders or rationed suppliers. We shall now study alternative concepts based on different premises which, in particular, make this more explicit. We shall now therefore study in more detail how transactions and quantity signals may be formed in a nonclearing market.

THE FUNCTIONING OF A NONCLEARING MARKET. In this and the two subsequent sections we shall study other non-Walrasian concepts due to Benassy (1975a, 1976, 1977b, 1982). A basic characteristic of these models is that a clear-cut difference is made between demands and supplies on the one hand, and the resulting transactions on the other. Agents express effective demands $\tilde{d}_{ih}$ or supplies $\tilde{s}_{ih}$ which are somehow signals to the market and the other agents, and which do not necessarily match on a specific market. However, the trading process will generate transactions, i.e. purchases d_{ih}^* and sales s_{ih}^* which identically balance on each market:

$$\sum_{i=1}^{n} d_{ih}^* = \sum_{i=1}^{n} s_{ih}^* \qquad \forall h.$$

A rationing process is thus necessary, which may take various forms, such as uniform rationing, queueing, priority systems, proportional rationing, etc.... To be more explicit, define:

$$\tilde{z}_{ih} = \tilde{d}_{ih} - \tilde{s}_{ih}, \qquad z_{ih}^* = d_{ih}^* - s_{ih}^*.$$

A rationing scheme on a market h is described by a set of n functions:

$$z_{ih}^* = F_{ih}(\tilde{z}_{1h}, \ldots, \tilde{z}_{nh}), \qquad i = 1, \ldots, n \qquad (1)$$

such that:

$$\sum_{i=1}^{n} F_{ih}(\tilde{z}_{1h}, \ldots, \tilde{z}_{nh}) \equiv 0.$$

We shall generally assumed that F_{ih} is continuous, non-decreasing in $\tilde{z}_{ih}$ and non-increasing in the other arguments. Let us now examine a few possible properties. The first one is that of voluntary exchange, according to which no one can be forced to trade more than he wants, which is expressed by:

$$d_{ih}^* \leqslant \tilde{d}_{ih} \qquad s_{ih}^* \leqslant \tilde{s}_{ih}$$

or

$$z_{ih}^* \cdot \tilde{z}_{ih} \geqslant 0 \qquad \text{and} \qquad |z_{ih}^*| \leqslant |\tilde{z}_{ih}|.$$

We shall now assume this property throughout. It allows to classify the agents in two categories: unrationed agents for which $z_{ih}^* = \tilde{z}_{ih}$, and rationed ones who trade less than they wanted. A second property we want to discuss is that of manipulability. A scheme is non-manipulable if an agent, when rationed, cannot increase the level of his transaction by increasing his demand or supply. Priority or uniform rationing schemes are non-manipulable, a proportional rationing scheme is manipulable. Rationing schemes which satisfy both voluntary exchange and non-manipulability can be expressed under the form:

$$d_{ih}^* = \min(\tilde{d}_{ih}, \bar{d}_{ih})$$
$$s_{ih}^* = \min(\tilde{s}_{ih}, \bar{s}_{ih}) \qquad (2)$$

with:

$$\bar{d}_{ih} = G_{ih}^d(\tilde{z}_{1h}, \ldots, \tilde{z}_{nh})$$
$$\bar{s}_{ih} = G_{ih}^s(\tilde{z}_{1h}, \ldots, \tilde{z}_{nh}) \qquad (3)$$

where $\bar{d}_{ih}$ and $\bar{s}_{ih}$, the quantity constraints faced by agent i, are actually functions only of demands other than $\tilde{z}_{ih}$ (hence the property of non-manipulability). We thus see that a rationing which takes the form of upper bounds on net trades results from both properties of voluntary exchange and non-manipulability, and we shall assume these in what follows (a more general theory covering other cases has been developed in Benassy, 1977b, 1982).

A third property which is often used, though it is not necessary for what follows, is that of market efficiency, according to which one should not find rationed demanders and rationed suppliers at the same time on a market. The intuitive idea behind it is that in an efficiently organized market a rationed buyer and a rationed seller should be able to meet, and would exchange until one of the two is not rationed. Of course this condition will be more often met in a small micro-market than on a large aggregated macro-market. Together with voluntary exchange it implies the 'short-side' rule according to which agents on the short side of the market may realize their desired transactions:

$$\tilde{z}_{ih}\left(\sum_j \tilde{z}_{jh}\right) \leqslant 0 \Rightarrow z_{ih}^* = \tilde{z}_{ih}.$$

FIXPRICE EQUILIBRIUM. The concept we shall describe here was developed in Benassy (1975a, 1977b, 1982). We have already seen in the previous section how transactions and quantity signals are formed in a market where effective demands and supplies have been expressed (equations (1) and (3)). All we need, in order, to obtain a fixprice equilibrium concept, is to show how optimal effective demands are expressed as a function of price and quantity signals.

For that each agent maximizes the utility of his transactions $U_i(\omega_i + z_i, m_i)$, knowing that the transactions he will obtain are related to his demands and supplies by formulas (2). A convenient solution (Benassy, 1977b, 1982) is to take the effective demand $\tilde{z}_{ih}$ as the solution (unique because of strict quasi-concavity) of the following programme:

Maximize $U_i(\omega_i + z_i, m_i)$ s.t.

$$\begin{cases} pz_i + m_i = \bar{m}_i \\ -\bar{s}_{ik} \leqslant z_{ik} \leqslant \bar{d}_{ik} \qquad k \neq h \end{cases}$$

which yields an effective demand function denoted as $\bar{\zeta}_{ih}(p, \bar{d}_i, \bar{s}_i)$, where $\bar{d}_i$ and $\bar{s}_i$ are the vectors of quantity constraints.

A fixprice equilibrium is now naturally defined as a set of effective demands, transactions and quantity constraints such that:

(a) $\qquad\qquad \tilde{z}_{ih} = \bar{\zeta}_{ih}(p, \bar{d}_i, \bar{s}_i) \qquad\qquad \forall i, \forall h$

(b) $\qquad\qquad z_{ih}^* = F_{ih}(\tilde{z}_{ih}, \dots, \tilde{z}_{nh}) \qquad\qquad \forall i, \forall h$

(c) $\qquad\qquad \bar{d}_{ih} = G_{ih}^d(\tilde{z}_{ih}, \dots, \tilde{z}_{nh}) \qquad\qquad \forall i, \forall h$

$\qquad\qquad\qquad \bar{s}_{ih} = G_{ih}^s(\tilde{z}_{1h}, \dots, \tilde{z}_{nh}) \qquad\qquad \forall i, \forall h.$

Equilibria defined by these equations exist for all positive prices and rationing schemes satisfying voluntary exchange and non-manipulability (Benassy, 1975a, 1982). Because the concept includes an explicit description of the rationing procedure, the equilibrium is unique for a given price system and rationing scheme under fairly natural assumptions (Schulz, 1983).

Equilibria is defined above also possess the optimality properties one would naturally expect: they are consistent at the market level because of (b), and individually rational since effective demands have been constructed to yield optimal transactions, given price and quantity constraints. If moreover the rationing scheme on a market h is efficient, then no demanders and suppliers are rationed at the same time on that market. This last remark suggests that, even though their respective logics of construction are quite different, under the added assumption of market efficiency the Benassy and Drèze concepts should yield similar allocations at given prices. This was shown indeed by Silvestre (1982, 1983) for both exchange and productive economies. Some efficiency (and inefficiency) properties of the corresponding allocations are studied in the entry FIXPRICE MODELS.

NON-WALRASIAN EQUILIBRIA WITH PRICE MAKERS. At this stage, the theory is still in need of a description of price making by agents internal to the system. We shall now describe a concept dealing with that problem (Benassy, 1976, 1977a, 1982), which synthesizes the previous developments and the theory of general equilibrium with monopolistic competition, as developed notably by Negishi (1961, 1972).

As indicated in the entry DISEQUILIBRIUM ANALYSIS, the idea behind the modelling of price making in such models is that each price maker uses the prices he controls to 'manipulate' the quantity constraints he faces. To make things more precise, assume that agent i controls the price of a subset H_i of the goods, with H_i and H_j disjoint so that the price of each good is determined by one agent at most. Agent i thus sets a vector of prices p_i,

$$p_i = \{p_h | h \in H_i\}.$$

He perceives that his sales constraint in a market h he controls, $\bar{s}_{ih}$ (this constraint is actually equal to the total demand of the other agents, since he is the only seller on that market) depends on the vector p_i through a function, the perceived demand curve, denoted as

$$\bar{S}_{ih}(p_i, \theta_i)$$

where θ_i is a vector of parameters. Symmetrically a demander who sets a price p_h has a perceived supply curve

$$\bar{D}_{ih}(p_i, \theta_i)$$

We assume that the parameters θ_i are estimated as a function of current signals $p, \bar{d}_i, \bar{s}_i$ (and of course any other signal available, including data of past periods. This formulation thus allows some learning about the demand curve). Because we are dealing with a general equilibrium concept, at equilibrium the perceived demand or supply curve must go through the observed point (Bushaw and Clower, 1957), i.e.

$$\bar{D}_{ih}(p_i, \theta_i) = \bar{d}_{ih}$$

$$\bar{S}_{ih}(p_i, \theta_i) = \bar{s}_{ih}. \tag{4}$$

We can now make explicit the procedure of price formation. Agent i, facing a price p_h and constraints $\bar{d}_{ih}$ and $\bar{s}_{ih}$ on markets $h \notin H_i$ will choose his price so as to maximize his utility, i.e. the solution in p_i to the programme

Maximize $U_i(\omega_i + z_i, m_i)$ s.t.

$$\begin{cases} pz_i + m_i = \bar{m}_i \\ -\bar{s}_{ih} \leqslant z_{ih} \leqslant \bar{d}_{ih}, \qquad h \notin H_i \\ -\bar{S}_{ih}(p_i, \theta_i) \leqslant z_{ih} \leqslant \bar{D}_{ih}(p_i, \theta_i) \qquad h \in H_i \end{cases}$$

which yields a function $\mathscr{P}_i^*(p, \bar{d}_i, \bar{s}_i)$ since the parameters θ_i are functions of $p, \bar{d}_i, \bar{s}_i$. A non-Walrasian equilibrium with price makers is then simply defined as an equilibrium where quantities are optimal given prices and no price maker has interest in changing his price i.e.:

(a) The quantities $\tilde{z}_{ih}, z_{ih}^*, \bar{d}_{ih}, \bar{s}_{ih}$ form a fixprice equilibrium for p^*

(b) $p_i^* = \mathscr{P}_i^*(p^*, \bar{d}_i, \bar{s}_i)$ $\qquad \forall i$.

We may note that under reasonable assumptions (though not necessarily always) a price maker will satisfy the demand addressed to him. Sufficient conditions are found in Benassy (1982).

We may note as a final remark that the consistency conditions (4) imposed on the parameters of the perceived demand and supply curves are minimal ones, which thus allows to cover a maximum number of cases, depending on the structure of information available to price makers. More demanding consistency conditions have been searched for (see notably the ideas of an objective demand curve in Nikaido (1975) or of rational conjectures in Hahn, 1978) but the problem has not yet received a general satisfactory solution, for lack of a well defined concept of a 'true' demand curve in a general equilibrium situation with price makers.

EXPECTATIONS AND NON-WALRASIAN EQUILIBRIA. Up to now we have dealt with an equilibrium structure in the period considered, implicitly a short-run one, but of course the economy extends further in the future, as we are reminded at least by the presence of money as a store of value. More generally the presence of stocks (inventories, capital goods, financial assets) makes it necessary to form expectations, and these will influence current equilibrium. How this occurs has been studied in Benassy (1975a, 1982), and we shall only briefly outline the method for dealing with that problem.

Each agent actually plans for the current and future periods. Expectations for future periods take the form of prices and quantity constraints (for price takers) or expected demand curves (for price makers). These may be deterministic or stochastic. These expectations are formed via expectations schemes, which link future price quantity expectations to all price quantity signals received in past and current periods. This formulation is thus quite general and covers any expectations scheme, 'rational' or not, based on actually available information.

By a standard dynamic programming technique, one can reduce the multi-period problem to a single period one, where the valuation of all stocks (and notably money) depends upon future expectations, and thus, via the expectations schemes, upon the current and past price-quantity signals. We are thus back to the one period formulation used in the previous section, with the only difference that current and past quantity signals must be added in the valuation functions. We should note that the inclusion of these expectations does not create any problem for the existence of an equilibrium when the prices are fully rigid, but may jeopardize existence when endogenous price setting is considered (see Benassy, 1982). We should also note that rational expectations are fully consistent with this type of model, as was pointed out in Neary and Stiglitz (1983).

The most important feature of the introduction of expectations in such models is that, whereas traditional market clearing models deal with price expectations only, these models deal with a richer menu of price and quantity expectations.

CONCLUDING REMARKS. The concepts of equilibria with rationing, or non-Walrasian equilibria described in this entry represent a useful generalization of the traditional Walrasian equilibrium concept in several directions: whereas the Walrasian model covers by definition only the case where all markets clear, these concepts consider more general price mechanisms including full or partial price rigidities or imperfect competition. They introduce quantity signals in addition to price signals in demand-supply theory and mixed price-quantity adjustments in the short run. They integrate quantity expectations as well as price expectations. All this is done with the same rigorous methods which have proved successful in Walrasian theory. Besides their evident microeconomic interest, non-Walrasian equilibria have been widely used in macroeconomics (see, for example, Benassy, 1986), where they allow, for example, to study more rigorously states of the economy with involuntary unemployment.

A great strength of the theory is that it gives a rigorous framework within which one can predict which allocations will occur when prices are not the Walrasian ones. It also provides the first steps of a theory of endogenous price making, in line with the traditional theories of imperfect competition in general equilibrium. This theory has certainly called for new interesting developments and applications as new modes of price making without an auctioneer will be integrated within that framework.

BIBLIOGRAPHY

Arrow, K.J. 1959. Towards a theory of price adjustment. In *The Allocation of Economic Resources*, ed. M. Abramowitz, Stanford: Stanford University Press.

Arrow, K.J. and Debreu, G. 1954. Existence of an equilibrium for a competitive economy. *Econometrica* 22, 265–90.

Arrow, K.J. and Hahn, F. 1971. *General Competitive Analysis*. San Francisco: Holden-Day.

Barro, R.J. and Grossman, H.I. 1971. A general disequilibrium model of income and employment. *American Economic Review* 61, 82–93.

Barro, R.J. and Grossman, H.I. 1976. *Money, Employment and Inflation*. Cambridge and New York: Cambridge University Press.

Bellman, R. 1957. *Dynamic Programming*. Princeton: Princeton University Press.

Benassy, J.P. 1975a. Neo-Keynesian disequilibrium theory in a monetary economy. *Review of Economic Studies* 42, 502–23.

Benassy, J.P. 1975b. Disequilibrium exchange in barter and monetary economies. *Economic Inquiry* 13, 131–56.

Benassy, J.P. 1976. The disequilibrium approach to monopolistic price setting and general monopolistic equilibrium. *Review of Economic Studies* 43, 69–81.

Benassy, J.P. 1977a. A neo-Keynesian model of price and quantity determination in disequilibrium. In *Equilibrium and Disequilibrium in Economic Theory*, ed. G. Schwödiauer, Boston: D. Reidel.

Benassy, J.P. 1977b. On quantity signals and the foundations of effective demand theory. *Scandinavian Journal of Economics* 79, 147–68.

Benassy, J.P. 1982. *The Economics of Market Disequilibrium*. New York: Academic Press.

Benassy, J.P. 1986. *Macroeconomics: An Introduction to the Non-Walrasian Approach*. New York: Academic Press.

Böhm, V. and Levine, P. 1979. Temporary equilibria with quantity rationing. *Review of Economic Studies* 46, 361–77.

Bushaw, D.W. and Clower, R. 1957. *Introduction to Mathematical Economics*. Homewood, Ill.: Richard D. Irwin.

Clower, R.W. 1965. The Keynesian counterrevolution: a theoretical appraisal. In *The Theory of Interest Rates*, ed. F.H. Hahn and F.P.R. Brechling, London: Macmillan; New York: St. Martin's Press.

Debreu, G. 1959. *Theory of Value*. New York: Wiley.

Dehez, P. and Drèze, J.H. 1984. On supply constrained equilibria. *Journal of Economic Theory* 33, 172–82.

Drèze, J.H. 1975. Existence of an exchange equilibrium under price rigidities. *International Economic Review* 16, 301–20.

Glustoff, E. 1968. On the existence of a Keynesian equilibrium. *Review of Economic Studies* 35, 327–34.

Grandmont, J.M. and Laroque, G. 1976. On Keynesian temporary equilibria. *Review of Economic Studies* 43, 53–67.

Greenberg, J. and Müller, H. 1979. Equilibria under price rigidities and externalities. In *Game Theory and Related Topics*, ed. O. Moeschlin and D. Pallaschke, Amsterdam: North-Holland.

Hahn, F.H. 1978. On non-Walrasian equilibria. *Review of Economic Studies* 45, 1–17.

Heller, W.P. and Starr, R.M. 1979. Unemployment equilibrium with myopic complete information. *Review of Economic Studies* 46, 339–59.

Hicks, J.R. 1939. *Value and Capital*. Oxford: Clarendon Press. 2nd edn, 1946; 2nd edn, New York: Oxford University Press, 1946.

Keynes, J.M. 1936. *The General Theory of Money, Interest and Employment*. New York: Harcourt, Brace.

Leijonhufvud, A. 1968. *On Keynesian Economics and the Economics of Keynes*. Oxford and New York: Oxford University Press.

Neary, J.P. and Stiglitz, J.E. 1983. Toward a reconstruction of Keynesian economics: expectations and constrained equilibria. *Quarterly Journal of Economics* 98, Supplement, 199–228.

Negishi, T. 1961. Monopolistic competition and general equilibrium. *Review of Economic Studies* 28, 196–201.

Negishi, T. 1972. *General Equilibrium Theory and International Trade*. Amsterdam: North-Holland.

Nikaido, H. 1975. *Monopolistic Competition and Effective Demand*. Princeton: Princeton University Press.

Schulz, N. 1983. On the global uniqueness of fixprice equilibria. *Econometrica* 51, 47–68.

Silvestre, J. 1982. Fixprice analysis of exchange economies. *Journal of Economic Theory* 26, 28–58.

Silvestre, J. 1983. Fixprice analysis in productive economies. *Journal of Economic Theory* 30, 401–9.

Triffin, R. 1940. *Monopolistic Competition and General Equilibrium Theory.* Cambridge, Mass.: Harvard University Press.

Van Der Laan, G. 1980. Equilibrium under rigid prices with compensation for the consumers. *International Economic Review* 21, 63–74.

Walras, L. 1874. *Eléments d'économie politique pure.* Lausanne: Corbaz. Definitive edition translated by W. Jaffé: *Elements of Pure Economics*, London: Allen & Unwin, 1954; New York: Orion, 1954.

Younés, Y. 1975. On the role of money in the process of exchange and the existence of a non-Walrasian equilibrium. *Review of Economic Studies* 42, 489–501.

Regular Economies

EGBERT DIERKER

General equilibrium theory describes those states of an economy in which the individual plans of many agents with partially conflicting interests are compatible with each other. Such a state is called an equilibrium. The concept of an equilibrium simply being based on a consistency requirement lends itself to the study of specific questions of quite different character. Indeed, equilibrium theory provides a unifying framework for the analysis of questions arising in various branches of economic theory. In our opinion it is fruitful to view equilibrium theory as a method of thinking applicable to a variety of problems of different origin.

Ideally one would like to have general principles which ensure that equilibria exist, that they are unique, and that, therefore, the equilibria resulting from different policy measures can equivocally be compared. Moreover, one would like to know whether equilibria have some desirable properties when no single agent can exert an essential influence on the global outcome to his personal advantage. These welfare questions are particularly interesting because the concept of an equilibrium itself is not based on the well-being of the economic agents. Finally, although the concept of an equilibrium as described above is static in nature, one would like to have a dynamic theory according to which some equilibrium is approached in the course of time.

These and related questions such as the computability of equilibria have been studied in the past with different degrees of success. There are general principles which yield the existence of an equilibrium in an astonishingly large variety of cases. Furthermore, the welfare properties of equilibria are well understood. However, it is easy to construct examples of economies with an infinite number of equilibria and it appears to be very difficult to provide conditions which lead, without being artificial or ad hoc, to the uniqueness of an equilibrium. As a consequence, comparative statics does not have a basis which makes it generally a well-defined problem. Also, the difficulties encountered when studying the uniqueness issue present severe obstacles for the development of a dynamic theory.

The theory of regular economies may be viewed as an effort to advance general equilibrium theory in the absence of a satisfactory uniqueness result. The seminal paper is Debreu (1970). Debreu explicitly allows for the multiplicity of equilibria. However, he requires each equilibrium to be *locally* unique. Each equilibrium is well determined and robust in the sense that it is not destroyed by a small change in the parameters.

A regular economy is an economy with a certain, finite number of equilibria, all of which respond continuously to small parameter changes. Hence each of these equilibria can be traced for some while during a parameter change. Thus there is a basis for doing comparative statics locally, that is to say as long as the equilibrium under consideration stays robust. If, at a certain point, it ceases to be robust, a drastic change is to be expected, the size and direction of which are probably hardly predictable. The focus of the theory of regular equilibria is more on the continuous behaviour of robust equilibria than on drastic changes.

It is most remarkable that Debreu (1970), by using concepts and techniques developed in the mathematical field of differential topology, has introduced a new kind of thought into economic analysis. In the meantime this way of thinking has penetrated many areas of economic theory at different levels. One of the first applications has occurred in the technically advanced area of core theory, where the continuous dependence of the set of price equilibria on the characteristics of the agents, which is guaranteed in a regular economy, plays an important role. An application on a purely conceptual level in oligopoly theory is incorporated in the notion of a demand function which an oligopolist faces in the Cournot–Nash context. The graph of this function is considered as given by the equilibria of an exchange economy with initial endowments as varying parameters.

The dependence of the equilibria on initial endowments will be discussed in detail in the next section because this case is particularly suited to illustrate basic ideas of the theory of regular economies.

DEBREU'S THEOREM ON REGULAR EQUILIBRIA. The purpose of this section is to describe the kind of reasoning typical for the theory of regular economies in a prototypical situation. It is desirable to deal with parameter variations taking place in some Euclidean space because the mathematical structures to be used are most familiar in this case. We shall study exchange economies which differ by the allocation of initial endowments.

There are l commodities and m consumers. Individual initial endowments are supposed to be positive in each component. If we denote the strictly positive orthant in $\mathbb{R}^l$ by P, then an initial allocation is a vector $(e_1, \ldots, e_m) \in P^m$. Since the demand function f_i of each consumer i is considered as fixed, an economy E is fully specified by $(e_1, \ldots, e_m)$. The space of all economics under consideration can thus be identified with P^m, an extremely simple subset of a Euclidean space. We want to examine how the exchange equilibria of an economy – there may be several such equilibria – depend on the particular economy $E \in P^m$.

We assume that all goods are desired so that attention may be restricted to strictly positive relative prices. Price systems are normalized; to be specific we consider price systems in

$$S = \left\{ p = (p_1, \ldots, p_l) \gg 0 \,\Big|\, \| p \| = \left(\sum_{h=1}^{l} p_h^2 \right)^{1/2} = 1 \right\}.$$

If consumer i initially possesses the commodity bundle e_i, his demand at the price system p is $f_i(p, p \cdot e_i) \in \mathbb{R}_+^l$, where $p \cdot e_i = w_i > 0$ is i's wealth. Hence the aggregate excess demand of the economy E, given by the initial allocation $(e_1, \ldots, e_m) \in P^m$, at p is

$$Z_E(p) = \sum_{i=1}^{m} [f_i(p, p \cdot e_i) - e_i].$$

We assume Walras's Law which states that the value $p \cdot Z_E(p)$ of the excess demand is identically equal to zero. Furthermore, every f_i is supposed to be continuous.

The desirability of all commodities will be captured in the following condition, which is always satisfied when consumers have strictly monotone preferences.

(D) If the price of at least one good approaches zero and the wealth $w_i > 0$ of every agent stays away from zero, then

$$\sum_{i=1}^{m} \| f_i(p, w_i) \|$$

tends to infinity.

An *equilibrium price system* of E is a price system $p \in S$ at which the consumption plans $f_i(p, p \cdot e_i)$ of all agents are consistent, i.e. a zero of the excess demand function Z_E. It is not difficult to show the following consequence of the desirability assumption (D) by a fixed point argument:

Every economy $E \in P^m$ has at least one equilibrium if (D) *holds.*

We would like to know how the equilibrium prices vary when the initial allocation is modified. Therefore we look at the graph Γ of the correspondence ('multi-valued function') Π which assigns to every economy $E \in P^m$ its set $\{p \in S \,|\, Z_E(p) = 0\}$ of equilibrium price systems. Defining $Z : P^m \times S \to \mathbb{R}^l$ by $Z(E, p) = Z_E(p)$ we get

$$\text{graph}\,(\Pi) = \Gamma = Z^{-1}(0).$$

Since Z is a continuous function, Γ is a closed set. It is well known that, in the case of a (single-valued) function, the closedness of the graph is intimately related to the continuity of the function. Here, where Π is a correspondence rather than a function, we obtain the following continuity result: *the graph Γ of the equilibrium price correspondence Π is upper hemicontinuous and compact-valued, if* (D) *holds.*

This is tantamount to the following explicit statement. If (E_n) is a sequence of economies in P^m converging to $E \in P^m$ and if $p_n \in \Pi(E_n)$ is an equilibrium price system of E_n for all n, then the sequence (p_n) has a subsequence which converges to an equilibrium price system of the limit economy E, provided (D) holds.

To improve our understanding of Γ, we assume that the demand functions f_i are continuously differentiable (C^1 for short) and we invoke the implicit function theorem in the following manner. Walras's Law allows us to disregard one market, say the lth, and to concentrate on

$$\hat{Z}: P^m \times S \to \mathbb{R}^{l-1}$$

which is obtained from Z by deleting the last component. Let p be an equilibrium price system of E, i.e. $\hat{Z}(E, p) = 0$. A simple calculation yields that the derivative $d\hat{Z}(E, p)$ has maximal rank at (E, p). Therefore, the graph Γ is given by a smooth surface of dimension lm. That is to say each point in Γ has a neighbourhood in Γ which can be mapped onto an open subset of $\mathbb{R}^{lm}$ by a C^1 diffeomorphism, i.e. a C^1 map with a C^1 inverse. Such a locally Euclidean space is called a C^1 manifold, see Figure 1.

We have seen that *the graph Γ of the equilibrium price correspondence Π is a C^1 manifold*, but Figure 1 suggests more. In Figure 1, Γ is not only locally Euclidean, there is even a global diffeomorphism between Γ and $\mathbb{R}^{lm}$. Indeed, one can show that this global equivalence holds (see Balasko, 1975).

The equilibrium price correspondence is continuous except at two points, E_1 and E_2. If a parameter variation leads through E_1 (or E_2) the equilibrium may be forced to jump. The equilibrium reached after the jump, however, is robust in the sense that no sudden change must occur when one passes through E_1 (or E_2) again. One can imagine a situation such as in E_1 takes place when a slight reduction in the supply of an important raw material leads to a drastic increase in its price. If later on the supply begins to increase again prices perhaps vary

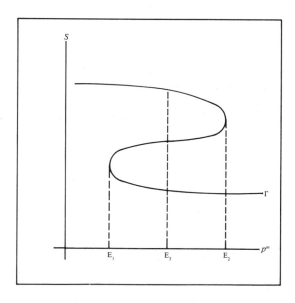

Figure 1

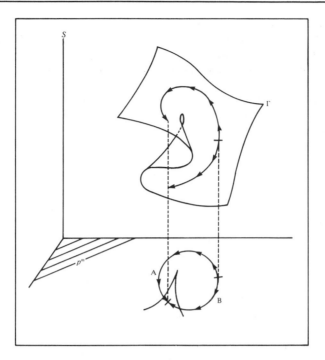

Figure 2

but stay at their high level. A reversion of this phenomenon may occur when the supply has reached the much higher level corresponding to E_2.

In Figure 2 we have drawn a two-dimensional parameter space. The following remarkable phenomenon may happen here.

There are two paths, A and B, in the parameter space which have their starting point and endpoint in common. Following either path there is no need for the equilibrium to jump. However, the two equilibria reached at the end are quite different equilibria of the same economy. In other words, if two or more policy variables are at one's disposal one must be aware of the possibility that the final outcome depends very well on the order in which the variables are utilized.

The economics E_1 and E_2 in Figure 1 are characterized by the fact that the graph Γ has a vertical tangent above E_1 and above E_2. Similarly, in Figure 2, Γ has vertical tangents above all points on the cusp drawn in the bottom plane, which represents P^m. Apparently qualitative changes of the equilibrium price set at an economy E are associated with vertical tangents of Γ above E. This motivates the following definitions. A *critical point* of the projection pr: $\Gamma \rightarrow P^m$ is a point in Γ at which the derivative of pr has rank less than dim $P^m = lm$. A *critical value* of pr: $\Gamma \rightarrow P^m$ is the image of a critical point. A *regular value* of pr: $\Gamma \rightarrow P^m$ is a point in P^m which is not a critical value. Figures 1 and 2 suggest that almost all points in P^m are regular values. Indeed, the concepts introduced above are defined

265

in differential topology in a quite general context and Sard's theorem, an analytical tool of great importance, asserts that the critical values of a sufficiently differentiable mapping are rare. More precisely, *Sard's theorem* applied to our particular problem yields that the set of critical values of pr: $\Gamma \to P^m$ is a (Lebesgue) null set.

Null sets are small in a probabilistic sense. At this point we make essential use of the space of economies P^m being part of a Euclidean space. If, for instance, consumers' demand functions or preferences are allowed to vary instead of consumers' endowments, it is not clear how null sets are to be defined. However, one can express quite easily when two demand functions or preference orderings are close to each other. That is to say metric structures are very often naturally given when there is no obvious way to define null sets. A set can then be defined to be small in a topological sense if its closure is nowhere dense.

Furthermore, if the concepts of smallness in the probabilistic and in the topological sense are both well-defined, as they are in the case of variable initial endowments, one has to be aware of the fact that the two variants of the intuitive notion of smallness apply to quite different sets. Defining a *critical economy* $E \in P^m$ as a critical value of pr: $\Gamma \to P^m$ and *regular economy* as a regular value of pr we ask ourselves whether the null set of critical economies has a null closure. We know already that the desirability assumption (D) implies that the equilibrium price correspondence is upper hemi-continuous and compact-valued or, in more intuitive terms, that Γ has only finitely many layers above some compact ball B of economies in P^m. Hence the points in Γ which lie above B and have a vertical tangent form a compact set. Projecting this set down to B yields a compact set, the set of critical economies in B. Since this set is also null by Sard's theorem, it is nowhere dense. We obtain:

The set of critical economies in P^m is a closed null set if (D) *holds.*

Let $E \in P^m$ be a regular economy. Then E has a finite number of equilibria and this number is locally constant. If E has r equilibria, then there is a neighbourhood U of E and there are $r C^1$ functions $g_1, \ldots, g_r$ such that the set $\Pi(E')$ of equilibrium price systems of any economy $E' \in U$ is given by $\{g_1(E'), \ldots, g_r(E')\}$. In particular, *the equilibrium price correspondence Π is continuous in a neighbourhood of a regular economy.*

These results, with minor differences, have been obtained by G. Debreu (1970), whose proof, however, differs from the exposition given here.

EXTENSIONS

When one wants to extend the theory of regular equilibria to more general spaces of economies, it is often useful to employ a definition of a regular economy which focuses on the given economy and does not refer to the graph Γ or to the parameter space. To motivate the following definition we contrast Figure 3, in which the excess demand of a critical economy such as E_1 or E_2 in Figure 1 is drawn, with Figure 4, which shows the graph of a regular economy such as E_3.

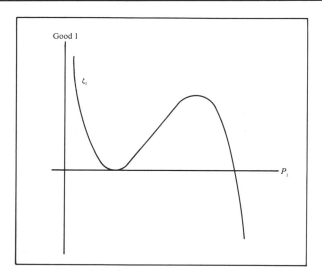

Figure 3

It is assumed that there are two goods so that it suffices, according to Walras's Law, to look at the excess demand ζ_1 for good 1.

In Figure 3 there is one equilibrium at which $d\zeta_1/dp_1$ vanishes. Shifting the graph of ζ_1 a little upwards destroys this equilibrium. In Figure 4, however, $d\zeta_1/dp_1$ does not vanish at any equilibrium and all equilibria are robust.

Let the excess demand function $\zeta: S \to \mathbb{R}^l$ of an economy E by C^1. A price system $p \in S$ is called a *regular equilibrium price system* if $\zeta(p) = 0$ and the matrix

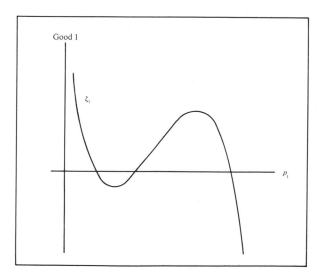

Figure 4

$$\left[\frac{\partial \zeta_h}{\partial p_k}(p)\right]_{h,k=1,\ldots,l-1}$$

is regular. A *regular economy* is an economy all equilibrium price systems of which are regular. One can show that this definition, introduced by E. and H. Dierker (1972), is independent of the way in which goods are indexed and that it is consistent with the definition given above.

The results on regular economies obtained in various frameworks are quite similar to those established in the previous section. It is shown that almost all economies, in an appropriate sense, are regular. Every regular equilibrium is locally unique and can be traced along its path when the economy varies gradually, as long as it stays regular. Economic models in which results of this kind have been precisely formulated and verified deal with variations in consumption and production (see, in particular, Smale, 1974). Also the case of many consumers, that is to say of consumption sectors described by the distribution of consumers' characteristics, has been treated. The basic mathematical tool is always some variant of Sard's Theorem. References can be found in my survey article (Dierker, 1982).

The study of regular equilibria has led to a revival of the differentiable viewpoint in general equilibrium theory and related areas. Readers interested in this modern development are referred to the excellent book by A. Mas-Colell (1985), which also contains an extensive, systematic presentation of the theory of regular equilibria.

BIBLIOGRAPHY

Balasko, Y. 1975. Some results on uniqueness and on stability of equilibrium in general equilibrium theory. *Journal of Mathematical Economics* 2, 95–118.

Debreu, G. 1970. Economies with a finite set of equilibria. *Econometrica* 38, 387–92.

Dierker, E. 1982. Regular economies. In *Handbook of Mathematical Economics*, ed. K. Arrow and M. Intriligator, Amsterdam: North-Holland, ch. 17, 795–830.

Dierker, E. and Dierker, H. 1972. The local uniqueness of equilibria. *Econometrica* 40, 867–81.

Mas-Colell, A. 1985. *The Theory of General Economic Equilibrium: A Differentiable Approach*. Econometric Society Monographs, Cambridge: Cambridge University Press.

Smale, S. 1974. Global analysis and economics IV: finiteness and stability of equilibria with general consumption sets and production. *Journal of Mathematical Economics* 1, 119–27.

Sequence Economies

ROSS M. STARR

A *sequence economy* is a general equilibrium model in discrete time including specific provision for the availability of markets at a sequence of dates (Radner, 1972). Markets reopen over time, and at each date firms and housholds act so that plans and prospects for actions on markets available in the future significantly affect their current actions.

This model is in contrast with the Arrow–Debreu model with a full set of futures markets (Debreu, 1959). There, all exchanges for current and future goods (including contingent commodities, futures contracts contingent on the realization of uncertain events) are transacted on a market at a single point in time. In the Arrow–Debreu model, there is no need for markets to reopen in the future; economic activity in the future consists simply of the execution of the contracted plans. The Arrow–Debreu model with a full set of futures markets appears unsatisfactory in that it denies commonplace observation: futures markets for goods and Arrow securities (contingent contracts payable in money) are not generally available for most dates or a sufficiently varied array of uncertain events; markets do reopen over time. The sequence economy model is an alternative that allows formalization and explanation of these observations.

The sequence economy model is particularly suitable for study of the store-of-value function of money. It is precisely because markets reopen over time that agents may find it desirable to carry abstract purchasing power from one date to succeeding date. Typically, this will take the form of transactions on spot markets at a succession of dates with money or other financial assets held over time to reflect the (net) excess value of prior sales over purchases. This may occur simply because the model does not provide for futures markets or because futures markets, though available in principle, are in practice inactive. Endogenously determined inactivity of futures markets is the result of transactions costs which tend to make the use of futures markets disproportionately costly compared with spot markets.

There are three principal reasons for the excess cost of futures markets:

(i) The necessarily greater complexity of futures contracts over time may simply imply use of more resources (e.g. for record keeping or enforcement) than spot markets;

(ii) The transactions costs of a futures contract are incurred (partly) at the transactions date, those of an equivalent spot transaction are incurred in the future. The present discounted value of the spot transactions costs incurred in the distant future may be lower than the futures market transaction cost incurred in the present, simply because of time-discounting;

(iii) Use of a full set of futures markets under uncertainty implies that most contracts transacted become otiose and are left unfulfilled as their effective dates pass and the events on which they were contingent do not occur. There is a corresponding saving in transaction costs associated with reducing the number of transactions required by use of a single spot transaction instead of many contingent commodity contracts, though this reduction may imply a different and inferior allocation of risk-bearing.

We now present a formal pure exchange sequence economy model with transactions costs (Kurz, 1974; Heller and Starr, 1976).

Commodity i for delivery at date τ may be bought spot at date τ or futures at any date t, $1 \leqslant t < \tau$. The complete system of spot and futures markets is available at each date (although some markets may be inactive). The time horizon is date K; each of H households is alive at time 1 and cares nothing about consumption after K. There are n commodities deliverable at each date; in the monetary interpretation of the model spot money is one of the goods. At each date and for each commodity, the household has available the current spot market, and futures markets for deliveries at all future dates. Spot and futures markets will also be available at dates in the future and prices on the markets taking place in the future are currently known. Thus in making his purchase and sale decisions, the household considers without price uncertainty whether to transact on current markets or to postpone transactions to markets available at future dates. There is a sequence of budget constraints, one for the market at each date. That is, for every date, the household faces a budget constraint on the spot and futures transactions taking place at that date, (4) below. The value of its sales to the market at each date (including delivery of money) must balance its purchases at that date.

In addition to a budget constraint, the agent's actions are restricted by a transactions technology. This technology specifies for each complex of purchases and sales at date t, what resources will be consumed by the process of transaction. It is because transactions costs may differ between spot and futures markets for the same good that we consider the reopening of markets allowed by the sequence economy model. Specific provision for transaction cost is introduced to allow an endogenous determination of the activity or inactivity of markets. In the special case where all transactions costs are nil, the model is unnecessarily complex; there is no need for the reopening of markets, and the equilibrium allocations are identical to those of the Arrow–Debreu model. Conversely, in the case where some futures markets are prohibitively costly to operate and others are costless, then there is an incomplete array of spot and futures markets and the model is an example of that of Radner (1972).

All of the n-dimensional vectors below are restricted to be non-negative.

$x_\tau^h(t)$ = vector of purchases for any purpose at date t by household h for delivery at date τ.

$y_\tau^h(t)$ = vector of sales analogously defined.

$z_\tau^h(t)$ = vector of inputs necessary to transactions undertaken at time t. The index τ again refers to the date at which these inputs are actually delivered.

$\omega^h(t)$ = vector of endowments at t for household h.

$s^h(t)$ = vector of goods coming out of storage at date t.

$r^h(t)$ = vector of goods put into storage at date t.

$p_\tau(t)$ = price vector on market at date t for goods deliverable at date τ.

With this notation, $p_{it}(t)$ is the spot price of good i at date t, and $p_{i\tau}(t)$ for $\tau > t$ is the futures price (for delivery at τ) of good i at date t.

The (non-negative) consumption vector for household h is

$$c^h(t) = \omega^h(t) + \sum_{\tau=1}^{t} [x_t^h(\tau) - y_t^h(\tau) - z_t^h(\tau)]$$
$$+ s^h(t) - r^h(t) \geq 0, \qquad (t = 1, \ldots, K). \qquad (1)$$

That is, consumption at date t is the sum of endowments plus all purchases past and present with delivery date t minus all sales for delivery at t minus transactions inputs with date t (including those previously committed) plus what comes out of storage at t minus what goes into storage. We suppose that households care only about consumption and not about which market consumption comes from. Thus, households maximize $U^h(c^h)$, where c^h is a vector of the $c^h(t)$'s, subject to constraint.

The household is constrained by its transaction technology, T^h, which specifies, for example, how much leisure time and shoeleather must be used to carry out any transaction. Let $x^h(t)$ denote the vector of $x_\tau^h(t)$'s [and similarly for $y^h(t)$ and $z^h(t)$]. We insist

$$[x^h(t), y^h(t), z^h(t)] \in T^h(t), \qquad (t = 1, \ldots, K). \qquad (2)$$

Naturally, storage input and output vectors must be feasible, so

$$[r^h(t), s^h(t+1)] \in S^h(t), \qquad (t = 1, \ldots, K-1). \qquad (3)$$

The budget constraints for household h are then:

$$p(t) \cdot x^h(t) \leq p(t) \cdot y^h(t), \qquad (t = 1, \ldots, K). \qquad (4)$$

Households may transfer purchasing power forward in time by using futures markets and by storage of goods that will be valuable in the future. Purchasing power may be carried backward by using futures markets. But these may be very costly transactions. In a monetary interpretation of the model, where money and

271

promissory notes are present, the household can either hold money as a store of wealth, or it can buy or sell notes.

Let $a^h(t) \equiv [x^h(t), y^h(t), z^h(t), r^h(t), s^h(t)]$, let a^h be a vector of the $a^h(t)$'s, and define x^h, y^h, z^h, r^h and s^h similarly. Define $B^h(p)$ as the set of a^h's which satisfy constraints (1)–(4). The household maximizes $U^h(c^h)$ over $B^h(p)$. Denote the demand correspondence (i.e. the set of maximizing a^h's) by $\gamma^h(p)$.

The model can be interpreted as monetary or non-monetary. We think of money as simply a 0th good that does not enter household preferences. Futures contracts in money are discounted promissory notes. $x_{0t}^h(t)$ is h's monetary recepits at t, $x_{0\tau}^h(t)$ is h's note purchase at t due at τ. Money is not treated as numeraire – positivity of its value cannot be assumed – it has price $p_{0t}(t)$.

The correspondences $\gamma_t^h(p)$ are always homogeneous of degree zero in $p(t)$, as is seen from the definition of $B^h(p)$. We can therefore restrict the price space to the simplex. Let S^t denote the unit simplex of dimensionality, $n(T - t + 1)$. Let $P = \mathbf{X}_{t=1}^T S^t$.

An *equilibrium* of the economy is a price vector $p^* \in P$ and an allocation a^{h*}, for each h, so that $a^{h*} \in \gamma^h(p^*)$ for all h and

$$\sum_{h=1}^H x^{h*} \leq \sum_{h=1}^H y^{h*} \tag{5}$$

(the inequality holds coordinate-wise), where for any good i, t, τ such that the strict inequality holds in (5) it follows that $p_{it}^*(t) = 0$. The equilibrium of a monetary economy is said to be *non-trivial* (that is, the economy is really monetary) if $p_{0t}^*(t) \neq 0$ for all t. Sufficient conditions for existence of equilibrium are continuity and convexity requirements typical of an Arrow–Debreu model appropriately extended. Transactions costs are often thought to be a non-convex, leading to approximate equilibrium rather than full equilibrium results (Heller and Starr, 1976). Existence of non-trivial monetary equilibrium requires additional restrictions designed to maintain positivity of the price of money (boundedness of the price level expressed in monetary terms). Monetary trade is actively used in non-trivial equilibrium in the case where transactions costs and storage losses of monetary trade are small relative to other means of intertemporal transfer of purchasing power.

In contrast to the Arrow–Debreu economy, an equilibrium allocation is not generally Pareto efficient. This is not due simply to the presence of transactions costs; transactions costs technically necessary to a reallocation must be incurred, and they represent no efficiency. The Arrow–Debreu model, however, uses a lifetime budget constraint. The corresponding constraint here is the sequence of constraints in (4). Transfer of purchasing power intertemporally – costless in the Arrow–Debreu model – is here a resource using activity; it requires purchase and sale of assets with resultant transactions cost. But the intertemporal transfer of purchasing power, unlike reallocation of goods among households, is needed not to satisfy technical or consumption requirements but rather to satisfy the administrative requirements of the market embodied in (4). Hence technically feasible Pareto-improving reallocations may be prevented in equilibrium by prohibitive transactions costs which would have to be incurred to satisfy the purely administrative requirements of crediting and debiting agents' budgets intertemporally (Hahn, 1971). If trade in monetary instruments is costless, however, then an equilibrium allocation is Pareto efficient (Starrett, 1973). Hence the sequence economy model provides a formal framework for the store-of-value role of money.

BIBLIOGRAPHY

Debreu, G. 1959. *Theory of Value.* New York: Wiley.

Hahn, F.H. 1971. Equilibrium with transaction costs. *Econometrica* 39(3), 417–39.

Heller, W.P. and Starr, R.M. 1976. Equilibrium with non-convex transactions costs: monetary and non-monetary economies. *Review of Economic Studies* 43(2), 195–215.

Kurz, M. 1974. Equilibrium in a finite sequence of markets with transactions cost. *Econometrica* 42(1), 1–20.

Radner, R. 1972. Existence of equilibrium of plans, prices, and price expectations in a sequence of markets. *Econometrica* 40(2), 289–303.

Starrett, D.A. 1973. Inefficiency and the demand for 'money' in a sequence economy. *Review of Economic Studies* 40, 437–48.

Sunspot Equilibrium

KARL SHELL

How does one explain the randomness which we see in the economy? Part of it can be traced to the randomness in the physical world which is transmitted through the economic fundamentals (such as endowments, technology and preferences). The weather provides an example. The randomness in rainfall causes randomness in crop yields which in turn generates randomness in agricultural outputs and agricultural prices. Since rainfall affects the economic fundamentals (in particular, it affects agricultural technology), it is said to be an intrinsic variable. Hence, uncertainty about rainfall is also an example of *intrinsic uncertainty* (see Cass and Shell, 1983, p. 194). The classic Arrow–Debreu extension of the general-equilibrium model to include uncertainty has long been the basis for analysing intrinsic uncertainty (see, e.g., Debreu, 1959, ch. 7).

Not all economic randomness can be explained in this way. Even if the fundamental parameters were non-random, economic outcomes would generally be random. This is because the economy is a social system composed of individual economic actors who are uncertain about each other's behaviour. In seeking to optimize his own actions, each participant in the market economy must attempt to predict the actions of the other participants. It is a complicated matter. Mr. A, in forecasting the market strategy of Mr. B, must forecast Mr. B's forecasts of the forecasts of others including that of Mr. A himself. And so on. Since market participants are not certain about the actions of others, they are uncertain about economic outcomes. Businessmen, for example, do not know what others will bid for their products, they do not know whether potential rivals will decide to enter or decide to hold back, they are uncertain about the inflation rate, and so forth.

Uncertainty of this sort is referred to as *market uncertainty* (see Peck and Shell, 1985). It is either created by the market economy or it is adopted from outside the economy as a means of coordinating the plans of the individual market participants. Market uncertainty is not transmitted through the fundamentals. It is, therefore, an instance of *extrinsic uncertainty*.

The interdependence of beliefs, even of 'rational' beliefs, is a central theme in the *General Theory*; see Keynes (1936, ch. 12). Keynes postulates that it is possible to encounter self-justifying expectations, beliefs which are individually rational but which may lead to socially irrational outcomes. The possible interdependence of individually rational beliefs is the central theme of the Townsend (1983) paper and the Frydman–Phelps (1983) volume. Nevertheless, it is fair to say that the formal modelling of market uncertainty has until recently lagged behind the modelling of uncertainty which is transmitted to the economy through its fundamental parameters. The recent work on 'Sunspot Equilibrium' introduced by Cass and Shell, reported in Shell (1977) and Cass–Shell (1983), is meant to provide a rigorous basis for the theory of market uncertainty. The Cass–Shell 'sunspots' are highly stylized. Contrary to fact and contrary to Jevons (1884), it is assumed that the sunspots represent purely extrinsic uncertainty: the economic fundamentals are assumed to be unaffected by the level of sunspot activity.

Can the level of sunspot activity affect the allocation of resources in a market economy? It has been known for some time that if probability beliefs (about sunspot activity) differ across individuals, then sunspots can matter. Consider the two-consumer, two-state, one-good, competitive exchange economy. Draw the usual Edgeworth box. Measure good consumption in state α on the horizontal. Measure good consumption in state β on the vertical. Because uncertainty is purely extrinsic, the box is a square: aggregate resources are independent of the state of nature. Also, because uncertainty is purely extrinsic, the endowment vector lies on the diagonal: individual endowments are independent of the state of nature. Assume that the consumers possess von Neumann–Morgenstern utility functions. Competitive equilibrium always exists. There are two cases: (1) The consumers have the same probability beliefs about the occurrence of states α and β. Indifference curve tangency, and hence contingent claims competitive equilibrium, occurs only on the diagonal. Sunspots do not matter. (2) The consumers have differing beliefs about the probabilities of α and β. Indifference curves will not be tangent on the diagonal. A contingent-claims competitive equilibrium will exist off the diagonal. Sunspots must matter.

There is a sense, however, in which the above sunspot equilibrium is unstable. Assume that the differences in probability beliefs are solely because of differences in information: the consumers share common prior beliefs, but because of differing information they have different posterior beliefs. The contingent-claims prices, however, reveal information. Indeed, in this example, the only competitive equilibrium in which individuals do not revise their beliefs from market information is based on common probability beliefs. Hence, we are especially interested in the special case where beliefs are commonly held. This might be thought of as the strong rational-expectations case.

Indeed, the original research on sunspot equilibrium was inspired by and in reaction to the rational-expectations macroeconomics literature as exemplified by Robert Lucas's (1972) classic paper in the *Journal of Economic Theory*. The Lucas paper was well received in some circles, while it was heavily criticized in others. Most of the critics took issue with the assumptions of individual rationality and perfect markets. Others, rather few in number at the time, were willing to ask whether or not the conclusions of the rational-expectations school follow from the assumptions. Does it follow that passive or simple 'monetary' rules are necessarily best? More generally, if individuals are rational and the government is nonerratic, will the social outcome be nonerratic?

Lucas gave us a formal model to shoot at. His model is based on the overlapping-generations model of Samuelson (1958), in which time is treated seriously and there is room for government debt (see Cass–Shell, 1980). In my Malinvaud lectures (Shell, 1977), I present an example of an overlapping-generations economy in which sunspots affect the allocation of resources solely because individuals believe that sunspot activity affects the price level. Their beliefs are rational: any single individual believing otherwise would be worse off. In the particular example, the best government policy is perpetually active and exhibits high variance. There is a continuum of perfect-foresight (nonsunspot) equilibria parametrized by the initial price of money and a vast multiplicity of sunspot equilibria partly parametrized by beliefs about the effects of sunspots. (The Shell (1977) model is in at least one way borderline: utility functions are linear. However, David Cass and I had presented similar results based on a non-linear overlapping-generations model at a Mathematical Social Science Board seminar in 1975.)

What features of this model allow for the existence of sunspot equilibria? The Shell (1977) model includes many of the salient features of decentralized, dynamic economies: Government debt is denominated in nominal (i.e. money) units. The time horizon is infinite. Market participation is restricted by natural lifetimes; that is, individuals cannot trade in markets which meet when they are not alive. Too much is included in the dynamic model of Shell (1977) to permit one to isolate 'the' source of sunspot equilibria.

Cass and Shell (1983) focus on only one of these aspects, the natural restrictions imposed on market participation. The model is finite. There is no government debt. Some individuals ('the old') can insure against the effects of sunspots; some individuals ('the young') cannot. If there were no restricted individuals ('no young'), there would be no sunspot equilibria. If there were no unrestricted individuals, a sunspot equilibrium would only be a randomization over nonsunspot equilibria. Otherwise, the typical sunspot equilibrium is not a mere lottery over nonsunspot equilibria. The set of equilibria has been expanded in a fundamental way: the classical Walrasian (nonsunspot) equilibria are only a subset of the set of equilibria. The new equilibria, the sunspot equilibria are never Pareto-optimal.

Cass and Shell (1983, Appendix) provide an example in which there is only one nonsunspot equilibrium but in which there is at least one sunspot equilibrium. The sunspot equilibrium cannot in this case be a randomization over nonsunspot equilibria, since there is only one nonsunspot equilibrium. What goes on in this simple example? Of course, the restricted consumers cannot transfer income across states of nature. The unrestricted consumers believe that relative prices

276

will differ from one state to another. The unrestricted consumers have tastes which differ: in particular, intrastate indifference curves differ and rates of risk aversion differ. Hence the unrestricted consumers may find it advantageous to transfer income across states of nature. Consequently, when conditions are right consumer beliefs in a sunspot equilibrium outcome are validated.

I showed in my overlapping-generations paper (Shell, 1971) that the set of perfect-foresight equilibria is unaffected by the natural restrictions on market participation. (In particular, the possible inoptimality of perfect-foresight competitive equilibria in the overlapping-generations model is *not* due to restricted participation. It is due to the 'double-infinity' of (dated) commodities and (dated) consumers.) Hence, the restriction on market participation which naturally arises in dynamic economies, while not a source of the inoptimality of some nonsunspot equilibria (the 'Samuelson' cases), is *a* source of the existence of sunspot equilibria, which are always Pareto inoptimal. Is restricted market participation the only source of sunspot equilibria in rational-expectations economies? The answer is no! Indeed, absence of sunspot equilibria seems to be the exception rather than the rule. If Pareto optimality is assured, then strong rational-expectations equilibria (based on shared beliefs) are not affected by sunspots. The so-called Philadelphia Pholk 'Theorem' is the assertion: in each 'class' of models in which Pareto-optimal allocations are not guaranteed, one can find an example of sunspot equilibrium. The 'proof' is based on several examples put together by Cass and me and our co-authors. We deviate from the preconditions for Pareto-optimality in only one aspect per example. Tested deviations giving rise to the existence of sunspot equilibria are: incomplete markets, externalities, imperfect competition, and the double-infinity of consumers and commodities (but with imagined unrestricted market participation). In this last case, sunspots can be a partial substitute for money. Sunspots offer the possibility of improved (but never Pareto-optimal) coordination. In general, sunspot equilibria are at best optimal in only a weak sense in which consumers are labelled in the conventional way but are also differentiated by the history of the prenatal states of nature (see Cass–Shell, 1983, pp. 215–18).

It is fair to say that the existence (indeed the prevalence) of proper sunspot outcomes came as a big surprise to many rational-expectations equilibrium theorists. Game theorists, on the other hand, long ago accepted the naturalness of stochastic solutions to nonstochastic games. Consider the well-known notion of mixed strategy or Aumann's (1974, 1985) generalization, correlated strategy. Mixed-strategy equilibria and, more generally, correlated equilibria are examples in which extrinsic uncertainty matters to the outcomes and payoffs of games. The possibility of asymmetric information is what makes correlated equilibrium an interesting generalization of Nash equilibrium.

Peck and Shell (1985) analyse market uncertainty in an imperfect-competition model. The particular model chosen is that of the *market game* due to Shapley and Shubik (1977). Any other model of imperfect competition might have served as well for analysing market uncertainty. The market-game model is, however, a perfect stage for comparing sunspot equilibrium (originally applied to competitive *market* models) and correlated equilibrium (originally applied to matrix *games*).

Peck and Shell establish the following: In the market game, there exists a proper (non-degenerate) correlated equilibrium if and only if the endowments are not Pareto-optimal. For correlated equilibrium the uncertainty device is outside the rules of the game. If the device becomes part of the rules of the game, we create from the market game the 'securities game', an imperfect-competition analogue of the Arrow (1964) securities model. Every correlated equilibrium allocation to the market game is also a pure-strategy Nash equilibrium allocation to the securities game. Proper correlated equilibria to the market game are sunspot equilibria to the securities game. Because the securities game allows for across-state transfers, some sunspot equilibrium allocations are not correlated equilibrium allocations (see Peck and Shell, 1985). Assuming common priors and common knowledge, we know that the set of correlated equilibrium allocations is equivalent to the set of Bayes-rational equilibrium allocations (see Peck and Shell, 1985, which follows Aumann, 1985).

Here, a subset of the sunspot equilibria arise as sophisticated solutions to simple games. The observed uncertainty is the rational consequence of the uncertainty that one player has about the moves of the others. All sunspot equilibria could be considered as simple solutions to sophisticated games. In the sophisticated games, securities are traded. These securities are intended to insure against disturbances caused by randomness in the natural world, even though the effect of this randomness on economic fundamentals is negligible. For examples of correlated equilibria and related sunspot equilibria, see Maskin and Tirole (1985), Aumann, Peck and Shell (1985) and Peck and Shell (1985).

The original impetus for sunspot equilibrium comes from intertemporal economics (cf. Shell, 1977). While the importance of the sunspot-equilibrium notion and related notions of market uncertainty – such as correlated equilibrium, Bayes-rational equilibrium and speculative bubbles (see Tirole, 1985) – are quite general, much of the development of the sunspot model itself has been closely related to economic dynamics. Azariadis (1981) and Azariadis and Guesnerie (1986) go back to the simplest overlapping-generations model from macro-economics with a stationary environment. Azariadis (1981) provides sufficient conditions for the existence of *stationary* stochastic business cycles based on sunspot activity. Azariadis and Guesnerie (1986) related the conditions for stationary sunspot cycles to the conditions for deterministic cycles. Spear (1985) challenges the view that the stationary sunspot cycles are 'likely' to be encountered when there is more than one commodity per period. Peck (1985) shows, however, that in simple overlapping generations models the existence of a continuum of nonsunspot equilibria (as 'often' arises in economies with taxes and transfers denominated in money units) implies the existence of (possibly nonstationary) sunspot equilibria. Peck's results do not depend on stationarity of the environment. Sunspot equilibria are not 'flukes'.

The connection between endogenous nonstochastic cycles and stationary sunspot equilibria is currently receiving substantial attention. It is too early to review this promising field. The interested reader should turn to the *Journal of Economic Theory* symposium issue (October 1986) on 'Nonlinear Economic Dynamics' edited by Jean-Michel Grandmont. There is a fair sampling of papers on these topics and related topics. The symposium issue also contains several references.

Sunspot equilibrium represents an example of the more general phenomenon, symmetry-breaking, in which symmetric problems have asymmetric solutions. See Balasko (1983) but expect to hear more from him on the subject of symmetry-breaking in economics.

BIBLIOGRAPHY

Arrow, K.J. 1964. The role of securities in the optimal allocation of risk-bearing. *Review of Economic Studies* 31, April, 91–6.

Aumann, R.J. 1974. Subjectivity and correlation in randomized strategies. *Journal of Mathematical Economics* 1(1), March, 67–96.

Aumann, R.J. 1987. Correlated equilibrium as an expression of Bayesian rationality. *Econometrica* 55(1), January, 1–18.

Aumann, R.J., Peck, J. and Shell, K. 1985. Correlated equilibrium in a market game, an example which is not based on perfectly correlated signals nor on uncorrelated signals. Mimeo, Center for Advanced Study in the Behavioral Sciences, Stanford, California, July.

Azariadis, C. 1981. Self-fulfilling prophecies. *Journal of Economic Theory* 25(3), December, 380–96.

Azariadis, C. and Guesnerie, R. 1986. Sunspots and cycles. *Review of Economic Studies* 53(5), October, 725–38.

Balasko, Y. 1983. Extrinsic uncertainty revisited. *Journal of Economic Theory* 31(2), December, 203–10.

Cass, D. and Shell, K. 1980. In defense of a basic approach. In *Models of Monetary Economies*, ed. J. Kareken and N. Wallace, Minneapolis: Federal Reserve Bank of Minneapolis, 25–60.

Cass, D. and Shell, K. 1983. Do sunspots matter? *Journal of Political Economy* 91(2), April, 193–227.

Debreu, G. 1959. *Theory of Value*, New York: Wiley.

Frydman, R. and Phelps, E.S. (eds) 1983. *Individual Forecasting and Aggregate Outcomes*. Cambridge: Cambridge University Press.

Jevons, W.S. 1884. *Investigations in Currency and Finance*. London: Macmillan. (The paper on 'The Periodicity of Commercial Crises and its Physical Explanation', read at the Meeting of the British Association, 19 August 1878.)

Keynes, J.M. 1936. *The General Theory of Employment, Interest and Money*. London: Macmillan; New York: Harcourt, Brace.

Lucas, R.E. 1972. Expectations and the neutrality of money. *Journal of Economic Theory* 4(2), April, 103–24.

Maskin, E. and Tirole, J. 1985. Imperfectly correlated equilibria: a note. Mimeo, Harvard University and MIT, May.

Peck, J. 1986. On the existence of sunspot equilibria in an overlapping-generations model. Mimeo, MEDS, Northwestern, April 1984. Revised 1986. Forthcoming in *Journal of Economic Theory*.

Peck, J. and Shell, K. 1985. Market uncertainty: sunspot equilibria in imperfectly competitive economies. CARESS Working Paper No. 85–21, July.

Samuelson, P.A. 1958. An exact consumption loan model of interest with or without the social contrivance of money. *Journal of Political Economy* 66(6), December, 467–82.

Shapley, L. and Shubik, M. 1977. Trade using one commodity as a means of payment. *Journal of Political Economy* 85(5), October, 937–68.

Shell, K. 1971. Notes on the economics of infinity. *Journal of Political Economy* 79(5), September–October, 1002–11.

Shell, K. 1977. Monnaie et allocation intertemporelle. Communication to Roy–Malinvaud seminar. Mimeo, Paris, November. (Title and abstract in French, text in English.)

Spear, S. 1985. Rational expectations in the overlapping generations model. *Journal of Economic Theory* 35(2), April, 251–75.

Tirole, J. 1985. Asset bubbles and overlapping generations. *Econometrica* 53(5), September, 1071–100.

Townsend, R.M. 1983. Equilibrium theory with learning and disparate expectations: some issues and methods. Ch. 9 in Frydman and Phelps (1983, eds), 169–97.

Tâtonnement and Recontracting

TAKASHI NEGISHI

In the current theory of general economic equilibrium, recontracting and tâtonnement (a French word meaning 'groping') are used interchangeably to denote a simplifying assumption that no actual transactions, and therefore no production and consumption activities, take place at disequilibria when prices are changed according to the law of supply and demand (Kaldor, 1934; Arrow and Hahn, 1971, pp. 264, 282). Historically speaking, however, this usage is somewhat confusing, since recontracting is originally due to Edgeworth who developed it in a direction different from that in which Walras developed his tâtonnement (Walker, 1973).

Though different interpretations are given as to whether Walras explicitly excluded disequilibrium transactions from the beginning (Patinkin, 1956, p. 533; Newman, 1965, p. 102; Jaffé, 1967, 1981), it is clear that Walras developed his theory of tâtonnement so as to exclude such transactions. To do this there are at least three methods of tâtonnement. First, we may assume price-taking traders facing market prices cried by the *auctioneer* reveal their plans of demand and supply to the auctioneer but do not make any trade contract among themselves until the auctioneer declares that equilibrium is established. Alternatively, traders may be assumed to make trade contracts (Walras, 1926, p. 242, suggested the use of tickets when production is involved) but recontract is assumed always to be possible, in the sense that contract can be cancelled without consent of the other party if market prices are changed. Finally, the effect of past contracts can be nullified by offering new demands (supplies) to offset past supplies (demands), even if it is assumed that past contracts are effective and would be carried out at the current prices when the equilibrium is established (Morishima, 1977, pp. 28–30). Since any changes in prices make the contract unfavourable to one of the parties which then wishes to cancel the trade contract, there is no difference between the three methods of tâtonnement in the behaviour of demand, supply and prices. Recontracting in this sense of tâtonnement is, however, quite different from that developed in Edgeworth's theory of recontract.

We shall start by the consideration of why this assumption of tâtonnement is necessary for the Walrasian theory of general equilibrium, which is the foundation of neoclassical economic theory. The reason lies in the structure of Walrasian economics, dichotomized between real and monetary theories. Then we analyse formal models of tâtonnement including the original one due to Walras and the modified version developed in modern theories of general equilibrium. It is followed by our assessment of the theoretical achievements and empirical relevance of Walrasian tâtonnement economics. Edgeworth's theory of recontract is reviewed in its relation to the Walrasian theory of tâtonnement. Finally, an evaluation is made on the recent studies of tâtonnement and recontracting, to show in which direction further progress should be made.

1. Walras ([1874–7] 1926) insisted that complicated phenomena can be studied only if the rule of proceeding from the simple to the complex is always observed. To understand the fundamental nature of Walrasian economics, it is convenient to make (as did Hicks, 1934) a comparison of Walrasian and Marshallian ways of applying this rule to the study of complicated economic phenomena. Both Walras and Marshall (1890) start with a very simple model of an economy and then proceed to more complex models. There is an important difference, however, between Walrasian general equilibrium analysis and Marshallian partial equilibrium analysis.

Walras first decomposes a complicated economy of the real world into several fundamental components like consumer-traders, entrepreneurs, consumers' goods, factors of production, newly produced capital goods, and money. He then composes a simple model of a pure exchange economy by picking up a very limited number of such components, that is, individual consumer-traders and consumer's goods, disregarding the existence of all other components. Travel from this simple model to the complex proceeds by adding one by one those components so far excluded, that is, entrepreneurs and factors of production first, then newly produced capital goods, and finally money. In this journey each intermediate model, enlarged from a simpler one and to be enlarged into a more complex one, is still a closed and self-compact logical system. However, each of them is as unrealistic as the starting model, with the exception of the last, into which all the components of a real world economy have been introduced.

Marshall on the other hand studies a whole complex of a real world economy as such. Of course, he also simplifies his study at first by confining his interest to a certain limited number of aspects of the economy. But he does it not by disregarding the existence of other aspects but by assuming that other things remain equal. In this sense most of Marshall's models of an economy, though realistic, are open and not self-sufficient, since some endogenous variables (i.e. the 'other things') remain unexplained and have to be given exogenously.

The simplest model of Walrasian economics is that studied in the theory of exchange, where goods to be exchanged among individual consumer-traders are assumed simply to be endowed to them and not considered as produced at cost. There exist no production activities in this hypothetical world. The corresponding simplest model of Marshall is that of the market day, in which goods to be sold are produced goods, although the amount available for sale is, for the time being, assumed to be constant. Production does exist in this temporary model, though the level of output is assumed to be unchanged. In that Walrasian model which includes production capital goods are introduced as a kind of factor of production but investment (i.e. the production of new capital goods) simply does not exist. On the other hand, in Marshallian short-run theory, which is also a theory of production, investment is actually undertaken though the amount of currently available capital is given. In all of the Walrasian models of exchange, of production and of credit and capital formation there exists no money at all, until it is finally introduced in the theory of circulation and money. In Marshallian models on the other hand money exists from the beginning, though its purchasing power is sometimes assumed to be constant.

In other words, Marshallian theories correspond respectively to special states of the real world economy. The market day (temporary) and short-run models are just as realistic as the long-run model, where capitals are fully adjusted. Thus Marshallian models are practically useful to apply to what Hicks (1934) called particular problems of history or experience. On the other hand, Walrasian models are in general not useful for such practical purposes. They are designed to show the fundamental significance of such components of the real world economy as entrepreneurs and production, investment and the rate of interest, inventories and money, etc., by successively introducing them into simple models which are then developed into more complex ones. Walras' theoretical interest was not in the solution of particular problems but in what Hicks called the pursuit of the general principles which underlie the working of a market economy.

From our standpoint we must emphasize that all exchanges have to be non-monetary (i.e. direct exchanges of goods for goods) in all the Walrasian theories of exchange, production and capital formation and credit, since money has not yet been introduced. Relative prices (including the rate of interest) and hence consumption and production activities are determined in non-monetary real models without using money, while the role of the model of circulation and money lies only in the determination of the level of absolute prices by the use of the money (Morishima, 1977, ch. 11; Negishi, 1979, ch. 2). Thus Walrasian economics is completely dichotomized between non-monetary real theories and monetary theory, in the sense that all non-monetary real variables are determined in the former and money is neutral, that is it does not matter for the determination of such variables. 'That being the case, the equation of monetary circulation, when money is not a commodity, comes very close, in reality, to falling outside the system of equations of (general) economic equilibrium' (Walras, 1926, pp. 326–7).

2. In each of his non-monetary theories Walras tried to show the existence of a general equilibrium in its corresponding self-compact closed model. General

equilibrium is of course a state in which not only each individual consumer-trader (entrepreneur) achieves the maximum obtainable satisfaction (profit) under given conditions but also demand and supply are equalized in all markets. In a large economy, how can we make such a situation possible without introducing money? What kind of process of exchange should we consider in order to establish a general equilibrium without using money? Even in the most simple case of an exchange economy, it seems in general almost impossible to satisfy all individual traders by barter exchanges, unless mutual coincidence of wants accidentally prevails everywhere. Walras ingeniously solved this difficulty by his famous tâtonnement, a preliminary process of price (and quantity) adjustment which preceeds exchange transactions and/or effective contracts.

Suppose that all the individual consumer-traders and entrepreneurs meet in a big hall. Since all of them are assumed to be competitive price takers it is convenient to assume (though Walras himself did not do so explicitly) the existence of an *auctioneer* whose only role is to determine prices. At the start the auctioneer calls all prices (including the price of a bond) at random. Individual consumers and entrepreneurs make decisions on the supply and demand of all goods, factors of production and of the bond, assuming that the prices cried by the auctioneer are fixed and that whatever amount they wish can actually be supplied and demanded at these prices. If total demand equals total supply for every good (including the factors of production and the bond) exchange takes place (or contracts are made) at these prices, and the problem is solved.

Generally, however, this will not be the case, in which event no exchange transaction should take place at all, even for a good for which total demand is equal to total supply, and every mutually agreed contract should be cancelled. The auctioneer cancels the earlier prices, which failed to establish a general equilibrium, and calls new prices by following the law of supply and demand, that is raising (lowering) the price of each good for which the demand is larger (smaller) than the supply. The same procedure is repeated until general equilibrium is established. Actual exchange transactions take place and enforceable contracts are made only when every party can actually realize its plan of demand and supply.

Prices change in the process of tâtonnement and it is generally impossible for a single trader to purchase or sell whatever amount he wishes at going prices. Nevertheless, each trader behaves on the assumption that prices are unchanged and that unlimited quantities of demand and supply can be realized at the current prices. This conjecture is justified by the very fact that no exchange transactions are made and no trade contracts are in effect during the tâtonnement, until general equilibrium is established where prices are no longer changed, and every trader can purchase and sell exactly the amount he wishes at going prices.

In a monetary economy of the real world, where of course the tâtonnement assumption cannot be made and some exchange transactions actually takes place before general equilibrium is established, even a competitive trader without power to control prices has to expect price changes and to try to sell when the prices is high and to buy when the price is low, though he may not always succeed in doing so. This leads to the separation of sales and purchases, a separation which is made possible only by the use of money as the medium of exchange and the store of value. In Walrasian non-monetary real models where the tâtonnement assumption is made, on the other hand, sales and purchases are synchronized when general equilibrium is established so that there is no need for money, and indeed there is no reason why the role of medium of exchange should be exclusively assigned to a single item called money. Since equilibrium prices are already fixed and unchanged almost any non-perishable good can be used if necessary as a medium of exchange.

Walras considered tâtonnement even in his final model, i.e. that of circulation and money. Since disequilibrium transactions are thus excluded and there is no uncertainty, there is no room here for money as a store of value. We have to assume therefore that people demand money only for the sake of convenience in transactions. Since all actual transactions are carried out at general equilibrium after the preliminary tâtonnement is over, however, this rationale for the demand for money is not at all convincing. The only role left for money is to determine its own price, that is the general level of prices.

3. Walras gave two solutions for general equilibrium of each of his non-monetary real models, as well as his monetary model. The first solution is the demonstration that the number of unknowns is equal to the number of independent equations, which Walras called the scientific or mathematical solution. But how can we find a solution of such equations, particularly when the number of equations is very large? The second solution of general equilibrium given by Walras (1926, pp. 162–3, 170–172) is tâtonnement itself, which is suggested by the mechanism of free competition in markets and is called the practical or empirical solution. Taking the example of the simple model of exchange these two solutions may be reformulated in modern notation as follows.

Consider an exchange economy of m goods and denote the price of and the excess demand for the jth good by p_j and E_j respectively. One condition for general equilibrium is that demand is equal to supply in all markets, that is

$$E_j(p_1, \ldots, p_m) = 0, \qquad j = 1, \ldots, m. \tag{1}$$

In view of Walras's Law that

$$\sum_j p_j E_j \equiv 0, \tag{2}$$

only $(m-1)$ equations of (1) are independent, while we can assign the role of numéraire to the mth good so that $p_m = 1$, since only relative prices are relevant in a non-monetary economy. Therefore (1) is replaced by

$$E_j(p_1, \ldots, p_{m-1}) = 0. \qquad j = 1, \ldots, m-1. \tag{3}$$

Equations (1) or (3) are derived from the competitive behaviour of individual consumer-traders. The ith consumer-trader is assumed to maximize his utility $U_i(x_{il}, \ldots, x_{im})$, subject to the budget constraint

285

$$\sum_j p_j x_{ij} = \sum_j p_j y_{ij} \qquad (4)$$

where x_{ij} and y_{ij} denote respectively the gross demand for the jth good by the ith consumer-trader and the given initial holding of the jth good of the ith consumer-trader. The excess demand for the jth good is then defined as

$$E_j = \sum_i x_{ij} - \sum_i y_{ij}. \qquad (5)$$

It is to be noted that excess demand is not defined in (1) and (3) explicitly as a function of the y_{ij}'s. The reason is that the y_{ij}'s are given constants and are assumed not to change through the process of exchange until the demand plans of all consumer-traders are simultaneously realized when general equilibrium is established. In other words the assumption of tâtonnement is already implicitly made in the mathematical or theoretical solution of general equilibrium.

The original form of Walrasian tâtonnement is the process of successive adjustment in each single market. Suppose the initial set of prices cried by the auctioneer $(p_1, \ldots, p_{m-1})$ does not satisfy the condition (3) of general equilibrium, and we are for example in a situation described by

$$E_1(p_1, \ldots, p_{m-1}) > 0$$

$$E_2(p_1, \ldots, p_{m-1}) < 0$$

$$E_{m-1}(p_1, \ldots, p_{m-1}) > 0 \qquad (6)$$

The price of the first good p_1 is now adjusted by reference to its excess demand E, and increased in the situation (3) until an equilibrium in the first market is established, that is

$$E_1(p_1', p_2, \ldots, p_{m-1}) = 0. \qquad (7)$$

Here E_1 is assumed to be decreasing with respect to p_1, an assumption which, writing the partial derivative of the excess demand function for the ith good with respect to the kth price by E_{jk}, may be symbolized by $E_{11} < 0$.

Under the new price system $(p_1', p_2, \ldots, p_{m-1})$ the remaining $m - 1$ markets may or may not be in equilibrium. If the second market is out of equilibrium, again under the assumption that $E_{22} < 0$, the price of the second good is changed from p_2 to p_2' so as to satisfy

$$E_2(p_1', p_2', p_3, \ldots, p_{m-1}) = 0. \qquad (8)$$

[Generally, this will upset the equilibrium in the first market (7).] Under the price system $(p_1', p_2', p_3, \ldots, p_{m-1})$, then, the price of the third good p_3 is adjusted if the third market (where $E_{33} < 0$) is out of equilibrium, upsetting the equilibrium in the second market (8) just established. In this way the last, $m - 1$th market, where $E_{m-1,m-1} < 0$, is eventually cleared by changing the price system from $(p_1', \ldots, p_{m-2}', p_{m-1})$ into $(p_1', \ldots, p_{m-2}', p_{m-1}')$ so as to satisfy

$$E_{m-1}(p_{m1}', \ldots, p_{m-2}', p_{m-1}') = 0. \qquad (9)$$

286

By this time all the markets except the last, which were once cleared successively, have generally been thrown out of their respective equilibria again. Neither the price system we have just arrived at, $(p'_1, \ldots, p'_{m-1})$, nor the initial system $(p_1, \ldots, p_{m-1})$, is part of a general equilibrium. The question then is which of the systems is closer to a true general equilibrium that satisfies (3). Walras argued that the former price system is closer to equilibrium than the latter since for example $E_1(p'_1, \ldots, p'_{m-1}) \neq 0$ is closer to 0 than $E_1(p_1, \ldots, p_{m-1}) \neq 0$. The reason for this, according to Walras, is that the change from p_1 to p'_1 which established (7) exerted a direct influence that was invariably in the direction of zero excess demand so far as the first good is concerned. But the subsequent changes from p_2 to $p'_2, \ldots, p_{m-1}$ to p'_{m-1}, which jointly moved the first excess demand away from zero exerted only indirect influences, some in the direction of equilibrium and some in the opposite direction, at least so far as the excess demand for the first good is concerned. So up to a certain point they cancelled each other out. Hence, Walras concluded, by repeating the successive adjustment of $m - 1$ markets along the same lines, that is changing prices according to the law of supply and demand, we can move closer and closer to general equilibrium.

4. Walras's argument for the convergence of the tâtonnement process to general equilibrium was intended to be, if successful, the first demonstration of the existence of competitive general equilibrium (Wald, 1936). As we said above, it was merely an argument for the plausibility of such convergence of the process of tâtonnement, and cannot be considered as a rigorous demonstration of existence of equilibrium. Whether indirect influences of the prices of other goods on the excess demand of a given good cancel each other out will certainly depend on substitutability and complementarity between goods. For example, indirect influence are *not* cancelled out and the excess demand of a good *is* increased if the prices of all gross substitutes are raised and the prices of all gross complements are lowered. In addition to the Walrasian stability condition for a single market, that is $E_{jj} < 0$ for all j, therefore, some conditions on the cross-effects of prices on excess demands, that is on $E_{jk}, j \neq k$ have to be imposed so as to demonstrate convergence.

It was Allais (1943, vol. 2, pp. 486–9) who first demonstrated the convergence of Walrasian tâtonnement by assuming gross substitutability, that is, $E_{jk} > 0$ for all $j = k$. To see whether the price system moves closer and closer to the general equilibrium, which he assumes to be at least locally unique, Allais defines the distance D of a price system from the equilibrium price system as the sum of the absolute values of the value of excess demand for all goods, including the numéraire. The convergence of tâtonnement is then demonstrated by showing that this distance D is always decreased by changes in prices that are made in accordance with the law of supply and demand. His demonstration may be reformulated in our notation as follows.

The distance to the general equilibrium is defined as

$$D = \sum_j |p_j E_j| \tag{10}$$

where the summation runs from $j = 1$ to $j = m$, and E_j is defined as a function of $p_1, \ldots, p_{m-1}$ as in (3). In view of Walras's Law (2), D can be replaced either by the summation of positive excess demands

$$D_1 = \sum_j p_j \max(0, E_j) \tag{11}$$

or by the summation of negative excess demands

$$D_2 = -\sum_j p_j \min(0, E_j) \tag{12}$$

where $\max(0, E_j)$ denotes E_j if it is positive and 0 if E_j is negative, and min $(0, E_j)$ denotes E_j if it is the negative and 0 if E_j is positive. From (2), that is $D_1 - D_2 = 0$, it is clear that

$$D = 2D_1 = 2D_2 \tag{13}$$

so that whether D is increasing or decreasing can be seen by checking whether D_1 or D_2 (whichever is more convenient) is increasing or decreasing.

Suppose E_1 to be positive as in (6) and that p_1 is raised following the law of supply and demand. From (12), we have

$$\partial D_2 / \partial p_1 < 0 \tag{14}$$

since $E_{j1} > 0$ for any j such that $E_j < 0$, from gross substitutability. In other words, a change in the price of the first good from p_1 to p_1' so as to satisfy (7) decreases the sum of negative excess demands D_2 and therefore the distance D to the general equilibrium. Suppose next that $E_2(p_1', p_2, \ldots, p_{m-1})$ is negative and p_2 is lowered to p_2' so as to satisfy (8). From (11) this time, we have

$$\partial D_1 / \partial p_2 > 0 \tag{15}$$

since $E_{j2} > 0$ for any j such that $E_j > 0$ from gross substitutability. In other words, a decrease in the price of the second good from p_2 to p_2' decreases the sum of positive excess demands D_1 and therefore the distance D to the general equilibrium.

Generally, if E_j is positive and p_j is raised D is decreased, which can be seen from the fact that D_2 is decreased. Similarly, if E_j is negative and p_j is lowered again D is decreased, which can be seen from the consideration of the behaviour of D_1. Out of the general equilibrium D remains positive and there exists at least one non-numéraire good with non-zero excess demand, so that its price is changing. The distance to the general equilibrium always decreases out of equilibrium, and therefore we can move closer and closer to that equilibrium by changing prices according to the law of supply and demand, provided that gross substitutability is assumed.

Though Walras discussed the behaviour of the process of successive adjustment, he was not against the consideration of *simultaneous adjustment processes* in all markets (Uzawa, 1960; Jaffé, 1981). If we assume that adjustments take place not only simultaneously but also continuously, the tâtonnement process that each rate of change of price is governed by excess demand can be described by a set of differential equations,

$$\mathrm{d}p_j/\mathrm{d}t = a_j E_j(p_1, \ldots, p_{m-1}), \qquad j = 1, \ldots, m-1, \qquad (16)$$

where t denotes time and the a_j's are positive constants signifying the speed of adjustment in the jth market. The study of the behaviour of the solutions of (16), that is prices as functions of t, which was initiated by Samuelson (1941) is called the study of the *stability of competitive equilibrium* and has been extensively carried out by many mathematical economists (Arrow and Hahn, 1971, pp. 263–323; Negishi, 1972, pp. 191–206). It is well known that gross substitutability is also a sufficient condition for the *convergence of adjustment processes* like (16).

5. The idea of tâtonnement was clearly suggested to Walras from the observation of how business is done in some well organized markets in the real world, like the stock exchanges, commercial markets, grain markets, fish markets. As a matter of fact, Walras was well informed of the actual operation of the Paris Stock Exchange where disequilibrium transactions actually did not occur (Jaffé, 1981). Tâtonnement is therefore not entirely unrealistic as a model of adjustment in such special markets.

However, it is certainly very unrealistic to apply such a model of special markets to the whole economy, since preliminary adjustments are usually not made before exchange transactions and effective contracts take place, even in markets where competition, though not so well organized, functions fairly satisfactorily. Of course, Walras would have admitted this, since tâtonnement was for him not so much a description of the process of adjustment in the markets of the real world as it was the demonstration of the existence of general equilibrium, that is a limit to which tâtonnement converges. It should be so interpreted not only in the case of successive tâtonnement, which reminds us of the Gauss–Seidel method of solving a set of simultaneous equations, but also in the case of simultaneous tâtonnement (16), where time t is not real calendar time, but hypothetical process time. This is no wonder, since Walrasian non-monetary models are not intended to be faithful descriptions of the real world. They are designed rather to make clear the significance of each component of the market economy and to uncover the general principles that underlie its working.

One may feel that such an interpretation of Walrasian tâtonnement is too strict and that the behaviour of not so well organized markets can be described approximately by the tâtonnement model. Walrasian tâtonnement may be interpreted as something like the laws of motion, that work strictly speaking only in the ideal frictionless world but which can be applied approximately to the real world. The law of supply and demand can certainly be applied even in markets where there is no auctioneer, traders are dispersed, and exchange transactions take place and effective contracts are made before equilibrium of demand and supply is established.

Prices are formed differently in each exchange transaction by negotiation between relevant parties of traders. The Law of Indifference tends to prevail, however, if the transmission of information is nearly perfect, since atomistic traders know the difficulty of purchasing (selling) at prices lower (higher) than the prices offered by competitors and there are, furthermore, arbitrage activities. If demand falls short of supply, it is suicidal for atomistic sellers to offer a price higher than the average market price, while an atomistic purchaser is unable to consider a price lower than the average market price when demand exceeds supply. With disequilibrium of supply and demand, exchange transactions can take place only if demanders (suppliers) can find suppliers (demanders). If demand is deficient therefore sellers consider cutting prices or increasing market costs in order to attract more purchasers, since a drastic increase in sales is expected from slight falls in price or slight increases in marketing costs when information is nearly perfect. By observing such behaviour by the sellers, the purchasers also insist on price cuts. Thus price falls in the face of excess supply. Similarly, market prices rise as the result of a similar process of disequilibrium exchange transactions in the face of excess demand, in which the roles of sellers and purchasers are interchanged from the case of excess supply.

Therefore, we can extend (16) to

$$dp_j/dt = a_j E_j(p_1, \ldots, p_{m-1}, y_{11}, \ldots, y_{nm}), \qquad j = 1, \ldots, m-1, \qquad (17)$$

where the E_j's are again derived from (5) but have now to be considered explicitly as functions of the y_{ij}'s, that is the stock of the jth good held by the ith consumer-trader, $i = 1, \ldots, n$, since the y_{ij}'s are no longer constants but instead are changed by disequilibrium transactions among the n consumer-traders. Here we cannot discuss in detail how the y_{ij}'s are changed as a result of transactions at disequilibria, and have to be content with the general assumption that their rates of change depend on everything, that is we have

$$dy_{ij}/dt = F_{ij}(p_1, \ldots, p_{m-1}, y_{11}, \ldots, y_{nm}), \qquad i = 1, \ldots, n, \quad j = 1, \ldots, m, \qquad (18)$$

where the F_{ij}'s are unknown functions incorporating rules for exchange transactions out of equilibria. Models of an economy with (17) and (18) are called non-tâtonnement models or *non-recontracting models*.

Generally, if a non-tâtonnement or non-recontracting process (17) and (18) converges, it does so to an equilibrium that is different from that arrived at by the tâtonnement process (16), since changes in the y_{ij}'s due to disequilibrium exchange transactions have effects on (17) which do not exist in the case of (16). As Newman (1965, p. 102) correctly pointed out, however, the difference can be safely neglected, if the speed of price adjustment in every market is very high [i.e. the a_j's in (17) are very large], since then markets arrive at equilibrium prices so rapidly that the effects of disequilibrium transactions are prevented from becoming serious. Although the possibility of disequilibrium transactions is not institutionally excluded and there may well be some, most transactions are actually carried out at equilibrium so that it looks as if the assumption of tâtonnement is satisfied. In this sense, tâtonnement models can be used to describe the behaviour of non-tâtonnement or non-recontracting markets in the real world.

6. Although the tâtonnement model can be applied to markets that are not so well organized if the transmission of information is nearly perfect and the speed of price adjustment is rapid, the general equilibrium tâtonnement model (16) is still not a realistic description of the real world economy. The reason is that the role of money as the medium of exchange and a store of value is very important in the real world, while as we saw it is highly limited in a model where most exchange transactions are simultaneously carried out at equilibrium. To make our model more realistic so that sales and purchases take place at disequilibria and are separated by the use of money, therefore, we have to get rid of tâtonnement by arguing that the speed of price adjustment is not rapid in (17), so that disequilibrium transactions cannot be ignored.

If the transmission of information is perfect, the law of supply and demand can be applied even in not so well organized markets where no auctioneer exists and disequilibrium transactions take place. This is because every seller (purchaser) perceives an infinitely elastic demand (supply) curve and expects that a drastic increase in sale (purchase) is made possible by a slight reduction (increase) in price. If total demand falls short of total supply in a market then, every trader willingly reduces price or accepts a reduction in it. Similarly, if total demand exceeds total supply in a market every trader willingly raises price or accepts a rise in it.

The transmission of information may not be so perfect, however, in markets where traders are dispersed and so cannot meet in a big hall as they do in the case of Walrasian tâtonnement. Suppose that a market is segmented and transmission of information is perfect among closely related traders, but that it is not so between different segments. Individual traders are assumed to keep contact with current trade partners and not to leave the segment of the market in which they are currently located in search of more favourable trade conditions, unless either they are well informed of such conditions in other segments or trade conditions change unfavourably in the original segment. Possibly because of consideration of cost, traders are constrained by inertia and do not move unless shocked by information on other segments or by changes in the original segment.

Then even an atomistic seller (purchaser) does not perceive an infinitely elastic demand (supply) curve. A seller expects that sales cannot be increased very much by reduction of price since only those purchasers who are currently buying from him are well informed of the price reductions, and this information is not perfectly transmitted to those purchasers who belong to other segments of the market and who are not buying from him. When total demand falls short of total supply and other sellers do not raise the price, it cannot be expected that 'their' purchasers leave them in search of cheaper sellers. The same seller has to expect, however, that sales will be drastically reduced if the price is raised, since those customers who are currently buying will be well informed of this and will leave to search for cheaper sellers, which they can find easily when total demand falls short of total supply and there are many other sellers willing to sell more at the unchanged price.

Atomistic sellers perceive kinked demand curves, with a downward sloping segment for levels of sale higher than the current one, and an almost infinitely elastic segment for levels of sale lower than the current one, when the market is in excess supply. It is very likely then that price does not fall and remains sticky in the face of excess supply (Reid, 1981, pp. 65–6, 96–9; Negishi, 1979, p. 36). It may not pay to reduce price if demand cannot be increased very much. Similarly, an atomistic purchaser perceives a kinked supply curve with an upward sloping segment for levels of purchase higher than the current one, and an almost infinitely elastic segment for levels of purchase lower than the current one, when the market is in excess demand. Since the transmission of information is imperfect and the purchaser cannot attract many sellers by raising price, it may not pay to raise price even if a larger purchaser is wanted at the current price. It is very likely, therefore, that price does not rise and remains sticky in the face of excess demand.

Thus prices may be sticky and may not be adjusted quickly by demand and supply in not-well-organized markets in the real world. The speed of adjustment in (17) need not be rapid enough to allow one to ignore the effects of disequilibrium transactions, so that the tâtonnement process (16) cannot then be regarded as a realistic description of adjustment in real-world markets. Walrasian tâtonnement models are, of course, not designed to describe such markets empirically. They are constructed to show how the market mechanism works beautifully under ideal conditions. No one can deny that Walrasian economics succeeded in accomplishing this purpose. The market mechanism, however, does not work so beautifully in the real world. It certainly manages to work somehow but quite often at the cost of prolonged disequilibria in markets, such as involuntary unemployment in the labour market and excess capacity in goods markets. This is why we have to supplement Walrasian economics by launching out into the study of non-Walrasian economics.

7. RECONTRACTING. Since the idea of recontracting is due originally to Edgeworth, who developed it in a way different from Walras's tâtonnement, the implication of Edgeworth's theory of recontract has to be carefully considered in its relation to the theory of tâtonnement in Walrasian economics. These two theories are different from each other in at least two ways, namely with respect to the Law of Indifference (the uniformity of prices) and to the provisional nature of revocability of trade contracts. The first problem is discussed below, while the second will be considered in the next section.

There have been different interpretations as to whether Edgeworth's *Mathematical Psychics* (1881) excluded disequilibrium transactions or assumed the irrevocability of contracts (Walker, 1973; Creedy, 1980). Even if we assume that disequilibrium transactions are excluded, however, the theory of recontract in Edgeworth is different from the theory of tâtonnement in Walrasian economics. The Law of Indifference (i.e. the existence of uniform market prices even in disequilibria) is imposed as an axiom in the original Walrasian as well as in modern Walrasian economic theories. This axiom may be justified either through arbitrage activities or by the existence of the auctioneer, and enables individual traders to act as price takers who have only to adjust their plans of supply and demand to the given prices. Such an axiom is not imposed in Edgeworth's recontracting model.

To demonstrate his famous limit theorem (Bewley, 1973), Edgeworth starts with a simple two-good two-individual model of exchange, where a trader X offers a good x to a trader Y in exchange for a good y. If we consider the so-called Edgeworth Box diagram, any point on the contract curve, where each of two individual traders is not worse off than before exchange, can be a final settlement of trade contract which cannot be varied by recontract. To narrow down the range of possible final settlements Edgeworth introduces a second X and a second Y, each respectively identical to the first, both in tastes and initial endowments. Since identical traders have to be treated equally in any final settlement, we can still use the same box diagram. Now it can be shown that no final settlement of contract can contain points on the contract curve which give 'small' gains from trade to the X traders. Otherwise, it is 'possible for *one* of the Ys (without the consent of the other) to *recontract* with the two Xs, so that for all those three parties the recontract is more advantageous than the previously existing contract' (Edgeworth, 1881, p. 35). Similarly, it is possible to exclude as final settlements those points which give 'small' trade gains to Y traders.

In this way Edgeworth shows that the range of possible final settlements shrinks as the number of identical traders grows. If there are infinitely many traders the only remaining final settlements turn out to be precisely the points of Walrasian equilibrium, each with a uniform price line, that is the common tangent to indifference curves of X and Y passing through the point of initial endowments. In the terminology of the modern theory of cooperative games, the core of the exchange game (i.e. those allocations not blocked by any coalitions of players) consists only of the Walrasian equilibria when the numbers of the Xs and the Ys are each infinitely large. Thus Edgeworth tries to show that the recontracting process in the large economy, where traders obtain a free flow of information through the making and breaking of provisional contracts, leads to the same uniform prices that are given by the auctioneer to price-taking traders in Walrasian equilibria. Though there are no uniform market prices and individual traders are not assumed to be price-takers in Edgeworth's recontracting process, the resulting equilibrium exchanges are the same as those obtained through Walrasian tâtonnement in a large economy. In such an economy, therefore, where information is perfect, we can safely argue as if there were uniform market prices and as if traders were price-takers. In a sense, Edgeworth justified the Walrasian axiom, since axioms of theories should be assessed not by themselves but by the results derived from them. Even if the Walrasian axiom is not itself realistic, the results derived from it can be as realistic as those derived from more realistic but more complicated axioms.

In later writings Edgeworth confirmed his early position on Walras and the uniformity of prices. Walras

describes *a* way rather than *the* way by which economic equilibrium is reached. ... Walras's laboured description of prices set up or 'cried' in the market is calculated to divert attention from a sort of higgling which may be regarded as more fundamental than his conception, the process of *recontract* . . . . The proposition that there is only one price in a perfect market may be regarded as *deducible* from the more axiomatic principle of recontract (*Mathematical Psychics*, p. 40 and context: Edgeworth, 1925, vol. 2, pp. 311–23).

We may add that even the existence of a uniform rate-of-exchange between any two commodities is perhaps not so much axiomatic as deducible from the process of competition in a perfect market (Edgeworth, 1925, vol. 2, p. 453).

8. It is possible to interpret Edgeworth's theory of bilateral exchange (Edgeworth, 1925, vol. 2, pp. 316–19) as a theory of a process where not only the rate of exchange is variable but also contracts are irrevocable. Starting from a situation with initial holdings, two goods are actually exchanged so as always to increase the utility of each of the two traders. Since exchanges are irrevocable, however, where on the contract curve this process of exchange will terminate depends on the path of exchanges as well as on the initial holdings. Hence it contrasts strongly with Walrasian tâtonnement, the equilibrium of which depends only on the initial holdings. There is no confusion, however, between this theory of Edgeworth and Edgeworth's theory of recontract interpreted in the sense of tâtonnement, since the modern extension of the former theory to the case of multiple traders is rightly called the theory of Edgeworth's *barter* process (Uzawa, 1962; Fisher, 1983, pp. 29–31).

Incidentally, Edgeworth's idea that exchanges necessarily take place only in the direction of increasing utilities can be relevant only in a barter economy. In a monetary economy an exchange of one good against another is decomposed into an exchange of the first good against money and an exchange of money against the second good. Even though the completed exchange of the two goods increases utility, its first half need not do so since in the course of the exchange process one may temporarily receive more money than one plans to keep eventually. In other words, one may impose a rule for non-monetary goods of no overfulfilment of demand and supply plans in the process of exchange, but this cannot be done for money, which has to act both as the medium of exchange and as a store of value beyond the current period.

In view of the current usage of the concept of recontracting in the sense of tâtonnement, what is confusing is the fact that Edgeworth sometimes, and particularly in his later writings, applied his recontracting model to situations where exchange transactions actually take place at disequilibria. To show that his model is of more than academic interest Edgeworth considered the case of a labour market, which each day ends in disequilibrium after exchange transactions have taken place at disequilibrium rates of exchange. From day to day, as the traders' knowledge of the state of disequilibrium in the market changes they progressively modify their behaviour, changing the rate of exchange in such a way that the market converges to equilibrium.

Since labour service is perishable within a day and the number and dispositions of the traders are assumed to be unchanged, this process over a sequence of days is formally equivalent to the recontracting process within a day, even though in the former process contracts made on the previous days are irrevocable while in the latter disequilibrium contracts are revocable. Edgeworth insisted that in this example of a process over a sequence of days (Edgeworth, 1925, vol. 1, p. 40) traders do recontract, in the full sense of *Mathematical Psychics*. Since contracts made in earlier days are irrevocable, however, in this case to recontract implies that a new contract is made which is different from that carried out on the previous day. It does not imply the cancellation of contracts already made.

Only a formal similarity exists between these two processes of recontracting, which is due to the assumption that disequilibrium exchange transactions do not really involve a permanent redistribution of wealth. Although labour service is perishable within a day, however, the money paid against labour service certainly is not and it is likely that a redistribution of wealth does take place over a sequence of days. Even from a formal point of view, then, Edgeworth's model of the labour market is rather a pioneering instance of *non-recontracting models*.

9. No one can deny that the rigorous demonstration of the dynamic stability of tâtonnement under certain sufficient conditions has substantially improved on the original argument for the plausibility of its convergence that was made by Walras. More importantly, however, the recent studies on stability have helped us to understand the underlying economic assumptions of the Walrasian tâtonnement process itself, and made us realize its considerable differences from most price adjustment processes in actual economies. The similar studies of Edgeworth's recontracting process have been helpful in the same way.

As we have shown, Walrasian tâtonnement is a realistic approximation to some actual adjustment processes, provided that the transmission of information is perfect and the speed of adjustment is rapid, as is roughly the case in well organized markets. The problem that remains to be studied, therefore, is the nature of adjustment processes when these conditions are not satisfied, that is, when markets are not so well organized. This is the problem of non-recontracting models in non-Walrasian or disequilibrium economies.

BIBLIOGRAPHY

Allais, M. 1943. *Traité d'économie pure.* Paris: Imprimerie Nationale, 2nd edn, 1952.

Arrow, K.J. and Hahn, F.H. 1971. *General Competitive Analysis.* San Francisco: Holden-Day.

Bewley, T.F. 1973. Edgeworth's conjecture. *Econometrica* 41(3), May, 425–54.

Creedy, J. 1980. Some recent interpretations of *Mathematical Psychics. History of Political Economy* 12(2), Summer, 267–76.

Edgeworth, F.Y. 1881. *Mathematical Psychics: An Essay on the Application of Mathematics to the Moral Sciences.* London: C. Kegan Paul & Co; reprinted New York: A.M. Kelley, 1967.

Edgeworth, F.Y. 1925. *Papers Relating to Political Economy.* 3 vols, London: Macmillan; New York: B. Franklin, 1963.

Fisher, F.M. 1983. *Disequilibrium Foundations of Equilibrium Economics.* Econometric Society Monographs in Pure Theory, Cambridge: Cambridge University Press.

Hicks, J.R. 1934. Léon Walras. *Econometrica* 2, October, 338–48.

Jaffé, W. 1967. Walras's theory of *tâtonnement*: a critique of recent interpretations. *Journal of Political Economy* 75(1), February, 1–19.

Jaffé, W. 1981. Another look at Léon Walras's theory of *tâtonnement*. *History of Political Economy* 13(2), Summer, 313–36.

Kaldor, N. 1934. A classificatory note on the determinateness of equilibrium. *Review of Economic Studies* 1, February, 122–36.

Marshall, A. 1890. *Principles of Economics*. London: Macmillan; New York: Macmillan, 1948.

Morishima, M. 1977. *Walras' Economics: A Pure Theory of Capital and Money*. Cambridge: Cambridge University Press.

Negishi, T. 1972. *General Equilibrium Theory and International Trade*. Amsterdam: North-Holland.

Negishi, T. 1979. *Microeconomic Foundations of Keynesian Macroeconomics*. Amsterdam: North-Holland.

Newman, P. 1965. *The Theory of Exchange*. Englewood Cliffs, NJ: Prentice-Hall.

Patinkin, D. 1956. *Money, Interest, and Prices: An Integration of Monetary Theory*. Evanston: Row, Peterson.

Reid, G.C. 1981. *The Kinked Demand Curve Analysis of Oligopoly: Theory of Evidence*. Edinburgh: Edinburgh University Press.

Samuelson, P.A. 1941. The stability of equilibrium: comparative statics and dynamics. *Econometrica* 9, April, 97–120.

Uzawa, H. 1960. Walras' tâtonnement in the theory of exchange. *Review of Economic Studies* 27(74), June, 182–94.

Uzawa, H. 1962. On the stability of Edgeworth's barter process. *International Economic Review* 3(2), May, 218–32.

Wald, A. 1936. Über einige Gleichungssysteme der mathematischen Ökonomie. *Zeitschrift für Nationalökonomie* 7, 637–70.

Walker, D.A. 1973. Edgeworth's theory of recontract. *Economic Journal* 83, March, 138–49.

Walras, L. 1874–7. *Éléments d'économie politique pure ou théorie de la richesse sociale*. Definitive edn, Lausanne, 1926. Trans. by W. Jaffé as *Elements of Pure Economics*. London: George Allen and Unwin; Homewood, Ill.: Richard D. Irwin, 1954.

Temporary Equilibrium

J.-M. GRANDMONT

1. THE CONCEPTUAL FRAMEWORK. The fact that trade and markets take place sequentially over time in actual economies is a trivial observation. It has nevertheless far-reaching implications. At any moment, economic units have to make decisions that call for immediate action, in the face of a future that is as yet unknown. Expectations about the unknown future play therefore an essential role in the determination of current economic variables. On the other hand, the expectations that traders hold at any time are determined by the information that they have at that date on the economy, in particular on its current and past states. Observed economic processes are thus the result of a strong and complex interaction between expectations of the traders involved and the actual realizations of economic variables.

Economists have long recognized that such an interaction should be at the heart of any satisfactory theory of economic dynamics. The temporary equilibrium approach was indeed designed quite a while ago by the Swedish school (Lindahl, 1939) and J.R. Hicks (1939, 1965), with the intent to establish a general conceptual framework that would enable economists to cope with the study of dynamical economic systems, and in particular to incorporate in their models the subtle interplay between expectations and actual realizations of economic variables that seem factually so important. Economic theorists have employed this framework in a systematic way over the last fifteen years or so, using in particular the powerful techniques of modern equilibrium and/or game theory; this effort has yielded important improvements of our understanding of monetary theory or of the choice-theoretic structure of traditional Keynesian models of unemployment, and more generally of the microeconomic foundations of macroeconomics.

Before reviewing briefly a few of these important advances, it may be worthwhile to make clear what are the basic characteristics of the temporary equilibrium approach, and to compare it with others.

To fix ideas, let us assume that time is divided into an infinite, discrete sequence of dates. We may envision first a specific institutional set-up, that was called a *futures economy* by Hicks (1946), and later generalized by Arrow and Debreu. Let us assume that markets for exchanging commodities are opened at a single date, say date 0; assume further that at that date, markets exist for contracts to deliver commodities at each and every future date $t \geqslant 0$. The specification of a 'commodity' will then involve not only the physical characteristics of the good or service to be delivered, but also the location and the circumstances ('state of nature') of the delivery. One gets then what has been called a 'complete' set of futures markets at the initial date $t = 0$ (Debreu, 1959, ch. 7).

It is clear that this framework is essentially timeless. Once an equilibrium is reached at date 0 (this equilibrium may be Walrasian or the result of any other game theoretic equilibrium notion), production and trade do take place sequentially in calendar time. But the coordination of the decisions of all traders is achieved at a single date through futures markets. There is no sequence of *markets* over time, and no role for expectations, money, financial assets, or stock markets.

Let us consider next another, more dynamic, type of organization, in which markets do open in every period. In this framework, traders would exchange at every date commodities immediately available on spot markets, promises to deliver specific commodities at later dates on futures markets, as well as money, financial assets and/or stock (of course markets must be 'incomplete' in the sense of Arrow–Debreu at every date, otherwise reopening markets would serve no purpose). To convey the following discussion most simply, let us assume away all sources of uncertainty and consider the case where the state of the economy at any date can be described by a single real number. To simplify matters further, let us assume that the state of the economy at t, say x_t, is completely determined by the forecasts $x^e_{i,t+1}$ made by all traders at date t about the future state, through the relation

$$x_t = f(x^e_{1,t+1}, \ldots, x^e_{i,t+1}, \ldots, x^e_{m,t+1}) \qquad (1)$$

The temporary equilibrium map f describes the result of the market equilibrating process at date t – be it Walrasian or not – for a given set of forecasts. Of course, in the study of any particular economy, the map f will be derived from the 'fundamental' characteristics of the economy: tastes, endowments, technologies, the rules of the game, the policies followed by the Government.

The foregoing formulation does seem to take into account the observed fact that markets unfold sequentially in calendar time. It is, however, incomplete since no specification of the way in which forecasts are made at each date has been offered at this stage.

We must first discuss a concept that was introduced by Hicks himself, that of an *intertemporal equilibrium*, with self-fulfilling expectations, and that has been extensively used recently in a variety of contexts. Such as intertemporal equilibrium is defined formally, in the present framework, as an infinite sequence of states $\{x_t\}$ and of forecasts $\{x^e_{i,t+1}\}$ satisfying (1) and

$$x^e_{i,t+1} = x_{t+1} \qquad (2)$$

for all dates. Although time appears explicitly in this formulation, it should be clear that this particular equilibrium concept is also intrinsically *timeless*. It is true, here again, that once an intertemporal equilibrium has been determined, production and exchange do take place sequentially in calendar time. But the inescapable truth is that all elements of the sequences of equilibrium states $\{x_t\}$ and of equilibrium forecasts $\{x_{i,t+1}^e\}$ are determined simultaneously by an outside observer. There is *no* sequential adjustment of the markets: past, present and future markets are equilibrated all at the same time. Furthermore, if one tries to give a dynamical interpretation of the foregoing equilibrium notion, in which markets do adjust sequentially, one finds that the dynamics go in the wrong direction. The formation of forecasts specified in (2) states indeed that the future equilibrium state x_{t+1} determines the current forecasts, which in turn determine the current equilibrium state x_t through (1).

The preceding discussion shows how we must proceed to describe a sequential adjustment of markets, in calendar time. We *must* add to the temporary equilibrium relationship (1) a specification of the way in which traders forecast the future at each date *as a function of their information on current and past states of the economy*. If we assume, for the simplicity of the exposition, that the only information available to traders at date t is represented by the sequence $(x_t, x_{t-1}, \ldots)$, that means that we have to add to (1), *m expectations functions* of the form

$$x_{i,t+1}^e = \psi_i(x_t, x_{t-1}, \ldots) \qquad (3)$$

The equations (1) and (3) describe then in a consistent way a sequential adjustment of markets – a sequence of *temporary equilibria* – in which time goes forward, as it should. Given past history $(x_{t-1}, x_{t-2}, \ldots)$, (1) and (3) determine the current temporary equilibrium state and forecasts. Once such a temporary equilibrium is reached, production and exchange takes place at date t, and the economy can move forward to date $t+1$, where the equilibrating process is repeated.

A formulation of the sort (1) plus (3) is thus the general formulation, in fact the *only* sort of formulation that is allowed, if one wishes to describe the evolution of the economy as a *sequence* of markets that adjust one after each other.

We claim that the temporary equilibrium approach, as sketched above, is general. One should expect it accordingly to include self-fulfilling expectations as a special case. It is not difficult to verify that it is indeed so, provided that the expectations functions ψ_i satisfy a number of restrictions. Choose a particular intertemporal equilibrium. Then the associated sequence of states, say $\{\bar{x}_t\}$, is a solution of the difference equation

$$\bar{x}_1 = F(\bar{x}_{t+1}) \qquad (4)$$

in which $F(x) = f(x, \ldots, x)$ for all x. Consider now the economy at date t, and assume that past states have been $(\bar{x}_{t-1}, \bar{x}_{t-2}, \ldots)$. Assume that the traders know the characteristics of the economy, or at least the map F, and further that the map F is invertible (we are voluntarily vague about the domain of definitions of the functions under consideration, to simplify the present methodological discussion, but these technical details can be fixed up). The traders are then able to detect the recurrence satisfied by current and past states. If they infer that this recurrence will obtain in the future as well, their forecasting rule should satisfy, for all $i = 1, \ldots, m$

$$\psi_i(\bar{x}_1, \bar{x}_{t-1}, \ldots) = F^{-1}(\bar{x}_t) \tag{5}$$

If this relation holds, $\bar{x}_t$ is indeed a temporary equilibrium state (i.e. it solves (1) and (3)) at date t, given past history $(\bar{x}_{t-1}, \bar{x}_{t-2}, \ldots)$. This will be true at all dates, and one will be able to generate any intertemporal equilibrium with self-fulfilling expectations as a sequence of temporary equilibria, provided that the traders' forecasting rules satisfy (5) at all dates, and for any sequence $(\bar{x}_t, \bar{x}_{t-1}, \ldots)$ that is part of an intertemporal equilibrium $\{\bar{x}_t\}$. The condition (5) is in fact necessary.

As we have just shown, the temporary equilibrium method includes self-fulfilling expectations as a special case. The approach is indeed much more general, since it permits to incorporate in the analysis the fact that traders usually learn the dynamics laws of their environment only gradually, and thus to study in principle how convergence toward self-fulfilling expectations may or may not obtain in the long run.

The preceding discussion was carried out in a simple one-dimensional world operating under certainty. It should be clear nevertheless that the qualitative conclusions we obtained hold as well in a more complex, multidimensional world operating under uncertainty. The general objective is, we recall, to design a conceptual framework that does justice to the fact that markets adjust sequentially in calendar time. The preceding discussion shows that, to this effect, one must specify beforehand two kinds of objects:

(1) The 'fundamental' characteristics of the economy (tastes, endowments, technologies, the institutional set up, the Government's policies, etc.). They should lead to the specification of a relation that describes, as in (1), how a temporary equilibrium is determined at any date, given past history and the current realization of exogenous variables, for a given 'state of expectations'.

(2) A description of the way in which traders form their expectations (these may be probability distributions or random variables), at any date, as a *function of the observations made in the current and past periods*. The process of expectations formation may be complex, it may involve sophisticated statistical inferences or estimations of unknown parameters, and/or it may be the result of a backward inductive procedure carried out by the traders. But the specification must generate in the end an *expectations function* for each trader, that links forecasts to current and past experience, as in (3).

The evolution of the economy is then described as a sequence of temporary equilibria, in which at each date, the current equilibrium states are determined by past history. In this framework, a number of issues arise naturally. First, one has to find the conditions under which the dynamic evolution of the economy is well defined. In other words, when does a temporary equilibrium exist? Second, does the corresponding dynamical system have long run equilibrium states, such as deterministic stationary states or cycles, and/or stationary stochastic processes, along which expectations are self-fulfilling? Under which conditions, in particular on the formation of expectations, do the sequences of temporary equilibria so generated converge to such a long run equilibrium? This is precisely the sort of questions that have attracted the attention of modern economic theorists working in temporary equilibrium theory over the last 15 years or so.

2. OVERVIEW. We turn now to a brief appraisal of this research effort, referring the interested reader to more extensive and more technical surveys that already exist in the literature, see for example Grandmont (1977, 1987).

Money and assets in comparative markets. Considering a sequence of markets opens immediately the possibility for traders to hold money and more generally, assets of various kinds for saving, borrowing, transactions purposes and/or insurance motives. The application of the modern techniques of temporary equilibrium theory to the study of monetary phenomena has led to a major reappraisal, in the seventies, of classical and neoclassical monetary theories in competitive environments. It has permitted in particular to solve an old problem that had puzzled economic theorists for some time (Hahn, 1965), namely why fiat money, which has no intrinsic value, should have a positive value in exchange in competitive markets. The answer provided by traditional neoclassical theory relied essentially upon unit-elastic price expectations and the presence of real balance or wealth effects (Patinkin, 1965). Modern temporary equilibrium methods have shown that sort of answer to be surely incomplete and presumably mistaken: intertemporal substitution effects have to play an important role, and this can be only achieved by abandoning the hypothesis of unit-elastic expectations and by introducing some degree of inelasticity of expectations with respect to current observations. The reappraisal of monetary theory by means of the temporary equilibrium method clarified greatly many confusing debates of the preceding literature: the relations between Walras's and Say's Law, the meaning and the validity of the Classical Dichotomy and the Quantity Theory of Money, the possibility of monetary authorities to manipulate the interest rates or the money supply, the existence of a 'liquidity trap' (Grandmont, 1983). The introduction of cash-in-advance constraints in temporary competitive equilibrium models of money (Grandmont and Younès, 1972, 1973) yielded important insights into the relations between its respective roles as a store of value and as a medium of exchange, and time preference, and permitted to make precise the microeconomic foundations of Milton Friedman's theory of optimum cash balances (1969). Such models of money using cash-in-advance constraints have been popular recently in macroeconomics, following the contribution of R.E. Lucas, Jr. (1980).

The introduction of assets of various kinds in competitive markets leads also to the possibility of speculation and arbitrage in capital markets. Different persons with different tastes or expectations will then be willing to trade such assets. An important question is to study the conditions ensuring the existence of a temporary equilibrium in that context. A neat answer to that problem was provided by J.R. Green (1973) and O.D. Hart (1974): there must be some agreement between the traders' expectations about future prices. That sort of result should remain at the centre of any theory of competitive financial markets.

Temporary equilibria with quantity rationing. As noted previously, a temporary equilibrium need not be Walrasian. In particular, one may consider cases where prices are set through monopolistic or oligopolistic competition at the beginning of each elementary period and remain temporarily fixed within that period. A temporary equilibrium corresponding to these prices is then achieved at each date by quantity rations that set upper or lower bounds on the traders' transactions.

It had been known for some time that traditional Keynesian macroeconomic models of unemployment involved, explicitly or implicitly, the assumption of temporarily fixed prices, as noted by Hicks himself (1965). The choice-theoretic structure of these models was rather unclear, however, which was a source of some confusion. The systematic study of temporary equilibrium models with quantity rationing undertaken in the seventies produced deep insights on this issue, and unveiled the hidden but central role played by quantity signals, as perceived by the traders in addition to the price system, to achieve an equilibrium in such models.

One major outcome of this research programme was the discovery that different types of unemployment could obtain, and even co-exist. 'Keynesian unemployment' corresponds to a situation where there is an excess supply on the labour and the goods markets. In such a situation, firms perceive constraints on their sales because demand is too low. Keynesian policies aiming at increasing aggregate demand do work in such a case. But unemployment may co-exist with an excess demand on the goods markets. In such a regime, called 'Classical unemployment' by Malinvaud (1977), the source of unemployment is rather the low profitability of productive activities. Keynesian policies do not work in that case; one has to resort to policies that restore profits, such as lowering real wages. In that respect, these results achieved a remarkably synthesis, within a unified and clear conceptual framework, between two paradigms that appeared fundamentally distinct beforehand.

The literature on this topic yielded numerous insights in particular of the connections between Keynesian models of unemployment and price-making in monopolistic or oligopolistic models of competition (see e.g. Hart, 1982), on the role of inventories and productive investment in such models, on the nature of unemployment in open economies. On these and related topics, the reader will benefit greatly from consulting the books of Barro and Grossman (1976), Benassy (1982, 1986), Malinvaud (1977, 1980), Negishi (1979), Picard (1985).

Stability and learning. As we mentioned earlier, the temporary equilibrium approach includes self-fulfilling expectations as a particular case, and is in fact more general, since it can incorporate learning in the formation of the traders' expectations. An important issue is then to know when the sequences of temporary equilibria that are associated to given learning processes or expectations functions converge eventually to a long run equilibrium along which forecasting mistakes vanish. This is a difficult question, on which much work has to be done. Progress has been made up to now by looking at the stability of stationary equilibria for given learning procedures, in particular examples. One of the lessons one can draw from these studies is that stability in the temporary equilibrium dynamics with learning may be *reversed* by comparison to the apparent stability properties one gets from the dynamics with self-fulfilling expectations. For more information, see Fuchs and Laroque (1976) and Grandmont (1987, ch. 1).

BIBLIOGRAPHY

Barro, R.J. and Grossman, H.I. 1976. *Money, Employment and Inflation*, Cambridge and New York: Cambridge University Press.

Benassy, J.P. 1982. *The Economics of Market Disequilibrium*. New York: Academic Press.

Benassy, J.P. 1986. *Macroeconomics: An Introduction to the Non-Walrasian Approach*. New York: Academic Press.

Debreu, G. 1959. *Theory of Value: an axiomatic analysis of economic equilibrium*. Cowles Foundation Monograph no. 17, New York: Wiley.

Friedman, M. 1969. *The Optimum Quantity of Money and Other Essays*. Chicago: Aldine.

Fuchs, G. and Laroque, G. 1976. Dynamics of temporary equilibria and expectations. *Econometrica* 44, 1157–78.

Grandmont, J.M. 1977. Temporary general equilibrium theory. *Econometrica* 45, 535–72.

Grandmont, J.M. 1983. *Money and Value: a reconsideration of classical and neoclassical monetary theories*. The Econometric Society, Monograph No. 5, Cambridge: Cambridge University Press.

Grandmont, J.M. (ed.) 1987. *Temporary Equilibrium: selected readings*. New York: Academic Press.

Grandmont, J.M. and Younès, Y. 1972. On the role of money and the existence of a monetary equilibrium. *Review of Economic Studies* 39, 355–72.

Grandmont, J.M. and Younès, Y. 1973. On the efficiency of a monetary equilibrium. *Review of Economic Studies* 40, 149–65.

Green, J.R. 1973. Temporary general equilibrium in a sequential trading model with spot and future transactions. *Econometrica* 41, 1103–23.

Hahn, F.H. 1965. On some problems of proving the existence of an equilibrium in a monetary economy. In *The Theory of Interest Rates*, ed. F.H. Hahn and F.P.R. Brechling, London: Macmillan; New York: St. Martin's Press.

Hart, O.D. 1974. On the existence of equilibrium in a securities model. *Journal of Economic Theory* 9, 293–311.

Hart, O.D. 1982. A model of imperfect competition with Keynesian features. *Quarterly Journal of Economics* 97, 109–38.

Hicks, J.R. 1939. *Value and Capital*. Oxford: Clarendon Press; 2nd edn, 1946; 2nd edn, New York: Oxford University Press, 1946.

Hicks, J.R. 1965. *Capital and Growth*. Oxford: Clarendon Press; New York: Oxford University Press, 1972.

Lindahl, E. 1939. *Theory of Money and Capital*. London: Allen and Unwin; New York: Holt, Rinehart and Winston.

Lucas, R.E., Jr. 1980. Equilibrium in a pure currency economy. *Economic Inquiry* 18, 203–220. Also in *Models of Monetary Economies*, ed. J.H. Kareken and N. Wallace, Minneapolis: The Federal Reserve Bank of Minneapolis, 1980.

Malinvaud, E. 1977. *The Theory of Unemployment Reconsidered*. Oxford: Basil Blackwell: New York: Wiley.

Negishi, T. 1979. *Microeconomic Foundations of Keynesian Macroeconomics*. Amsterdam: North-Holland.

Patinkin, D. 1965. *Money, Interest and Prices*. 2nd edn, New York: Harper & Row.

Picard, P. 1985. *Théorie du déséquilibre et politique économique*. Paris: Economica.

Uncertainty and General Equilibrium

ROY RADNER

One of the notable intellectual achievements of economic theory during the past years has been the rigorous elaboration of the Walras–Pareto theory of value; that is, the theory of the existence and optimality of competitive equilibrium. Although many economists and mathematicians contributed to this development, the resulting edifice owes so much to the pioneering and influential work of Arrow and Debreu that in this paper I shall refer to it as the 'Arrow–Debreu theory'. (For comprehensive treatments, together with references to previous work, see Debreu, 1959, and Arrow and Hahn, 1971.)

The Arrow–Debreu theory was not originally put forward for the case of uncertainty, but an ingenious device introduced by Arrow (1953), and further elaborated by Debreu (1953), enabled the theory to be reinterpreted to cover the case of uncertainty about the availability of resources and about consumption and production possibilities. (See Debreu, 1959, ch. 7, for a unified treatment of time and uncertainty.)

Subsequent research has extended the Arrow–Debreu theory to take account of (1) differences in information available to different economic agents, and the 'production' of information, (2) the incompleteness of markets, and (3) the sequential nature of markets. The consideration of these complications has stimulated the developments of new concepts of equilibrium, which will be discussed in this article under the headings: (1) temporary equilibrium, (2) equilibrium of plans, prices, and price expectations, and (3) rational expectations equilibrium. The consideration of these features of real-world markets has also made possible a general-equilibrium analysis of money and securities markets, institutions about which the original Arrow–Debreu theory could provide only limited insights.

REVIEW OF THE ARROW–DEBREU MODEL OF A COMPLETE MARKET FOR PRESENT AND FUTURE CONTINGENT DELIVERY. In this section I review the approach of Arrow

(1953) and Debreu (1959) to incorporating uncertainty about the environment into a Walrasian model of competitive equilibrium. The basic idea is that commodities are to be distinguished, not only by their physical characteristics and by the location and dates of their availability and/or use, but also by the environmental event in which they are made available and/or used. For example, ice cream made available (at a particular location on a particular date) if the weather is hot may be considered to be a different commodity from the same kind of ice cream made available (at the same location and date) if the weather is cold. We are thus led to consider a list of 'commodities' that is greatly expanded by comparison with the corresponding case of certainty about the environment. The standard arguments of the theory of competitive equilibrium, applied to an economy with this expanded list of commodities, then require that we envisage, a 'price' for each commodity in the list, or, more precisely, a set of price ratios specifying the rate of exchange between each pair of commodities.

Just what institutions could, or do, effect such exchanges is a matter of interpretation that is, strictly speaking, outside the models. I shall present one straightforward interpretation, and then comment briefly on an alternative interpretation.

First, however, it will be useful to give a more precise account of concepts of environment and event that I shall be employing. The description of the 'physical world' is decomposed into three sets of variables: (1) decision variables, which are controlled (chosen) by economic agents; (2) environmental variables, which are not controlled by any economic agent; and (3) all other variables, which are completely determined (possibly jointly) by decisions and environmental variables. A state of the environment is a complete specification (history) of the environmental variables from the beginning to the end of the economic system in question. An event is set of states; for example, the event 'the weather is hot in New York on July 1, 1970' is the set of all possible histories of the environment in which the temperature in New York during the day of July 1, 1970, reaches a high of at least (say) 75°F. Granted that we cannot know the future with certainty, at any given date, there will be a family of elementary observable (knowable) events, which can be represented by a partition of the set of all possible states (histories) into a family of mutually exclusive subsets. It is natural to assume that the partitions corresponding to successive dates are successively finer, which represents the accumulation of information about the environment.

We shall imagine that a 'market' is organized before the beginning of the physical history of the economic system. An elementary contract in this market will consist of the purchase (or sale) of some specified number of units of a specified commodity to be delivered at a specified location and date, if and only if a specified elementary event occurs. Payment for this purchase is to be made now (at the beginning), in 'units of account', at a specified price quoted for that commodity-location-date-event combination. Delivery of the commodity in more than one elementary event is obtained by combining a suitable set of elementary contracts. For example, if delivery of one quart of ice cream (at a specified location and date) in hot weather costs $1.50 (now) and delivery of one-quart in non-hot weather costs $1.10, then sure delivery of one quart (i.e., whatever the weather) costs $1.50 + $1.10 = $2.60.

There are two groups of economic agents in the economy: producers and consumers. A producer chooses a production plan, which determines his input and/or output of each commodity at each date in each elementary event. (I shall henceforth suppress explicit reference to location, it being understood that the location is specified in the term commodity.) For a given set of prices, the present value of a production plan is the sum of the values of the inputs minus the sum of the values of the outputs. Each producer is characterized by a set of production plans that are (physically) feasible for him: his production possibility set.

A consumer chooses a consumption plan, which specifies his consumption of each commodity at each date in each elementary event. Each consumer is characterized by: (1) a set of consumption plans that are (physically, psychologically, etc.) feasible for him, his consumption possibility set; (2) preferences among the alternative plans that are feasible for him; (3) his endowment of physical resources, i.e., a specification of the quantity of each commodity, e.g., labour, at each date in each event, with which he is exogenously endowed; and (4) his shares in each producer, that is, the fraction of the present value of each producer's production plan that will be credited to the consumer's account. (For any one producer, the sum of the consumers' shares is unity.) For given prices and given production plans of all the producers, the present net worth of a consumer is the total value of his resources plus the total value of his shares of the present values of producers' production plans.

An equilibrium of the economy is a set of prices, a set of production plans (one for each producer), and a set of consumption plans (one for each consumer), such that (a) each producer's plan has maximum present value in his production possibility set; (b) each consumer's plan maximizes his preferences within his consumption possibility set, subject to the additional (budget) constraint that the present cost of his consumption plan not exceed his present net worth; (c) for each commodity at each date in each elementary event, the total demand equals the total supply; i.e., the total planned consumption equals the sum of the total resource endowments and the total planned net output (where inputs are counted as negative outputs).

Notice that (1) producers and consumers are 'price takers'; (2) for given prices there is no uncertainty about the present value of a production plan or of given resource endowments, nor about the present cost of a consumption plan; (3) therefore, for given prices and given producers plans, there is no uncertainty about a given consumer's present net worth; (4) since a consumption plan may specify that, for a given commodity at a given date, the quantity consumed is to vary according to the event that actually occurs, a consumer's preferences among plans will reflect not only his 'tastes' but also his subjective beliefs about the likelihoods of different events and his attitude towards risk (Savage, 1954).

It follows that beliefs and attitudes towards risk play no role in the assumed behaviour of producers. On the other hand, beliefs and attitudes towards risk do play a role in the assumed behaviour of consumers, although for given prices and production plans each consumer knows his (single) budget constraint with certainty.

I shall call the model just described an 'Arrow–Debreu' economy. One can demonstrate, under 'standard conditions': (1) the existence of an equilibrium, (2) the Pareto optimality of an equilibrium, and (3) that, roughly speaking, every Pareto optimal choice of production and consumption plans is an equilibrium relative to some price system for some distribution of resource endowments and shares (Debreu, 1959).

In the above interpretation of the Arrow–Debreu economy, all accounts are settled before the history of the economy begins, and there is no incentive to revise plans, reopen the market or trade in shares. There is an alternative interpretation, which will be of interest in connection with the rest of this entry but which corresponds to exactly the same formal model. In this second interpretation, there is a single commodity at each date – let us call it 'gold' – that is taken as a numeraire at the date. A 'price system' has two parts: (1) for each date and each elementary event at that date, there is a price, to be paid in gold at the beginning date, for one unit of gold to be delivered at the specified date and event; (2) for each commodity, date, and event at that date, there is a price, to be paid in gold at that date and event, for one unit of the commodity to be delivered at that same date and event. The first part of the price system can be interpreted as 'insurance premiums' and the second part as 'spot prices' at the given date and event. The insurance interpretation is to be made with some reservation, however, since there is no real object being insured and no limit to the amount of insurance that an individual may take out against the occurrence of a given event. For this reason, the first part of the price system might be better interpreted as reflecting a combination of betting odds and interest rates.

Although the second part of the price system might be interpreted as spot prices it would be a mistake to think of the determination of the equilibrium values of these prices as being deferred in real time to the dates to which they refer. The definition of equilibrium requires that the agents have access to the complete system of prices when choosing their plans. In effect, this requires that at the beginning of time all agents have available a (common) forecast of the equilibrium spot prices that will prevail at every future date and event.

EXTENSION OF THE ARROW–DEBREU MODEL TO THE CASE IN WHICH DIFFERENT AGENTS HAVE DIFFERENT INFORMATION. In an Arrow–Debreu economy, at any one date each agent will have incomplete information about the state of the environment, but all the agents will have the same information. This last assumption is not tenable if we are to take good account of the effects of uncertainty in an economy. I shall now sketch how, by a simple reinterpretation of the concepts of production possibility set and consumption possibility set, we can extend the theory of the Arrow–Debreu economy to allow for differences in information among the economic agents.

For each date, the information that will be available to a given agent at that date may be characterized by a partition of the set of states of the environment. To be consistent with our previous terminology, we should assume that each such information partition must be at least as coarse as the partition that describes the elementary events at that date; i.e. each set in the information partition must contain a set in the elementary event partition for the same date.

For example, each set in the event partition at a given date might specify the high temperature at that date, whereas each set in a given agent's information partition might specify only whether this temperature was higher than 75°F. or not. Or the event partition at a given date might specify the temperature at each date during the past month, whereas the information partition might specify only the mean temperature over the past month.

An agent's information restricts his set of feasible plans in the following manner. Suppose that at a given date the agent knows only that the state of the environment lies in a specified set A (one of the sets in his information partition at that date), and suppose (as would be typical) that the set A contains several of the elementary events that are in principle observable at that date. Then any action that the agent takes at that date must necessarily be the same for all elementary events in the set A. In particular, if the agent is a consumer, then his consumption of any specified commodity at that date must be the same in all elementary events contained in the information set A; if the agent is a producer, then his input or output of any specified commodity must be the same for all events in A. (I am assuming that consumers know what they consume and producers what they produce at any given date.)

Let us call the sequence of information partitions for a given agent his information structure and let us say that this structure is fixed if it is given independent of the actions of himself or any other agent. Furthermore, in the case of a fixed information structure, let us say that a given plan (consumption or production) is compatible with that structure if it satisfies the conditions described in the previous paragraph, at each date.

Suppose that consumption and production possibility sets of the Arrow–Debreu economy are interpreted as characterizing, for each agent, those plans that would be feasible if he had 'full information' (i.e. if his information partition at each date coincided with the elementary event partition at that date). The set of feasible plans for any agent with a fixed information structure can then be obtained by restricting him to those plans in the full information possibility set that are also compatible with his given information structure.

From this point on, all of the machinery of the Arrow–Debreu economy (with some minor technical modifications) can be brought to bear on the present model. In particular, we get a theory of existence and optimality of competitive equilibrium relative to fixed structures of information for the economic agents. I shall call this the 'extended Arrow–Debreu economy'. (For a fuller treatment, see Radner, 1968, 1982.)

CHOICE OF INFORMATION. There is no difficulty in principle in incorporating the choice of information structure into the model of the extended Arrow–Debreu economy. I doubt, however, that it is reasonable to assume that the technological conditions for the acquisition and use of information generally satisfy the hypotheses of the standard theorems on the existence and optimality of competitive equilibrium.

The acquisition and use of information about the environment typically require the expenditure of goods and services; i.e., of commodities.

If one production plan requires more information for its implementation than another (i.e., requires a finer information partition at one or more dates), then the list of (commodity) inputs should reflect the increased inputs for information. In this manner a set of feasible production plans can reflect the possibility of choice among alternative information structures.

Unfortunately, the acquisition of information often involves a 'set-up cost'; i.e., the resources needed to obtain the information may be independent of the scale of the production process in which the information is used. This set-up cost will introduce a nonconvexity in the production possibility set, and thus one of the standard conditions in the theory of the Arrow–Debreu economy will not be satisfied (Radner, 1968).

Even without set-up costs, *there is a general tendency for the value of information to exhibit 'increasing returns', at least at low levels*, provided that the structure of information varies smoothly with its cost. This striking phenomenon leads to discontinuities in the demand for information. (For a precise statement, see Radner and Stiglitz, 1984.)

There is another interesting class of cases in which an agent's information structure is not fixed, namely, cases in which the agent's information at one date may depend upon production or consumption decisions taken at previous dates, but all actions can be scaled down to any desired size. Unfortunately space limitations prevent me from discussing this class in the present article.

CRITIQUE OF THE EXTENDED ARROW–DEBREU ECONOMY. If the Arrow–Debreu model is given a literal interpretation, then it clearly requires that the economic agents possess capabilities of imagination and calculation that exceed reality by many orders. Related to this is the observation that the theory requires in principle a complete system of insurance and futures markets, which appears to be too complex, detailed, and refined to have practical significance. A further obstacle to the achievement of a complete insurance market is the phenomenon of 'moral hazard' (Arrow, 1965).

A second line of criticism is that the theory does not take account of at least three important institutional features of modern capitalist economies: money, the stock market, and active markets at every date.

These two lines of criticism have an important connection, which suggests how the Arrow–Debreu theory might be improved. If, as in the Arrow-Debreu model, each production plan has a sure unambiguous present value at the beginning of time, then consumers have no interest in trading in shares, and there is no point in a stock market. If all accounts can be settled at the beginning of time, then there is no need for money during the subsequent life of the economy; in any case, the standard motives for holding money are not applicable.

On the other hand, once we recognize explicitly that there is a sequence of markets, one for each date, and no one of them complete (in the Arrow–Debreu sense), then certain phenomena and institutions not accounted for in the Arrow–Debreu model become reasonable. First, there is uncertainty about the prices that will hold in future markets, as well as uncertainty about the environment.

Second, producers do not have a clear-cut natural way of comparing net revenues at different dates and states. Stockholders have an incentive to establish a stock exchange since it enables them to change the way their future revenues depend on the states of the environment. As an alternative to selling his shares in a particular enterprise, a stockholder may try to influence the management of the enterprise in order to make the production plan conform better to his own subjective probabilities and attitude towards risk.

Third, consumers will typically not be able to discount all of their 'wealth' at the beginning of time, because (a) their shares of producers' future (uncertain) net revenues cannot be so discounted and (b) they cannot discount all of their future resource endowments. Consumers will be subject to a sequence of budget constraints, one for each date (rather than to a single budget constraint relating present cost of his consumption plan to present net worth, as in the Arrow–Debreu economy).

Fourth, economic agents may have an incentive to speculate on the prices in future markets, by storing goods, hedging, etc. Instead of storing goods, an agent may be interested in saving part of one date's income, in units of account, for use on a subsequent date, if there is an institution that makes this possible. There will thus be a demand for 'money' in the form of demand deposits.

Fifth, agents will be interested in forecasting the prices in markets at future dates. These prices will be functions of both the state of the environment and the decisions of (in principle, all) economic agents up to the date in question.

Sixth, if traders have different information at a particular date, then the equilibrium prices at that date will reflect the pooled information of the traders, albeit in a possibly complicated way. Hence traders who have a good model of the market process will be able to infer something about other traders' information from the market prices.

EXPECTATIONS AND EQUILIBRIUM IN A SEQUENCE OF MARKETS. Consider now a sequence of market at successive dates. Suppose that no market at any one date is complete in the Arrow–Debreu sense; i.e., at every date and for every commodity there will be some future dates and some events at those future dates for which it will not be possible to make current contracts for future delivery contingent on those events. In such a model, several types of 'equilibrium' concept suggest themselves, according to the hypotheses we make about the way traders form their expectations.

Let us place ourselves at a particular date-event pair; the excess supply correspondence at the date-event pair reflects the traders' information about past prices and about the history of the environment up through that date. If a given trader's excess supply correspondence is generated by preference satisfaction, then the relevant preferences will be conditional upon the information available. If, furthermore, the trader's preferences can be scaled in terms of utility and subjective probability, and conform to the Expected Utility Hypothesis, then the relevant probabilities are the conditional probabilities given the available information. These conditional probabilities express the trader's expectations regarding the future. Although a general theoretical treatment of our problem does not necessarily require us to assume that traders' preferences conform to the Expected Utility Hypothesis, it will be helpful in the following heuristic discussion to keep in mind this particular interpretation of expectations.

A trader's expectations concern both future environmental events and future prices. Regarding expectations about future environmental events, there is no conceptual problem. According to the Expected Utility Hypothesis, each trader is characterized by a subjective probability measure on the set of complete histories of the environment. Since, by definition, the evolution of the environment is exogenous, a trader's conditional subjective probability of a future event, given the information to date, is well defined.

It is not so obvious how to proceed with regard to traders' expectations about future prices. I shall contrast two possible approaches. In the first, which I shall call the *perfect foresight* approach, let us assume that the behaviour of traders is such as to determine, for each complete history of the environment, a unique corresponding sequence of price system, say $\phi_t^*(e_t)$, where e_t is the particular event at date t. If the 'laws' governing the economic system are known to all, then every trader can calculate the sequence of functions ϕ_t^*. In this case, at any date-event pair a trader's expectations regarding future prices are well defined in terms of the functions ϕ_t^* and his conditional subjective probability measures on histories of the environment, given his current information. Traders need not agree on the probabilities of future environmental events, and therefore they need not agree on the probability distribution of future prices, *but they must agree on which future prices are associated with which events*. I shall call this last type of agreement the condition of *common price expectation functions*.

Thus, the perfect foresight approach implies that, in equilibrium, traders have common price expectation functions. These price expectation functions indicate, for each date-event pair, what the equilibrium price system would be in the corresponding market at that date-event pair. Pursuing this line of thought, it follows that, in equilibrium, the traders would have strategies (plans) such that, if these strategies were carried out, the markets would be cleared at each date-event pair. Call such plans *consistent*. A set of common price expectations and corresponding consistent plans is called an *equilibrium of plans, prices, and price expectations*.

This model of equilibrium can be extended to cover the case in which different traders have different information, just as the Arrow–Debreu model was so

312

extended. In particular, one could express in this way the hypothesis that a trader cannot observe the individual preferences and resource endowments of other traders. Indeed, one can also introduce into the description of the state of the environment variables that, for each trader, represent his alternative hypotheses about the 'true laws' of the economic system. In this way the condition of common price expectation functions can lose much of its apparent restrictiveness.

The situation in which traders enter the market with different non-price information presents an opportunity for agents to learn about the environment from prices, since current market prices reflect, in a possibly complicated manner, the non-price information signals received by the various agents. To take an extreme example, the 'inside information' of a trader in a securities market may lead him to bid up the price to a level higher than it otherwise would have been. In this case, an astute market observer might be able to infer that an insider has obtained some favourable information, just by careful observation of the price movement. More generally, *an economic agent who has a good understanding of the market is in a position to use market prices to make inferences about the (non-price) information received by other agents.*

These inferences are derived, explicitly or implicitly, from an individual's 'model' of the relationship between the non-price information received by market participants and the market prices. On the other hand, the true relationship is determined by the individual agents' behaviour, and hence by their individual models. Furthermore, economic agents have the opportunity to revise their individual models in the light of observations and published data. Hence, there is a feedback from the true relationship to the individual models. An equilibrium of this system, in which the individual models are identical with the true model, is called *rational expectations equilibrium.*

This concept of equilibrium is more subtle, of course, than the ordinary concept of the equilibrium of supply and demand. In a rational expectations equilibrium, not only are prices determined so as to equate supply and demand, but individual economic agents correctly perceive the true relationship between the non-price information received by the market participants and the resulting equilibrium market prices. This contrasts with the ordinary concept of equilibrium in which the agents respond to prices but do not attempt to infer other agents' non-price information from the actual market prices.

Research on rational expectations equilibrium is quite recent, and the subject has not been fully explored. Nevertheless, several important insights have already been obtained; these insights will be sketched below.

Although it is capable of describing a richer set of institutions and behaviour than is the Arrow–Debreu model, the perfect foresight approach is contrary to the spirit of much of competitive market theory in that it postulates that individual traders must be able to forecast, in some sense, the equilibrium prices that will prevail in the future under all alternative states of the environment. Even if one grants the extenuating circumstances mentioned in previous paragraphs, this approach still seems to require of the traders a capacity for imagination and computation far beyond what is realistic. An equilibrium of plans and price expectations might be appropriate as a conceptualization of the ideal goal of indicative planning, or of a long-run steady state toward which the economy might tend in a stationary environment.

These last considerations lead us in a different direction, which I shall call the *bounded rationality* approach. This approach is much less well defined, but expresses itself in terms of various retreats from the hypothesis of 'fully rational' behaviour by traders, e.g., by assuming that the trader's planning horizons are severely limited, or that their expectation formation follows some simple rules-of-thumb. An example of the bounded-rationality approach is the theory of *temporary equilibrium*.

In the evolution of a sequence of monetary equilibria, each agent's expectations will be successively revised in the light of new information about the environment and about current prices. Therefore, the evolution of the economy will depend upon the rules or processes of expectation formation and revision used by the agents. In particular, there might be interesting conditions under which such a sequence of momentary equilibria would converge, in some sense, to a (stochastic) steady state. This steady state, for example stationary probability distribution of prices, would constitute a fourth concept of equilibrium.

Of the four concepts of equilibrium, the first two are perhaps the closest in the spirit to the Arrow–Debreu theory. How far do the conclusions of the Arrow–Debreu theory (existence and optimality of equilibrium) extend to this new situation? We turn now to this question.

EQUILIBRIUM OF PLANS, PRICES AND PRICE EXPECTATIONS. Consider now the model of perfect-foresight equilibrium sketched above, in which the agents have common information at every date-event pair (for a precise description of the model, see Radner, 1972). Three features of the situation are different from the Arrow–Debreu model: (1) there is a sequence of markets (or rather a 'tree' of markets), one for each date-event pair, no one of which is complete; (2) for each agent, there is a separate budget constraint corresponding to each date-event pair; (3) even if there is a natural bound on consumption and production, there is no single natural bound on the *positions* that traders can take in the markets for securities, if short sales are permitted, (4) there is no obvious objective for each firm to pursue, since each firm's profit is defined only for each date-event pair.

To deal with points (3) and (4), make the following assumptions. Regarding (3), although there is no *single* natural bound on traders' positions, *some* bound is natural; for example, a commitment to deliver a quantity of a commodity vastly greater than the total supply would not be credible to moderately well-informed traders. Regarding (4), assume that the manager of each firm has preferences on the sequence of net revenues that can be represented by a continuous, strictly concave utility function. In other respects, we make the 'standard' assumptions of the Arrow–Debreu model.

I first discuss the question of existence of equilibrium, but before paraphrasing the existence theorem I must define what I shall call a *pseudo-equilibrium*.

The definition of pseudo-equilibrium is obtained from the definition of equilibrium by replacing the requirement of consistency of plans by the condition that each date and each event the difference between total saving and total investment (by consumers) is smaller at the pseudo-equilibrium prices than at any other prices.

One can prove (Radner, 1972) that under assumptions about technology and consumer preferences similar to those used in the Arrow–Debreu theory, and with the additional assumptions sketched above: (1) there exists a pseudo-equilibrium; (2) if in a pseudo-equilibrium the current and future prices on the stock market are all strictly positive, then the pseudo-equilibrium is an equilibrium; (3) in the case of a pure exchange economy, there exists an equilibrium.

The crucial difference between this theorem and the corresponding one in the Arrow–Debreu theory seems to be due to the form taken by Walras's Law, which in this model can be paraphrased by saying that saving must be at least equal to investment at each date in each event. This form derives from the replacement of a single budget constraint (in terms of present value) by a sequence of budget constraints, one for each date-event pair.

Hart (1975) has shown that without a bound on traders' positions an equilibrium need not exist, even in pure-exchange economies. Geanakoplos and Polemarchakis (1986) have shown that, in a pure-exchange economy, if all securities (for future delivery) are denominated in the same real commodity (possibly composite), then equilibrium exists. Duffie and Shafer (1985, 1986, 1987) have demonstrated the *generic* existence of equilibrium with a general structure of incomplete asset markets. (Roughly speaking, equilibrium is said to exist *generically* in a given model if, for any vector of parameters for which an equilibrium does not exist, there are arbitrarily small perturbations of the parameters for which an equilibrium does exist.)

In the above model with production the 'shareholders' have *un*limited liability, and therefore have a status more like that of partners than of shareholders, as these terms are usually understood. One way to formulate limited liability for shareholders is to impose the constraint on producers that their net revenues be non-negative at each date-event pair. However, in this case producers' correspondences may not be upper semicontinuous. This is analogous to the problem that arises when, for a given price system, the consumer's budget constraints force him to be on the boundary of his consumption set. In the case of the consumer, this situation is avoided by some assumption; see Debreu (1959, notes to ch. 5, pp. 88–9) and Debreu (1962). However, for the case of the producer, it is not considered unusual in the standard theory of the firm that, especially in equilibrium, the maximum profit achievable at the given price system could be zero (e.g., in the case of constant returns to scale).

What are conditions on the producers and consumers that would directly guarantee the existence of an equilibrium, not just a pseudo-equilibrium? In other words, under what conditions would the share markets be cleared at every date-event pair? Notice that if there is an excess supply of shares of a given producer j at a date-event pair (t, e), then at date $(t + 1)$ only part of the producer's revenue will be 'distributed'. One would expect this situation to arise only if his revenue is to be negative in at least one event at date $t + 1$; thus at such a date-event pair the producer would have a deficit covered neither by 'loans' (i.e. not offset by forward contracts) nor by shareholders' contributions. In other words, the producer would be 'bankrupt' at that point.

One approach might be to eliminate from a pseudo-equilibrium all producers for whom the excess supply of shares is not zero at some date-event pair, and then search for an equilibrium with the smaller set of producers, etc. successively reducing the set of producers until an equilibrium is found. This procedure has the trivial consequence that an equilibrium always exists, since it exists for the case of pure exchange (the set of producers is empty)! This may not be the most satisfactory resolution of the problem, but it does point up the desirability of having some formulation of the possibility of 'exit' for producers who are not doing well.

Generic existence of equilibrium with production (and stock markets) has been demonstrated under sufficiently strong 'regularity' conditions (e.g. smoothness of preferences and production sets, etc.). (See Duffie and Shafer, 1986; Burke (1986); and the references cited below.)

Although the above model with production does not allow for 'exit' of producers (except with the modification described in the preceding paragraph), it does allow for 'entrance' in the following limited sense. A producer may have zero production up to some date, but plans to produce thereafter; this is not inconsistent with a positive demand for shares at preceding dates.

The creation of new 'equity' in an enterprise is also allowed for in a limited sense. A producer may plan for a large investment at a given date-event pair, with a negative revenue. If the total supply of shares at the preceding date-event pair is nevertheless taken up by the market, this investment may be said to have been 'financed' by shareholders.

The above assumptions describe a model of producer behaviour that is not influenced by the shareholders or (directly) by the prices of shares. A common alternative hypothesis is that a producer tries to maximize the current market value of this enterprise. There seem to me to be at least two difficulties with this hypothesis. First, there are different market values at different date-event pairs, so it is not clear how these can be maximized simultaneously. Second, the market value of an enterprise at any date-event pair is a price, which is supposed to be determined, along with other prices, by an equilibrium of supply and demand. The 'market-value-maximizing' hypothesis would seem to require the producer to predict, in some sense, the effect of a change in his plan on a price *equilibrium*: in this case, the producers would no longer be price-takers, and one would need some sort of theory of general equilibrium for monopolistic competition.

There is one circumstance in which the value of the firm can be defined unambiguously, given the sytem of present prices and common expectations about future prices. Call a price system *arbitrage-free* if it is not possible to make a sure, positive cash flow from trading, without a positive investment. An equilibrium price system is, *a fortiori*, arbitrage-free. One can show (see Radner,

1967; Harrison and Kreps, 1979; Duffie and Shafer, 1986) that an arbitrage-free price system implicitly determines a system of 'insurance premiums' for a corresponding family of events. This means that, by suitable trading one can insure oneself against the occurrence of any of these events. If these events include all of the uncertain events that may affect the (uncertain) revenues of the firm, then they can be used in a natural way to define a present value of the firm at any date-event pair, for any production plan of the firm, and no probability judgements are needed to calculate the value. On the other hand, if the family of 'insurable events' is not rich enough, then the value is a random variable, and stockholders may not agree on its probability distribution.

OPTIMALITY. Recall that in the extended Arrow–Debreu model, under 'standard' conditions, equilibria are Pareto-optimal, and (roughly speaking) vice-versa. The same results do not hold for the case of incomplete markets. Of course, if markets are incomplete, one could at best expect equilibria to be optimal relative to some constrained set of resource allocations. With a fairly natural definition of 'constrained optimality', Geanakoplos and Polemarchakis (1986) have shown that, generically, equilibria of pure exchange are not optimal. Indeed, Hart (1975) gave an example of a model of incomplete markets in which there is a multiplicity of equilibria, which can be ranked by the Pareto criterion.

RATIONAL EXPECTATIONS EQUILIBRIUM. In a market for commodities whose future utility is uncertain, the equilibrium prices will reflect the information and beliefs that the traders bring to the market, as well as their tastes and endowments. If the traders have different nonprice information, this situation presents an opportunity for each trader to make inferences from the market prices about other traders' information. An example of this phenomenon is recognized by the everyday expression, 'judging quality by price'. The term *rational expectations equilibrium* is applied to a model of market equilibrium that takes account of this potential informational feedback from market prices.

We may take the convention that the future utility of the commodities to each trader depends on the *state of the environment*. With this convention, we can model the inferences that a trader makes from the market prices and his own nonprice information signal by a family of conditional probability distributions of the environment given the market prices and his own nonprice information. We shall call such a family of conditional distributions the trader's *market model*. Given such a market model, the market prices will influence a trader's demand in two ways: first, through his budget constraint, and second, through his conditional expected utility function. It is this second feature, of course, that distinguished theories of rational expectations equilibrium from earlier models of market equilibrium.

Given the traders' market models, the equilibrium prices will be determined by the equality of supply and demand in the usual way, and thus will be a deterministic function of the joint nonprice information that the traders bring to the market. In order for the market models of the traders to be 'rational', they must be consistent with that function. To make this idea precise, it will be useful to have some formal notation. Let p denote the vector of market prices, e denote the (utility-relevant) state of the environment, and s_i denote traders i's nonprice information signal ($i = 1, \ldots, I$). The joint nonprice information of all traders together will be denoted by $s = (s_1, \ldots, s_I)$. We shall call s the 'joint signal'. (The term 'state of information' is also commonly applied to this array.) Trader i's market model, say m_i, is a family of conditional probability distributions of e, given s_i and p. Given the traders' market models, the equilibrium price vector will be some (measurable) function of the joint nonprice information, say $p = \phi(s)$.

To model the required rationality of the traders' models, suppose that, for each i, trader i has (subjective) prior beliefs about the environment and the information signals that are expressed by a joint probability distribution, say Q_i, of e and s. These prior beliefs need not, of course, be the same for all traders. Given the price function ϕ, a *rational* market model for trader i would be the family of conditional probability distributions of e, given s_i and p, that are derived from the distribution Q_i and the price function ϕ; thus (supposing e and s to be discrete variables),

$$m_i(e'|s_i', p') = \text{Prob}_{Q_i}(e = e'|s_i' \quad \text{and} \quad \phi(s) = p'). \tag{1}$$

A given price function ϕ, together with the rationality condition (1), would determine the total market excess supply for each price vector p and each joint information signal s, say $Z(p, s, \phi)$. Note that the excess supply for any p and s *depends also on the price function ϕ*, since (in principle) the entire price function is used to calculate the conditional distribution in (1). I can now define a *rational expectations equilibrium* (REE) to be a price function ϕ^* such that, for (almost) every s, excess supply is zero at the price vector $\phi^*(s)$, i.e.,

$$Z(\phi^*(s), s, \phi^*) = 0, \qquad \text{for a.e. } s. \tag{2}$$

The formal study of rational expectations equilibrium was introduced by Radner (1967); it was taken up independently by Lucas (1972) and Green (1973), and further investigated by Grossman, Jordan, and others. We shall make no attempt here to provide complete bibliographic notes on the subject; for this the reader is referred to Radner (1982, Sec. 7.1, 7.4). The particular definition given above can be criticized on several grounds, and we shall return to this point below.

I should emphasize that I am concerned here with the aspect of 'rational expectations' in which traders make inferences from market prices about other traders' information, a phenomenon that is only of interest when traders do not all have the same nonprice information. The term 'rational expectations equilibrium' has also been used to describe a situation in which traders correctly forecast (in some sense or other) the probability distribution of future prices. (See Radner (1982) for references to the work of Muth and others on this topic.)

The concept of REE has been used to make a number of interesting predictions about the behaviour of markets (see, for example, Futia (1979, 1981) and the references cited there). A sound foundation for such applications requires the investigation of conditions that would ensure the existence and stability of REE, and this investigation has revealed a set of problems that are more difficult and more subtle than those encountered in ordinary equilibrium analysis.

If markets are incomplete, the existence of REE is not assured by the 'classical' conditions of ordinary general equilibrium analysis. Even under such conditions, if traders condition their expected utilities on market prices, then their demands can be discontinuous in the price function. Specific examples of the nonexistence of REE due to such discontinuities were given by Kreps (1977), Green (1977), and others.

These examples naturally led theorists to question whether the absence of REE is pervasive or is confirmed to a 'negligible' set of such examples. Indeed, this question was already anticipated by Green, whose example is robust to perturbations of the density function describing the environment, but not to perturbations of traders' characteristics. The work of Radner, Allen, and Jordan (see Jordan and Radner, 1982, for references) provided – in a certain context – an essentially complete answer, which can be loosely summarized in the statement that *REE exists generically except when the dimension of the space of private information is equal to the dimension of the price space.* (Recall that REE exists *generically* in a given model if, for any vector of parameters values for which REE does not exist, there are arbitrarily small perturbations of the parameters for which REE does exist.) Furthermore, if the dimension of the space of private information is strictly *less* than the dimension of the price space, then generically there is a REE that is *fully revealing*, i.e., in which the price reveals to each trader all the nonprice information used by *all* traders (Radner, 1979; Allen, 1981).

EQUILIBRIUM AND LEARNING WITH IMPERFECT PRICE MODELS. The nonexistence of rational expectations equilibrium illustrated in section 2 can be traced to discontinuities in the demand function with respect to the price function. In a sense, these discontinuities arise because the theory postulates that, in equilibrium, *the traders know the price function perfectly, and the price function is perfectly accurate.* To see this, consider the example of section 2, in which there are two traders, one who is initially fully informed about the environment and one who is initially uninformed. Suppose that there are two possible information signals, s', and s'', let ϕ_n be a sequence of price functions, and define

$$p'_n = \phi_n(s'), p''_n = \phi_n(s'').$$

Suppose that, for every n, $p'_n \neq p''_n$, but that the two sequences, (p'_n) and (p''_n), both converge to a common value, say p_0. Finally, define the price function ϕ_0 by $\phi_0(s') = \phi_0(s'') = p_0$. Thus each price function in the sequence is revealing, but the limit price function is not. Therefore, for each $n > 0$ the second trader's demands at the two prices will be different, and these differences will not tend to zero as n increases because although the differences between p'_n and p''_n are tending to zero the two prices reveal the respective signals, s' and s'', as long as the prices are different. On the other hand, in the limit trader 2 cannot infer the information signal from the price, since the limit price function is not revealing. Hence, in the limit, trader 2's expected utility will not be conditioned on the signal s, and so his demand will (typically) have a discontinuity at the limit price function. This follows from the (implicit) assumption that, *no matter how close* $\phi(s')$ and $\phi(s'')$ are, if they are different then trader 2 can infer the signal s from the price.

Let us now modify the description of the market, by replacing the assumption that each trader knows a (perfectly accurate) forecast function with the assumption that each trader has an 'econometric' model of how equilibrium prices are determined. Let E denote the set of environments e, let S denote the set of pooled information signals s, and let Δ denote the set of all nonnegative price vectors, normalized so that the sum of all prices is unity. Trader i's econometric model of the price determination, which we shall call his *price model*, is characterized by a family, $\psi_i(p|s)$, of strictly positive conditional probability density functions on the set Δ of possible price vectors. (This includes, as a special case, the typical econometric model in which a 'disturbance' with a probability density function is added to a deterministic relationship.) The joint probability distribution, for trader i, of the variables e, s, and p is determined by his probability distribution Q_i on $E \times S$ together with his price model, ψ_i.

One can show that, for each trader i, maximizing conditional expected utility given s_i and p is equivalent to maximizing

$$E_{Q_i}[u_i(x_i, e)\psi_i(p|s)|s_i], \tag{3}$$

where $E_{Q_i}[\cdot|s_i]$ denotes conditional expectation with respect to the probability measure Q_i, given s_i. Given s, an equilibrium is characterized by a price vector p^* and an I-tuple (x_i^*) of demand vectors such that, for each i, x_i^* maximizes (3) subject to $x_i \geqslant 0$ and a budget constraint, and such that excess demand is zero.

One can show that, with suitable assumptions, *an equilibrium exists for almost every s*. The assumptions are in two sets.

Those in the first set concern the trader's models of price determination. They express the two ideas that (1) each trader's price model is appropriately continuous in the price vector p, and (2) no trader's price model could predict the equilibrium price perfectly from the joint signal s. Formally, we assume that, for every trader i:

$\psi(\cdot|s)$ is continuous on Δ, and strictly positive on its interior, for almost every s;

$$\tag{4a}$$

$\psi_i(p|\cdot)$ is majorized in absolute value by an integrable function on S, *uniformly in p*. (4b)

The assumptions in the second set are standard in the theory of exchange equilibrium and in expected utility theory; they are omitted here (see Jordan and Radner, 1982, section 4).

With only these assumptions, the resulting equilibrium has no obvious 'self-fulfilling' or 'rational' expectations property. A minimal requirement along these lines is that an equilibrium price p^* not be 'inconsistent' with any trader's model of price determination. One way to express this formally is to require that

p^* be in the support of $\psi_i(\cdot|s)$, considered as a probability density on Δ. But this follows from the assumption that $\psi_i(p|s)$ is strictly positive on the interior of Δ. This expresses the idea that, given any exogenous signal s_i, trader i's model ψ_i *does not exclude as impossible any open set of equilibrium price vectors.*

A more stringent 'rational expectations' requirement would concern the opportunities that traders might have for learning from experience. For example, suppose that there is a market at each of a succession of dates t, and that the successive exogenous vectors (e_t, s_t) are independent and identically distributed. Suppose further that at the beginning of date t trader i knows the *past* history of environments, prices, and his own nonprice information. On the basis of this history he updates his initial market model to form a current market model. These current market models, together with the nonprice information signals at date t, then determine an equilibrium price at date t, say p_t^*, as above. The updating of models constitutes the *learning* process of the traders. For a given learning process, one might ask whether the process converges in any useful sense, and if so, whether the models are asymptotically consistent with the (endogenously determined) actual relationship between signals and equilibrium prices, i.e. whether they converge to a REE. In this case one would say that the REE is *stable* (relative to the learning process).

Thus far, answers to this question are only fragmentary. Bray (1982) has studied a simple linear asset-market model in which, at each date, each trader i updates his model by calculating an ordinary least-squares estimates of the regression of e on p and s_i, using all the past values (e_i, p_t^*, s_{it}). For this example, Bray proves stability.

On the other hand, Blume and Easley (1982) present a somewhat less optimistic view of the possibility of learning rational expectations. They define a class of learning procedures by which traders use successive observations to form their subjective models, where the term model for trader i means a conditional distribution of s, given s_i and p. They show that rational expectations equilibria are at least 'locally stable' under learning, but that learning processes may also get stuck at a profile of subjective models that is not an REE. The learning procedures defined by Blume and Easley are applied to a fairly general class of stochastic exchange environments that do not process the special linear structure of the above example. However, to accommodate this additional generality, Blume and Easley constrain traders to choose their subjective models from a fixed finite set of models and convex combinations thereof. Hence for some profiles of subjective models, market clearing may result in a 'true' model that lies outside the admissible set. It is then intuitively plausible that a natural learning procedure could get stuck at a profile of subjective models that differs from the resulting true model but is in some sense the best admissible approximation to the true model, even if the admissible set contains an REE model. This phenomenon is illustrated in section 5 of their paper.

BIBLIOGRAPHY

Most of the literature on incomplete markets and on rational expectations equilibrium is quite recent, and many interesting papers are still unpublished at the time this is being written. Further results and references can be found in (Radner, 1982), Jordan and Radner (1982), Younès (1985), Allen (1986), Geanakoplos and Polemarchakis (1986), Duffie and Shafer (1986).

Allen, B. 1981. Generic existence of completely revealing equilibria for economies with uncertainty when prices convey information. *Econometrica* 49, 1173–99.

Allen, B. 1986. General equilibrium with rational expectations. Ch. 1 of *Contributions to Mathematical Economics: Essays in Honor of Gerard Debreu*, ed. A. Mas-Colell and W. Hildenbrand, Amsterdam: North-Holland, 1–23.

Arrow, K.J. 1953. Le rôle de valeurs boursières pour la répartition la meilleure des risques. *Econométrie*, 41–48. Trans. as 'The role of securities in the optimal allocation of risk-bearing', *Review of Economic Studies* 31, (1964), 91–6.

Arrow, K.J. 1965. *Aspects of the Theory of Risk-Bearing*. Helsinki: Yrjo Johansson Foundation.

Arrow, K.J. and Hahn, F.H. 1971. *General Competitive Analysis*. San Francisco: Holden-Day.

Blume, L.E. and Easley, D. 1982. Learning to be rational. *Journal of Economic Theory* 26, 340–51.

Bray, M. 1982. Learning, estimation, and the stability of rational expectations. *Journal of Economic Theory* 26, 318–39.

Burke, J. 1986. Existence of equilibrium for incomplete market economies with production and stock trading. Texas A & M University (unpublished).

Debreu, G. 1953. Une économie de l'incertain. Electricité de France, Paris, mimeo.

Debreu, G. 1959. *Theory of Value*. New York: Wiley.

Debreu, G. 1962. New concepts and techniques for equilibrium analysis. *International Economic Review* 3, 257–73.

Duffie, D. and Shafer, W. 1985. Equilibrium in incomplete markets I: a basic model of generic existence. *Journal of Mathematical Economics* 14, 285–300.

Duffie, D. and Shafer, W. 1986. Equilibrium and the role of the firm in incomplete markets. Research Paper No. 915, Graduate School of Business, Stanford University, November.

Duffie, D. and Shafer, W. 1987. Equilibrium in incomplete markets II: Generic existence in stochastic economies. *Journal of Mathematical Economics* 15, 199–216.

Futia, C.A.1979. Stochastic business cycles. AT & T Bell Laboratories, Murray Hill, N.J. (unpublished).

Futia, C.A. 1981. Rational expectations in stationary linear models. *Econometrica* 49, 171–92.

Geanakoplos, J. and Polemarchakis, H. 1986. Existence, regularity, and constrained suboptimality of competitive allocations when the asset market is incomplete. In *Uncertainty, Information and Communication: Essays in Honor of Kenneth Arrow*, ed. W.P. Heller, R.M. Starr, and D.A. Starrett, Vol. III, 65–95.

Green, J. 1973. Information, inefficiency, and equilibrium. Discussion Paper 284, Harvard Institute of Economic Research, Cambridge.

Green, J. 1977. The nonexistence of informational equilibria. *Review of Economic Studies* 44, 451–63.

Harrison, J.M. and Kreps, D.M. 1979. Martingales and arbitrage in multiperiod securities markets. *Journal of Economic Theory* 20, 381–408.

Hart, O. 1975. On the optimality of equilibrium when the market structure is incomplete. *Journal of Economic Theory* 11, 418–43.

Jordan, J.S. and Radner, R. 1982. Rational expectations in microeconomic models: an overview. *Journal of Economic Theory* 26, 201–23.

Kreps, D.M. 1977. A note on 'fulfilled expectations' equilibria. *Journal of Economic Theory* 14, 32–43.

Lucas, R.E. 1972. Expectations and the neutrality of money. *Journal of Economic Theory* 4, 103–24.

Radner, R. 1967. Equilibria des marchés à terme et au comptant en cas d'incertitude. *Cahiers d'Econométrie CNRS*, Paris, 4, 35–52.

Radner, R. 1968. Competitive equilibrium under uncertainty. *Econometrica* 36, 31–58.

Radner, R. 1972. Existence of equilibrium of plans, prices, and price expectations in a sequence of markets. *Econometrica* 40, 289–304.

Radner, R. 1979. Rational expectations equilibrium: generic existence and the information revealed by prices. *Econometrica* 47, 655–7.

Radner, R. 1982. Equilibrium under uncertainty. Ch. 20 in *Handbook of Mathematical Economics*, ed. K.J. Arrow and M.D. Intriligator, Vol. II, Amsterdam: North-Holland, 923–1006.

Radner, R. and Stiglitz, J.E. 1984. A nonconcavity in the value of information. In *Bayesian Models of Economic Theory*, ed. M. Boyer and R.E. Kihlstrom, Amsterdam: North-Holland, 33–52.

Savage, L.J. 1954. *The Foundations of Statistics.* New York: Wiley.

Younès, Y. 1985. Competitive equilibrium and incomplete market structures. Economics Department, University of Pennsylvania, revised October 1986 (unpublished).

Uniqueness of Equilibrium

MICHAEL ALLINGHAM

In general equilibrium theory, equilibrium prices may be interpreted as those prices which coordinate the buying and selling plans of all the various agents in the economy; equivalently, they may be interpreted as the values of the commodities. Such values will only be well defined if there is only one system of coordinating prices, that is, if the equilibrium is unique. If this does not obtain then at least the set of equilibrium price systems should not be too large, that is, there should be only a finite number of equilibria.

The question of uniqueness was first posed by Walras (1874–7), but received its first systematic treatment by Wald (1936). In the present discussion we commence with a formal definition of uniqueness. We then note that there may be multiple, and even infinitely many, equilibria, but show that the latter possibility is unlikely. In the light of this we examine various conditions which are sufficient to ensure that equilibrium is unique. Finally, we note some problems which may arise in the presence of multiple equilibria.

We may represent an economy with n commodities by the excess demand function $f: S \to R^n$, where $S = R^n_+ - 0$. The interpretation of this is that $f(p)$ is the vector of aggregate excess demands (positive) or excess supplies (negative) expressed at the price system p. Under some reasonable assumptions on the underlying parameters of the economy, that is the individual preferences and endowments, this excess demand function has the following properties:

Homogeneity: $f(tp) = f(p)$ for all positive t.

Walras's Law: $p \cdot f(p) = 0$ for all p.

Desirability: $f_i(p)$ is infinite if $p_i = 0$.

Differentiability: f is continuously differentiable.

The price system p is an equilibrium price system if $f(p) = 0$. Because of desirability it is clear that if p is an equilibrium then p is strictly positive. We shall denote by E the set of equilibrium prices. Now if p is in E then so is tp for any positive t (because of Homogeneity), so we take the equilibrium p to be unique if q is in E implies that $q = tp$ for some positive t. Equivalent formulations specify that the equilibrium p is unique if it is the only equilibrium in the unit simplex in R^n, or if it is the only equilibrium with, say, $p_n = 1$. Of course, the question of uniqueness of equilibrium only arises if there is at least one equilibrium: however, under the above four conditions on the excess demand function this existence is assured (Debreu, 1959).

The first point to note is that equilibrium may well not be unique: indeed, there may be infinitely many equilibria. This follows from the fact that the above four conditions are, at the most, the only restrictions which economic theory places on the excess demand function (Debreu, 1970). It is therefore straightforward to construct examples of economies with many equilibria, and even of economies in which all positive prices are equilibrium prices.

In the light of this point we first consider the likelihood of encountering an infinite number of equilibria. Let $F(p)$ be the Jacobian of excess supply, that is of $-f$, at p with the last row and last column deleted. We lose no information in working with F rather than with the full Jacobian: simply because we can set $p_n = 1$ without loss of generality (Homogeneity) and because if $f_i(p) = 0$ for all i other than n then $f_n(p) = 0$ (Walras's Law). The economy is said to be regular if $F(p)$ is of full rank at all p in E. The importance of this is that almost all economies are regular, in that the set of economies which are not regular, or critical economies, is a closed null subset of the set of all economies, as may be shown using Sard's theorem (Debreu, 1970).

With this in mind we may now observe that the number of equilibria in a regular economy is finite. This may be shown, using the Poincaré–Hopf index theorem, by defining the index $i(p) = 1$ if the determinant $\det F(p) > 0$ and $i(p) = -1$ if $\det F(p) < 0$ and noting that the sum of $i(p)$ over all p in E is 1 (Dierker, 1972). This result has two immediate corollaries: the first is that the number of equilibria in a regular economy is odd; the second is that if $\det F(p)$ is positive for all p in E then equilibrium is unique. Taking the above two results together we note that in almost all economies the number of equilibria is finite.

The economic interpretation of $\det F(p)$ being positive in the two-dimensional case is that excess demand is 'downward-sloping' (or excess supply 'upward-sloping'). It is intuitively clear that this ensures uniqueness. In the general case, however, the economic interpretation of this property is not so clear; we therefore examine some more interpretable properties which ensure uniqueness.

An economy with excess demand function f has the revealed preference property if $p \cdot f(q) > 0$ wherever p is in E and q is not in E. It is well known that if g is an individual's excess demand function then $q \cdot g(p) \leqslant 0$ (that is $g(p)$ is available to the individual at price q) implies that $p \cdot g(q) > 0$ (that is $g(q)$ is not available at price p). If all individuals are identical this property will hold in aggregate, where, if p is in E, $q \cdot f(p) = 0$ immediately, so that $p \cdot f(q) > 0$ if q is not in E. Thus if all agents are identical the economy has the revealed preference property. In fact the essential reason why the property holds if all agents are identical is that there is then no trade at equilibrium. It can readily be seen that the property holds if there is no trade at equilibrium for whatever reason. This becomes relevant if we consider today's endowments as being the result of yesterday's trading, with no intervening consumption or production.

Now assume f has the revealed preference property and let p and q be in E but suppose that r, a proper linear combination of p and q, is not in E. Then $p \cdot f(r) > 0$ and $q \cdot f(r) > 0$ so that $r \cdot f(r) > 0$, which contradicts Walras's Law. This shows that E is convex. Since in almost all economies E is finite, and the only finite convex set is a singleton, it follows that in almost all economies with the revealed preference property equilibrium is unique.

An economy with excess demand function f has the gross substitute property if $p_i > q_i$ and $p_j = q_j$ for each $j \neq i$ imply that $f_j(p) > f_j(q)$ for each $j \neq i$. If this property obtains then Walras's Law implies that excess demand must be 'downward-sloping'. The interpretation of this is that all commodities are substitutes for each other (in the gross sense, that is including income effects as well as substitution effects). In fact, the gross substitutes property implies the revealed preference property; instead of showing this implication we will demonstrate directly that the gross substitutes property ensures uniqueness.

Let p be in E and for any $q \neq p$ define $m = \max_i q_i / p_i = q_k / p_k$ say, and let $r = mp$. Then $r_i \geq q_i$ for each i with equality for $i = k$ and inequality for some $i \neq k$, so by repeated use of the gross substitutes property we have $f_k(r) > f_k(q)$. But by Homogeneity $f(r) = f(p) = 0$, so that $f_k(q) < 0$ and q is not in E. Thus equilibrium is unique.

If $p_i > q_i$ and $p_j = q_j$ for each $j \neq i$ imply that $f_j(p) \geq f_j(p)$ for each $j \neq i$ then the economy has the weak gross substitutes property. Arguments analogous to that above show that in this case E is convex, so that in almost all economies equilibrium is unique. Alternatively, if the economy is, in addition, connected in some specific sense, then equilibrium is definitely unique.

Finally, we should note that these properties of revealed preference and gross substitutes do not depend on differentiability. If we accept differentiability there are other properties which ensure uniqueness. One such is diagonal dominance, which is that F has a positive diagonal and that there are some units in which commodities can be measured such that each of their excess demands are more sensitive to a change in their own price then they are to a change in all other non-numeraire prices combined.

It is clear from the above discussion that uniqueness is a strong property. If it does not obtain equilibrium prices will still coordinate individual agents' plans, but they will not, of course, define values uniquely.

One more specific problem which arises under multiple equilibria concerns stability. Assume that we have a process for changing prices such that no change is made in equilibrium and define an equilibrium price p to be stable under this process if prices converge to p whatever their initial values. Then if there are two equilibria, say p and q, neither can be stable: the path starting at p will remain at p so that q is not stable, and conversely. This problem may be avoided by considering only system stability, that is by defining the set E of equilibrium prices to be stable if all paths converge to E. It may also be avoided by considering only local stability, that is by defining p to be stable if prices converge to p given initial values sufficiently close to p. It is clear that even local stability requires equilibria to be separated, and thus finite. As we have seen, this applies in a regular economy; in this case the index theorem then implies that if there are $2k + 1$ equilibria (we know the number to be odd) then $k + 1$ will typically be locally stable and k unstable.

A further specific problem which arises under multiple equilibria concerns comparative statics. Assume that we want to compare the set of equilibria E of the economy with the set of equilibria E' of some new economy obtained from the original economy by some specified parameter change. If there are multiple equilibria we may be able to say very little: for example if p is in E and both p' and q' are in E' and $p' < p < q'$ all comparative statics results are ambiguous. However, in regular economies, where not only are equilibria separated but also the elements of E and of E' correspond to one another in a natural one-to-one way, this problem may be avoided by considering only local comparative statics, interpreted analogously to local stability.

BIBLIOGRAPHY

Debreu, G. 1959. *Theory of Value*. New York: Wiley.

Debreu, G. 1970. Economies with a finite set of equilibria. *Econometrica* 38(3), May, 387–92.

Dierker, E. 1972. Two remarks on the number of equilibria of an economy. *Econometrica* 40(5), September, 867–81.

Wald, A. 1936. Über einige Gleichungssysteme der mathematischen Ökonomie. *Zeitschrift für Nationalökonomie* 7; trans. as: On some systems of equations of mathematical economics, *Econometrica* 19, October 1951, 368–403.

Walras, L. 1874–7. *Eléments d'économie politique pure*. Definitive edn, Lausanne: Corbaz, 1926. Translated by W. Jaffé as *Elements of Pure Economics*. London: George Allen & Unwin, 1954; New York: Orion.

Walras's Law

DON PATINKIN

Walras's Law (so named by Lange, 1942) is an expression of the interdependence among the excess-demand equations of a general-equilibrium system that stems from the budget constraint. Its name reflects the fact that Walras, the father of general-equilibrium economics, himself made use of this interdependence from the first edition of his *Eléments d'économie politique pure* (1874, §122) through the fourth (1900, §116), which edition is for all practical purposes identical with the definitive one (1926). I have cited §116 of this edition because it is the one cited by Lange (1942, p. 51, n.2), though in a broader context than Walras's own discussion there (see below). In this section, Walras presents the argument for an exchange economy. In accordance with his usual expository technique (cf. his treatment of the *tâtonnement*), he repeats the argument as he successively extends his analysis to deal first with a simple production economy and then with one in which capital formation also takes place (ibid., §§206 and 250, respectively.)

For reasons that will become clear later, I shall derive Walras's Law in a more general – and more cumbersome – way than it usually has been. Basically, however, the derivation follows that of Arrow and Hahn (1971, pp. 17–21), with an admixture of Lange (1942) and Patinkin (1956, chs I–III and Mathematical Appendix 3:a).

Let x_i^h be the decision of household h with respect to good i ($i = 1, \ldots, n$), where 'goods' also include services and financial assets (securities and money). If $x_i^h \geqslant 0$, it is a good purchased by the household; if $x_i^h < 0$, it is a good (mainly, labour or some other factor-service) sold. Similarly, let y_i^f be the decision of firm f with respect to good i; if $y_i^f \geqslant 0$, it is a good produced and sold by the firm (i.e., a product-output); if $y_i^f < 0$, it is a factor-input.

Assume that firm f has certain initial conditions (say, quantities of fixed factors of production) presented by the vector $\mathbf{k}^f$ and operates in accordance with a certain production function. Following Patinkin (1956), let us conduct the conceptual individual-experiment of confronting the firm with the vector of variables $\mathbf{v}$ (the nature of which will be discussed below) while keeping $\mathbf{k}^f$

constant and asking it to designate (subject to its production function) the amounts that it will sell or buy of the various goods and services. By repeating this conceptual experiment with different values of the respective elements of **v**, we obtain the behaviour functions of firm f,

$$y_i^f = y_i^f(\mathbf{v}: \mathbf{k}^f) \qquad (i = 1, \ldots, n). \tag{1}$$

For $y_i \geqslant 0$, this is a supply function; for $y_i < 0$, it is a demand function for the services of factors of production. Profits (positive or negative) of firm f are then

$$R^f = \sum_i p_i y_i^f(\mathbf{v}; \mathbf{k}^f). \tag{2}$$

Let d^{hf} represent the proportion of the profits of firm f received by the household h. Its total profits received are then $\Sigma_f d^{hf} R^f$ and its budget constraint is accordingly

$$\sum_i p_i x_i^h = \sum_f d^{hf} R^f, \tag{3}$$

which assumes that households correctly estimate the profits of firms (cf. Buiter, 1980, p. 7; I shall return to this point below). As with the firm, let us, *mutatis mutandis*, conduct individual-experiments with household h (with its given tastes), subject to its budget constraint (3) by varying the elements of **v**, while keeping its initial endowment (represented by the vector $\mathbf{e}^h$) constant. This yields the behaviour functions

$$x_i^h = x_i^h(\mathbf{v}; \mathbf{e}^h) \qquad (i = 1, \ldots, n). \tag{4}$$

For $x_i \geqslant 0$, this is a demand function for goods; for $x_i < 0$, it is a supply function (e.g., of factor-services).

Substituting from (2) and (4) into (3) then yields

$$\sum_i p_i x_i^h(\mathbf{v}; \mathbf{e}^h) = \sum_f d^{hf} \sum_i p_i y_i^f(\mathbf{v}; \mathbf{k}^f), \tag{5}$$

which holds identically for all **v**, $\mathbf{e}^h$, $\mathbf{k}^f$ and p_i. Summing up over all households then yields

$$\sum_h \sum_i p_i x_i^h(\mathbf{v}; \mathbf{e}^h) = \sum_h \sum_f d^{hf} \sum_i p_i y_i^f(\mathbf{v}; \mathbf{k}^f), \tag{6}$$

which we rewrite as

$$\sum_i p_i \sum_h x_i^h(\mathbf{v}; \mathbf{e}^h) = \sum_i p_i \sum_f \left(\sum_h d^{hf} \right) y_i^f(\mathbf{v}; \mathbf{k}^f). \tag{7}$$

On the assumption that firm f distributes all its profits,

$$\sum_h d^{hf} = 1 \qquad \text{for all } f, \tag{8}$$

329

so that (7) reduces to

$$\sum_i p_i[X_i(\mathbf{v}; \mathbf{E}) - Y_i(\mathbf{v}; \mathbf{K})] = 0 \qquad (9)$$

identically in all $\mathbf{v}$, $\mathbf{E}$, $\mathbf{K}$ and p_i, where

$$X_i(\mathbf{v}; \mathbf{E}) = \sum_h x_i^h(\mathbf{v}; \mathbf{e}^h) \qquad \text{and} \qquad Y_i(\mathbf{v}; \mathbf{K}) = \sum_f y_i^f(\mathbf{v}; \mathbf{k}^f) \qquad (10)$$

represent the aggregate demand and supply functions, respectively, for good i; $\mathbf{E}$ is a vector containing all the $\mathbf{e}^h$; and $\mathbf{K}$ a vector containing all the $\mathbf{k}^f$. If $X_i(\mathbf{v}; \mathbf{E}) - Y_i(\mathbf{v}; \mathbf{K}) > 0$, an excess demand is said to exist in the market; if $X_i(\mathbf{v}; \mathbf{E}) - Y_i(\mathbf{v}; \mathbf{K}) < 0$, an excess supply; and if $X_i(\mathbf{v}; \mathbf{E}) = Y_i(\mathbf{v}; \mathbf{K})$, equilibrium.

Equation (9) is a general statement of Walras's Law. Its most frequent application in the literature has been (as in Walras's *Eléments* itself) to the general-equilibrium analysis of a system of perfect competition, in which the behaviour functions of firms are derived from the assumption that they maximize profits subject to their production function; and those of households are derived from the assumption that they maximize utility subject to their budget constraint. In this context, the vector $\mathbf{v}$ is the price vector $(p_1, \ldots, p_{n-1})$, with the nth good being money and serving as numéraire (i.e., $p_n = 1$), so that there are only $n - 1$ prices to be determined. Ignoring for simplicity vectors $\mathbf{E}$ and $\mathbf{K}$, which remain constant in the conceptual market-experiment, equation (9) then becomes

$$\sum_{i=1}^n p_i[X_i(p_1, \ldots, p_{n-1}) - Y_i(p_1, \ldots, p_{n-1})] = 0 \qquad \text{identically in the } p_i.$$
$$(11)$$

(Though it does not bear on the present subject, I should note that under the foregoing assumptions, and in the absence of money illusion, each of the demand and supply functions is homogeneous of degree zero in $p_1, \ldots, p_{n-1}$ and in whatever nominal financial assets are included in $\mathbf{E}$ and $\mathbf{K}$ (e.g., initial money holdings): see Patinkin, 1956, ch. III: 4.) Thus Walras's Law states that no matter what the p_i, the aggregate value of excess demands in the system equals the aggregate value of excess supplies. This is the statement implicit in Lange's presentation (1942, p. 50).

Walras himself, however, sufficed with a particular and narrower application of this statement, and was followed in this by, *inter alia*, Hicks (1939, chs. IV: 3 and XII: 4–5), Modigliani (1944, pp. 215–16) and Patinkin (1956, ch. III: 1–3). Assume that it has been shown that a certain price vector $(p_1^0, \ldots, p_{n-1}^0)$ equilibrates all markets but the jth. Since (11) holds identically in the p_i, it must hold for this price vector too. Hence substituting the $n - 1$ equilibrium conditions into (11) reduces it to

$$p_j^0[X_j(p_1^0, \ldots, p_{n-1}^0) - Y_j(p_1^0, \ldots, p_{n-1}^0)] = 0. \qquad (12)$$

Thus if $p_j^0 > 0$, the price vector $(p_1^0, \ldots, p_{n-1}^0)$ must also equilibrate the jth market, which means that only $n - 1$ of the equilibrium equations are independent. In this way Walras (and those who followed him) established the equality between the number of independent equations and the number of price-variables to be determined. (Though such an equality is not a sufficient condition for the existence of a unique solution with positive prices, it is a necessary – though not sufficient – condition for the peace-of-mind of those of us who do not aspire to the rigour of mathematical economists.)

It should however be noted that at tne end of §126 of Walras's *Eléments* (1926), there is a hint of Lange's broader statement of the Law: for there Walras states that if at a certain set of prices 'the total demand for some commodities is greater (or smaller) than their offer, then the offer of some of the other commodities must be greater (or smaller) than the demand for them'; what is missing here is the quantitative statement that the respective aggregate values of these excesses must be equal.

Since the contrary impression might be gained from some of the earlier literature (cf., e.g., Modigliani, 1944, pp. 215–16), it should be emphasized that no substantive difference can arise from the choice of the equation to be 'dropped' or 'eliminated' from a general-equilibrium system by virtue of Walras's Law. For identity (11) can be rewritten as

$$X_j(p_1,\ldots,p_{n-1}) - Y_j(p_1,\ldots,p_{n-1})$$

$$= -\frac{1}{p_j}\sum_{\substack{i=1\\i\neq j}}^{n} p_i[X_i(p_1,\ldots,p_{n-1}) - Y_i(p_1,\ldots,p_{n-1})]$$

identically in the p_i. (13)

Thus the properties of the 'eliminated' equation are completely reflected in the remaining ones. Correspondingly, no matter what equation is 'eliminated', the solution for the equilibrium set of prices obtained from the remaining equations must be the same. (From this it is also clear that the heated 'loanable-funds *versus* liquidity-preference' debate that occupied the profession for many years after the appearance of the *General Theory*, was largely misguided; see Hicks, 1939, pp. 157–62; see also Patinkin, 1956, ch. XV: 3, and 1958, pp. 300–302, 316–17.)

In this influential article, Lange (1942, pp. 52–3) also distinguished between Walras's Law and what he called Say's Law, and I digress briefly to discuss this. As before, let the first $n-1$ goods represent commodities and the nth good money. Then Say's Law according to Lange is

$$\sum_{i=1}^{n-1} p_i X_i(p_1,\ldots,p_{n-1}) = \sum_{i=1}^{n-1} p_i Y_i(p_1,\ldots,p_{n-1}) \qquad \text{identically in the } p_i.$$

(14)

That is, the aggregate value of commodities supplied at any price vector $(p_1,\ldots,p_{n-1})$ must equal the aggregate value demanded: supply always creates its own demand.

On both theoretical and doctrinal grounds, however, I must reject Lange's

331

treatment of Say's Law. First of all, Lange himself demonstrates (ibid., p. 62) that identity (14) implies that money prices are indeterminate. In particular, subtracting (14) from (11) yields

$$X_n(p_1, \ldots, p_{n-1}) = Y_n(p_1, \ldots, p_{n-1}) \qquad \text{for all } p_i. \qquad (15)$$

That is, no matter what the price vector, the excess-demand equation for money must be satisfied, which in turn implies that money prices cannot be determined by market forces. But it is not very meaningful to speak of a money economy whose money prices are indeterminate even for fixed initial conditions as represented by the vectors $\mathbf{E}$ and $\mathbf{K}$. So if we rule out this possibility, we can say that Say's Law in Lange's sense implies the existence of a barter economy. Conversely, in a barter economy (i.e., one in which there exist only the $n-1$ commodities) Say's Law is simply a statement of Walras's Law. Thus from the above viewpoint, a necessary and sufficient condition for the existence of Say's Law in Lange's sense is that the economy in question be a barter economy: it has no place in a money economy (Patinkin, 1956, ch. VIII: 7).

Insofar as the doctrinal aspect is concerned, identity (14) cannot be accepted as a representation of Say's actual contention. For Say's concern was (in today's terminology) not the short-run viewpoint implicit in this identity, but the viewpoint which denied that in the long run inadequacy of demand would set a limit to the expansion of output. In brief and again in today's terminology, Say's concern was to deny the possibility of secular stagnation, not that of cyclical depression and unemployment. Thus, writing in the first quarter of the 19th century, Say (1821a, p. 137) adduces evidence in support of his thesis from the fact 'that there should now be bought and sold in France five or six times as many commodities, as in the miserable reign of Charles VI' – four centures earlier. Again, in his *Letters to Malthus* (1821b, pp. 4–5) Say argues that the enactment of the Elizabethan Poor Laws (codified at the end of the 16th century) proves that '*there was* no employ in a country which since then has been able to furnish enough for a double and triple number of labourers' (italics in original). Similarly, Ricardo, the leading contemporary advocate of Say's *loi des débouchés*, discusses this law in chapter 21 of his *Principles* (1821), entitled 'Effects of Accumulation on Profits and Interest'; on the other hand, he clearly recognizes the short-run 'distress' that can be generated by 'Sudden Changes in the Channels of Trade' (title of ch. 19 of his *Principles*, for further discussion see Patinkin (1956), Supplementary Note L.).

Let me return now to the general statement of Walras's Law presented in equation (9) above. This statement holds for any vector $\mathbf{v}$ and not only for that appropriate to perfect competition. *In particular, Walras's Law holds also for the case in which households and/or firms are subject to quantity constraints.* In order to bring this out, consider the macroeconomic analysis of a disequilibrium economy presented in chapter XIII: 2 of Patinkin (1956) and illustrated by Figure 1. In this figure, w is the money wage-rate, p the price level, N the quantity of labour, $N^d = Q(w/p, K_0)$ the firms' demand curve for labour as derived from profit-maximization as of a given stock of physical capital K_0; and $N^s = R(w/p)$ is the supply curve of labour as derived from utility maximization subject to the budget constraint (these perfect-competition curves are what Clower (1965, p. 119) subsequently denoted as 'notional curves'). Assume that because of the firms' awareness that at the real wage rate $(w/p)_1$ they face a quantity constraint and will not be able to see all of the output corresponding to their profit-maximizing input of labour N_1, they demand only N_2 units of labour, represented by point P in Figure 1. This constraint also operates on workers, who can sell only the foregoing quantity of labour instead of their optimal one N_3, represented by point H. In brief, at point P, both firms and workers are off their notional curves. In order to depict this situation, the notional curves must accordingly be replaced by quantity-constrained ones; namely, the kinked demand curve TAN_2 and kinked supply curve OUE. Note that for levels of employment before they become kinked, the curves coincide respectively with the notional ones (but see Patinkin, 1956, ch. XIII: 2, n. 9, for a basic analytical problem that arises with respect to the kinked demand curve TAN_2).

The obverse side of these constraints in the labour market are corresponding constraints in the commodity market. In particular, as Clower (1965, pp. 118–21) has emphasized, the demands of workers in this market are determined by their constrained incomes. Clower also emphasizes that it is this quantity constraint which rationalizes the consumption function of Keynes's *General Theory*, in which income appears as an independent variable. For in the absence of such a constraint, the individual's income is also a dependent variable, determined by the optimum quantity of labour he decides to sell at the given real wage rate in

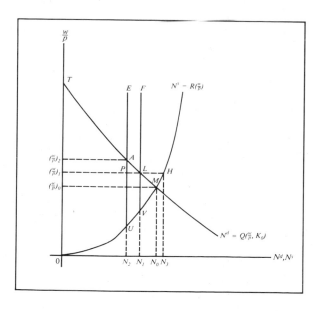

Figure 1

accordance with the labour-supply function $N^S = R(w/p)$ in Figure 1; and he makes this decision simultaneously with the one with respect to the optimum quantities of commodities to buy. If, however, his income is determined by a quantity constraint which prevents him from selling his optimum quantity of labour, the individual can decide on his demands for commodities only after his income is first determined. This is the so-called 'dual decision hypothesis' (Clower, ibid.). To this I would add (and its significance will become clear below) that the quantity constraint also rationalizes the form of Keynes's liquidity preference function, for this too depends on income (*General Theory*, p. 199). Furthermore, if the behaviour functions in the markets for labour, commodities, and money balances are thus quantity-constrained, so too (by the budget constraint) will be that for bonds – the fourth market implicitly (and frequently explicitly) present in the Keynesian system. (The theory of the determination of equilibrium under quantity constraints – in brief, disequilibrium theory – has been the subject of a growing literature, most of it highly technical; for critical surveys of this literature, see Grandmont, 1977; Drazen, 1980; Fitoussi, 1983; and Gale, 1983, ch. 1.)

In the *General Theory* (ch. 2), Keynes accepted the 'first classical postulate' that the real wage is equal to the marginal product of labour, but rejected the second one, that it always also measures the marginal disutility of labour. In terms of Figure 1 this means that while firms are always on their demand curve $N^d = Q(w/p, K_0)$, workers are not always on their supply curve $N^s = R(w/p)$. Thus, for example, at the level of employment N_2, the labour market will be at point A on the labour-demand curve, corresponding to the real wage rate $(w/p)_2$; but the marginal utility of the quantity of commodities that workers then buy with their real-income $(w/p)_2 \cdot N_2$ is greater than the marginal disutility of that level of employment. And Keynes emphasizes that only in a situation of full-employment equilibrium (represented by intersection point M in Figure 1) will both classical postulates be satisfied.

Consider now the commodity market as depicted in the usual Keynesian-cross diagram (Figure 2). The 45° line represents the amounts of commodities which firms produce and supply as they move along their labour-demand curve from point T to M. Thus Y_0 represents the output (in real terms) of N_0 units of labour. Note too that the negative slope of the labour-demand curve implies that the real wave declines as we move rightwards along the 45° line.

Curve E represents the aggregate demand curve, which is the vertical sum of the consumption function of workers (E_L) and capitalists (E_C), respectively, and of the investment function (I). For simplicity, these last two are assumed to be constant. The fact that curve E does not coincide with the 45° line reflects Keynes's assumption that in a monetary economy, Say's Law (in Keynes's sense, which is the macroeconomic counterpart of Lange's subsequent formulation) does not hold (ibid., pp. 25–6).

Consider now the consumption function of workers. The income which they have at their disposal is their constrained income as determined by the labour-demand curve in Figure 1. Thus assume that Y_1 and Y_2 in Figure 2 are the outputs corresponding to the levels of employment N_1 and N_2, respectively.

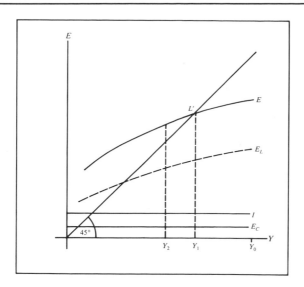

Figure 2

The corresponding incomes of workers at these levels are $(w/p)_1 \cdot N_1$ and $(w/p)_2 \cdot N_2$. On the assumption that the elasticity of demand for labour is greater than unity, the higher the level of employment the greater the income of workers and hence their consumption expenditures. From Figure 2 we see that at income Y_2 there is an excess demand for commodities. This causes firms to expand their output to, say, Y_1, and hence their labour-input to, say, N_1, thus causing the constrained labour supply curve to shift to the right to the kinked curve $OUVLF$. By construction, Y_1 is the equilibrium level of output.

What must now be emphasized is that Walras's Law holds in this situation too – *provided we relate this Law to excess-demand functions of the same type*. Thus if within our four-good Keynesian model we *consistently* consider notional behaviour functions, the excess supply of labour LH in Figure 1 corresponds to an excess demand for commodities which is generated by workers' planned consumption expenditures at the real wage rate $(w/p)_1$ and level of employment N_3 as compared with firms' planned output at that wage rate and lower level of employment N_2; and there will generally also exist a net excess planned demand for bonds and money. Alternatively, if we *consistently* consider constrained functions, then constrained equilibria exist in both the labour market (point L), the commodity market (point L'), the bond market, and the money market. Similarly, the broader form of Walras's Law states that a constrained (say) excess supply in the commodity market corresponds to a constrained net excess demand in the bond and money markets, while the labour market is in constrained equilibrium. In brief, a sufficient condition for the validity of Walras's Law is that the individual's demand and supply functions on which it is ultimately based are all derived from the same budget constraint, whether quantity-constrained or not. (This is the implicit assumption of Patinkin's (1956, p. 229; 1958, pp. 314–16) application of Walras's Law to a disequilibrium economy with unemployment, and the same is true for Grossman (1971) and Barrow and Grossman (1971; 1976, p. 58).)

I must admit that the validity of Walras's Law in this Keynesian model depends on our regarding the kinked curve $OUVLF$ as a labour-supply curve, and that this is not completely consistent with the usual meaning of a supply curve or function. For such a function usually describes the behaviour of an agent under constraints which leave him some degree of freedom to choose an optimum, whereas no such freedom exists in the vertical part of $OUVLF$. However, I prefer this inconsistency to what I would consider to be the logical – and hence more serious – inconsistency that lies at the base of the rejection of Walras's Law, and which consists of lumping together behaviour functions derived from different budget constraints.

It is thus clear that the foregoing constrained equilibrium in the labour market is not an equilibrium in the literal sense of representing a balance of opposing market forces, but simply the reflection of the passive adjustment by workers of the amount of labour they supply to the amount demanded by firms (cf. Patinkin, 1958, pp. 314–15). From this viewpoint, the constrained equilibrium in the labour market always exists and simply expresses the fact that, by definition, every ex post purchase is also an ex post sale. In contrast, as we have seen in the discussion of Figure 2 above, the corresponding constrained equilibrium in the commodity market is a true one; for, in accordance with the usual Keynesian analysis, were the level of Y to deviate from Y_1, automatic market forces of excess demand or supply would be generated that would return it to Y_1. And a similar statement holds, *mutatis mutandis*, for the constrained equilibria in the bond and money markets.

Note, however, that in the commodity market too there is an ex post element. This element is a basic, if inadequately recognized, aspect of the household behaviour implied by Clower's 'dual decision hypothesis': namely, that households' constrained decisions on the amount of money to spend on commodities is based on their ex post knowledge of the amount of money received from the constrained sale of their factor services. And to this I again add that a similar statement holds for their constrained decisions with reference to the amounts of bonds and money balances, respectively, that they will want to hold. (Note that an analysis in terms of constrained decisions can also be applied to the case in which households do not correctly estimate firms' profits in equation (3) above, and are thus forced to base their effective (say) consumption decisions on the ex post knowledge of these profits.)

In his treatment of an economy with constrained functions, Clower (1965, pp. 122–3) has claimed that under these conditions Walras's Law does not hold. This is not true for the Law as hitherto discussed. What Clower seems to have in mind, however, is that though the excess supply of labour LH in Figure 1 is notional, it nevertheless exerts pressure on workers to reduce their money wages; in contrast, the notional excess demand for commodities corresponding to LH

(see above) cannot – because of their constrained incomes – lead households to exert expansionary pressures on the commodity market. Thus there exists no *effective* excess demand for commodities to match the *effective* excess supply of labour. Accordingly, no 'signal' to the market is generated that will lead to the expansion of output and consequent reduction of unemployment (cf. also Leijonhufvud, 1968, pp. 81–91). And it is the absence of such a 'signal' that Leijonhufvud (1981, ch. 6) subsequently denoted as 'effective demand failure'.

This 'failure', however – and correspondingly the failure of Walras's Law to hold in Clower's sense – is not an absolute one: for though there is no direct signal to the commodity market, an indirect one may well be generated. In particular, the very fact that the constrained equilibrium in the labour market does not represent a balancing of market forces means that the unemployed workers in this market are a potential source of a downward pressure on the money wage rate. And if this pressure is to some extent effective, the resulting decline in money wages will generate an increase in the real quantity of money, hence a decrease in the rate of interest, hence an increase in investment and consequently in aggregate demand – and this process may be reinforced by a positive real-balance effect (see chapter 19 of the *General Theory*, which, however, also emphasizes how many weak – and possibly perverse – links there are in this causal chain). Thus a sufficient condition for absolute 'effective demand failure' is the traditional classical one of absolute rigidity of money wages and prices.

An analogy (though from a completely different field) may be of help in clarifying the nature of the foregoing equilibrium in the labour market. Consider a cartel of (say) oil-producing firms, operating by means of a Central Executive for the Production of Oil (CEPO) which sets production quotas for each firm. The total quantity-constrained supply so determined, in conjunction with the demand conditions in the market, will then determine the equilibrium price for crude oil, and that equilibrium position is the relevant one for Walras's Law. But this will not be an equilibrium in the full sense of the term, for it coexists with market pressures to disturb it. In particular, the monopolistic price resulting from CEPO's policy is necessarily higher than the marginal cost of any individual member of the cartel. Hence it is to the interest of every firm in the cartel that all other firms adhere to their respective quotas and thus 'hold an umbrella' over the price, while it itself surreptitiously exceeds the quantity constraint imposed by its quota and thus moves closer to its notional supply curve as represented by its marginal-cost curve. And since in the course of time there will be some firms who will succumb to this temptation, a temptation that increases inversely with the ratio of its quota to the total set by CEPO, actual industry output will exceed this total, with a consequent decline in the price of oil. Indeed, if such violations of cartel discipline should become widespread, its very existence would be threatened.

This analogy is, of course, not perfect. First of all, unlike workers in the labour market, the member-firms of CEPO have themselves had a voice in determining the quantity constraints. Second, and more important, any individual firm knows that by 'chiselling' and offering to sell even slightly below the cartel price, it can readily increase its sales. But analogies are never perfect: that is why they remain only analogies.

A final observation: the discussion until now has implicitly dealth with models with discrete time periods. In models with continuous time, there are two Walras's Laws: one for stocks and one for flows: one for the instantaneous planned (or constrained) purchases and sales of assets (primarily financial assets) and one for the planned (or constrained) purchases and sales of flows (cf. May, 1970; Foley and Sidrauski, 1971, pp. 89–91; Sargent, 1979, pp. 67–9; Buiter, 1980; for a dissenting view, see Harrison, 1980). On the other hand, in a discrete-time intertemporal model, in which there exists a market for each period, there is only one Walras's Law: for such a model, all variables have the time-dimension of a stock (see Patinkin, 1972, ch. 1).

BIBLIOGRAPHY

Arrow, K.J. and Hahn, F.J. 1971. *General Competitive Analysis.* San Francisco: Holden-Day; Edinburgh: Oliver and Boyd.

Barro, R. and Grossman, H.I. 1971. A general disequilibrium model of income and employment. *American Economic Review* 61, March 82–93.

Barro, R. and Grossman, H.I. 1976. *Money, Employment and Inflation.* Cambridge and New York: Cambridge University Press.

Buiter, W. H. 1980. Walras's law and all that: budget constraints and balance sheet constraints in period models and continuous time models. *International Economic Review* 21, February, 1–16.

Clower, R. 1965. The Keynesian counterrevolution: a theoretical appraisal. In *The Theory of Interest Rates,* ed. F.H. Hahn and F.P.R. Brechling, London: Macmillan, 103–25; New York: St. Martin's Press.

Drazen, A. 1980. Recent developments in macroeconomic disequilibrium theory. *Econometrica* 48, March, 283–306.

Fitoussi, J.P. 1983. Modern macroeconomic theory: an overview. In *Modern Macroeconomic Theory* ed. J.P. Fitoussi, Oxford: Basil Blackwell, 1–46.

Foley, D.K. and Sidrauski, M. 1971. *Monetary and Fiscal Policy in a Growing Economy.* London: Macmillan.

Gale, D. 1983. *Money: in Disequilibrium.* Cambridge: Cambridge University Press.

Grandmont, J.M. 1977. Temporary general equilibrium theory. *Econometrica* 45, April, 535–72.

Grossman, H.I. 1971. Money, interest, and prices in market disequilibrium. *Journal of Political Economy* 79, September–October, 943–61.

Harrison, G.W. 1980. The stock-flow distinction: a suggested interpretation. *Journal of Macroeconomics* 2, Spring, 111–28.

Hicks, J.R. 1939. *Value and Capital.* Oxford: Clarendon Press 2nd edn, New York: Oxford University Press, 1946.

Keynes, J.M. 1936. *The General Theory of Employment, Interest and Money.* London: Macmillan; New York: Harcourt, Brace.

Lange, O. 1942. Say's Law: A restatement and criticism. In *Studies in Mathematical Economics and Econometrics: In Memory of Henry Schultz,* ed. Oscar Lange et al., Chicago: University of Chicago Press, 49–68.

Leijonhufvud, A. 1981. *Information and Coordination: Essays in Macroeconomic Theory.* Oxford: Oxford University Press.

May, J. 1970. Period analysis and continuous analysis in Patinkin's macroeconomic model. *Journal of Economic Theory* 2, 1–9.

Modigliani, F. 1944. Liquidity preference and the theory of interest and money. *Econometrica* 12, January, 45–88. As reprinted in *Readings in Monetary Theory*, ed F.A. Lutz and L.W. Mints, Philadelphia: Blakiston, for the American Economic Association, 1951, 186–240.

Patinkin, D. 1956. *Money, Interest and Prices.* Evanston, Ill.: Row, Peterson. (The material referred to appears unchanged in the second, 1965 edition.)

Patinkin, D. 1958. Liquidity preference and loanable funds: stock and flow analysis. *Economica* 25, November, 300–318.

Patinkin, D. 1972. *Studies in Monetary Economics.* New York: Harper & Row.

Ricardo, D. 1821. *On the Principles of Political Economy and Taxation*, 3rd edn. As reprinted in *The Works and Correspondence of David Ricardo*, Vol. I, ed. P. Sraffa, Cambridge: Cambridge University Press, 1951; New York: Cambridge University Press, 1973.

Sargent, T.J. 1979. *Macroeconomic Theory.* New York: Academic Press.

Say, J.B. 1821a. *Traité d'économie politique*, 4th edn, Paris: Deterville. As translated by C.R. Prinsep under the title *A Treatise on Political Economy*, Philadelphia, Grigg R. Elliot: 1834.

Say, J.B. 1821b. *Letters to Thomas Robert Malthus on Political Economy and Stagnation of Commerce.* London. As reprinted with an Historical Preface by H.J. Laski, London: George Harding's Bookshop, 1936; Wheeler Economic and Historical Reprints No. 2.

Walras, L. 1874. *Eléments d'économie politique pure.* Paris: Guillaumin (Sections I–III of the work).

Walras, L. 1900. *Eléments d'économie politique pure.* 4th edn, Paris: F. Pichon.

Walras, L. 1926. *Eléments d'économie politique pure.* Definitive edition. Paris: F. Pichon (for our purposes, identical with 4th edition). As trans. by William Jaffé under the title *Elements of Pure Economics*, London: George Allen and Unwin, 1954; New York: Orion.

Contributors

Michael Allingham Professor of Economic Theory, University of Kent. 'Tâtonnement stability', *Econometrica* 40 (1972); 'Equilibrium and stability', *Econometrica* 42 (1974); *General Equilibrium* (1975); 'Stability of monopoly', *Econometrica* 44 (1976); *Value* (1983); *Theory of Markets* (1989).

Yves Balasko Professor of Mathematics and Economics, University of Geneva. 'Some results on uniqueness and on stability of equilibrium in general equilibrium theory', *Journal of Mathematical Economics* 2 (1975); *Foundations of the Theory of General Equilibrium* (1986).

Jean-Pascal Benassy Directeur de Rechérche, CNRS and CEPREMAP. Fellow, Econometric Society. 'Neo-Keynesian disequilibrium theory in a monetary economy', *Review of Economic Studies* 42 (1975); 'The disequilibrium approach to monopolistic price setting and general monopolistic equilibrium', *Review of Economic Studies* 43 (1976); 'A neo-Keynesian model of price and quantity determination in disequilibrium', in *Equilibrium and Disequilibrium in Economic Theory* (ed. G. Schwödiauer, 1977); *The Economics of Market Equilibrium* (1982); *Macroeconomics: An Introduction to the Non-Walrasian Approach* (1986); 'Non-Walrasian equilibria, money and macroeconomics', in *Handbook of Monetary Economics* (ed. B. Friedman and F. Hahn, 1988).

Theodore C. Bergstrom Professor of Economics, University of Michigan. 'A "Scandinavian consensus" solution for efficient income distribution among non-malevolent consumers', *Journal of Economic Theory* (1970); 'Private demands for public goods', (with R. Goodman) *American Economic Review* (June 1973); 'Collective choice and the Lindahl allocation mechanism', *Economics of Externalities* (ed. S.Y. Lin, 1977); 'When is a man's life worth more than his human capital', in *Value of Human Life and Safety* (ed. Jones-Lee, 1982); 'Independence of allocative efficiency from distribution in the theory of public goods', (with R. Cornes) *Econometrica* (1983); 'On the private provision of public goods', (with L. Blume and H. Varian) *Journal of Public Economies* (1986).

Gerard Debreu University Professor of Economics and of Mathematics, University of California at Berkeley. Fellow, Econometric Society; Member, National Academy of Sciences of the USA; Distinguished Fellow, American Economic Association, 1982; Nobel Memorial Prize in Economics, 1983; Member, American Philosophical Society; Foreign Associate, French Academy of Sciences. *Theory of Value, An Axiomatic Analysis of Economic Equilibrium* (1959); *Mathematical Economics, Twenty Papers of Gerard Debreu* (1983).

E. Dierker Professor of Economics, University of Vienna. 'Two remarks on the number of equilibria of an economy', *Econometrica* 40 (1972); 'The local uniqueness of equilibria', (with H. Dierker) *Econometrica* 40 (1972); *Topological Methods in Walrasian Economics* (1974); 'Gains and losses at core allocations', *Journal of Mathematical Economics* 2 (1975); 'Regular economies', in *Handbook of Mathematical Economics* (ed. K. Arrow and M. Intriligator, 1982); 'Price-dispersed preferences and C mean demand', (with H. Dierker and W. Trockel) *Journal of Mathematical Economics* 13 (1984); 'When does marginal cost pricing lead to Pareto efficiency?', *Journal of Economics* (1986).

John Eatwell Fellow, Director of Studies and Lecturer in Economics, Trinity College, Cambridge. Editor, *Contributions to Political Economy* (series). *An Introduction to Modern Economics* (with Joan Robinson, 1973); *Whatever Happened to Britain?* (1982); *Keynes's Economics and the Theory of Value and Distribution* (ed., with Murray Milgate, 1983).

Franklin M. Fisher Professor of Economics, Massachusetts Institute of Technology. John Bates Clark Award, American Economic Association; Fellow, Econometric Society; Fellow, American Academy of Arts and Sciences; President, Econometric Society, 1979. *The Identification Problem in Econometrics* (1966); 'The existence of aggregate production functions: reply', *Econometrica* 39 (1971); *The Economic Theory of Price Indices* (with Karl Shell, 1972); 'On the misuse of accounting rates of return to infer monopoly profits' (with John J. McGowan), *American Economic Review* 73 (March 1983); *Folded, Spindled, and Mutilated: Economic Analysis and U.S. v. IBM* (with John J. McGowan and Joan E. Greenwood, 1983); *Disequilibrium Foundations of Equilibrium Economics* (1983).

John D. Geanakoplos Professor of Economics, Yale University. 'We can't disagree forever', (with H. Polemarchakis) *Journal of Economic Theory* (1982); 'Real indeterminacy with financial assets', (with A. Mas-Colell, 1985), *Journal of Economic Theory*, forthcoming; 'Multimarket oligopoly: strategic substitutes and complements', (with J. Bulow and P. Klemperer) *Journal of Political Economy* 93(3), (June 1985); 'Walrasian indeterminacy and Keynesian macroeconomics', (with H. Polemarchakis) *Review of Economic Studies* 1986; 'The revelation of information in strategic market games: a critique of rational expectations equilibrium' (with P. Dubay and M. Shubik) *Journal of Mathematical Economics* 16(2), (1987). 'Existence, regularity, and constrained suboptimality of equilibrium with incomplete asset markets', (with H. Polemarchakis) in *Essays in Honour of Kenneth J. Arrow* (1988).

Giorgio Gilibert Professor of Political Economy, University of Modena. 'Production conjointe et valeurs-travail negatives', *Ricardiens, Keynesiens et Marxistes* (1972); *Quesnay. La costruzione della "macchina della prosperità"* (1977); 'Evaluation of aggregates in terms of labour-values: a critical appraisal', *Economic Notes* 8 (1979); 'Isnard, Cournot, Walras, Leontief. Evoluzione di un modello', *Annali della Foundazione L. Einaudi* 15 (1981); 'La teoria oggettiva dei prezzi', (with M. Egidi) *Economica Politica* 1 (1984); 'François Quesnay', *Klassiker des ökonomischen Denkens* (ed. J. Starbatty, 1989).

Jean-Michel Grandmont Directeur de Recherches, CNRS and CEPREMAP, Paris. Fellow, Econometric Society; Vice-President, Econometric Society, 1988. 'On temporary Keynesian equilibria', (with G. Laroque) *Review of Economic Studies* (1976); 'Temporary general equilibrium theory', *Econometrica* (1977); *Money and Value* (1983); 'On endogenous competitive business cycles', *Econometrica* (1985); *Nonlinear Economic Dynamics* (ed., 1987); *Temporary Equilibrium. Selected Readings* (ed., 1988).

Frank Hahn Professor of Economics and Fellow, Churchill College, Cambridge. Fellow, British Academy; President, Econometric Society; Foreign Honorary Member, American Academy of Arts and Sciences. *General Equilibrium Analysis* (with K.J. Arrow, 1971); *The Share of Wages in the National Income* (1972); *Money-Inflation* (1982).

Werner Hildenbrand Professor in Economics, University of Bonn. Fellow, Economic Society; Member, Akademie der Wissenschaften; Leibniz-Preis, Deutsche Forschungsgemeinschaft, 1987. *Core and Equilibria of a Large Economy* (1974); *Introduction to Equilibrium Analysis* (with A. Kirman, 1976); 'Short-run production functions based on microdata', *Econometrica* (1981); 'Core of an economy', in *Handbook of Mathematical Economics* (1982); 'On the law of demand', *Econometrica* (1983).

M. Ali Khan Abraham G. Hutzler Professor of Political Economy, Johns Hopkins University. Gonner Prize, 1969. 'Some remarks on the core of a large economy', *Econometrica* 44 (1974); 'Some equivalence theorems', *Review of Economic Studies* 41 (1974); 'The Harris–Todaro hypothesis and the Heckscher–Ohlin–Samuelson trade model', *Journal of International Economics* 10 (1980); 'Development policies in less developed countries with several ethnic groups: a theoretic analysis', (with T. Chauduri) *Zeitschrift für Nationalökonomie* 45 (1985); 'Equilibrium points of non-atomic games over a Banach space', *Transactions of the American Mathematical*

Society 293 (1986); 'An extension of the second welfare theorem to economics with non-convexities and public goods', (with R. Vahra) *Quarterly Journal of Economics* (1987).

Timothy J. Kehoe Lecturer and Fellow, Clare College, Cambridge. 'Regular production economies', *Journal of Mathematical Economics* 10 (1982); 'Regularity and index theory for economies with smooth production technologies', *Econometrica* 51 (1983); 'Computing all of the equilibria in economies with two factors of production', *Journal of Mathematical Economics* 13 (1984); 'Intertemporal separability in overlapping generations models', (with David K. Levine) *Journal of Economic Theory* 34 (1984); 'An observation on gross substitutibility and the weak axiom of revealed preference', (with Andrew Mas-Colell) *Economics Letters* 15 (1984); 'Regularity in overlapping generations exchange commodities', (with David K. Levine) *Journal of Mathematical Economics* 13 (1984).

Edmond Malinvaud Professor au Collège de France. President, International Economic Association, 1974–7; President, European Economic Association, 1988. *Statistical Methods of Econometrics* (1966); *Lectures on Microeconomic Theory* (1972); *French Economic Growth* (with J.J. Carre and P. Dubois, 1975); *The Theory of Unemployment Reconsidered* (1977); *Théorie macroéconomique* (1981).

Lionel W. McKenzie Wilson Professor of Economics, University of Rochester. Fellow, Econometric Society; American Academy of Arts and Sciences; National Academy of Sciences. 'Equality of factor prices in world trade', *Econometrica* (1955); 'Specialization in production and the production possibility locus', *Review of Economic Studies* (1956); 'On the existence of general equilibrium for a competitive market', *Econometrica* (1959); 'Turnpike theorems for a generalized Leontief model', *Econometrica* (1963); 'The classical theorem on existence of competitive equilibrium', *Econometrica* (1981); 'Optimal economic growth, turnpike theorems, and comparative dynamics', in *Handbook of Mathematical Economics* (ed. K.J. Arrow and M.D. Intriligator, 1986).

Takashi Negishi Professor of Economics, University of Tokyo. Nikkei Prize; Matsunaga Science Foundation Prize, 1977; Fellow, Econometric Society; President, Japan Association of Economics and Econometrics, 1985; Member, Science Council of Japan, 1985–8. *General Equilibrium Theory and International Trade* (1972); *Microeconomic Foundations of Keynesian Macroeconomics* (1979); *Economic Theories in a Non-Walrasian Tradition* (1985); *Disequilibrium Trade Theories* (with Motoshige Itoh, 1987); *Recent Developments in Japanese Economics* (ed., with R. Sato, 1987); *History of Economic Theory* (1988).

Peter Newman Professor of Economics, Johns Hopkins University. *Costs in Alternative Locations: The Clothing Industry* (with D.C. Hague, 1952); 'The erosion of Marshall's theory of value', *Quarterly Journal of Economics* 74 (1960); *British Guiana: Problems of Cohesion in an Immigrant Society* (1964); *The Theory of Exchange* (1965); *Malaria Eradication and Population Growth* (1965); 'Some properties of concave functions', *Journal of Economic Theory* 1 (1969).

Hukukane Nikaido Professor of Economics, Department of Commerce, Tokyo International University. Fellow, Econometric Society. 'On the classical multilateral exchange problem', *Metroeconomica* 8(2), (1956); 'Persistence of continual growth near the von Neumann ray: a strong version of the Radner turnpike theorem', *Econometrica* 32(1/2), (1964); *Convex Structures and Economic Theory* (1968); *Introduction to Sets and Mappings in Modern Economics* (1970); *Monopolistic Competition and Effective Demand* (1975); 'Dynamics of growth and capital mobility in Marx's scheme of reproduction', *Zeitschrift für Nationalökonomie* 45(3), (1985).

Don Patinkin Professor of Economics, Hebrew University of Jerusalem. Rothschild Prize 1959; Israel Prize 1970; President, Econometric Society, 1974; President, Israel Economic Association, 1976; various honorary degrees and fellowships. *Money, Interest, and Prices: an Integration of Monetary and Value Theory* (1956); *The Israel Economy: The First Decade* (1959); *Studies in Monetary Economics* (1972); *Keynes' Monetary Thought: A Study of Its Development* (1976); *Essays On and In the Chicago Tradition* (1981); *Anticipations of the General Theory? and other essays on Keynes* (1982).

Joseph M. Ostroy Professor of Economics, University of California. 'The informational efficiency of monetary exchange', *American Economic Review* 63(4), (1973); 'Money and the decentralization of exchange', *Econometrica* (1974); 'The no-surplus condition as a characterisation of perfectly competitive equilibrium', *Journal of Economic Theory* 22(2), (1980); 'Vickrey–Clarke–Groves mechanisms and perfect competition', (with L. Makouski) *Journal of Economic Theory* 42(2), (1987).

J. Trout Rader Professor of Economics, Washington University in St. Louis. 'The existence of a utility function to represent preferences', *Review of Economic Studies* 30 (1963); 'Resource allocation with increasing returns to scale', *American Economic Review* 60 (1970); 'General equilibrium theory with complementary factors', *Journal of Economic Theory* 4 (1972); *Theory of General Economic Equilibrium* (1972); 'Induced preferences on trades when preferences may be intransitive and incomplete', *Econometrica* 46 (1978); 'Factor price equalization with more industries than factors', in *General Equilibrium Growth and Trade* (ed. Green and Scheintmann, 1979).

Roy Radner Distinguished Member of Technical Staff, AT & T Bell Laboratories; Research Professor of Economics, New York University. Member, National Academy of Sciences, USA; Fellow, American Academy of Arts and Sciences;

President, Econometric Society, 1972–3; Distinguished Fellow, American Economic Association; Guggenheim Fellow, 1961, 1965. 'Paths of economic growth that are optimal with regard to final states: a turnpike theorem', *Review of Economic Studies* 28 (1961); *Economic Theory of Teams* (with J. Marschak, 1972); 'Existence of equilibrium of plans, prices, and price expectations in a sequence of markets', *Econometrica* 40 (1972); 'Satisficing', *Journal of Mathematical Economics* 2 (1975); 'Equilibrium under uncertainty', in *Handbook of Mathematical Economics* (ed. K.J. Arrow and M. Intriligator, 1981); 'Decision and information', in *Information, Incentives, and Economic Mechanisms* (ed., with T. Groves and S. Reiter, 1987).

John Roberts Jonathan B. Lovelace Professor of Economics and Associate Dean, Graduate School of Business, Stanford University. Fellow, Econometric Society; CORE Faculty Research Fellow, 1974–5; Associate Editor, *Econometrica* (1985–87); *Games and Economic Behaviour* (1988–); *Journal of Economic Theory* (1977–). 'Existence of Lindahl equilibrium with a measure space of consumers', *Journal of Economic Theory* 6 (1973); 'On the foundations of the theory of monopolistic competition', (with Hugo Sonnenschein), *Econometrica* 45 (1977); 'Limit pricing and entry under incomplete information: an equilibrium analysis', (with Paul Milgrom) *Econometrica* 50 (1982); 'Predation, reputation and entry deterrence', (with Paul Milgrom) *Journal of Economic Theory* 27 (1982); 'An equilibrium model with involuntary employment at flexible, competitive prices and wages', *American Economic Review* 77 (1987); 'An economic approach to influence activities in organizations', (with Paul Milgrom) *American Journal of Sociology* 94 (Supplement, July 1988).

Herbert E. Scarf Sterling Professor of Economics, Cowles Foundation for Research in Economics, Yale University. Fellow, National Science Foundation, Princeton University, 1952–3; Fellow, Econometric Society; Fellow, American Academy of Arts and Sciences; Lancaster Prize, Operations Society of America, 1974; Member, National Academy of Sciences, 1976; Von Neumann Medal, Operations Research Society of America, 1983. 'The optimality of (S, s) policies in the dynamic inventory problem', First Stanford Symposium on Mathematics in the Social Sciences (1960); 'Some examples of global instability of the competitive equilibrium', *International Economic Review* 1(3), (1960); 'A limit theorem on the core of an economy', (with Gerard Debreu) *International Economic Review* (1963); 'The core of an N-person game', *Econometrica* (1967); 'The approximation of fixed points of a continuous mapping' *SIAM Journal of Applied Mathematics* 15(5), (1967); *The Computation of Economic Equilibria*, Cowles Foundation Monograph 24 (1973).

Karl Shell Robert Julius Thorne Professor of Economics and Director, Center for Analytic Economics, Cornell University. Fellow, Center for Advanced Study in the Behavioral Sciences; Fellow, Guggenheim Foundation; Fellow, Econometric Society; Fellow, Ford Foundation; Fellow, Woodrow Wilson

Foundation. 'Public debt, taxation, and capital intensiveness', (with E.S. Phelps) *Journal of Economic Theory* (1969 and 1970); 'Notes on the economics of infinity', *Journal of Political Economy* (1971); *The Economic Theory of Price Indices: Two Essays on the Effects of Taste, Quality and Technological Change* (with F.M. Fisher, 1972); 'The overlapping-generations model', (with Y. Balasko) *Journal of Economic Theory* (1980/81); 'Do sunspots matter?', (with D. Cass) *Journal of Political Economy* (1983); 'Market uncertainty: correlated equilibrium and sunspot equilibrium in imperfectly competitive economies' (with J. Peck) Center for Analytic Economics Working Paper No. 88-22 (1987).

Joaquim Silvestre Professor of Economics, University of California. 'A model of a general equilibrium with monopolistic behaviour', *Journal of Economic Theory* 16(2), (1977); 'General monopolistic equilibrium under non-convexitites', *International Economic Review* 18(2), (1977); 'Increasing returns in general non-competitive analysis', *Econometrica* 46(2), (1978); 'Voluntariness and efficiency in the provision of public goods', *Journal of Public Economics* 24(2), (1984).

Steve Smale Professor of Mathematics and Economics, University of California at Berkeley. Fields Medal, International Union of Mathematicians. 'Dynamics in general equilibrium theory', *American Economic Review* 66 (1976); 'Global analysis and economics', *Journal of Mathematical Economics* 3 (1976); 'The qualitative analysis of a difference equation of population growth', (with R.F. Williams) *Journal of Mathematical Biology* 3 (1976); 'On the differential equations of specie in competition', *Journal of Mathematical Biology* 3 (1976); 'A convergent process of price adjustment', *Journal of Mathematical Economics* 3 (1976); 'Exchange processes with price adjustment', *Journal of Mathematical Economics* 3 (1976).

Ross M. Starr Professor of Economics, University of California, San Diego. Guggenheim Fellow, 1978–9. 'Quasi-equilibria in markets with non-convex preferences', *Econometrica* 37(1), (1969); 'Optimal production and allocation under uncertainty', *Quarterly Journal of Economics* (1973); 'Money and the decentralization of exchange', (with Joseph M. Ostroy) *Econometrica* 42(6), (1974); 'Equilibrium with nonconvex transaction costs: monetary and non-monetary economies', (with Walter P. Heller) *Review of Economic Studies* 43(2), (1976); 'U.S. money demand 1960–1984', (with Yoshihisa Baba and David F. Hendry) UCSD Economics Department Discussion Paper No. 88-8 (1987); *General Equilibrium Models of Monetary Economics: Studies in the Static Foundations of Monetary Theory* (ed., 1988).

Ian Steedman Professor of Economics, University of Manchester. *Marx after Sraffa* (1977); *Trade amongst Growing Economies* (1979); *Sraffian Economics* (ed., 1988); *From Exploitation to Altruism* (1989).